W9-AGE-035

ELFQUEST:
THE GRAND QUEST
VOLUME SEVEN

ELFQUEST CREATED BY
**WENDY &
RICHARD PINI**

ELFQUEST:
**THE GRAND
QUEST**
VOLUME **SEVEN**

WRITTEN BY
WENDY & RICHARD PINI

PENCIL ART BY
WENDY PINI

INKS BY
JOE STATON

LETTERING BY
JANICE CHIANG

ELFQUEST: THE GRAND QUEST VOLUME SEVEN
Published by DC Comics. Cover, timeline, character
bios and compilation copyright © 2005 Warp
Graphics, Inc. All Rights Reserved.

Originally published in single magazine form in
ELFQUEST: SIEGE AT BLUE MOUNTAIN 1-3.
Copyright © 1986 Warp Graphics, Inc. All Rights
Reserved. All characters, their distinctive like-
nesses and related elements featured in this
publication are trademarks of Warp Graphics, Inc.
The stories, characters and incidents featured in
this publication are entirely fictional. DC Comics
does not read or accept unsolicited submissions
of ideas, stories or artwork.

DC Comics, 1700 Broadway, New York, NY 10019
A Warner Bros. Entertainment Company
Printed in Canada. First Printing.
ISBN: 1-4012-0503-8

Cover illustration by Wendy Pini

Dan DiDio
   VP-Executive Editor
Richard Pini
   Editor-original series
Robert Greenberger
   Senior Editor-collected edition
Robbin Brosterman
   Senior Art Director
Paul Levitz
   President & Publisher
Georg Brewer
   VP-Design & Retail Product Development
Richard Bruning
   Senior VP-Creative Director
Patrick Caldon
   Senior VP-Finance & Operations
Chris Caramalis
   VP-Finance
Terri Cunningham
   VP-Managing Editor
Alison Gill
   VP-Manufacturing
Rich Johnson
   VP-Book Trade Sales
Hank Kanalz
   VP-General Manager, WildStorm
Lillian Laserson
   Senior VP & General Counsel
Jim Lee
   Editorial Director-WildStorm
David McKillips
   VP-Advertising & Custom Publishing
John Nee
   VP-Business Development
Gregory Noveck
   Senior VP-Creative Affairs
Cheryl Rubin
   Senior VP-Brand Management
Bob Wayne
   VP-Sales & Marketing

The ElfQuest Saga is an ever-unfolding story spanning countless millennia that follows the adventures of humans, trolls and various elfin tribes. Some of the events that occur prior to the time of this volume are outlined below using the very first published ElfQuest story as a benchmark.

OUR STORY BEGINS HERE...

7 YEARS LATER

Recognition has given Cutter and Leetah twin children, *Ember* and *Suntop*. One day, however, nomadic humans arrive in the remote oasis, and the elves realize they are no safer than before. Cutter and Skywise set out to find and unite other elfin tribes. Their journey leads them through the mysterious Forbidden Grove where they encounter fairylike Petalwing, one of the Preservers.

After a harrowing series of adventures, Cutter and Skywise are reunited with Leetah, the twin cubs and the Wolfriders. Together, they enter the fabled Blue Mountain where they meet bizarre, winged *Tyldak* and the beautiful, enigmatic Winnowill, who jealously protects her control over the mountain and its secrets. *Lord Voll*, though, is enchanted by the Wolfriders and once more stirs with ancient memories.

Voll desires to find the long-lost Palace of the High Ones. But on the way to the frozen northlands, Voll is killed by brutal mountain trolls, and the Wolfriders are barely saved by the Go-Back elves. Their leader, *Kahvi*, convinces Cutter to help them finish the age-old war between elves and trolls once and for all.

The fight is brutal but the elves emerge victorious. The Palace is theirs but Cutter discovers that as one quest ends, another begins. The Wolfriders determine to recreate their lost holt in the forest near the Palace...

2,000 - 3,000 YEARS BEFORE

Goodtree, eighth chief of the Wolfriders, founds a new Holt deep in the woods and creates the Father Tree where the Wolfriders can all live. Her son, *Mantricker*, is the first in several generations to have to deal with nomadic humans again.

Mantricker's son, *Bearclaw*, discovers Greymung's trolls who live in the caverns and tunnels beneath the Holt. Bearclaw becomes the Wolfriders' tenth chief.

In the distant Forbidden Grove near Blue Mountain, *Petalwing* and the preservers tirelessly protect their mysterious wrapstuff bundles.

Among the Wolfriders, *Treestump, Clearbrook, Moonshade, Strongbow, One-Eye, Redlance, Pike, Rainsong* and *Woodlock* are born.

4,000 YEARS BEFORE

Freefoot leads the Wolfriders during a prosperous time. Game is plentiful, and life is easy.

Freefoot's son, Oakroot, subsequently becomes chief and later takes the name *Tanner*.

9,000 YEARS BEFORE

Wolfrider chief Timmorn feels the conflict between his elf and wolf sides, and leaves the tribe to find his own destiny. *Rahnee the She-Wolf* takes over as leader, followed by her son *Prey-Pacer*.

10,000 YEARS BEFORE

Over time, the early High Ones become too many for their faraway planet to support. *Timmain's* group discovers the World of Two Moons, but as the crystalline ship approaches, the trolls revolt. The High Ones lose control and crash-land far in the new world's past. Ape-like primitive humans greet them with brutality, and the elfin High Ones scatter into the surrounding forest.

In order to survive, Timmain magically takes on a wolf's form and hunts for the other elves. In time, the High Ones adapt, making a spartan life for themselves. *Timmorn*, first chief of the Wolfriders, is born to Timmain and a true wolf.

| 0 |
| 1,000 |
| 2,000 |
| 3,000 |
| 4,000 |
| 5,000 |
| 6,000 |
| 7,000 |
| 8,000 |
| 9,000 |
| 10,000 |

FIRE & FLIGHT

The peace is an illusion, and humans burn the Wolfriders from their forest home. Cutter and his band are driven into a vast desert where, at the end of their strength, they discover a second tribe of elves, the Sun Folk. Cutter recognizes the Sun Folk's healer Leetah, and the two groups unite in an uneasy alliance.

6 YEARS BEFORE

The feud between elves and humans ends – seemingly – with the death of Bearclaw. Cutter takes the chief's lock and assumes leadership of the tribe.

25 YEARS BEFORE

Joyleaf gives birth to a son, *Cutter,* who forms a fast friendship with Skywise. The two become brothers "in all but blood."

475 YEARS BEFORE

Bearclaw begins a long feud with a tribe of humans who have claimed the land near the Wolfriders' Holt. Though both sides suffer over the years, neither can prevail, and neither will give in.

7,000 YEARS BEFORE

Swift-Spear, fourth chief, goes to war for the first time against the humans of a nearby village. The humans are forced to leave, and he earns the name *Two-Spear.*

Two-Spear has strange dreams of the humans returning and believes the elves are no longer safe. He becomes obsessed by the dreams and tries repeatedly to convince the Wolfriders they must wipe out the human threat for all time. When his sister *Huntress Skyfire* challenges his chieftainship, the tribe splits. Two-Spear leaves with his followers, and Skyfire becomes chief of the remaining tribe.

600 YEARS BEFORE

In an oasis called the Sun Village deep in the desert to the south of the Holt, *Rayek* is born to villagers Jarrah and Ingen. *Leetah* is born to Suntoucher and Toorah twelve years later.

10,000 – 8,000 YEARS BEFORE

In a long diaspora, descendants of the High Ones wander the world. *Savah* and her family settle the Sun Village in the desert at Sorrow's End. Lord Voll and the Gliders move into Blue Mountain and shut themselves away from the world.

Guttlekraw becomes king of the trolls, who have fled to the cold north.

Ekuar and two rock-shaper companions discover the abandoned palace-ship of the High Ones but are enslaved by Guttlekraw. Glaciers force the trolls to move south, tunneling under the future Holt of the Wolfriders.

Greymung rebels against Guttlekraw. Guttlekraw and his cohorts return north, and the three rock-shaper elves escape in the melee.

Winnowill leaves Blue Mountain, finds the troll, seduces him and gives birth to *Two-Edge.* She later kills the troll.

Timeline markers (left axis):
0
475
600
1,000
2,000
3,000
4,000
5,000
6,000
7,000
8,000
9,000
10,000

The ElfQuest saga spans thousands of years and to date has introduced readers to hundreds of characters. At the time of the stories in this volume, these are the major characters you will meet and get to know.

THE ELVES

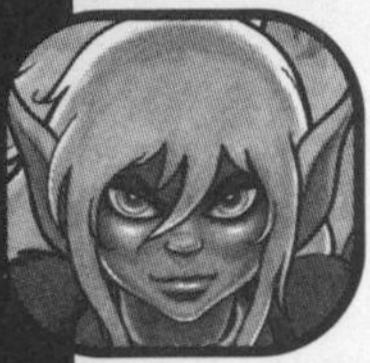

CUTTER

While his name denotes his skill with a sword, Cutter is not a cold and merciless death-dealer. Strong in his beliefs, he will nevertheless bend even the most fundamental of them if the well-being of his tribe is at stake. Skywise believes that what sets Cutter apart from all past Wolfrider chieftains is his imagination and ability to not only accept change, but take advantage of it.

LEETAH

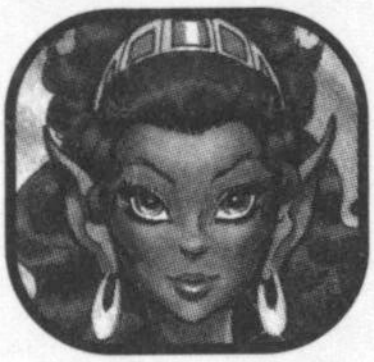

Her name means "healing light" and – as the Sun Folk's healer – she is the village's most precious resource. For over 600 years she has lived a sheltered life, surrounded by love and admiration, knowing little of the world beyond her desert oasis. Though delicate-seeming, beneath her beauty lies a wellspring of strength that has yet to be tested. She dislikes the death she has caused but understands it is The Way.

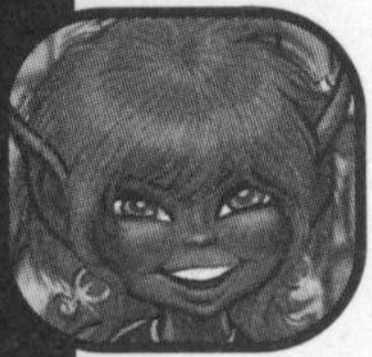

EMBER

Named for her fire-red hair, Ember is destined to be the next chief of the Wolfriders. As such, she constantly watches and learns from her father's actions; she also learns gentler skills from Leetah. As Cutter was a unique blend of his own parents' qualities, so too is Ember. She shares a close bond with her twin brother Suntop, giving her strength.

SUNTOP

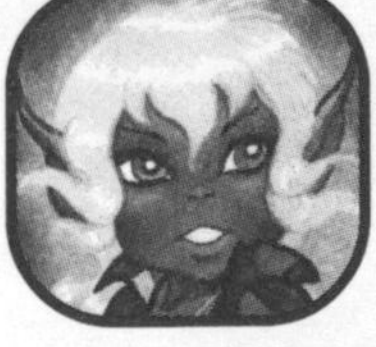

Suntop is the gentle, enigmatic son of Cutter and Leetah. Although a true Wolfrider, Suntop was born in the Sun Village and considers it home. Content that Ember will become chief of the Wolfriders, he says of himself, "I'll be what I'll be." Suntop has powerful mental abilities; his "magic feeling," as he calls it, alerts him when magic is being used by other elves.

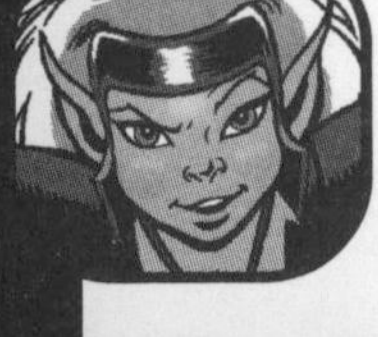

SKYWISE

Orphaned at birth, Skywise is the resident stargazer of the Wolfriders, and only his interest in elf maidens rivals his passion for understanding the mysteries of the universe. Skywise is Cutter's counselor, confidant, and closest friend. While he is capable of deep seriousness, nothing can diminish Skywise's jovial and rakish manner.

STRONGBOW

Strongbow is the reserved, silent master archer of the Wolfriders. Ever the devil's advocate, he is often proved right but finds no value in saying "I told you so." Strongbow is extremely serious, rarely smiles, and prefers sending to audible speech. He is completely devoted to his lifemate, Moonshade, and intensely proud of their son Dart, who has remained in the Sun Village to train its people in the art of combat.

MOONSHADE

Moonshade is the Wolfriders' tanner. Though the process can be lengthy and tedious, she enjoys the quiet hours spent bringing the beauty out of a supple hide. Moonshade, like her lifemate Strongbow, is very much a traditionalist, strong-minded and with unshakable beliefs. Completely devoted to her mate, Moonshade will defend him even when she knows he's wrong.

SCOUTER

Scouter has the sharpest eyes of all the Wolfriders. He is steadfast, loyal, and often overprotective. He is also extremely intolerant of anyone, tribemates included, whom he perceives as putting his loved ones in jeopardy. Dewshine and Scouter have been lovemates for most of their lives, yet are not Recognized.

DEWSHINE

Swift and graceful as a deer, Dewshine is the most agile and free-spirited of the Wolfriders — and that takes some doing! She has a beautiful voice, full of melody and laughter. Song and dance are passions with her, and she has a talent for mimicking birdsong. Dewshine came to Recognition early and unexpectedly, with the shapechanged Glider Tyldak. Dewshine and Scouter have been lovemates for most of their lives, yet are not Recognized.

RAYEK

Vain and prideful, Rayek is chief hunter for the Sun Village and never tires of boasting of his superior skills. The same age as Leetah, he has spent nearly all those years as the healer's friend – always hoping that she will see him as more than simply that. He is a superb athlete, and skilled in both magic and weaponry. Thought lost, he returned with the Go-Backs and helped save Cutter's life. He now resides within the Palace.

KAHVI

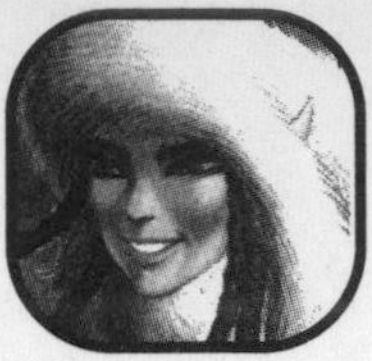

Kahvi is the devil-may-care leader of the northern elf tribe called the Go-Backs (so named because they hope someday to "go back" to the Palace of the High Ones). She is a superb fighter, even to the point of recklessness, who believes that life is to be lived to the fullest every day, for one never knows when death is just around the corner. She recently endured the loss of her daughter Vaya.

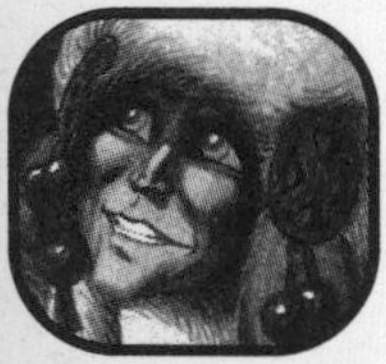

EKUAR

Ekuar is one of the most ancient elves on the World of Two Moons. He is a rock-shaper, who long ago was abducted by trolls who forced him to use his powers to search for precious metals and gems. To keep him in line, the trolls tortured and maimed the gentle elf, but rather than becoming bitter, Ekuar has turned his misfortune into an outlook that is amazingly life-affirming!

WINNOWILL

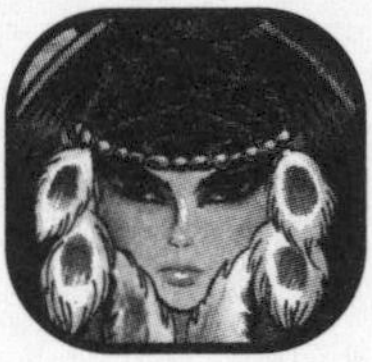

Beautiful, seductive, manipulative, enigmatic, black-hearted... Winnowill is all this, but she was not always thus. Countless centuries of boredom and uselessness have caused her healing powers to fester and turn in on themselves, taking her down into a subtle madness. Her only known child is the half-elf/half-troll Two-Edge, and she is not above lying, abduction, or even murder in order to realize her ends.

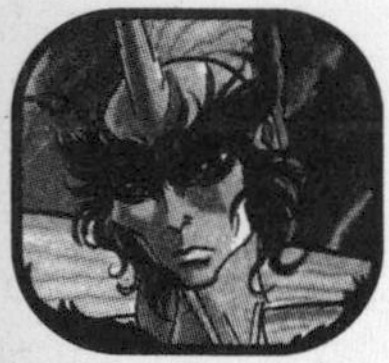

TYLDAK

Tyldak is a Glider elf who wished desperately to fly, rather than merely glide or levitate as the rest of his folk do. He begged Winnowill to use her flesh-shaping powers to give him true wings that he might ride on air currents and soar with the birds!

AROREE

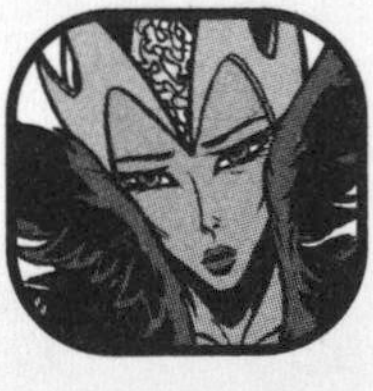

Aroree was one of the Gliders' Chosen Eight. When she met Skywise, he opened her eyes to a wider world. Aroree saw in Skywise a spark — one that was missing from her life. She desperately wanted to flee Blue Mountain and lead a life far from its shadow.

OTHER

PETALWING

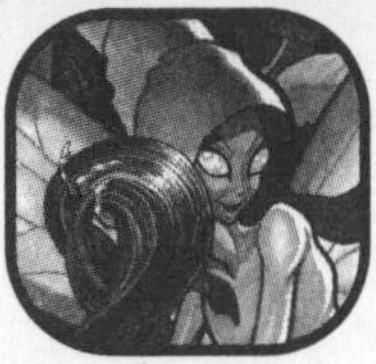

Petalwing is a Preserver – a carefree, fairylike creature that arrived on the World of Two Moons with the original High Ones. Petalwing lives under the grand illusion that "highthings" (elves) cannot live without it, and must be watched over and protected. Petalwing is the closest thing that the Preservers have to a leader. Cutter considers Petalwing to be a major annoyance; the sprite is unperturbed by this.

TROLLS

PICKNOSE

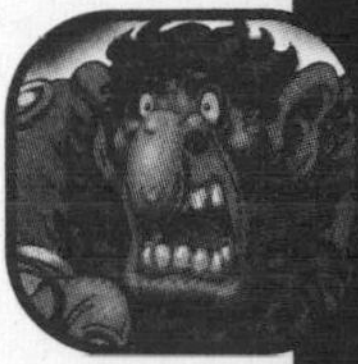

His name was inspired by his most prominent facial feature, which resembles the curved business end of a pick. The success of Picknose's interactions with the Wolfriders has been mixed at best, for while he does possess a sort of honor, he is also an opportunist of the first water. Despite his nature, he allied himself with the wolfriders to help overthrow the vile King Guttlekraw. Picknose now leads the trolls.

TWO-EDGE

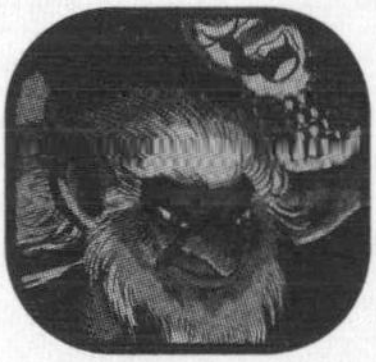

Two-Edge is the son of Winnowill and a troll named Smelt. He is an ingenious mastersmith and inventor. Immortal, he has already lived for many thousands of years. Two-Edge is unique on the World of Two Moons — a half-elf, half-troll hybrid. Emotionally abused as a child by Winnowill, Two-Edge was devastated when she killed his father and ever since has played a bizarre cat-and-mouse mind game with his mother...

IN THE PREVIOUS VOLUME

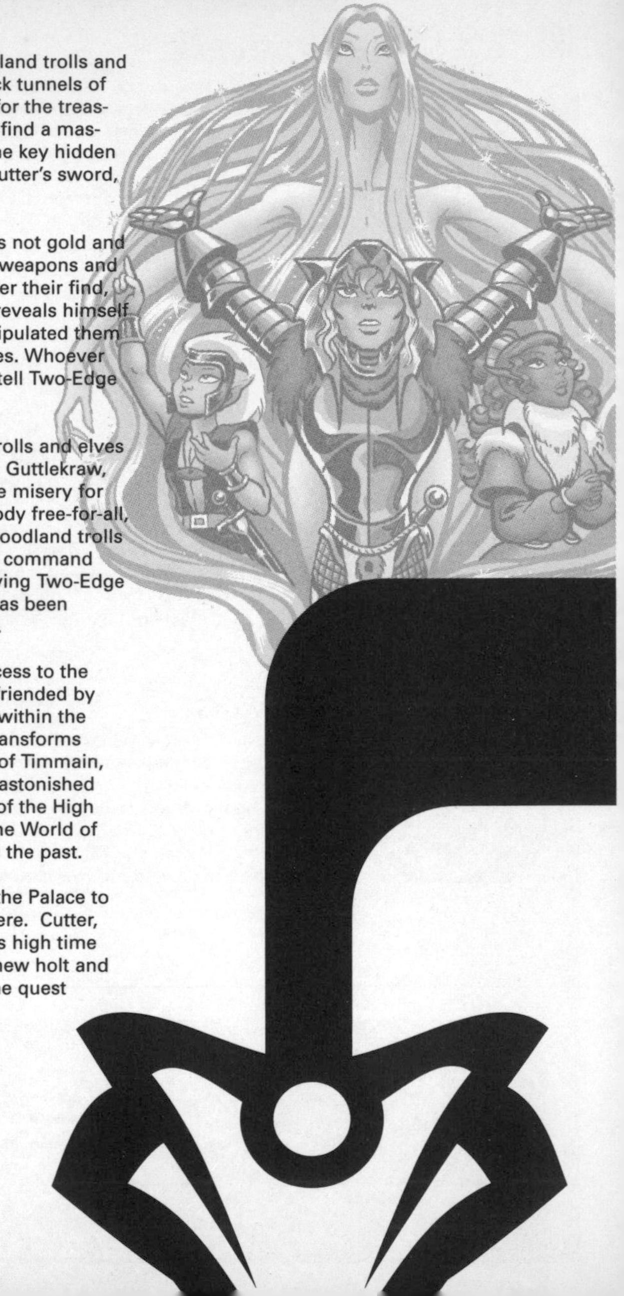

The reluctant alliance of woodland trolls and elves goes deep within the rock tunnels of the northern trolls, searching for the treasure of Two-Edge. Finally they find a massive doorway; Skywise uses the key hidden in the handle of New Moon, Cutter's sword, to unlock the entry.

The treasure chamber contains not gold and jewels, but beautifully crafted weapons and armor. Just as the elves ponder their find, Two-Edge, the mad half-troll, reveals himself and explains how he has manipulated them into fighting among themselves. Whoever wins — elf or troll — that will tell Two-Edge "who he truly is."

To the trickster's dismay, the trolls and elves unite against the larger threat: Guttlekraw, who has caused immeasurable misery for all. The battle becomes a bloody free-for-all, but ultimately the elves and woodland trolls are victorious. Picknose takes command from the slain Guttlekraw, leaving Two-Edge lost, wondering what lesson has been learned from his insane game.

At long last, the elves gain access to the Palace. One of the wolves befriended by the Wolfriders behaves oddly within the magical place and suddenly transforms back into its true form — that of Timmain, first of the High Ones. To the astonished elves, she reveals the secrets of the High Ones and how they came to the World of Two Moons countless years in the past.

Rayek chooses to stay within the Palace to study it, feeling he belongs there. Cutter, on the other hand, decides it is high time for the Wolfriders to create a new holt and so they set out, completing one quest and beginning another.

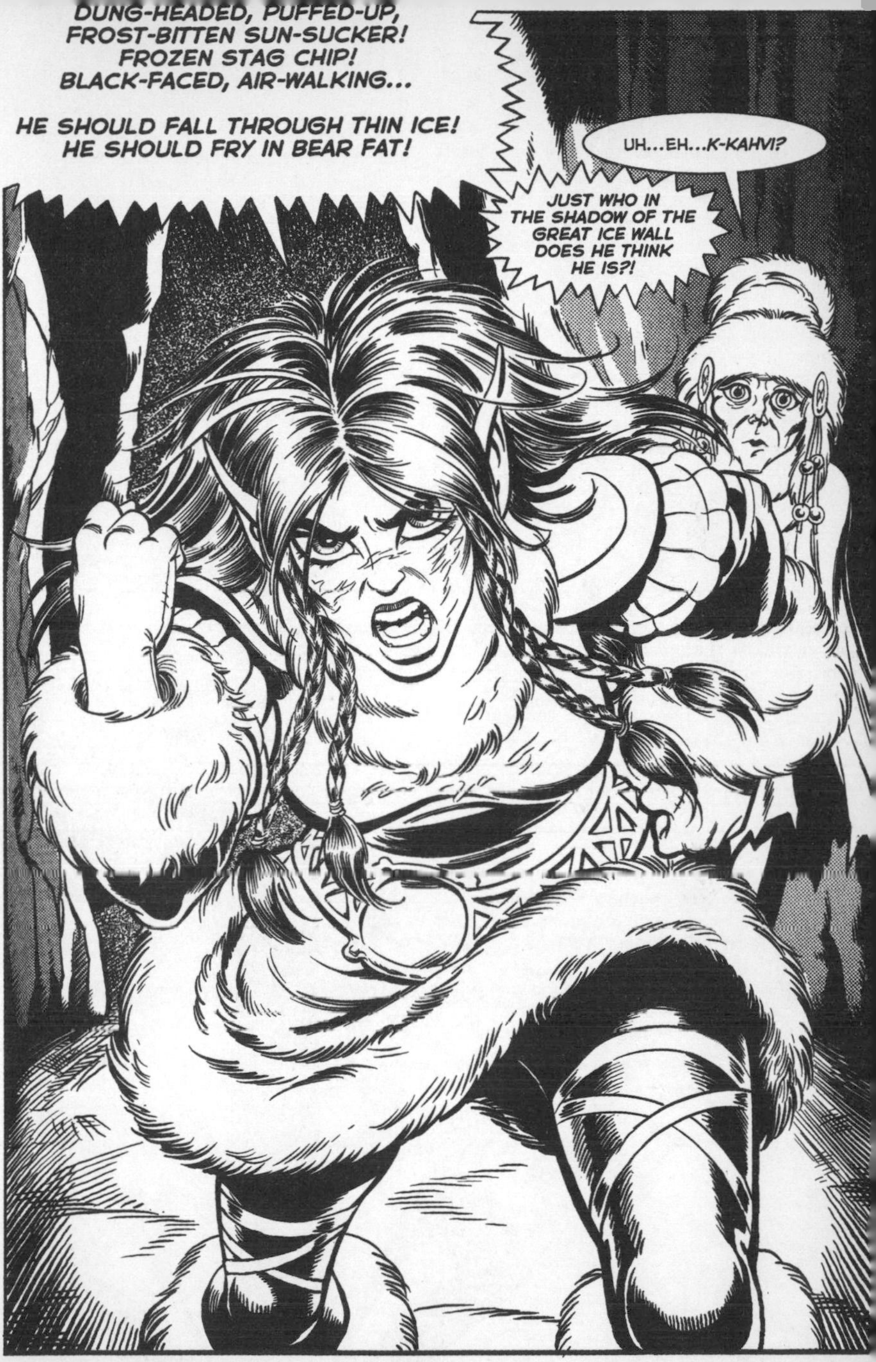
DUNG-HEADED, PUFFED-UP, FROST-BITTEN SUN-SUCKER! FROZEN STAG CHIP! BLACK-FACED, AIR-WALKING...
HE SHOULD FALL THROUGH THIN ICE! HE SHOULD FRY IN BEAR FAT!
JUST WHO IN THE SHADOW OF THE GREAT ICE WALL DOES HE THINK HE IS?!
UH...EH...K-KAHVI?

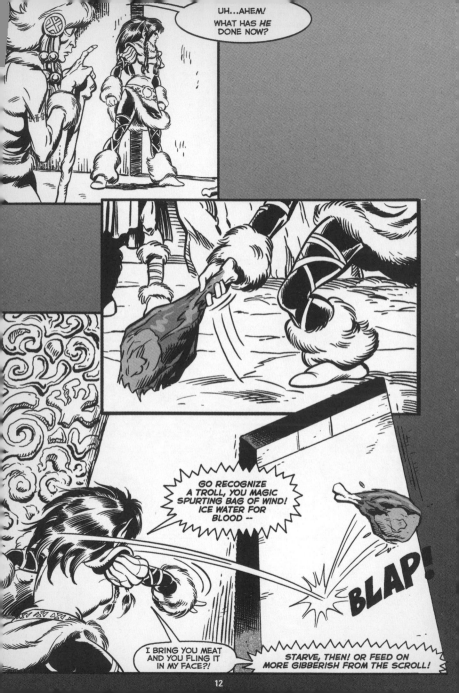

UH...AHEM!
WHAT HAS *HE*
DONE NOW?

GO RECOGNIZE
A TROLL, YOU MAGIC
SPURTING BAG OF WIND!
ICE WATER FOR
BLOOD --

BLAP!

I BRING YOU MEAT
AND YOU FLING IT
IN MY FACE?!

STARVE, THEN! OR FEED ON
MORE GIBBERISH FROM THE SCROLL!

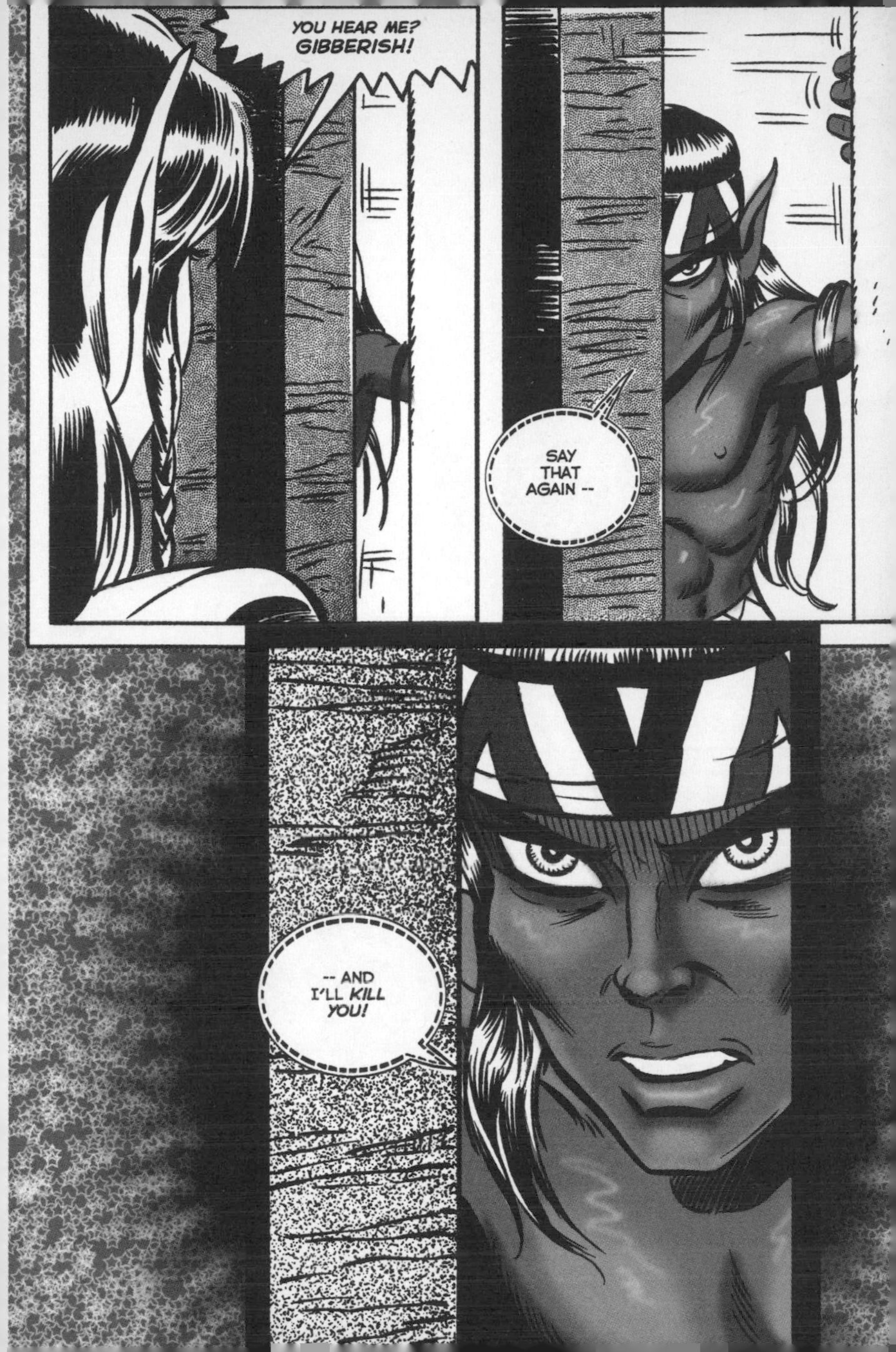
YOU HEAR ME? GIBBERISH!
SAY THAT AGAIN --
-- AND I'LL *KILL* YOU!

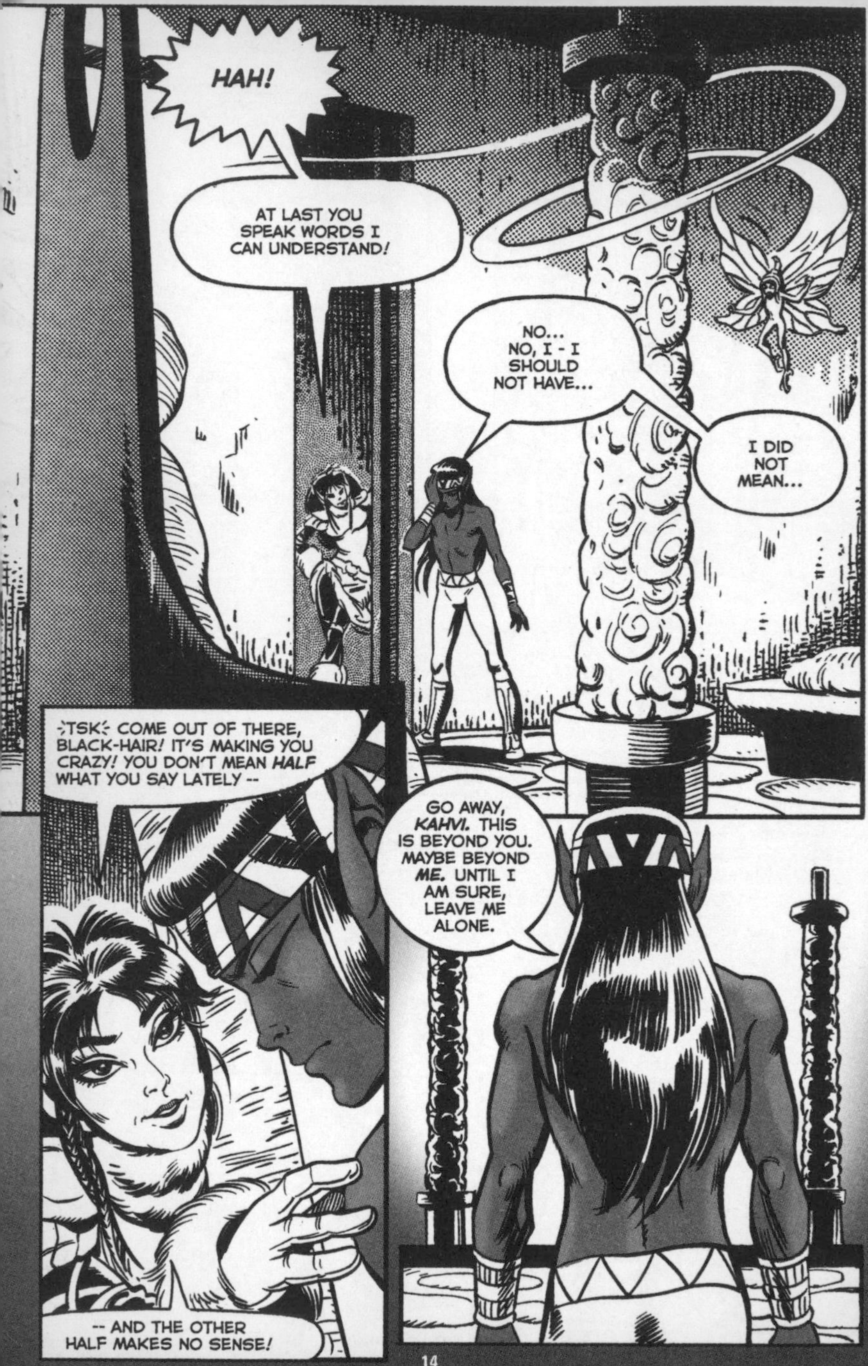
HAH!
AT LAST YOU SPEAK WORDS I CAN UNDERSTAND!
NO... NO, I - I SHOULD NOT HAVE...
I DID NOT MEAN...
-TSK- COME OUT OF THERE, BLACK-HAIR! IT'S MAKING YOU CRAZY! YOU DON'T MEAN HALF WHAT YOU SAY LATELY --
GO AWAY, KAHVI. THIS IS BEYOND YOU. MAYBE BEYOND ME. UNTIL I AM SURE, LEAVE ME ALONE.
-- AND THE OTHER HALF MAKES NO SENSE!

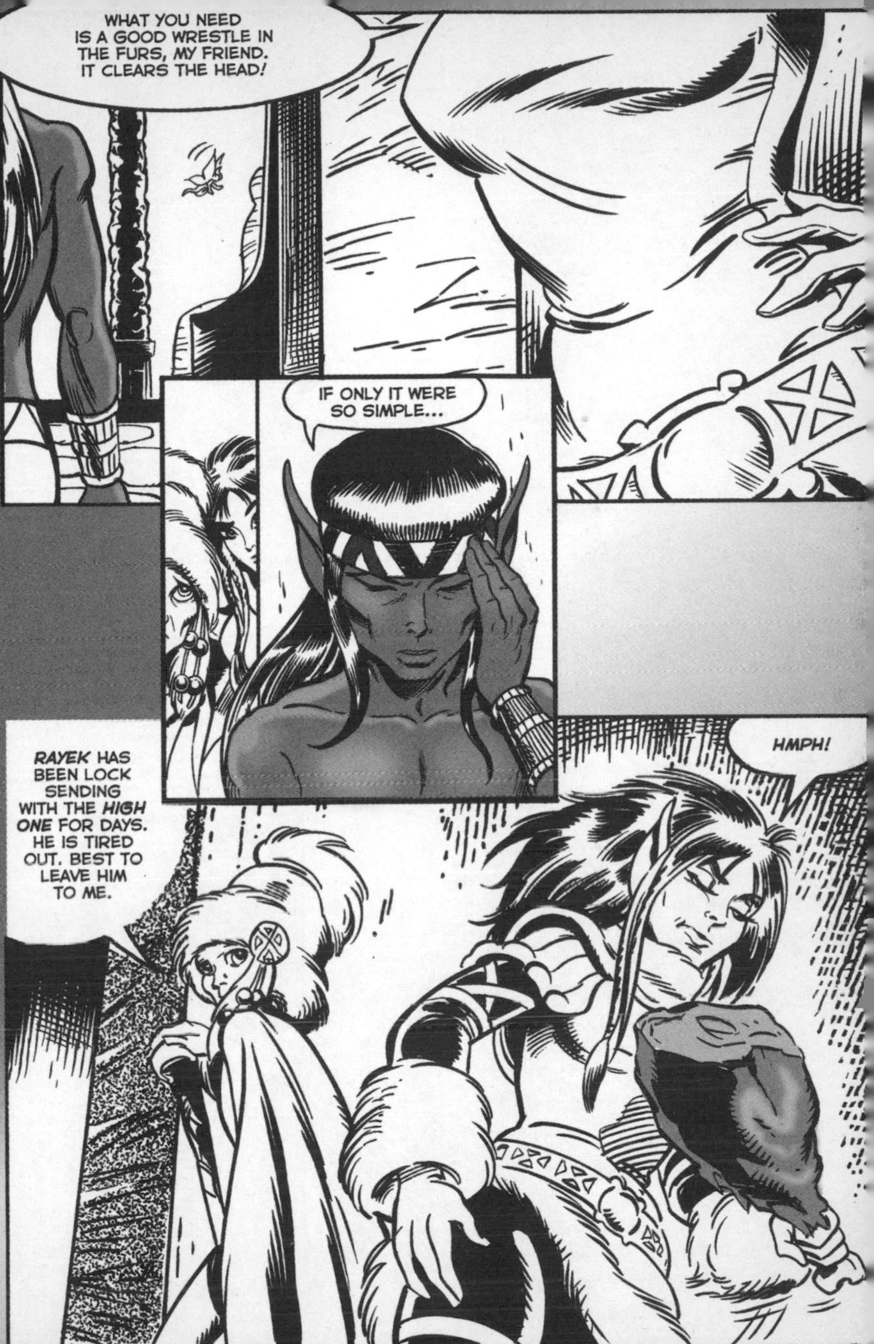
WHAT YOU NEED IS A GOOD WRESTLE IN THE FURS, MY FRIEND. IT CLEARS THE HEAD!
IF ONLY IT WERE SO SIMPLE...
RAYEK HAS BEEN LOCK SENDING WITH THE HIGH ONE FOR DAYS. HE IS TIRED OUT. BEST TO LEAVE HIM TO ME.
HMPH!

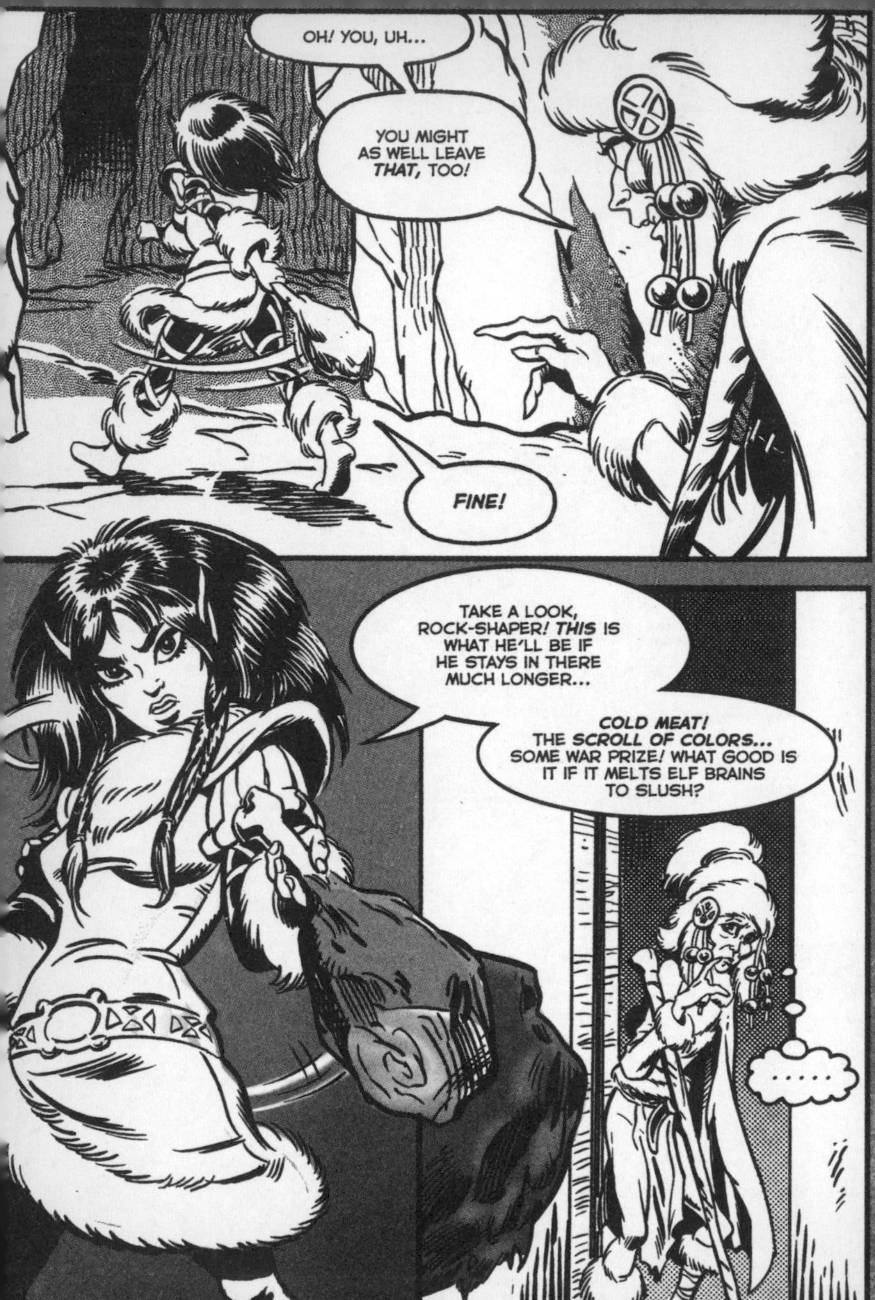
OH! YOU, UH...
YOU MIGHT AS WELL LEAVE *THAT,* TOO!
FINE!
TAKE A LOOK, ROCK-SHAPER! *THIS* IS WHAT HE'LL BE IF HE STAYS IN THERE MUCH LONGER...
COLD MEAT! THE *SCROLL OF COLORS...* SOME WAR PRIZE! WHAT GOOD IS IT IF IT MELTS ELF BRAINS TO SLUSH?
.....

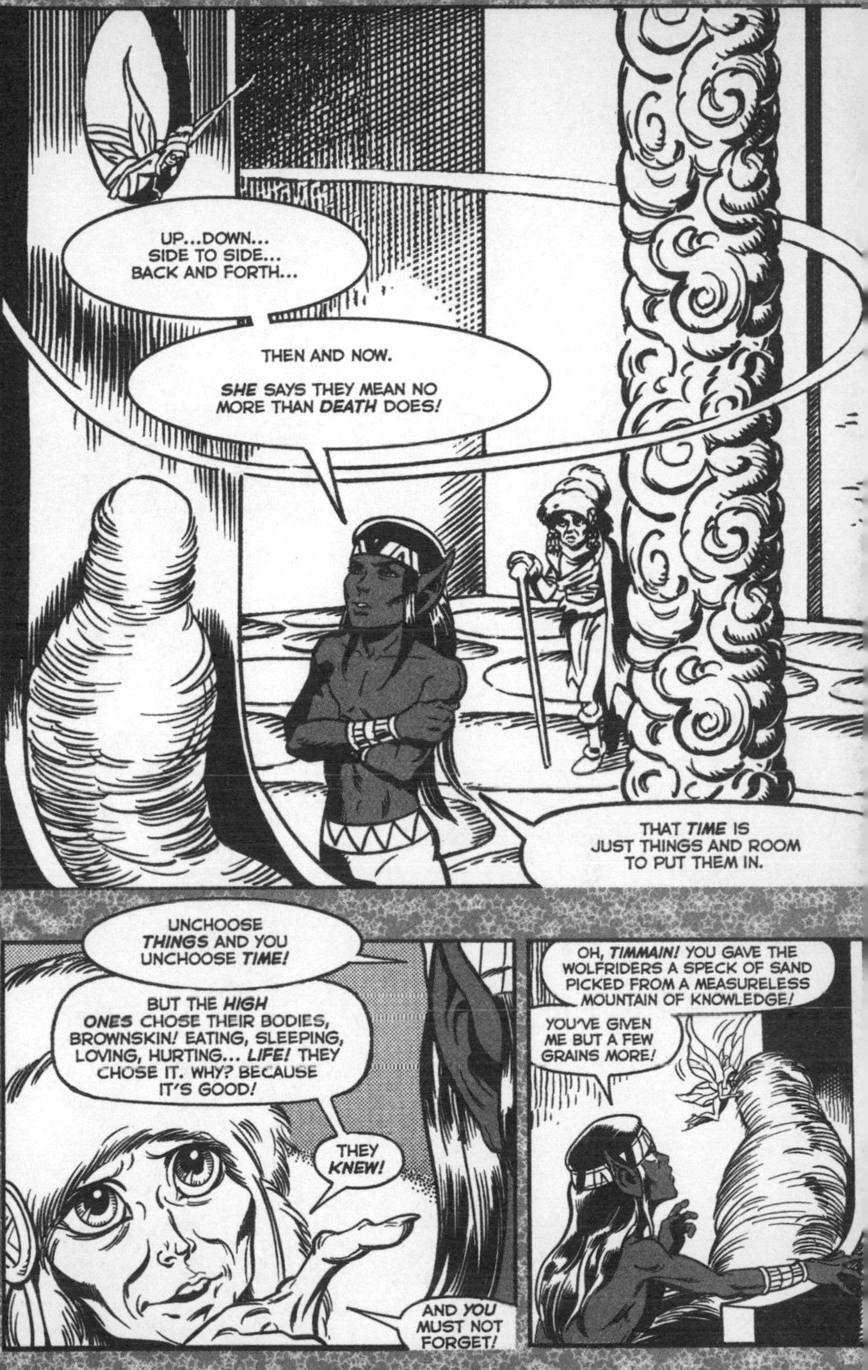

UP...DOWN... SIDE TO SIDE... BACK AND FORTH...
THEN AND NOW.
SHE SAYS THEY MEAN NO MORE THAN *DEATH* DOES!
THAT *TIME* IS JUST THINGS AND ROOM TO PUT THEM IN.
UNCHOOSE *THINGS* AND YOU UNCHOOSE *TIME!*
BUT THE *HIGH ONES* CHOSE THEIR BODIES, BROWNSKIN! EATING, SLEEPING, LOVING, HURTING... *LIFE!* THEY CHOSE IT. WHY? BECAUSE IT'S GOOD!
THEY *KNEW!*
AND *YOU* MUST NOT FORGET!
OH, *TIMMAIN!* YOU GAVE THE WOLFRIDERS A SPECK OF SAND PICKED FROM A MEASURELESS MOUNTAIN OF KNOWLEDGE!
YOU'VE GIVEN ME BUT A FEW GRAINS MORE!

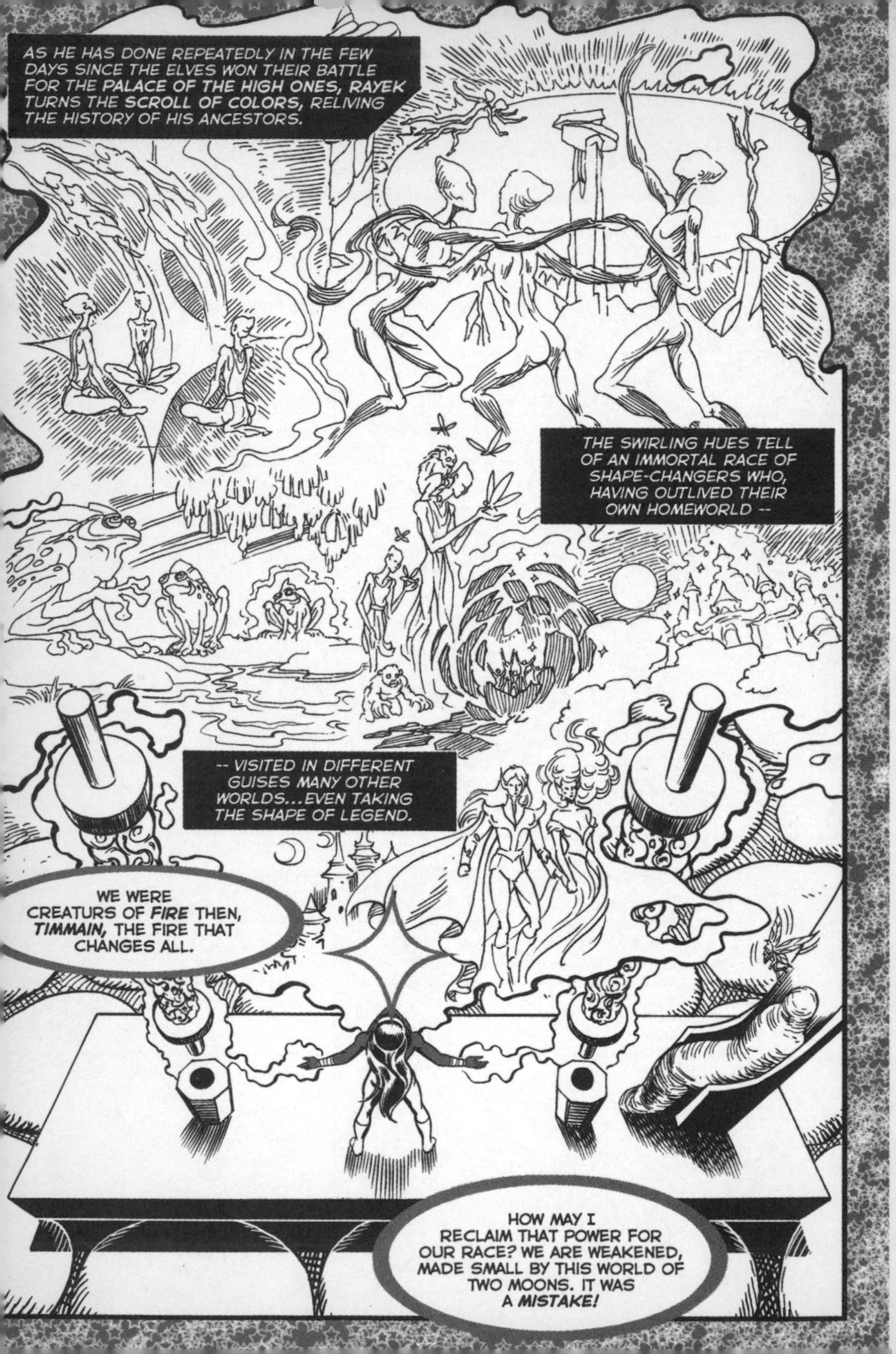
AS HE HAS DONE REPEATEDLY IN THE FEW DAYS SINCE THE ELVES WON THEIR BATTLE FOR THE PALACE OF THE HIGH ONES, RAYEK TURNS THE SCROLL OF COLORS, RELIVING THE HISTORY OF HIS ANCESTORS.
THE SWIRLING HUES TELL OF AN IMMORTAL RACE OF SHAPE-CHANGERS WHO, HAVING OUTLIVED THEIR OWN HOMEWORLD --
-- VISITED IN DIFFERENT GUISES MANY OTHER WORLDS...EVEN TAKING THE SHAPE OF LEGEND.
WE WERE CREATURES OF FIRE THEN, TIMMAIN, THE FIRE THAT CHANGES ALL.
HOW MAY I RECLAIM THAT POWER FOR OUR RACE? WE ARE WEAKENED, MADE SMALL BY THIS WORLD OF TWO MOONS. IT WAS A MISTAKE!

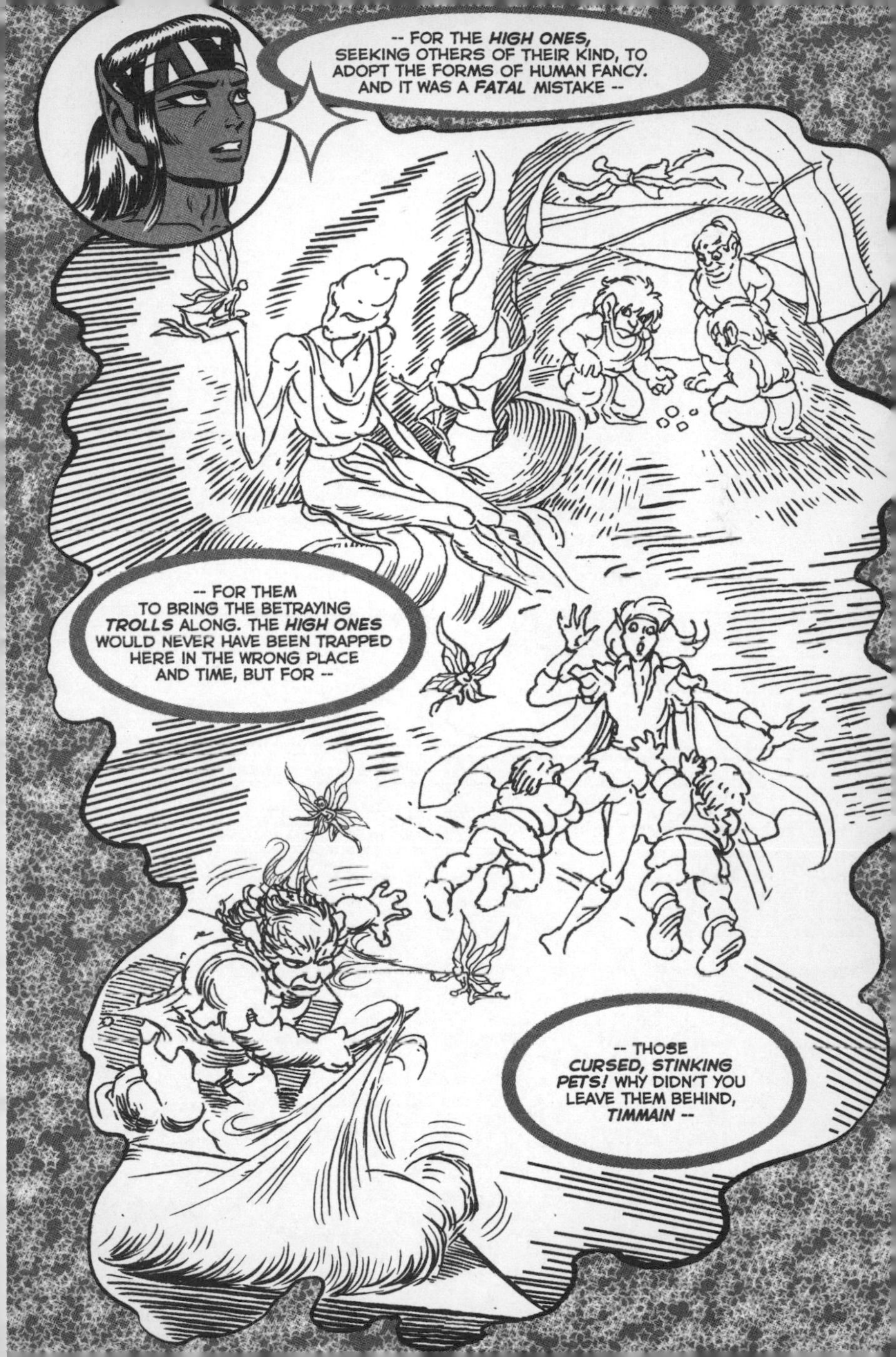
-- FOR THE *HIGH ONES*, SEEKING OTHERS OF THEIR KIND, TO ADOPT THE FORMS OF HUMAN FANCY. AND IT WAS A *FATAL* MISTAKE --
-- FOR THEM TO BRING THE BETRAYING *TROLLS* ALONG. THE *HIGH ONES* WOULD NEVER HAVE BEEN TRAPPED HERE IN THE WRONG PLACE AND TIME, BUT FOR --
-- THOSE *CURSED, STINKING PETS!* WHY DIDN'T YOU LEAVE THEM BEHIND, *TIMMAIN* --

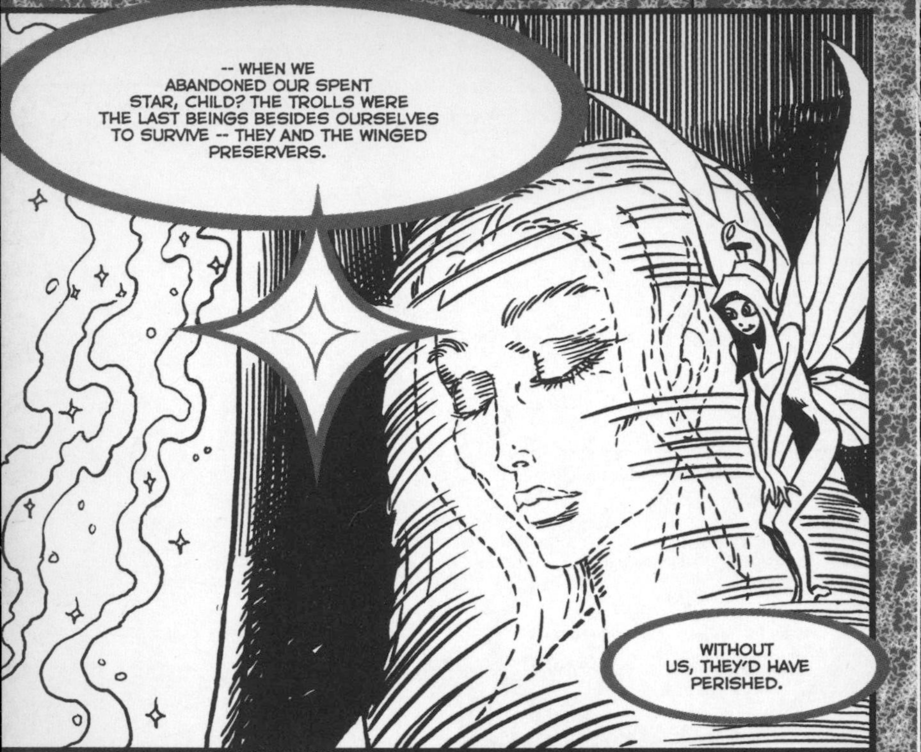
-- WHEN WE ABANDONED OUR SPENT STAR, CHILD? THE TROLLS WERE THE LAST BEINGS BESIDES OURSELVES TO SURVIVE -- THEY AND THE WINGED PRESERVERS.
WITHOUT US, THEY'D HAVE PERISHED.

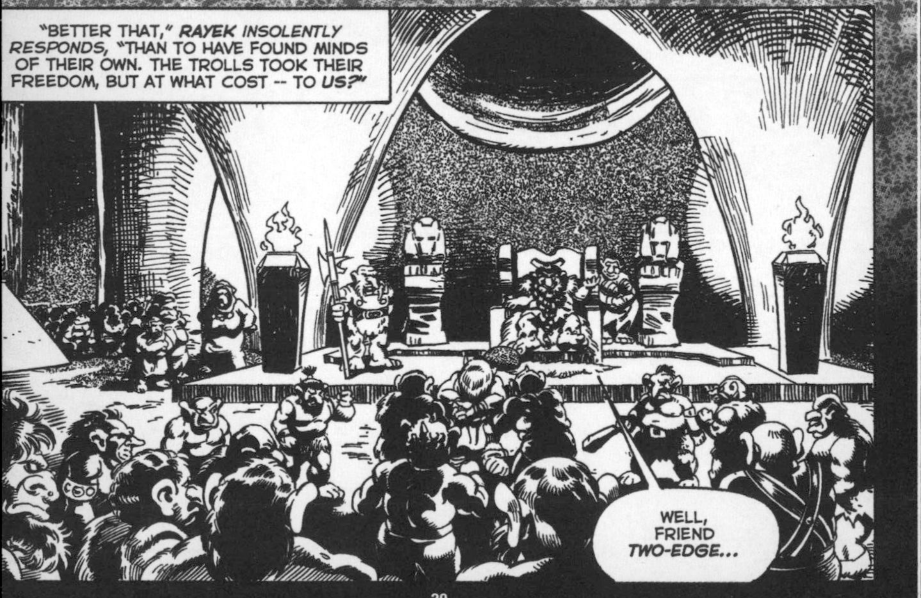
"BETTER THAT," *RAYEK INSOLENTLY RESPONDS,* "THAN TO HAVE FOUND MINDS OF THEIR OWN. THE TROLLS TOOK THEIR FREEDOM, BUT AT WHAT COST -- TO *US?*"
WELL, FRIEND *TWO-EDGE...*

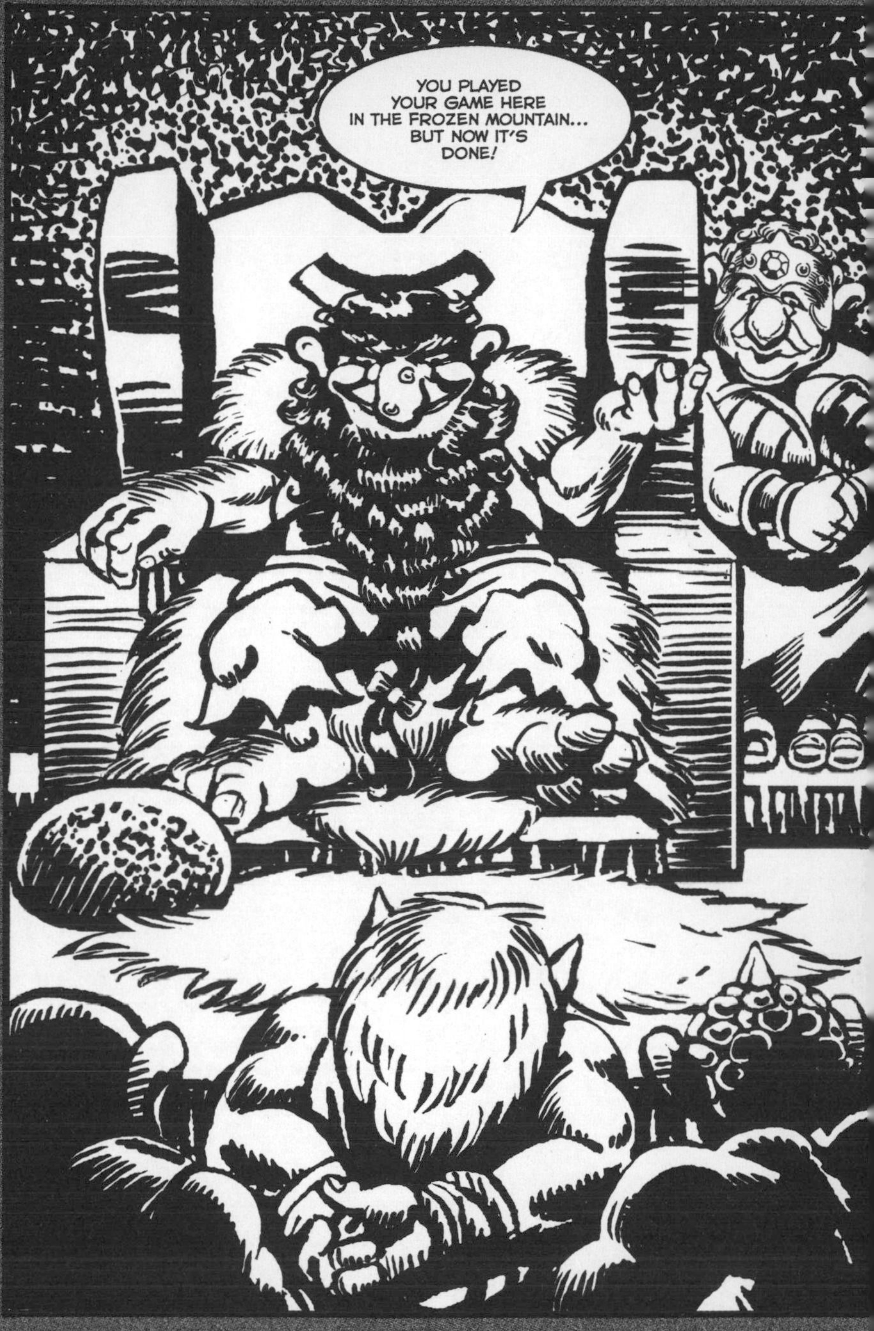
YOU PLAYED YOUR GAME HERE IN THE FROZEN MOUNTAIN... BUT NOW IT'S DONE!

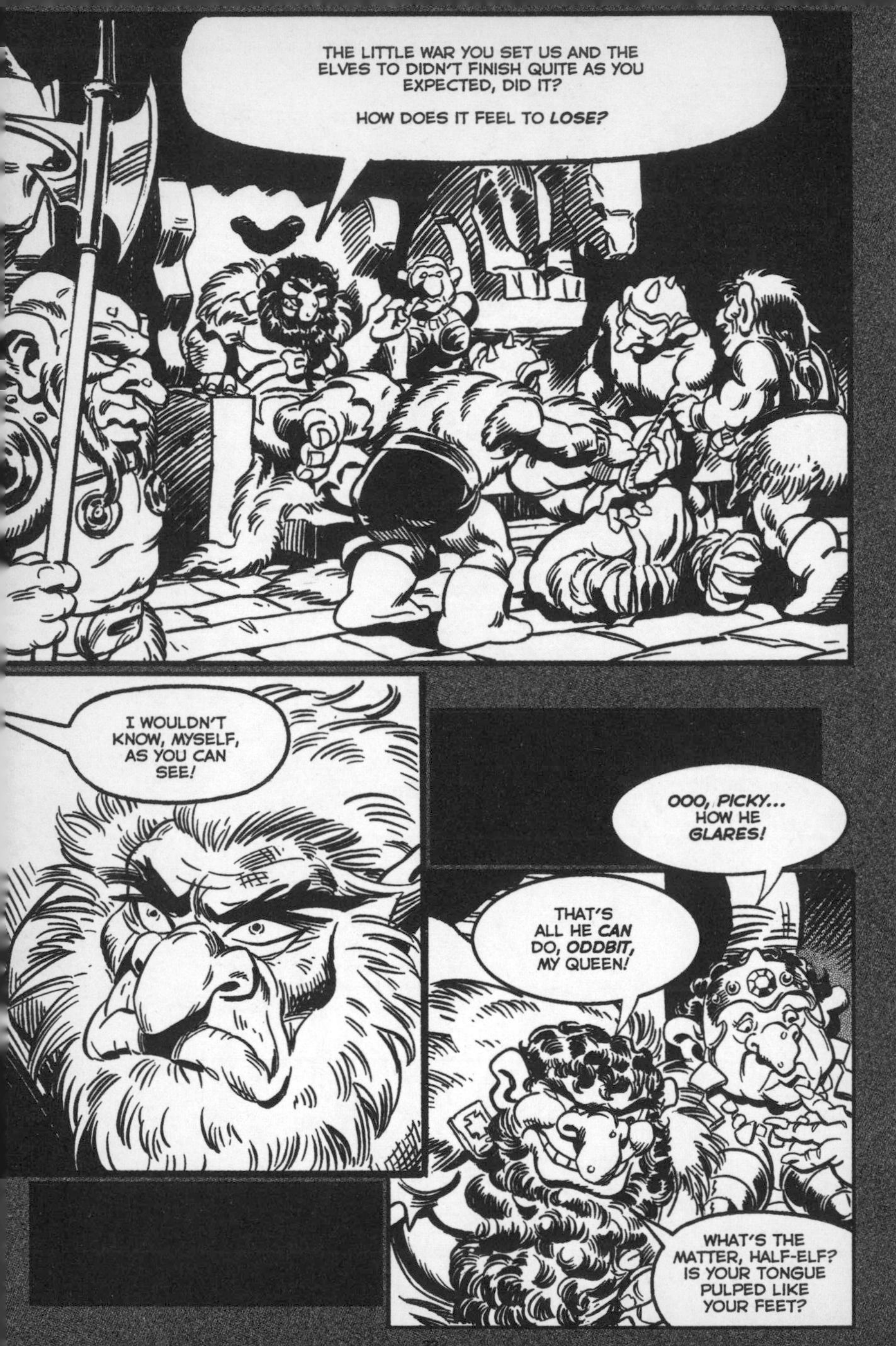
THE LITTLE WAR YOU SET US AND THE ELVES TO DIDN'T FINISH QUITE AS YOU EXPECTED, DID IT?
HOW DOES IT FEEL TO *LOSE?*
I WOULDN'T KNOW, MYSELF, AS YOU CAN SEE!
OOO, PICKY... HOW HE *GLARES!*
THAT'S ALL HE *CAN* DO, *ODDBIT,* MY QUEEN!
WHAT'S THE MATTER, HALF-ELF? IS YOUR TONGUE PULPED LIKE YOUR FEET?

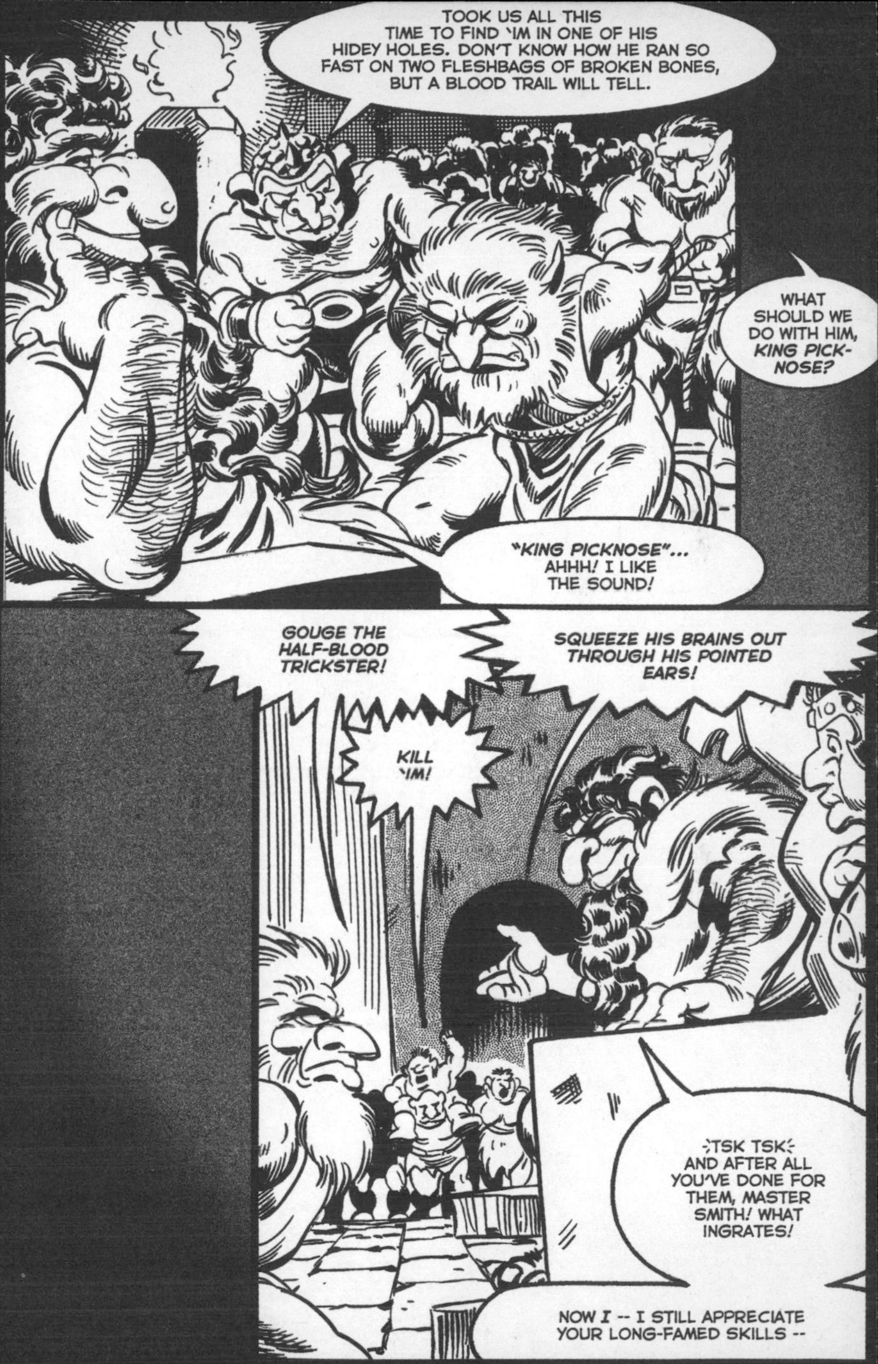
TOOK US ALL THIS TIME TO FIND 'IM IN ONE OF HIS HIDEY HOLES. DON'T KNOW HOW HE RAN SO FAST ON TWO FLESHBAGS OF BROKEN BONES, BUT A BLOOD TRAIL WILL TELL.
WHAT SHOULD WE DO WITH HIM, *KING PICK-NOSE?*
"KING PICKNOSE"... AHHH! I LIKE THE SOUND!
GOUGE THE HALF-BLOOD TRICKSTER!
SQUEEZE HIS BRAINS OUT THROUGH HIS POINTED EARS!
KILL 'IM!
TSK TSK AND AFTER ALL YOU'VE DONE FOR THEM, MASTER SMITH! WHAT INGRATES!
NOW *I* -- I STILL APPRECIATE YOUR LONG-FAMED SKILLS --

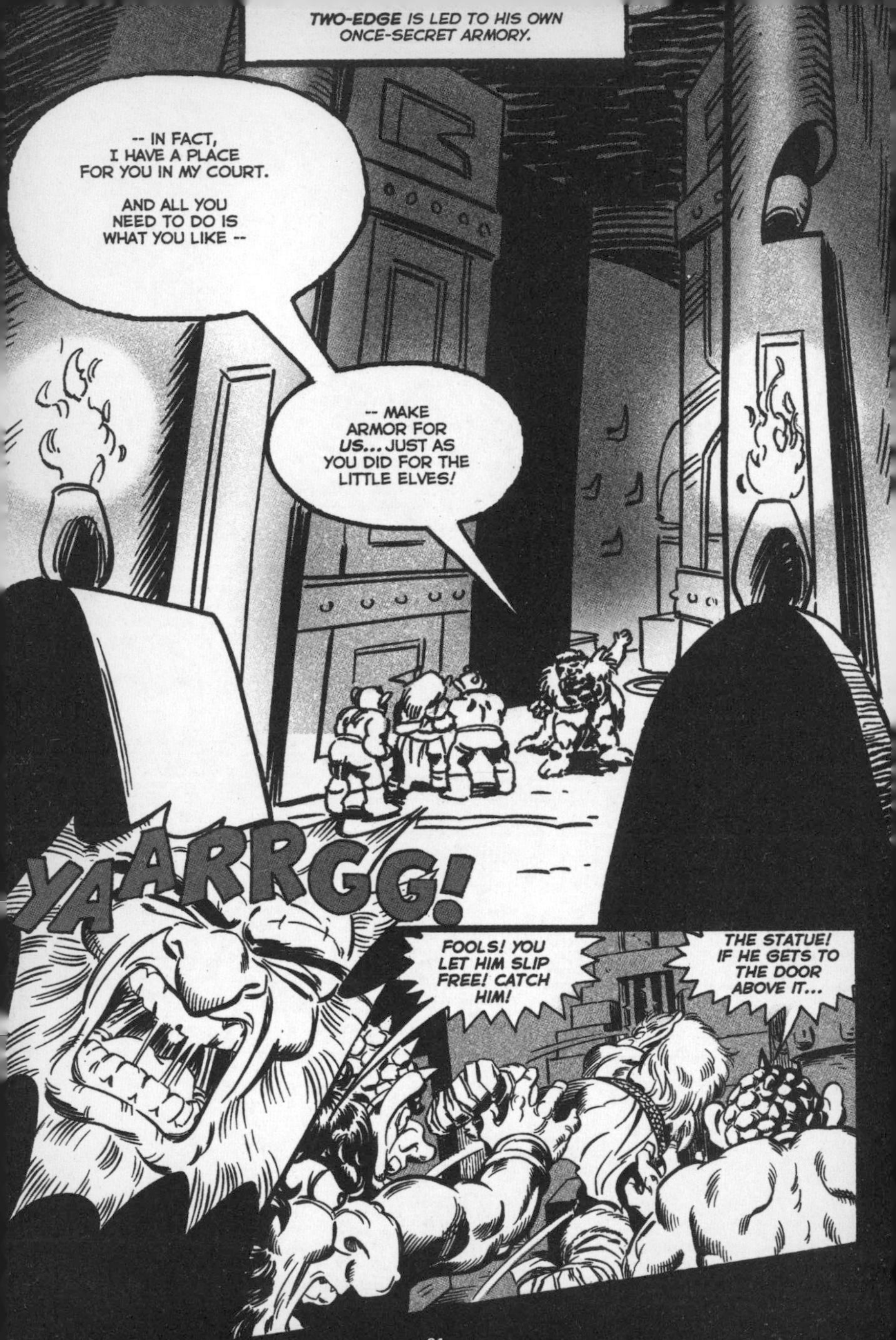
TWO-EDGE IS LED TO HIS OWN ONCE-SECRET ARMORY.
-- IN FACT, I HAVE A PLACE FOR YOU IN MY COURT.
AND ALL YOU NEED TO DO IS WHAT YOU LIKE --
-- MAKE ARMOR FOR US... JUST AS YOU DID FOR THE LITTLE ELVES!
YAARRGG!
FOOLS! YOU LET HIM SLIP FREE! CATCH HIM!
THE STATUE! IF HE GETS TO THE DOOR ABOVE IT...

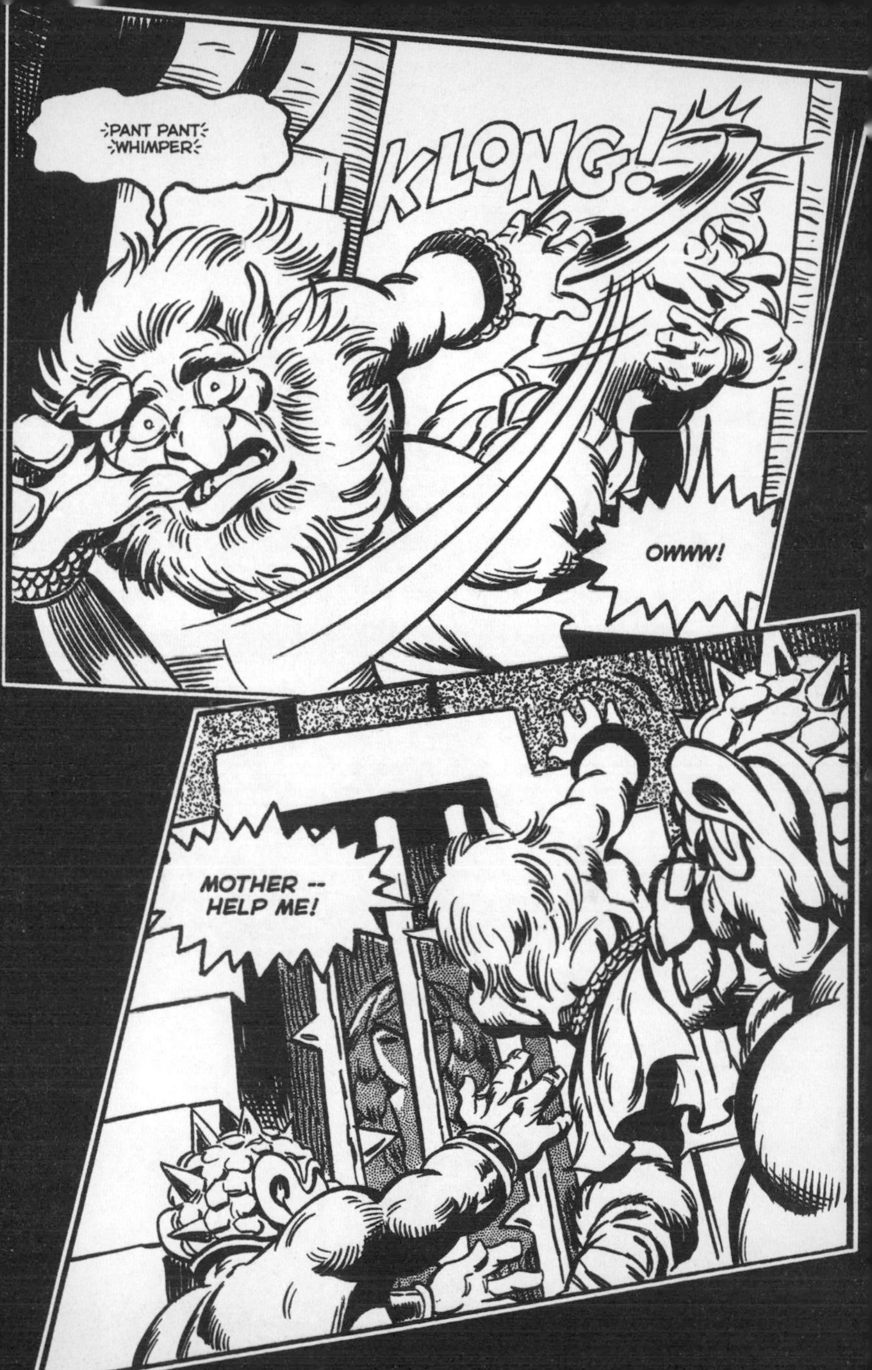
PANT PANT
WHIMPER
KLONG!
OWWW!
MOTHER -- HELP ME!

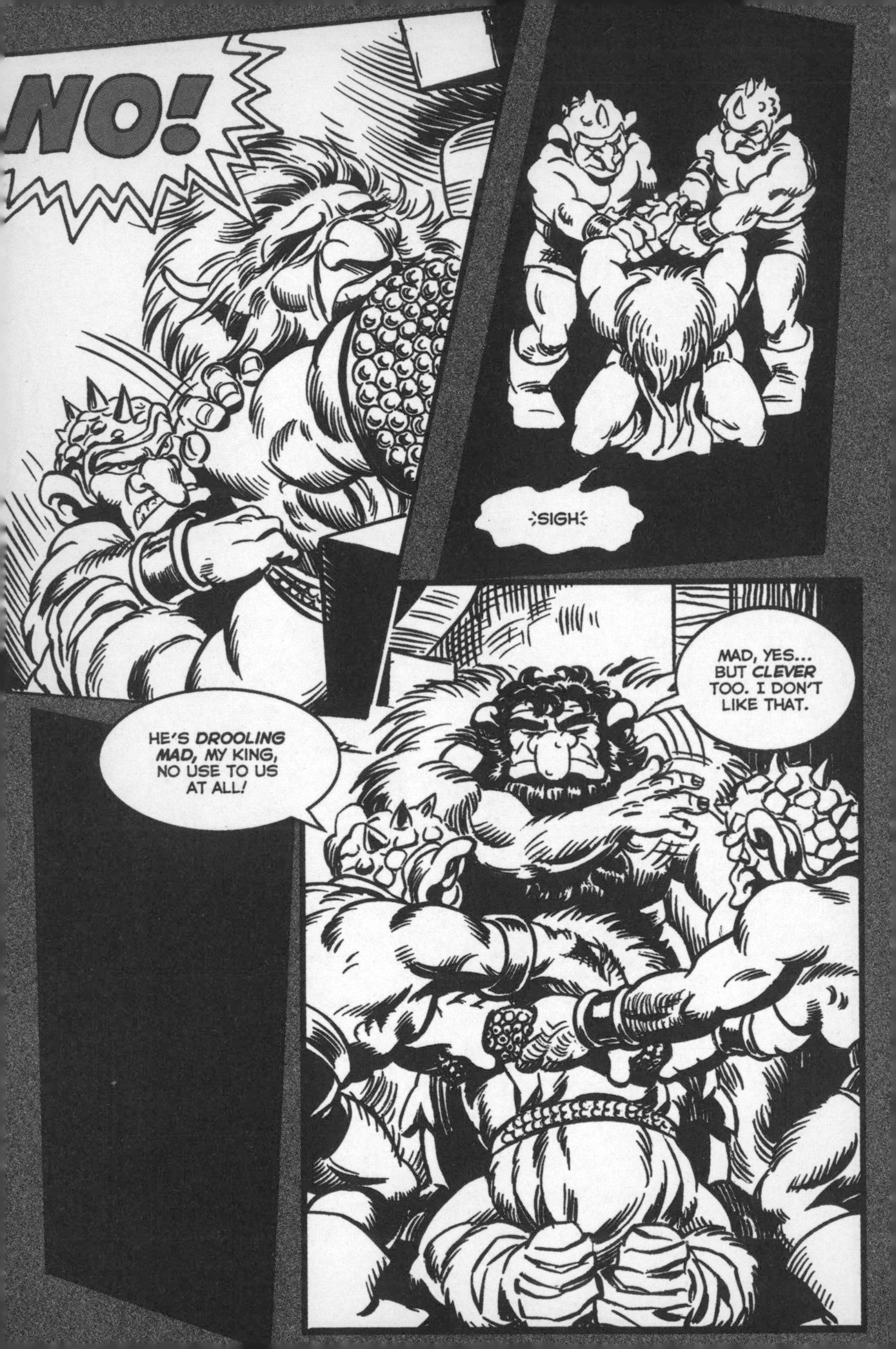
NO!
:SIGH:
HE'S DROOLING MAD, MY KING, NO USE TO US AT ALL!
MAD, YES... BUT CLEVER TOO. I DON'T LIKE THAT.

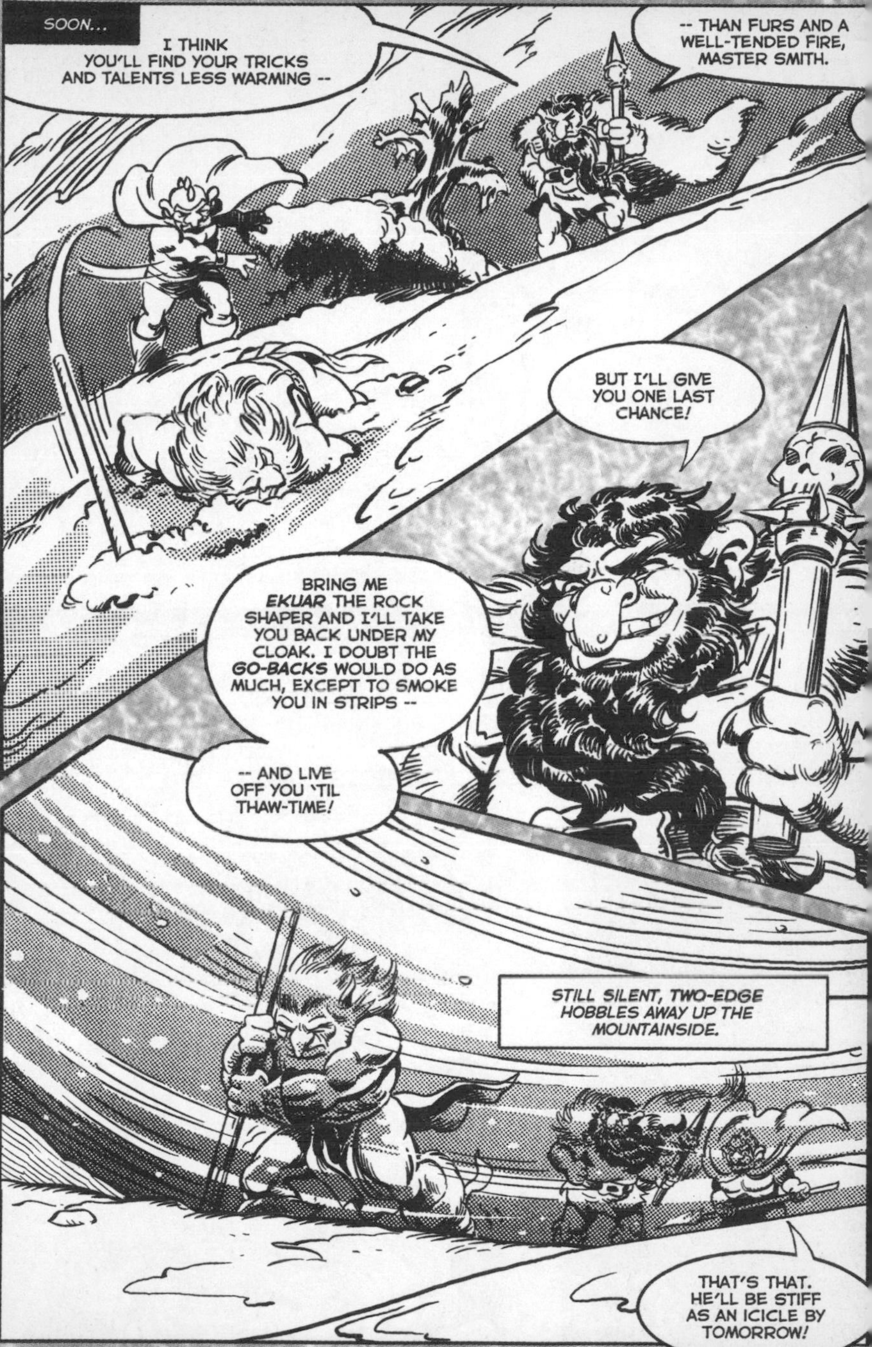
SOON...
I THINK YOU'LL FIND YOUR TRICKS AND TALENTS LESS WARMING --
-- THAN FURS AND A WELL-TENDED FIRE, MASTER SMITH.
BUT I'LL GIVE YOU ONE LAST CHANCE!
BRING ME EKUAR THE ROCK SHAPER AND I'LL TAKE YOU BACK UNDER MY CLOAK. I DOUBT THE GO-BACKS WOULD DO AS MUCH, EXCEPT TO SMOKE YOU IN STRIPS --
-- AND LIVE OFF YOU 'TIL THAW-TIME!
STILL SILENT, TWO-EDGE HOBBLES AWAY UP THE MOUNTAINSIDE.
THAT'S THAT. HE'LL BE STIFF AS AN ICICLE BY TOMORROW!

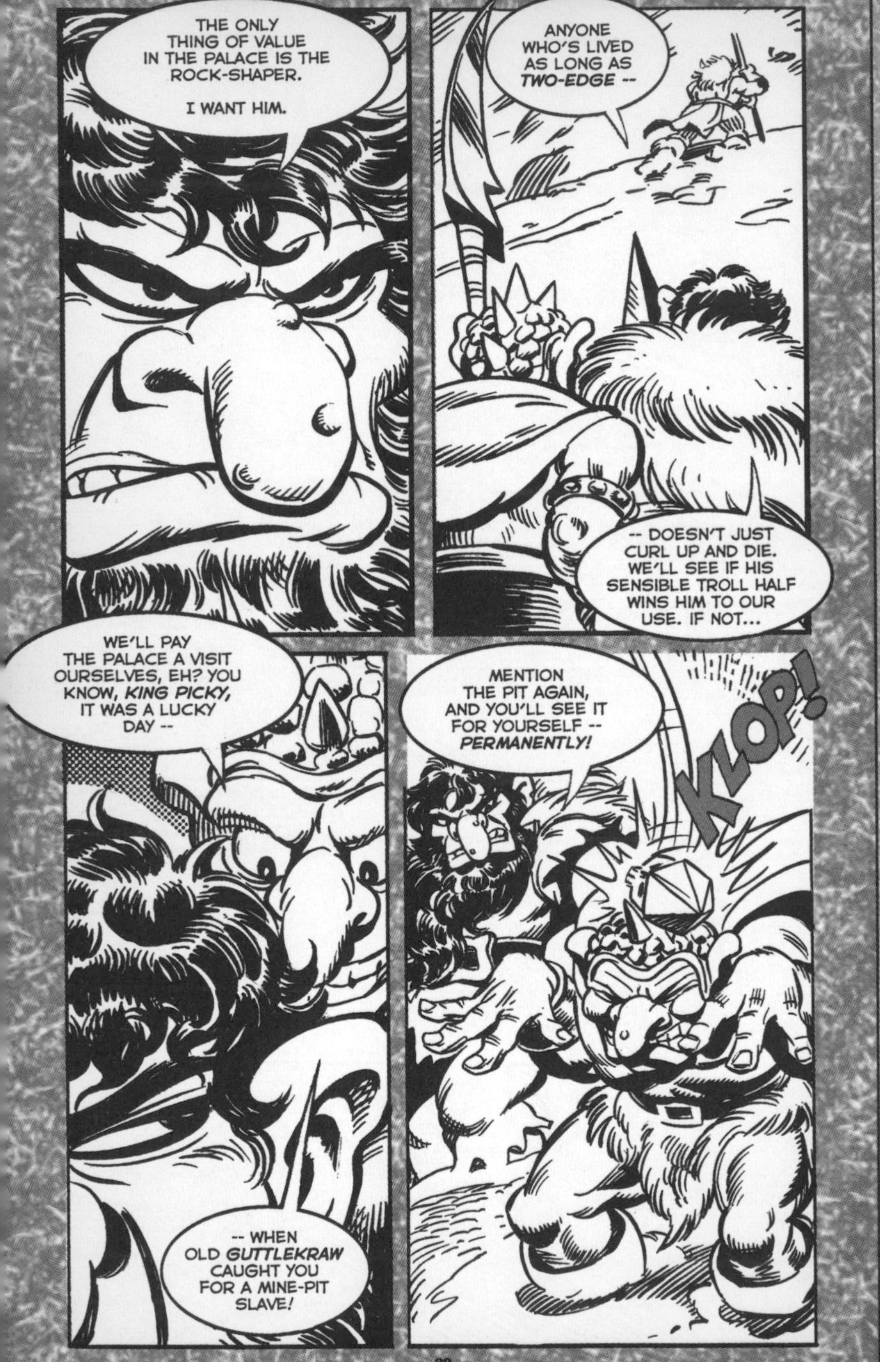
THE ONLY THING OF VALUE IN THE PALACE IS THE ROCK-SHAPER.
I WANT HIM.
ANYONE WHO'S LIVED AS LONG AS *TWO-EDGE* --
-- DOESN'T JUST CURL UP AND DIE. WE'LL SEE IF HIS SENSIBLE TROLL HALF WINS HIM TO OUR USE. IF NOT...
WE'LL PAY THE PALACE A VISIT OURSELVES, EH? YOU KNOW, *KING PICKY,* IT WAS A LUCKY DAY --
-- WHEN OLD *GUTTLEKRAW* CAUGHT YOU FOR A MINE-PIT SLAVE*!*
MENTION THE PIT AGAIN, AND YOU'LL SEE IT FOR YOURSELF -- *PERMANENTLY!*
KLOP!

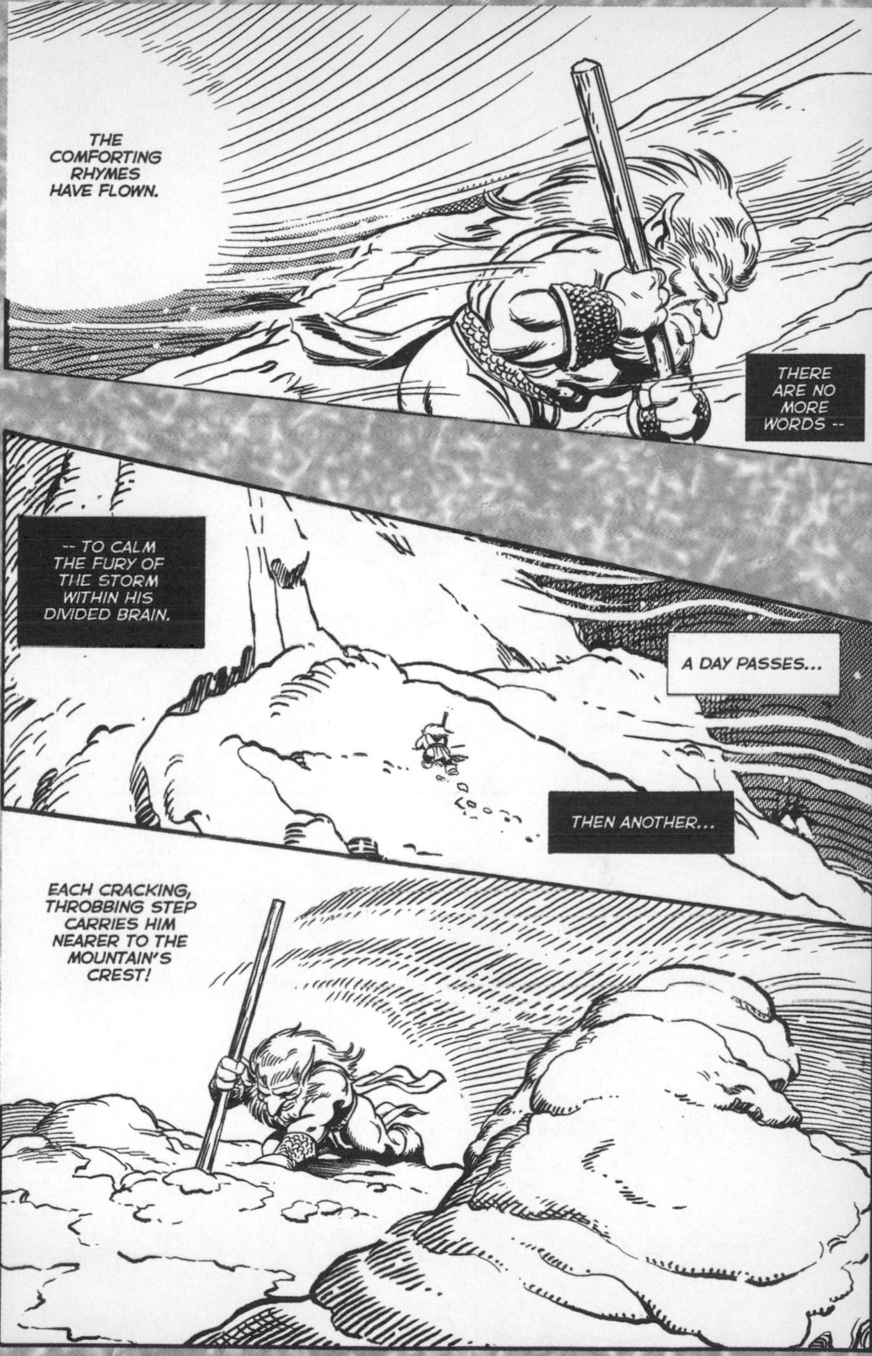
THE COMFORTING RHYMES HAVE FLOWN.
THERE ARE NO MORE WORDS --
-- TO CALM THE FURY OF THE STORM WITHIN HIS DIVIDED BRAIN.
A DAY PASSES...
THEN ANOTHER...
EACH CRACKING, THROBBING STEP CARRIES HIM NEARER TO THE MOUNTAIN'S CREST!

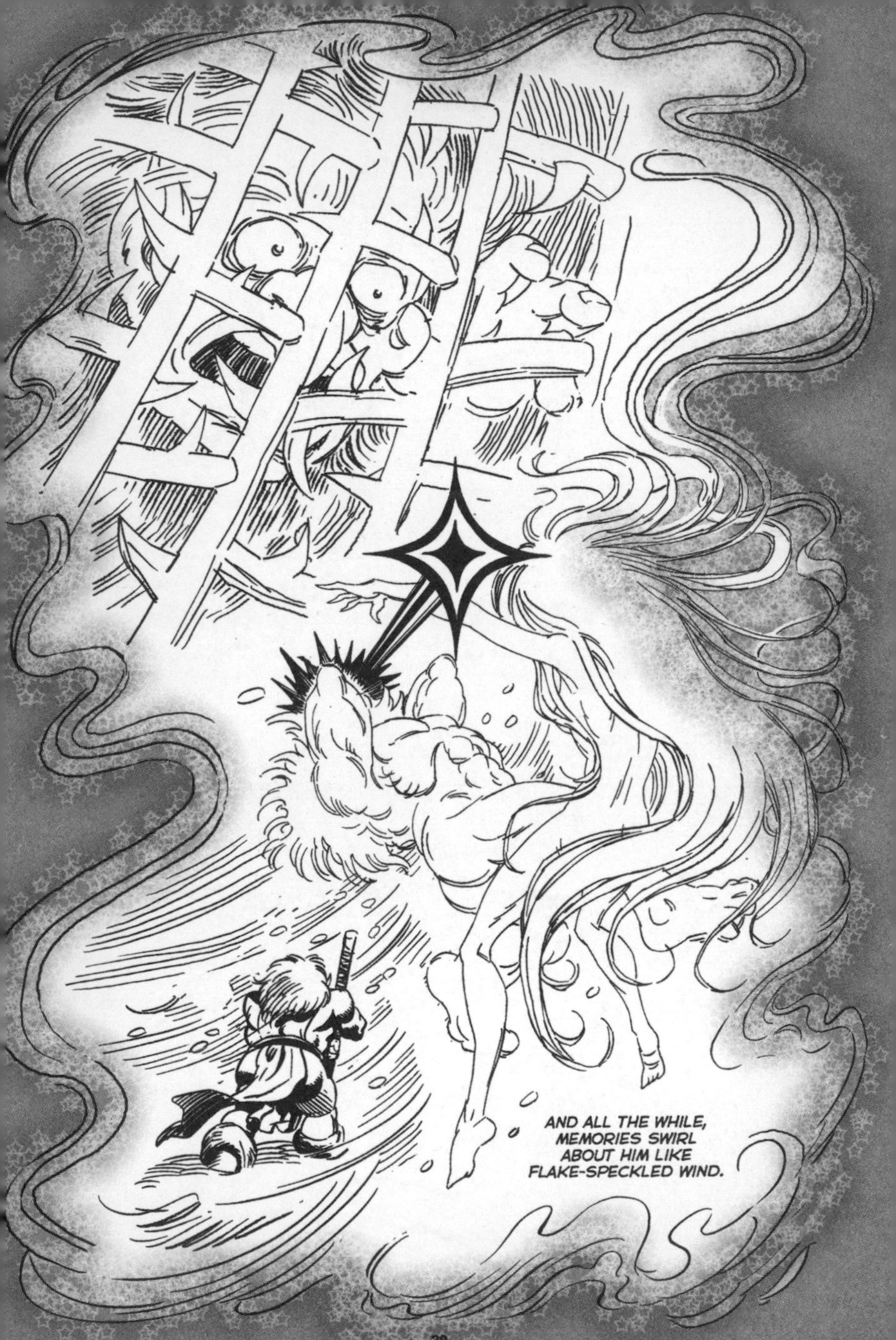
AND ALL THE WHILE, MEMORIES SWIRL ABOUT HIM LIKE FLAKE-SPECKLED WIND.

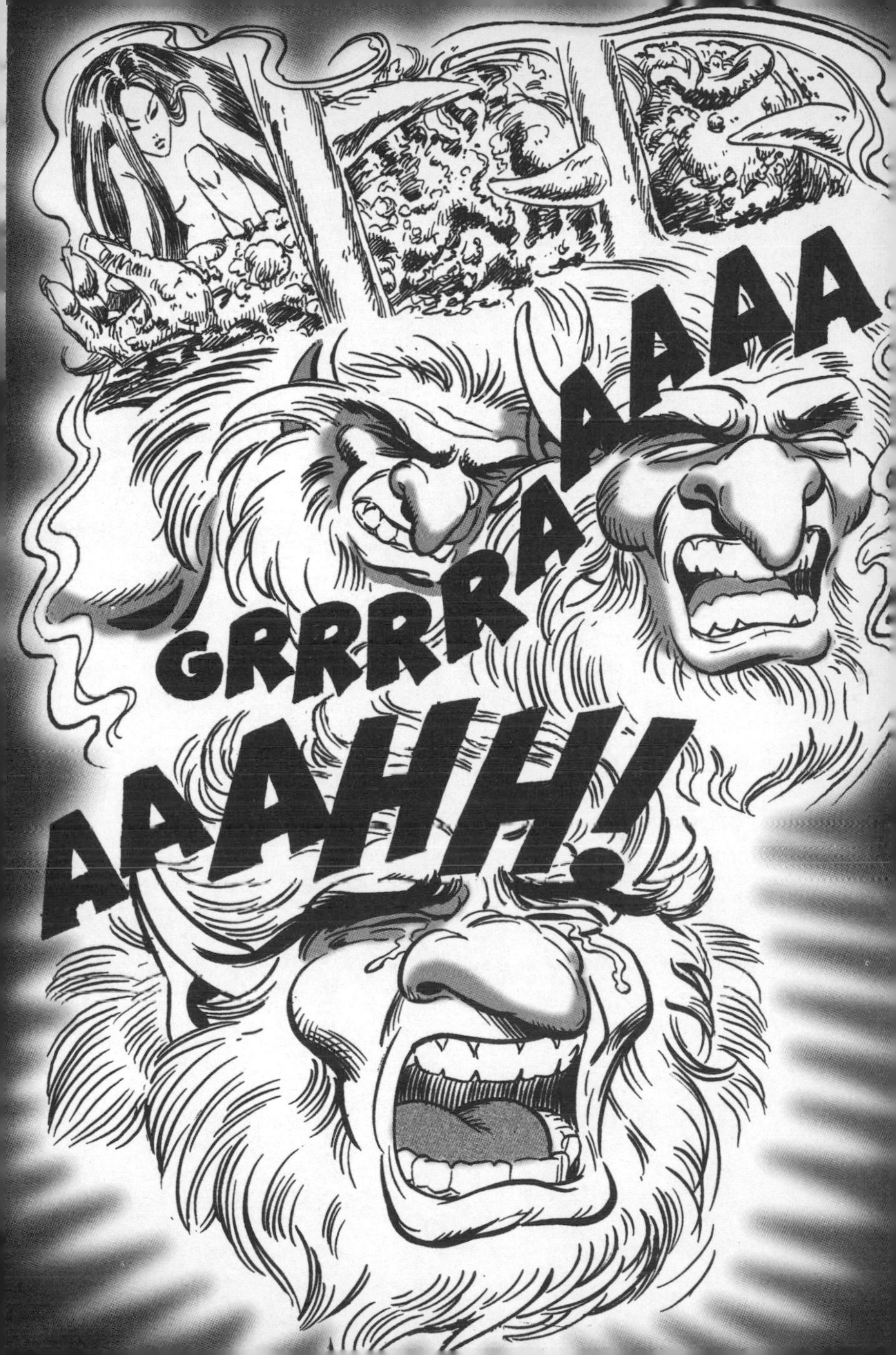
GRRRRAAAAA
AAAHH!

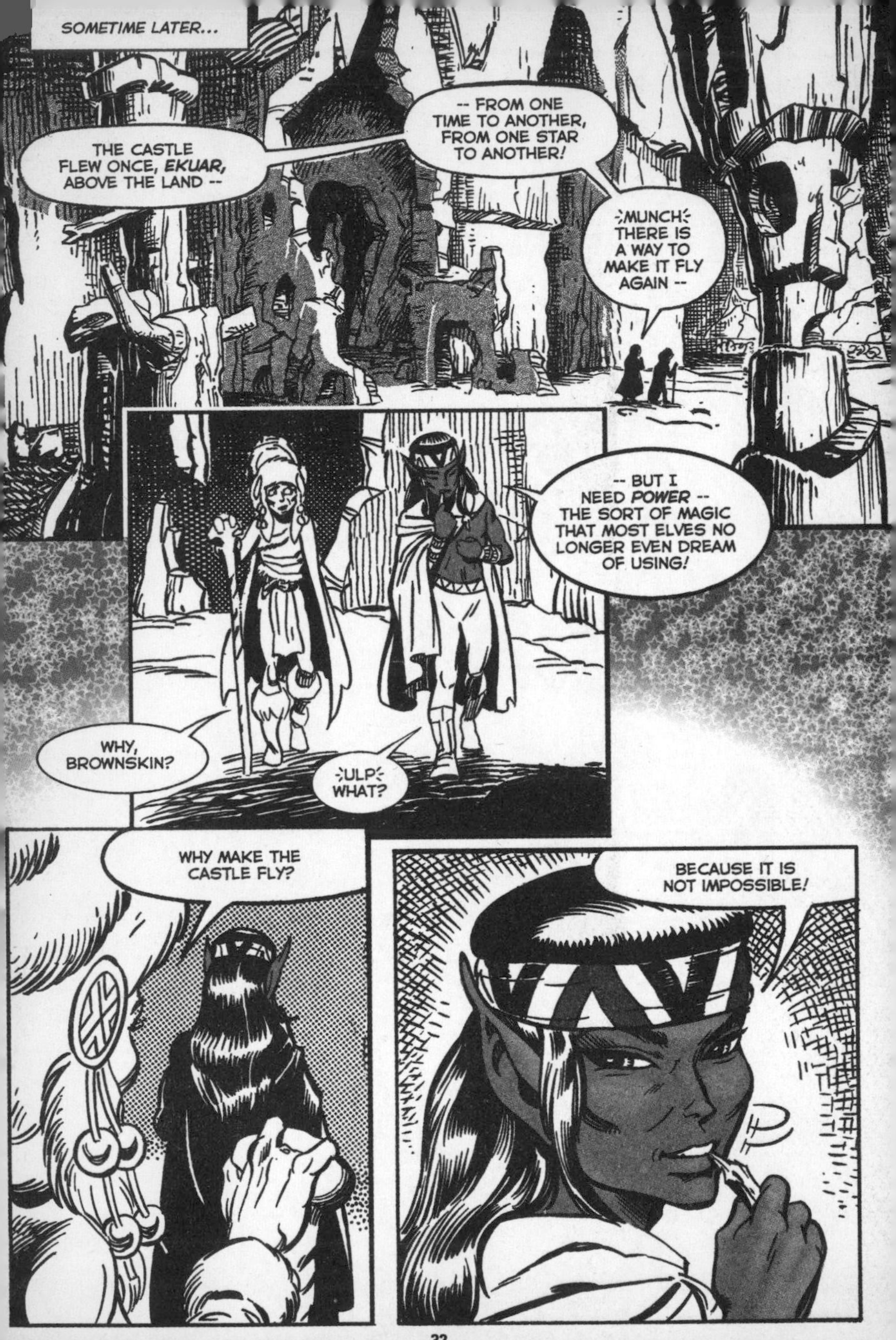
SOMETIME LATER...
THE CASTLE FLEW ONCE, EKUAR, ABOVE THE LAND --
-- FROM ONE TIME TO ANOTHER, FROM ONE STAR TO ANOTHER!
MUNCH THERE IS A WAY TO MAKE IT FLY AGAIN --
-- BUT I NEED POWER -- THE SORT OF MAGIC THAT MOST ELVES NO LONGER EVEN DREAM OF USING!
WHY, BROWNSKIN?
ULP WHAT?
WHY MAKE THE CASTLE FLY?
BECAUSE IT IS NOT IMPOSSIBLE!

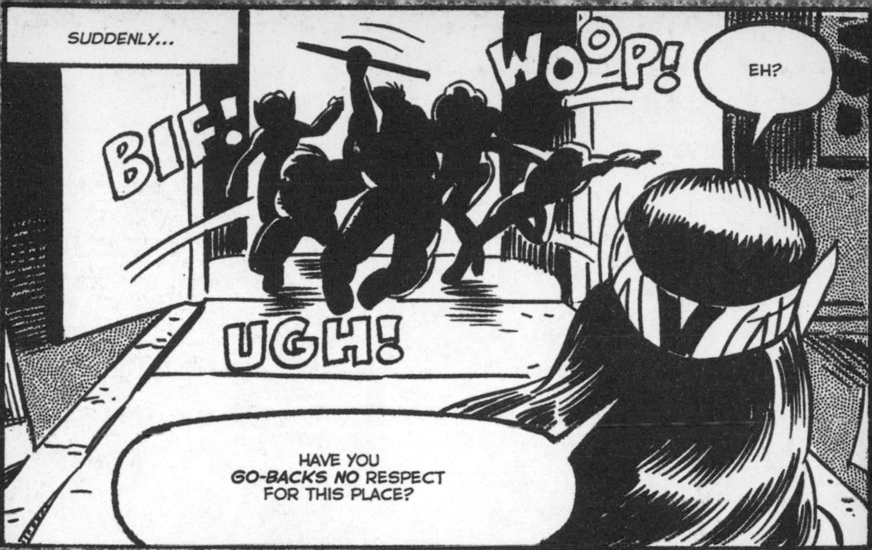
SUDDENLY...
BIF!
WOOP!
EH?
UGH!
HAVE YOU GO-BACKS NO RESPECT FOR THIS PLACE?

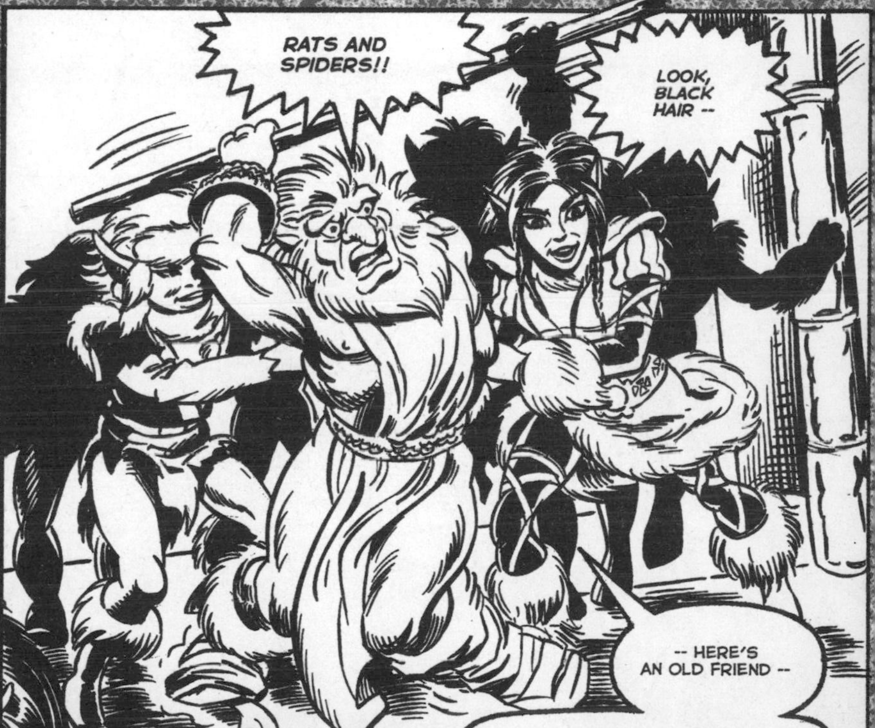
RATS AND SPIDERS!!
LOOK, BLACK HAIR --
-- HERE'S AN OLD FRIEND --
-- WE HAVEN'T SEEN FOR A FEW DAYS!

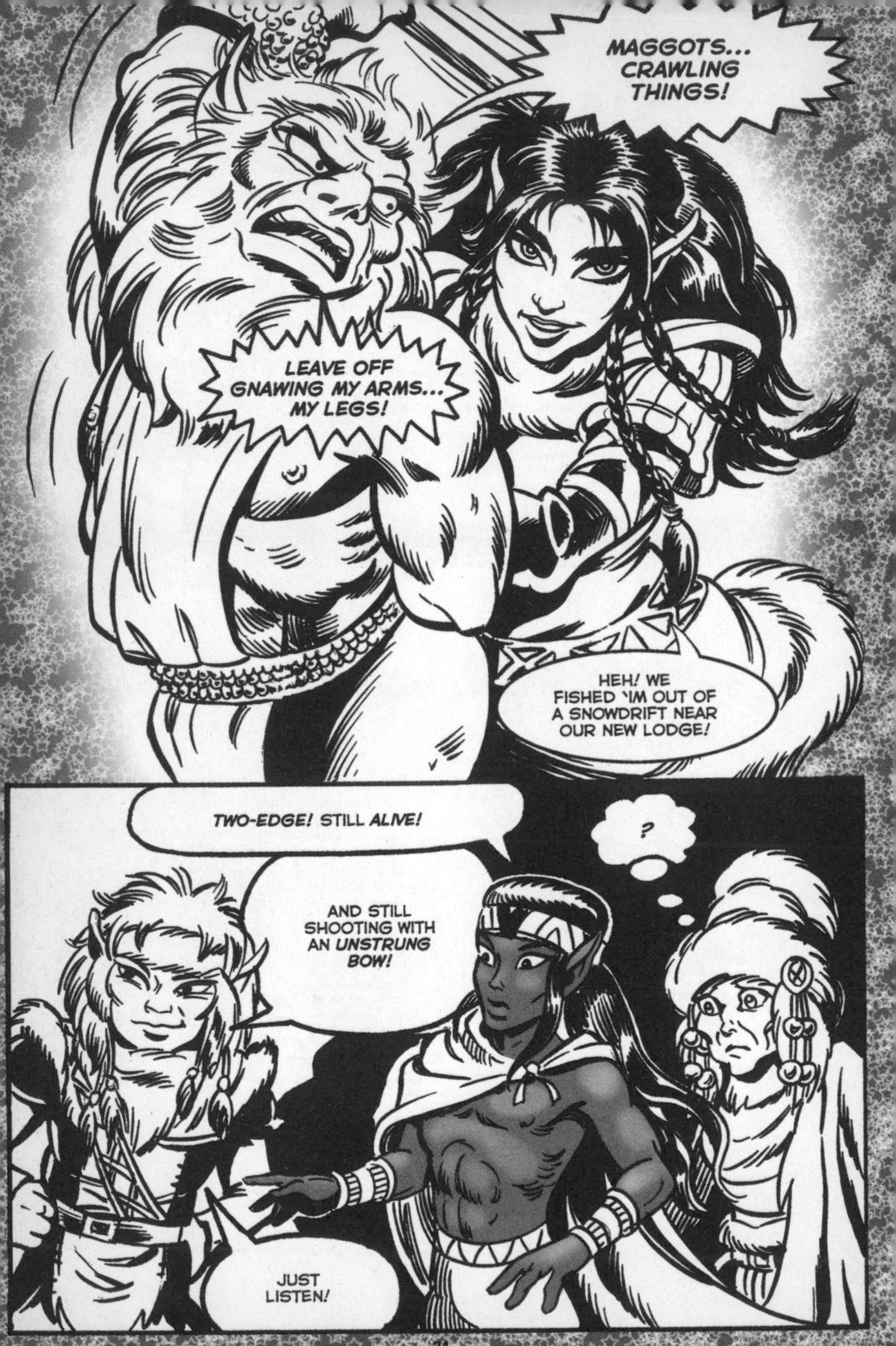
MAGGOTS... CRAWLING THINGS!
LEAVE OFF GNAWING MY ARMS... MY LEGS!
HEH! WE FISHED 'IM OUT OF A SNOWDRIFT NEAR OUR NEW LODGE!
TWO-EDGE! STILL ALIVE!
?
AND STILL SHOOTING WITH AN UNSTRUNG BOW!
JUST LISTEN!

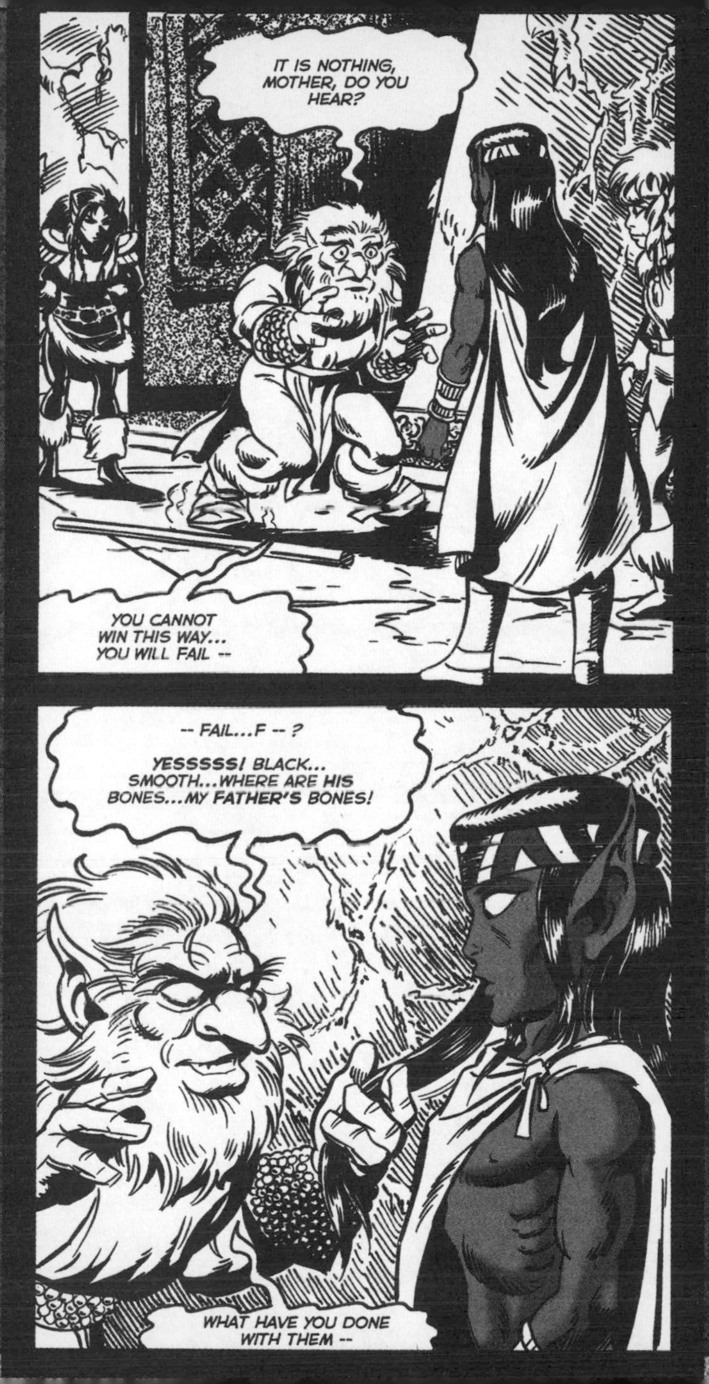
IT IS NOTHING, MOTHER, DO YOU HEAR?
YOU CANNOT WIN THIS WAY... YOU WILL FAIL --
-- FAIL...F -- ?
YESSSSS! BLACK... SMOOTH...WHERE ARE HIS BONES...MY FATHER'S BONES!
WHAT HAVE YOU DONE WITH THEM --

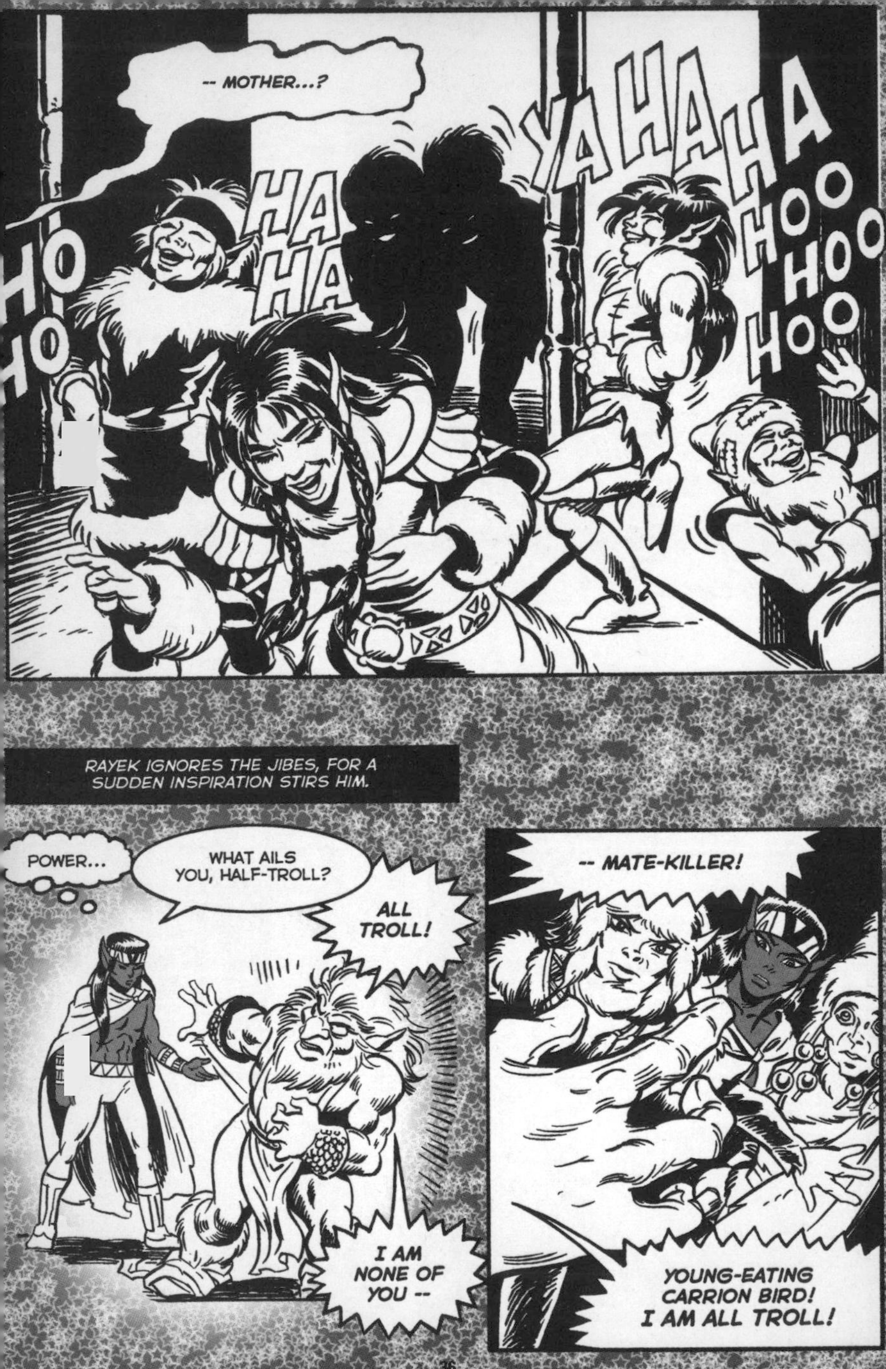
-- MOTHER...?
HO HO
HA HA
YAHAHAHA
HOO HOO HOO
RAYEK IGNORES THE JIBES, FOR A SUDDEN INSPIRATION STIRS HIM.
POWER...
WHAT AILS YOU, HALF-TROLL?
ALL TROLL!
I AM NONE OF YOU --
-- MATE-KILLER!
YOUNG-EATING CARRION BIRD! I AM ALL TROLL!

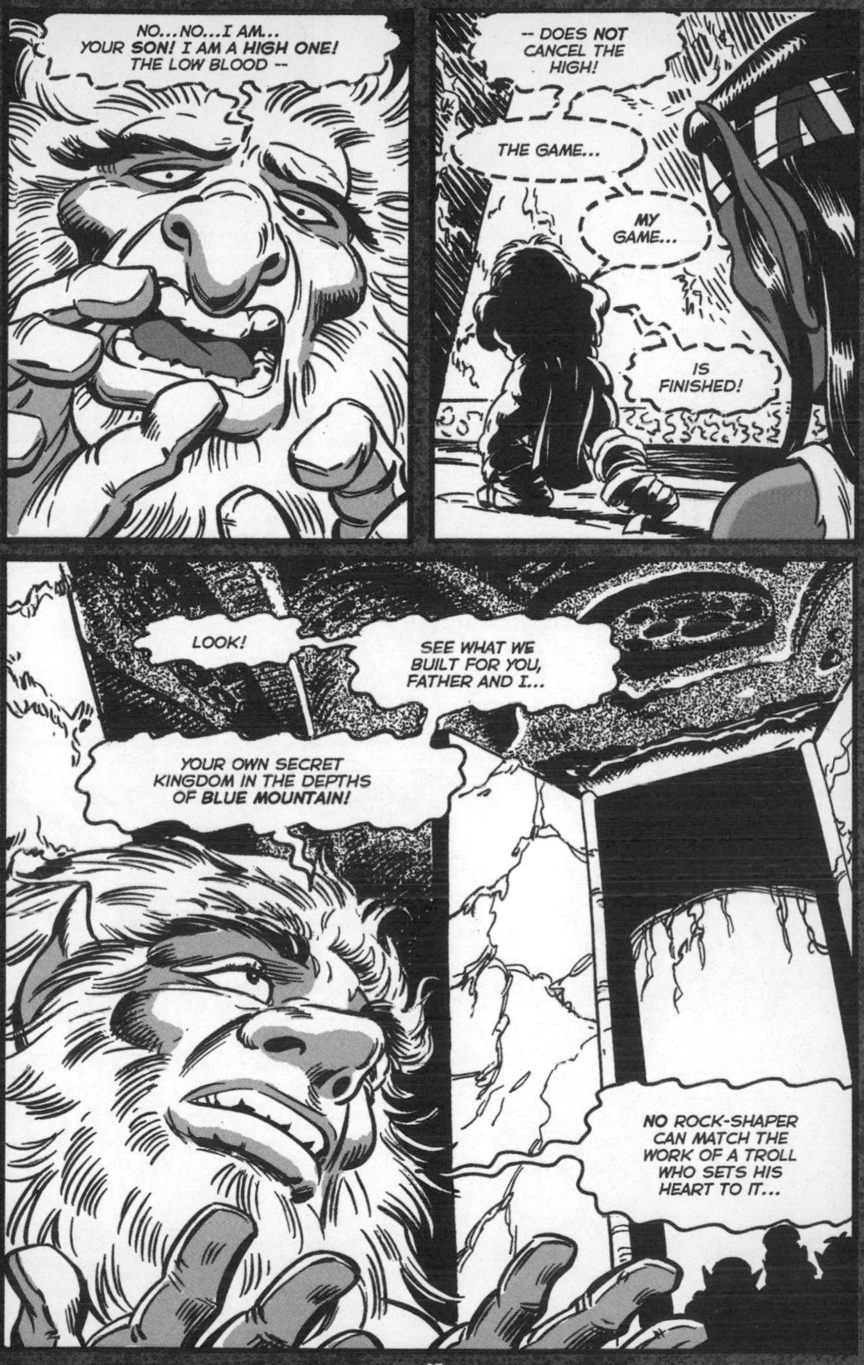
NO...NO...I AM... YOUR SON! I AM A HIGH ONE! THE LOW BLOOD --
-- DOES NOT CANCEL THE HIGH!
THE GAME...
MY GAME...
IS FINISHED!
LOOK!
SEE WHAT WE BUILT FOR YOU, FATHER AND I...
YOUR OWN SECRET KINGDOM IN THE DEPTHS OF BLUE MOUNTAIN!
NO ROCK-SHAPER CAN MATCH THE WORK OF A TROLL WHO SETS HIS HEART TO IT...

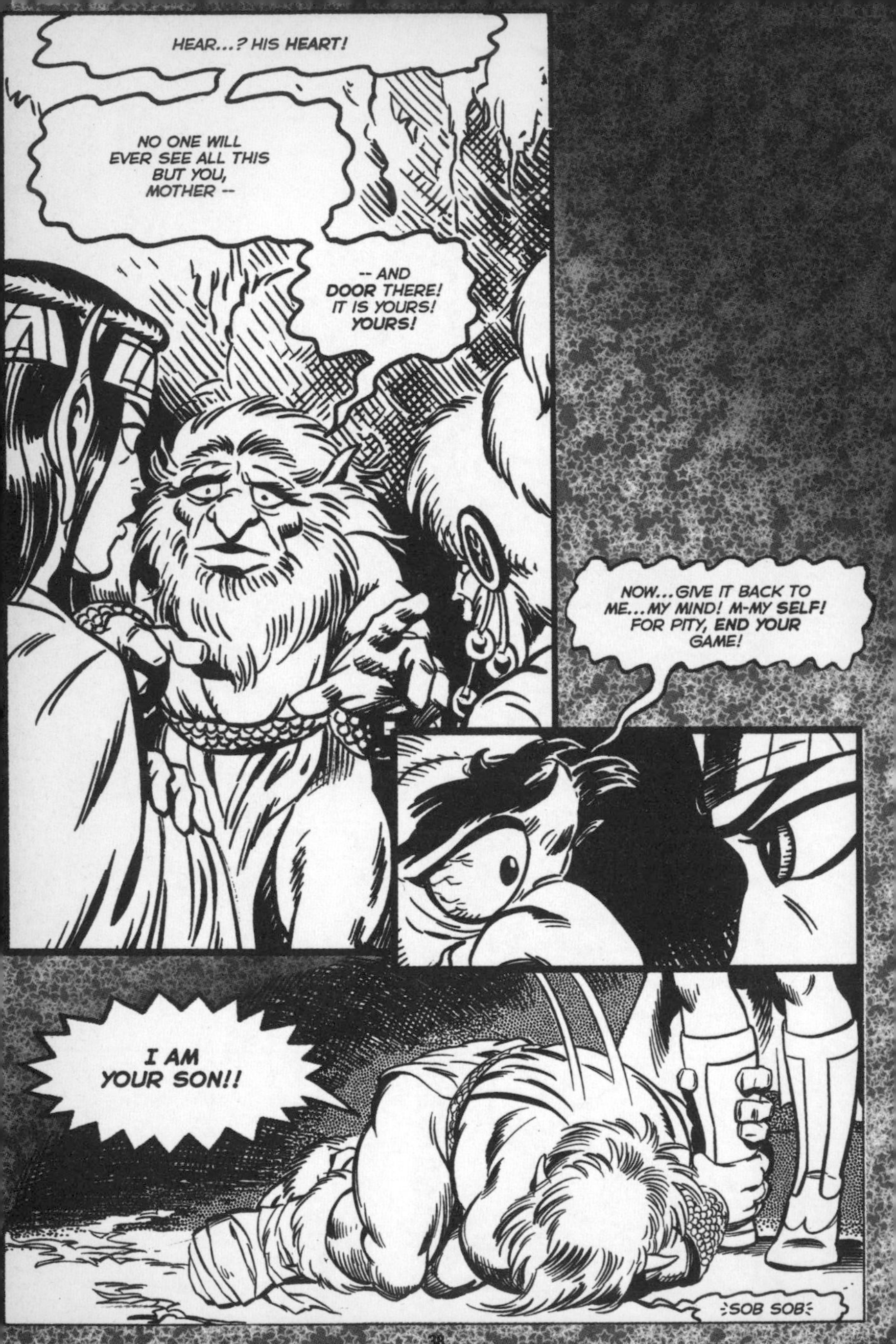
HEAR...? HIS HEART!
NO ONE WILL EVER SEE ALL THIS BUT YOU, MOTHER --
-- AND DOOR THERE! IT IS YOURS! YOURS!
NOW...GIVE IT BACK TO ME...MY MIND! M-MY SELF! FOR PITY, END YOUR GAME!
I AM YOUR SON!!
SOB SOB

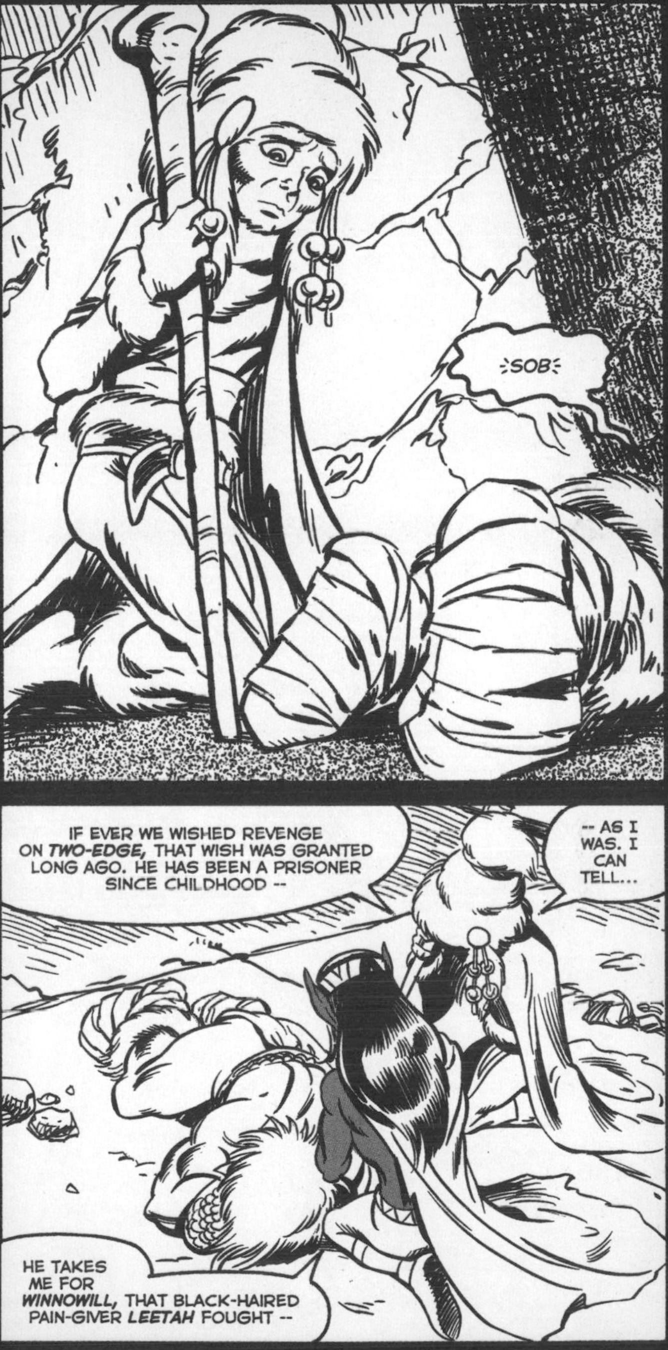
SOB
IF EVER WE WISHED REVENGE ON TWO-EDGE, THAT WISH WAS GRANTED LONG AGO. HE HAS BEEN A PRISONER SINCE CHILDHOOD --
-- AS I WAS. I CAN TELL...
HE TAKES ME FOR WINNOWILL, THAT BLACK-HAIRED PAIN-GIVER LEETAH FOUGHT --

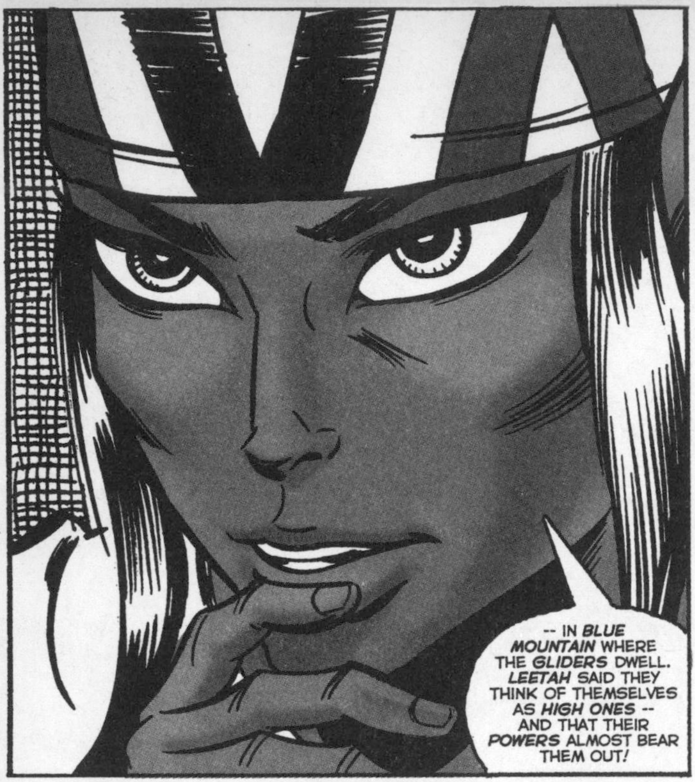
-- IN BLUE MOUNTAIN WHERE THE GLIDERS DWELL. LEETAH SAID THEY THINK OF THEMSELVES AS HIGH ONES -- AND THAT THEIR POWERS ALMOST BEAR THEM OUT!

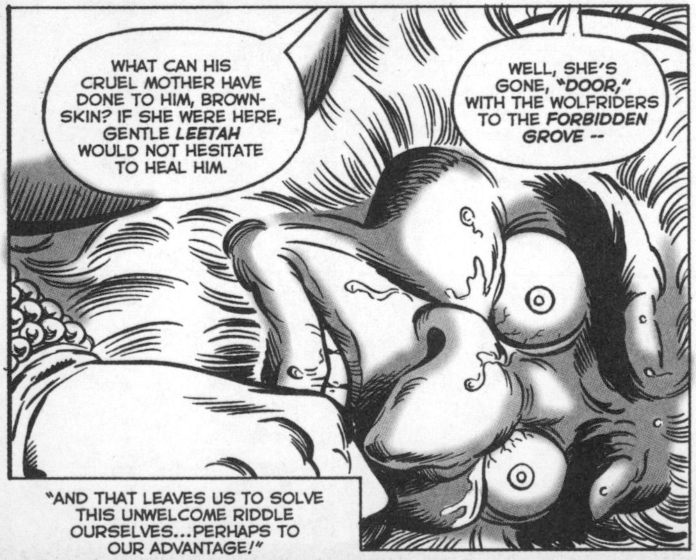
WHAT CAN HIS CRUEL MOTHER HAVE DONE TO HIM, BROWN-SKIN? IF SHE WERE HERE, GENTLE LEETAH WOULD NOT HESITATE TO HEAL HIM.
WELL, SHE'S GONE, "DOOR," WITH THE WOLFRIDERS TO THE FORBIDDEN GROVE --
"AND THAT LEAVES US TO SOLVE THIS UNWELCOME RIDDLE OURSELVES...PERHAPS TO OUR ADVANTAGE!"

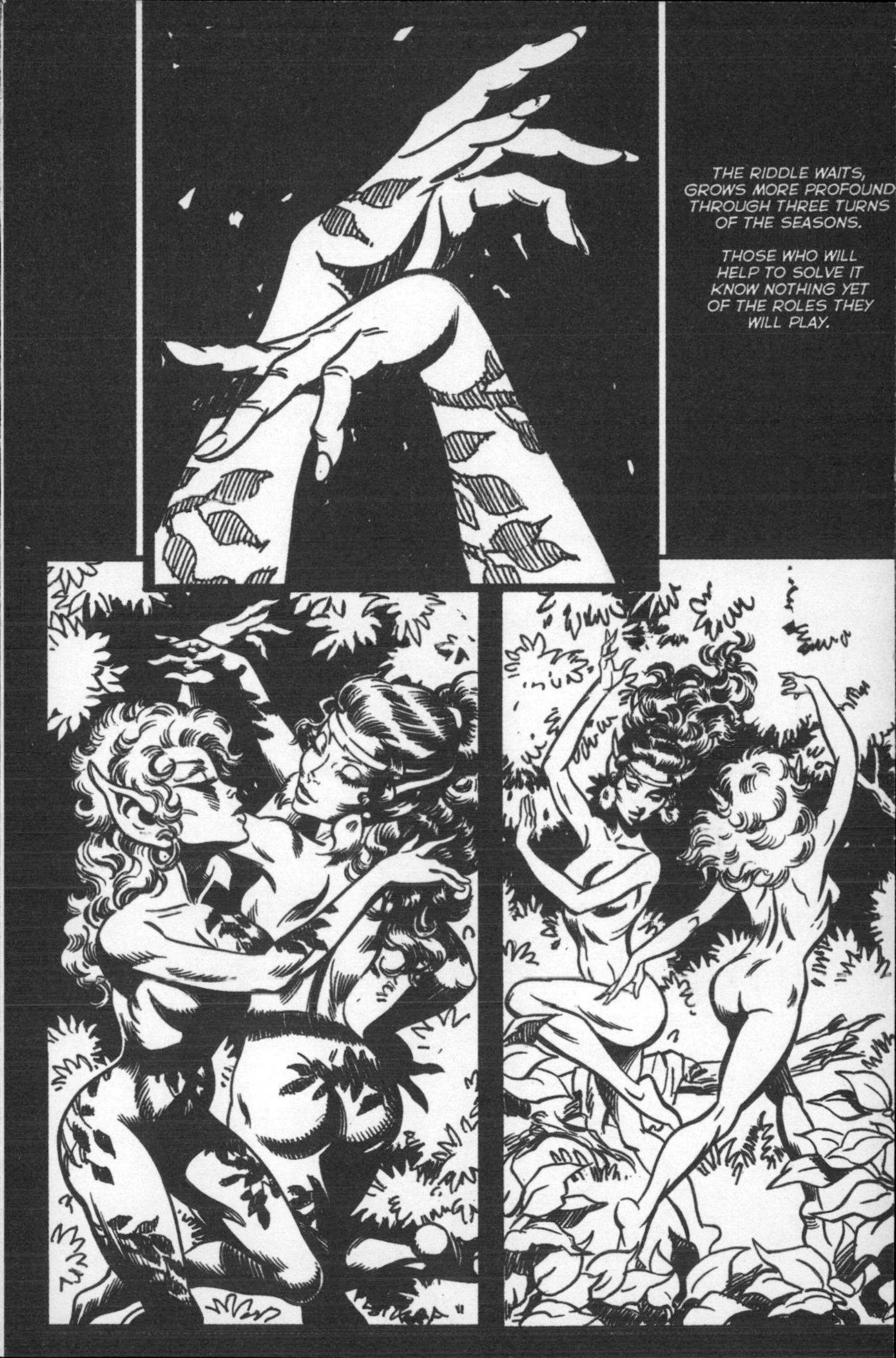
THE RIDDLE WAITS, GROWS MORE PROFOUND THROUGH THREE TURNS OF THE SEASONS.
THOSE WHO WILL HELP TO SOLVE IT KNOW NOTHING YET OF THE ROLES THEY WILL PLAY.

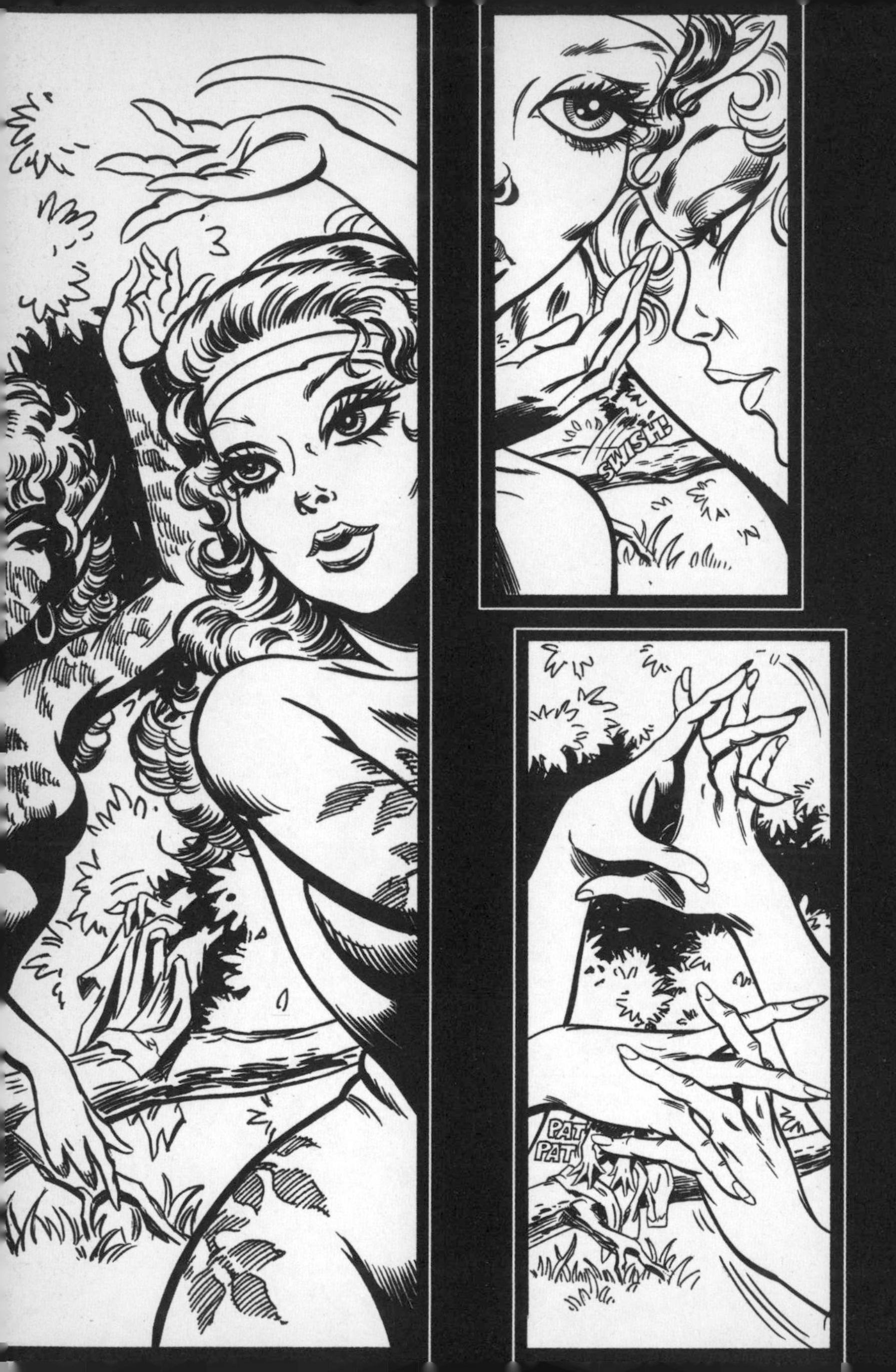
SWISH!
PAT PAT

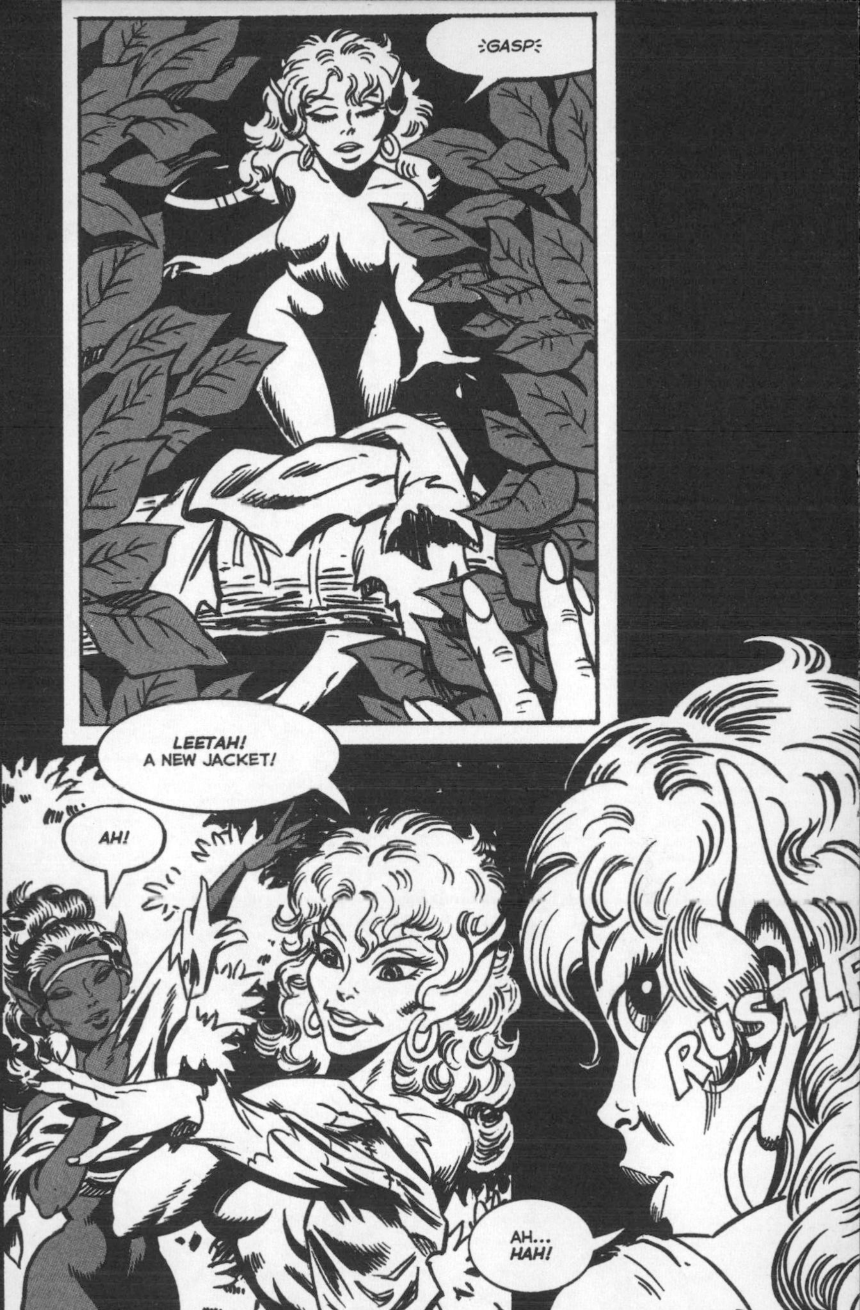

⁝GASP⁝
LEETAH!
A NEW JACKET!
AH!
AH...
HAH!

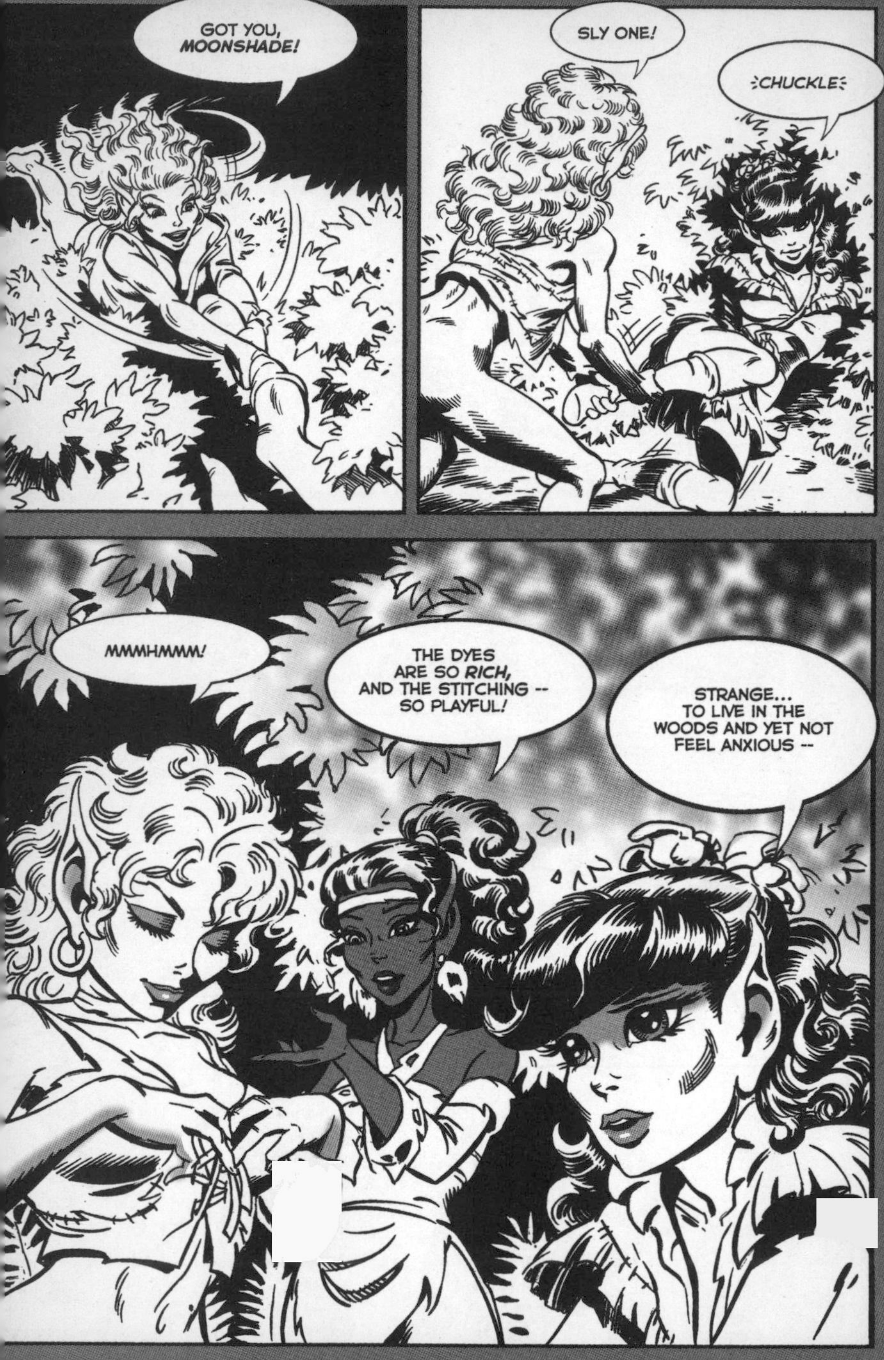
GOT YOU, *MOONSHADE!*
SLY ONE!
:CHUCKLE:
MMMHMMM!
THE DYES ARE SO *RICH,* AND THE STITCHING -- SO PLAYFUL!
STRANGE... TO LIVE IN THE WOODS AND YET NOT FEEL ANXIOUS --

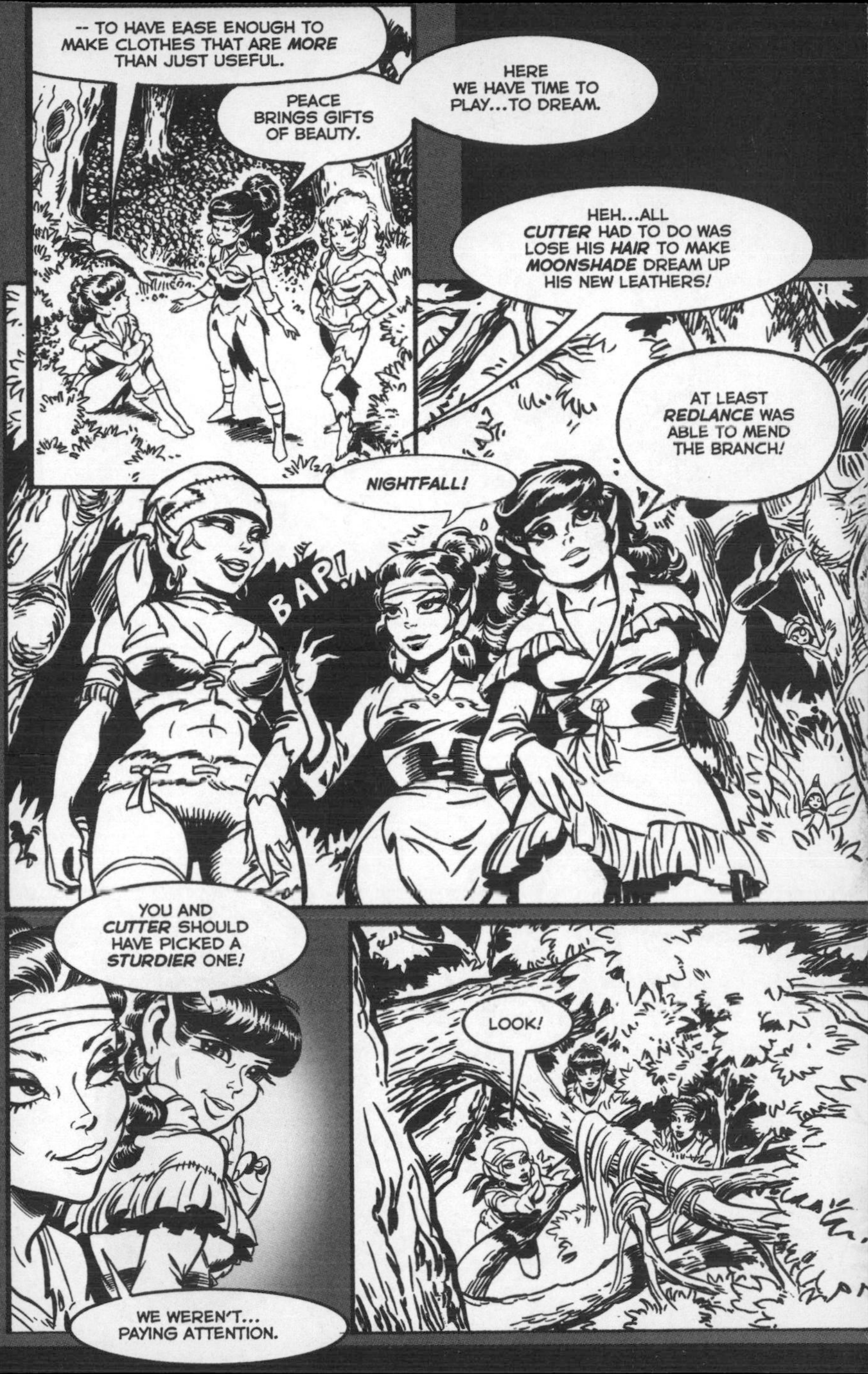
-- TO HAVE EASE ENOUGH TO MAKE CLOTHES THAT ARE *MORE* THAN JUST USEFUL.
PEACE BRINGS GIFTS OF BEAUTY.
HERE WE HAVE TIME TO PLAY... TO DREAM.
HEH... ALL *CUTTER* HAD TO DO WAS LOSE HIS *HAIR* TO MAKE *MOONSHADE* DREAM UP HIS NEW LEATHERS!
AT LEAST *REDLANCE* WAS ABLE TO MEND THE BRANCH!
NIGHTFALL!
BAP!
YOU AND *CUTTER* SHOULD HAVE PICKED A *STURDIER* ONE!
WE WEREN'T... PAYING ATTENTION.
LOOK!

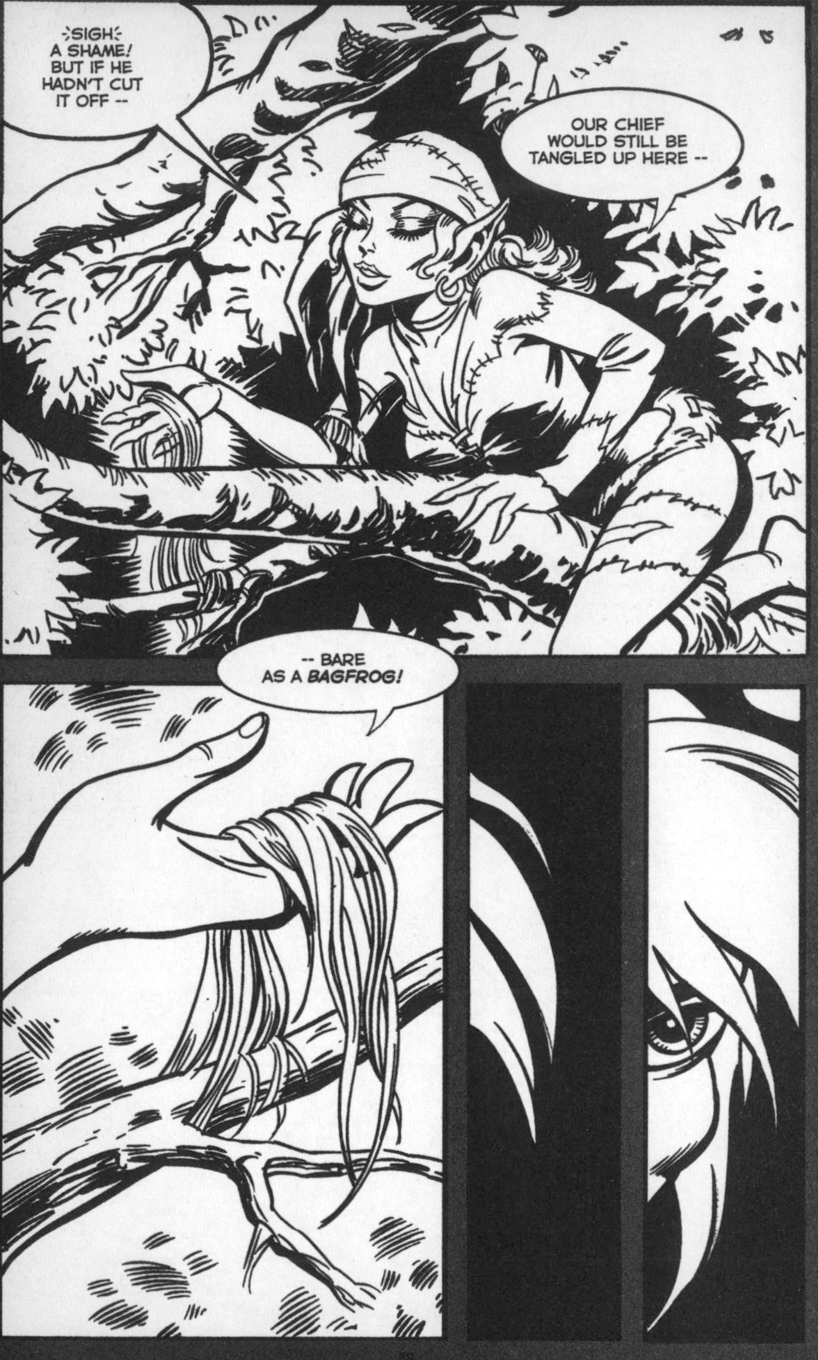

SIGH A SHAME! BUT IF HE HADN'T CUT IT OFF --
OUR CHIEF WOULD STILL BE TANGLED UP HERE --
-- BARE AS A *BAGFROG!*

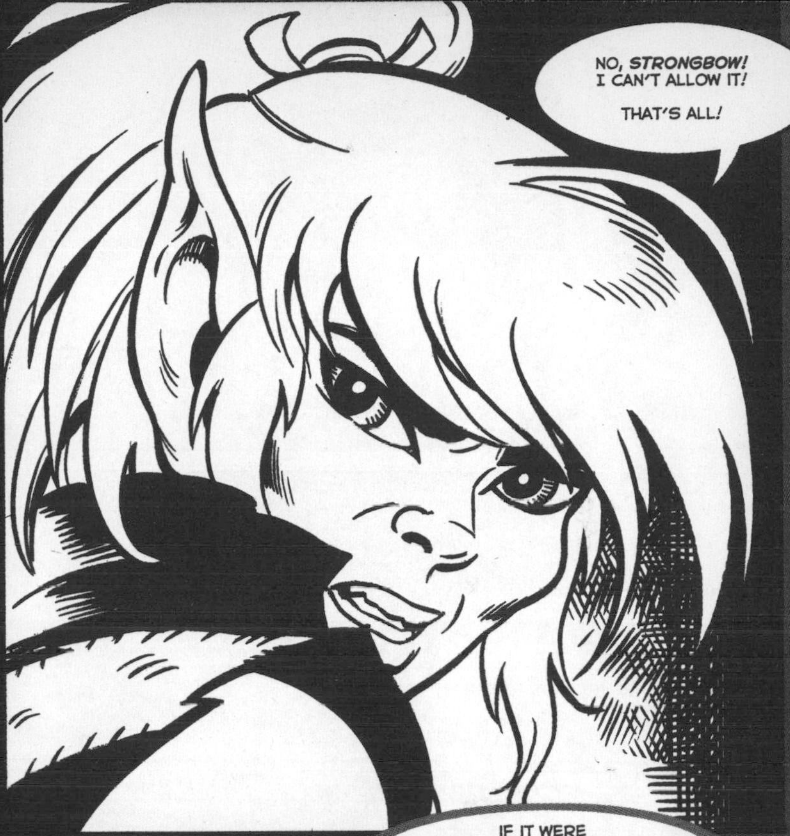
NO, *STRONGBOW!* I CAN'T ALLOW IT!
THAT'S ALL!
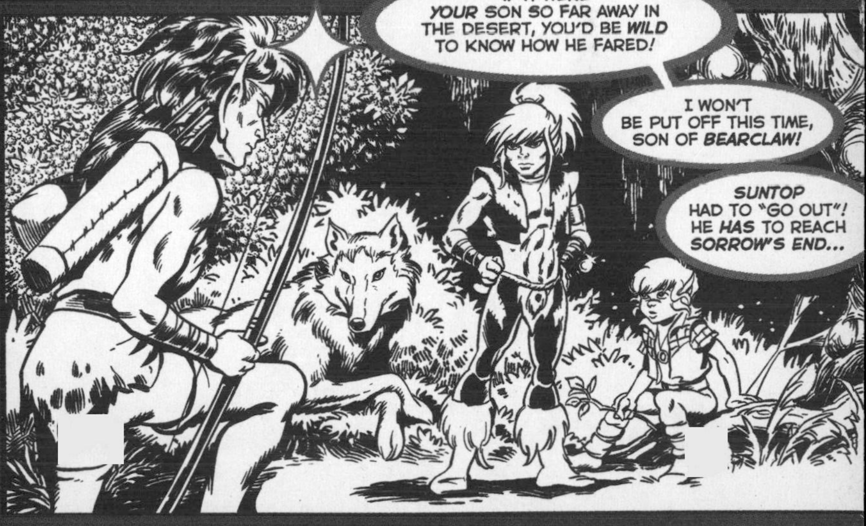
IF IT WERE *YOUR* SON SO FAR AWAY IN THE DESERT, YOU'D BE *WILD* TO KNOW HOW HE FARED!
I WON'T BE PUT OFF THIS TIME, SON OF *BEARCLAW!*
SUNTOP HAD TO "GO OUT"! HE *HAS* TO REACH *SORROW'S END...*

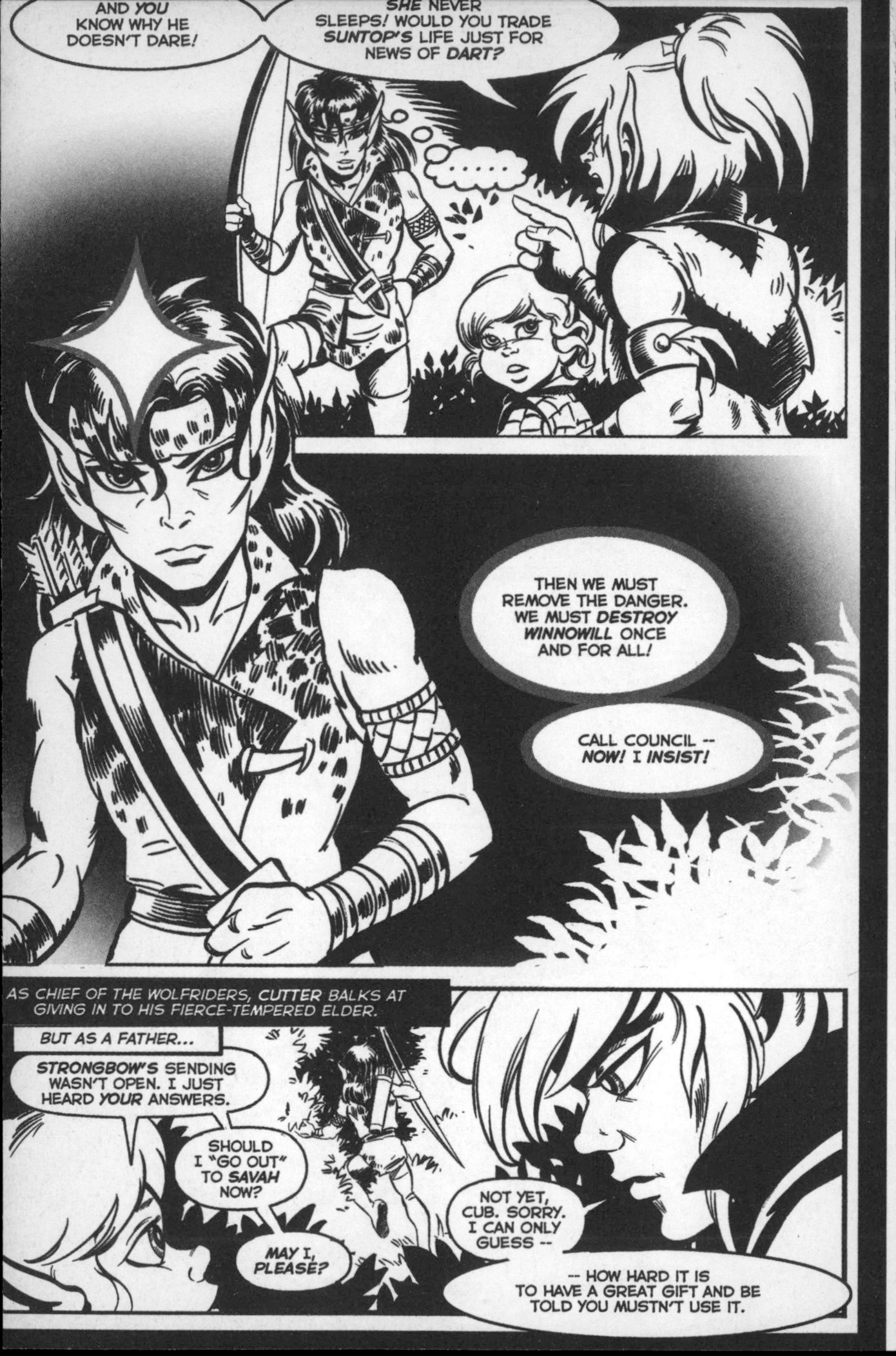
AND YOU KNOW WHY HE DOESN'T DARE!
SHE NEVER SLEEPS! WOULD YOU TRADE SUNTOP'S LIFE JUST FOR NEWS OF DART?
.....
THEN WE MUST REMOVE THE DANGER. WE MUST DESTROY WINNOWILL ONCE AND FOR ALL!
CALL COUNCIL -- NOW! I INSIST!
AS CHIEF OF THE WOLFRIDERS, CUTTER BALKS AT GIVING IN TO HIS FIERCE-TEMPERED ELDER.
BUT AS A FATHER...
STRONGBOW'S SENDING WASN'T OPEN. I JUST HEARD YOUR ANSWERS.
SHOULD I "GO OUT" TO SAVAH NOW?
MAY I, PLEASE?
NOT YET, CUB. SORRY. I CAN ONLY GUESS --
-- HOW HARD IT IS TO HAVE A GREAT GIFT AND BE TOLD YOU MUSTN'T USE IT.

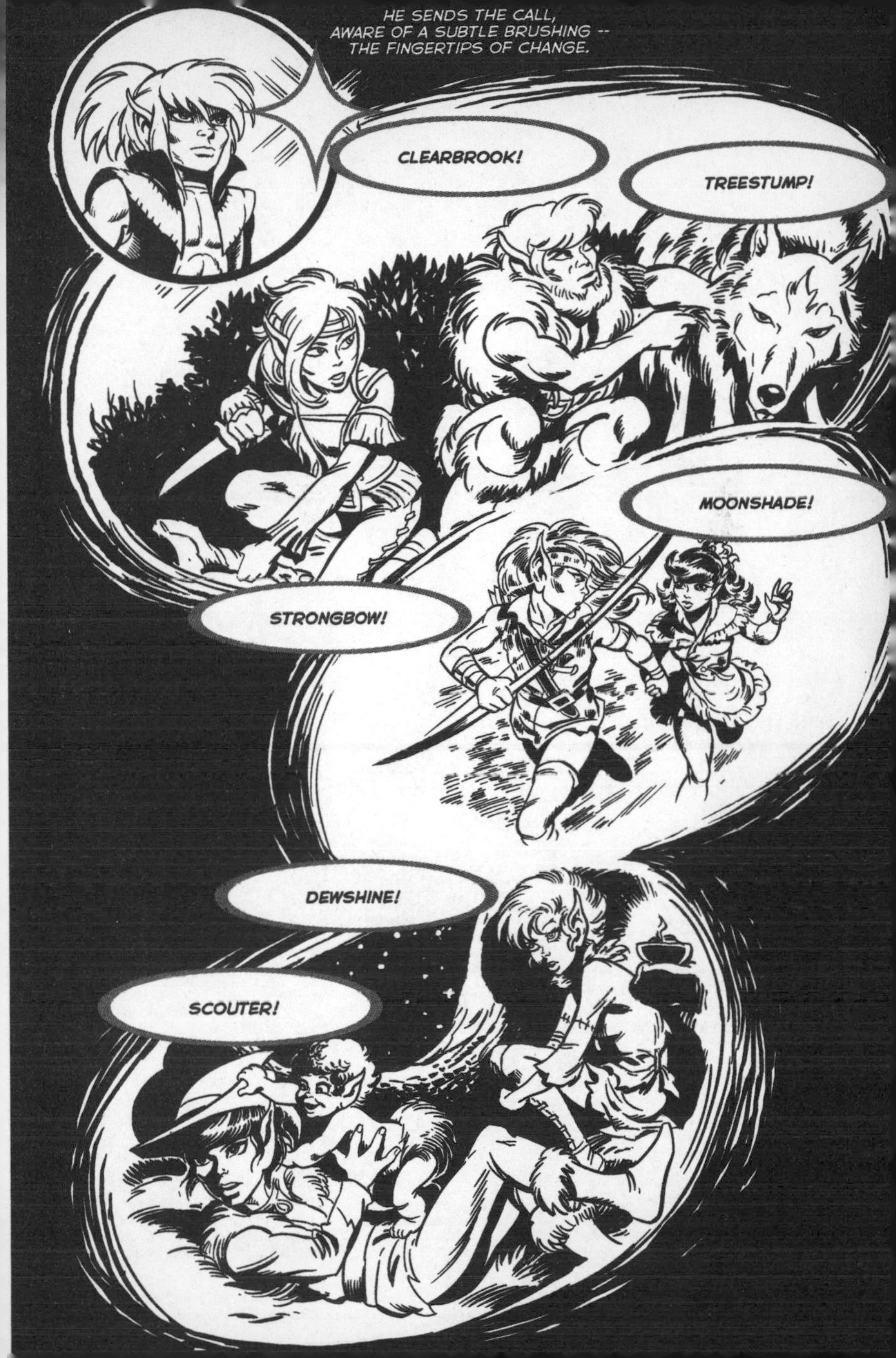
HE SENDS THE CALL,
AWARE OF A SUBTLE BRUSHING --
THE FINGERTIPS OF CHANGE.
CLEARBROOK!
TREESTUMP!
MOONSHADE!
STRONGBOW!
DEWSHINE!
SCOUTER!

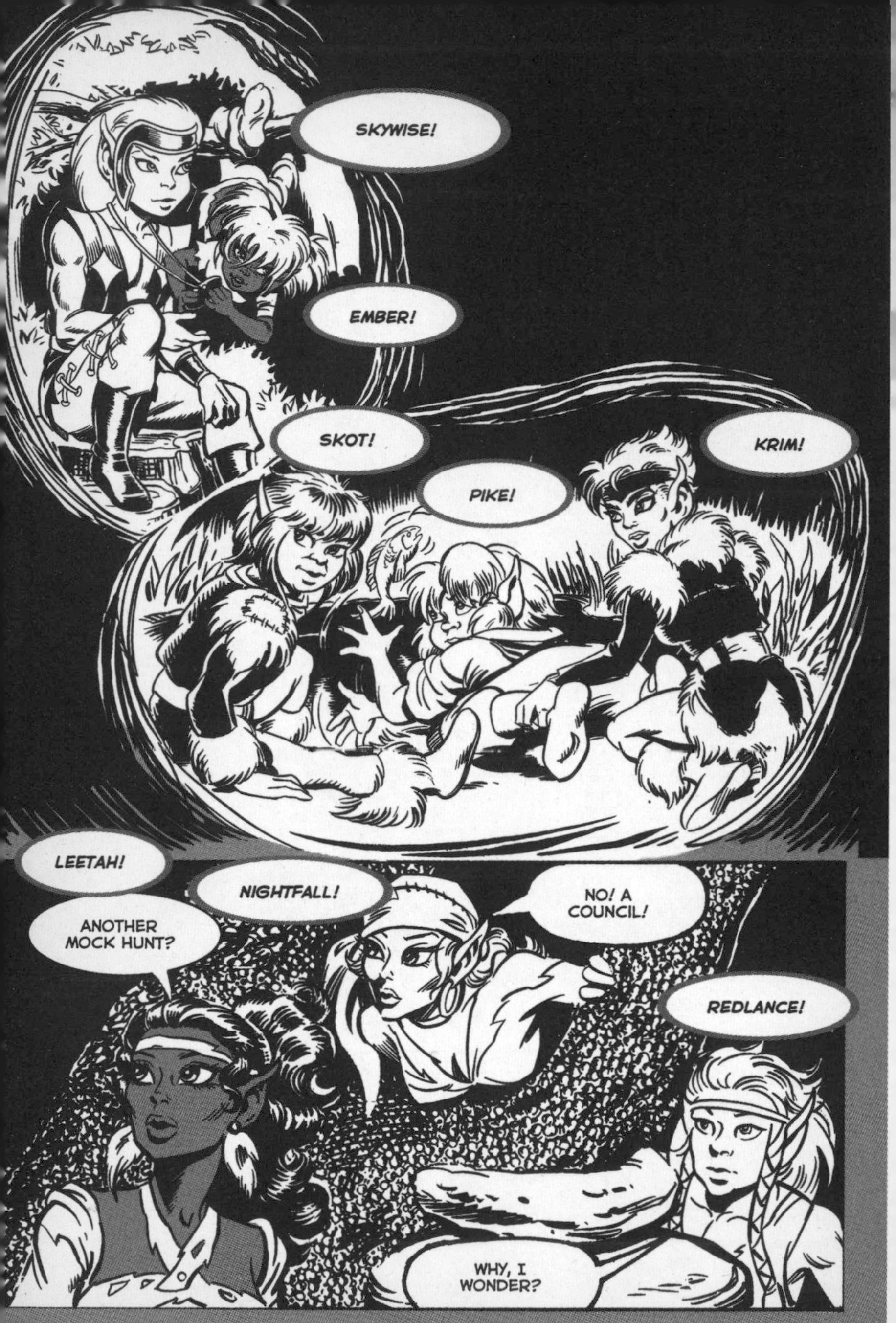
SKYWISE!
EMBER!
SKOT!
PIKE!
KRIM!
LEETAH!
NIGHTFALL!
ANOTHER MOCK HUNT?
NO! A COUNCIL!
REDLANCE!
WHY, I WONDER?

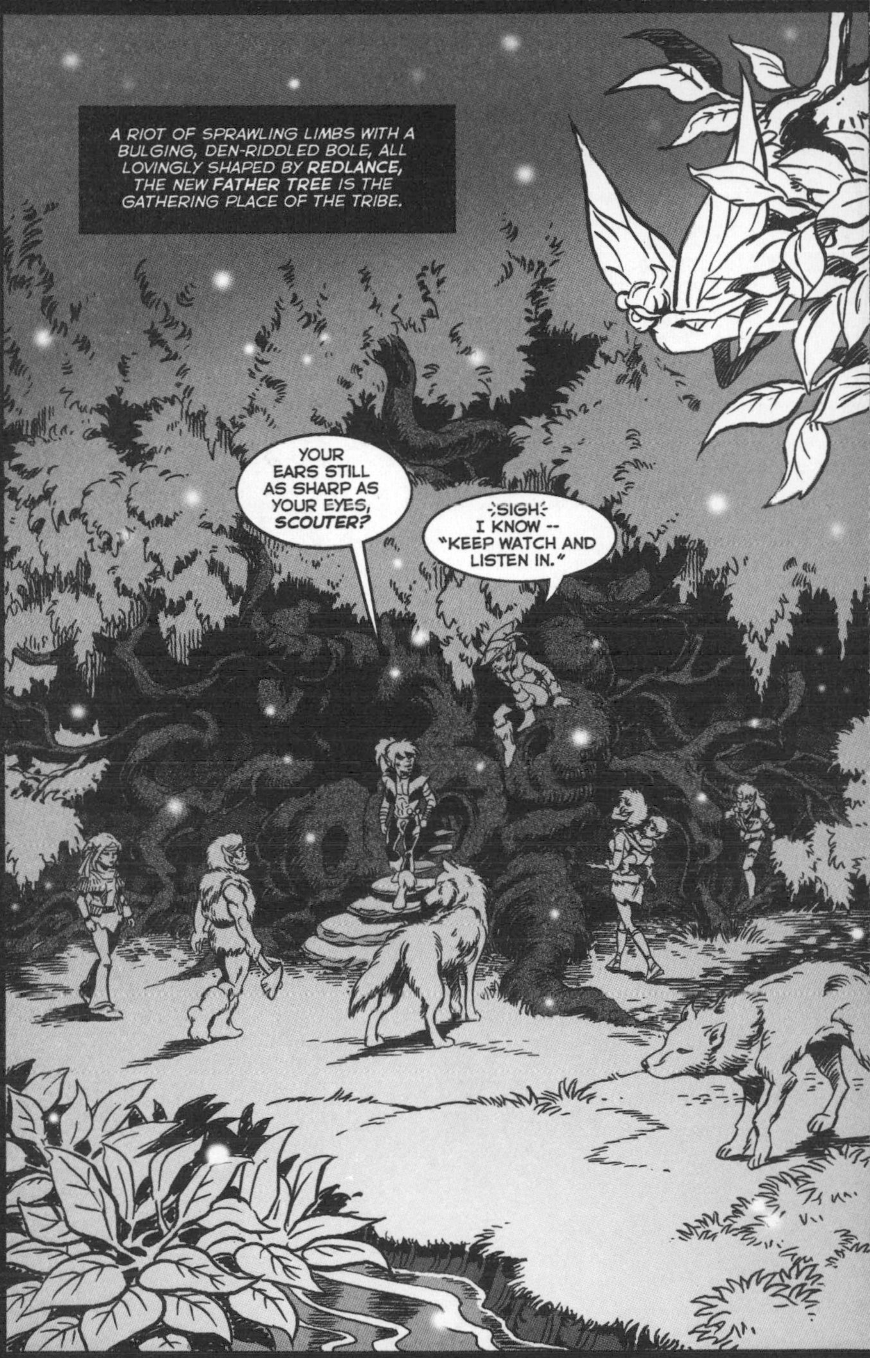
A RIOT OF SPRAWLING LIMBS WITH A BULGING, DEN-RIDDLED BOLE, ALL LOVINGLY SHAPED BY REDLANCE, THE NEW FATHER TREE IS THE GATHERING PLACE OF THE TRIBE.
YOUR EARS STILL AS SHARP AS YOUR EYES, SCOUTER?
SIGH I KNOW -- "KEEP WATCH AND LISTEN IN."

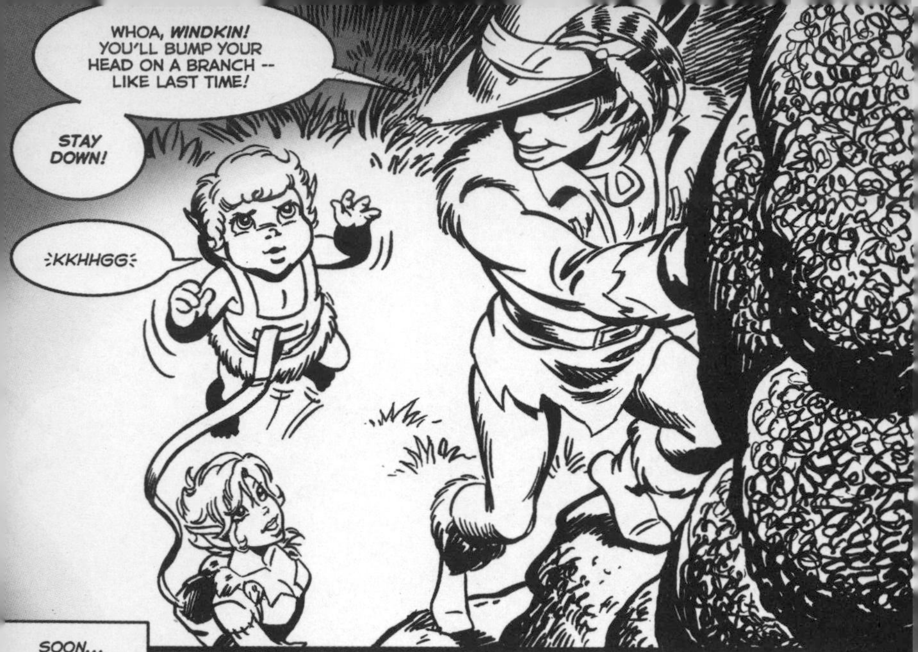
WHOA, WINDKIN! YOU'LL BUMP YOUR HEAD ON A BRANCH -- LIKE LAST TIME!
STAY DOWN!
KKHHGG
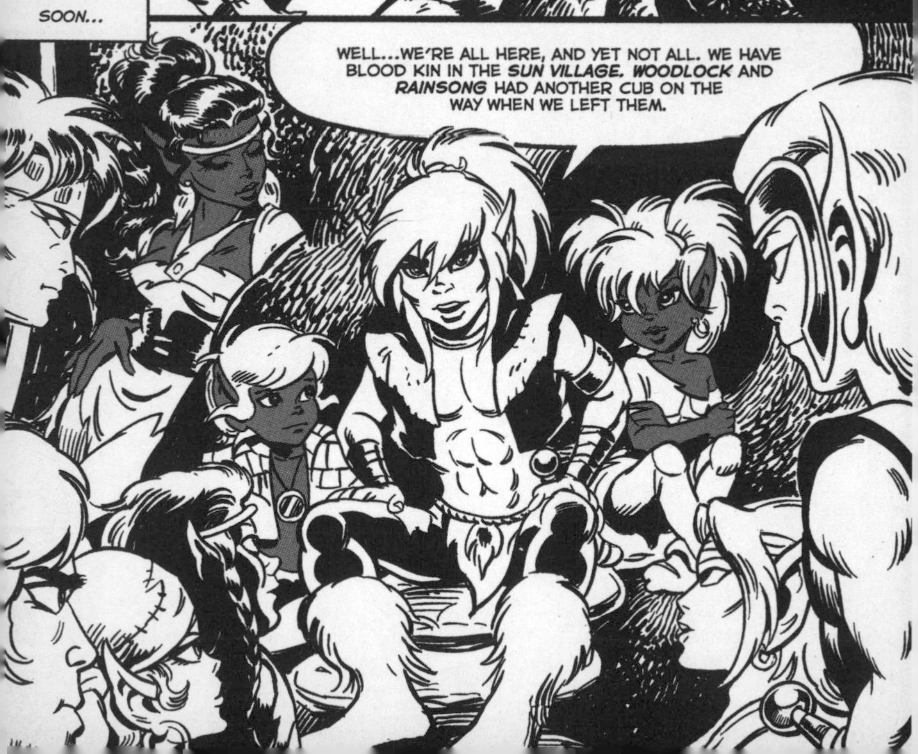
SOON...
WELL...WE'RE ALL HERE, AND YET NOT ALL. WE HAVE BLOOD KIN IN THE SUN VILLAGE. WOODLOCK AND RAINSONG HAD ANOTHER CUB ON THE WAY WHEN WE LEFT THEM.

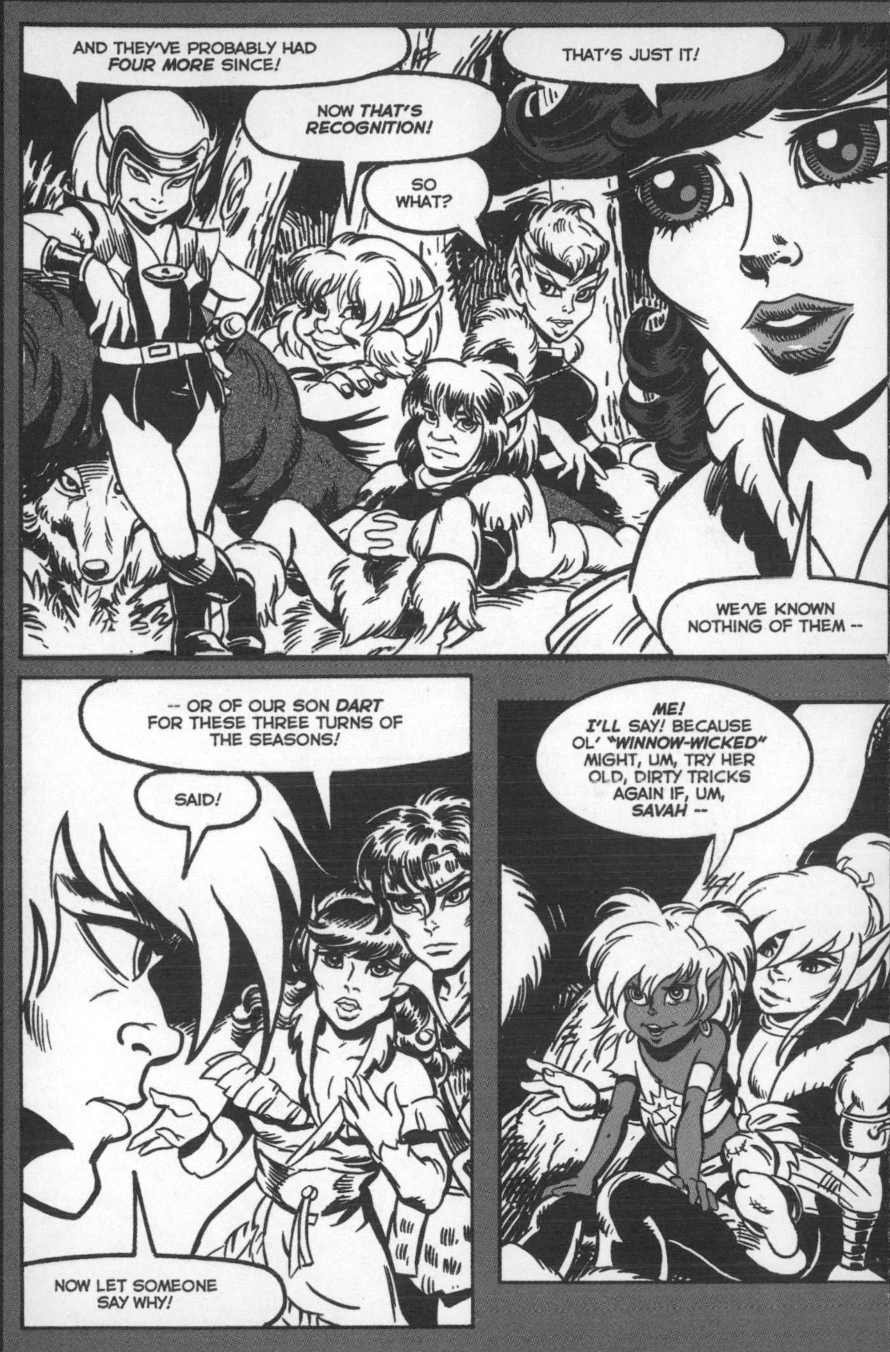
AND THEY'VE PROBABLY HAD *FOUR MORE* SINCE!
NOW *THAT'S RECOGNITION!*
SO WHAT?
THAT'S JUST IT!
WE'VE KNOWN NOTHING OF THEM --
-- OR OF OUR SON *DART* FOR THESE THREE TURNS OF THE SEASONS!
SAID!
NOW LET SOMEONE SAY WHY!
ME! I'LL SAY! BECAUSE OL' *"WINNOW-WICKED"* MIGHT, UM, TRY HER OLD, DIRTY TRICKS AGAIN IF, UM, *SAVAH* --

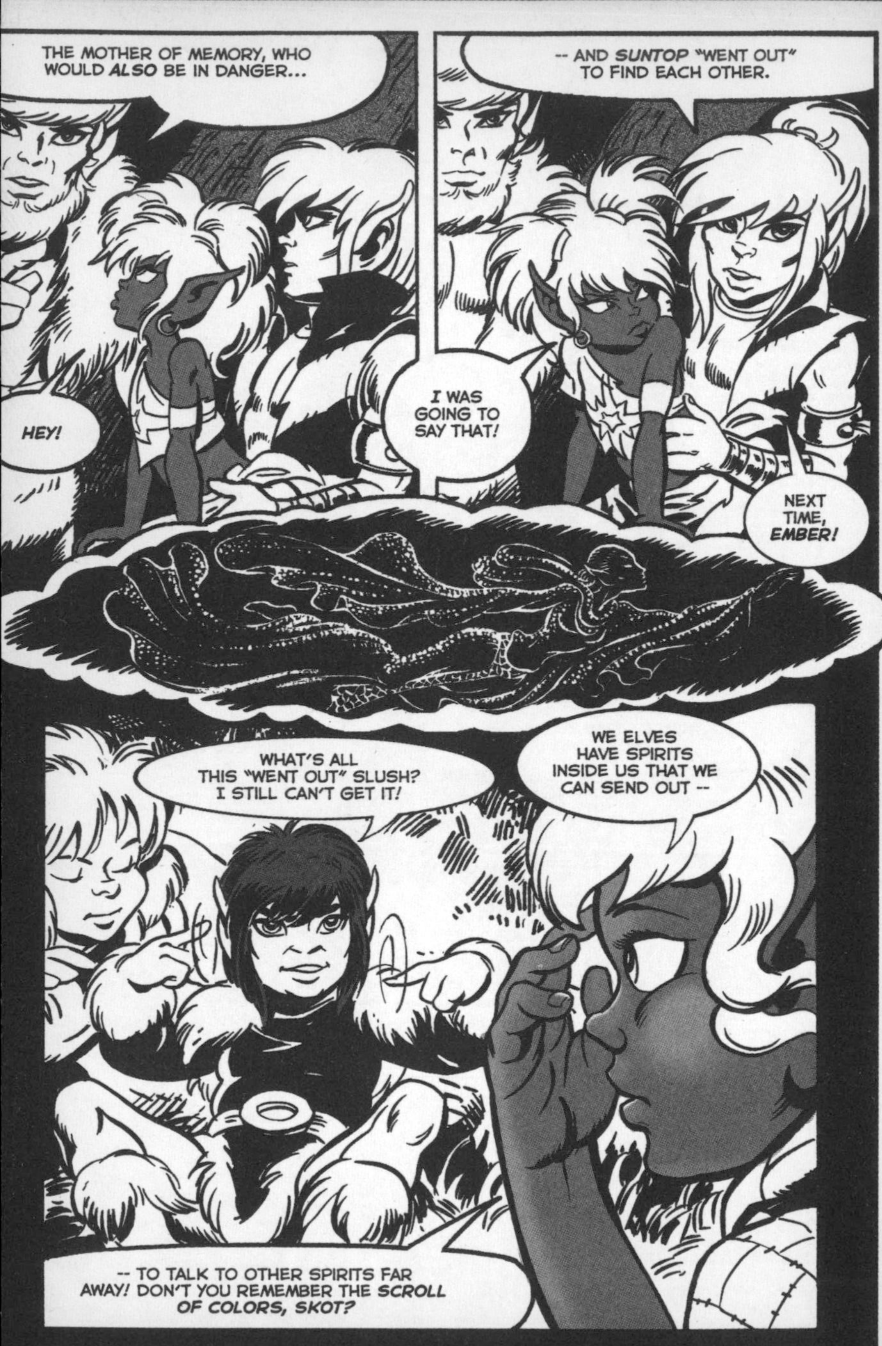

THE MOTHER OF MEMORY, WHO WOULD *ALSO* BE IN DANGER...
HEY!
-- AND *SUNTOP* "WENT OUT" TO FIND EACH OTHER.
I WAS GOING TO SAY THAT!
NEXT TIME, *EMBER!*
WHAT'S ALL THIS "WENT OUT" SLUSH? I STILL CAN'T GET IT!
WE ELVES HAVE SPIRITS INSIDE US THAT WE CAN SEND OUT --
-- TO TALK TO OTHER SPIRITS FAR AWAY! DON'T YOU REMEMBER THE *SCROLL OF COLORS, SKOT?*

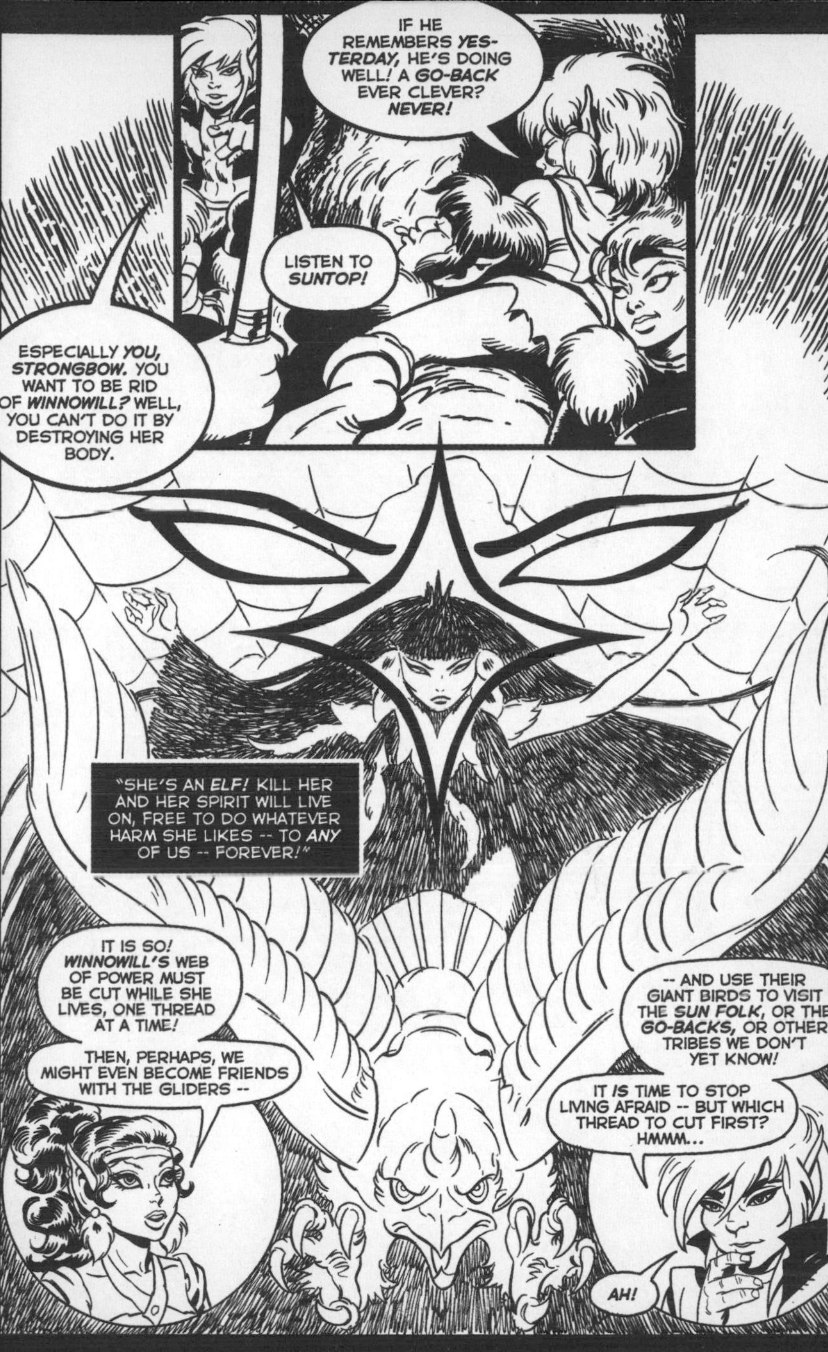
IF HE REMEMBERS YESTERDAY, HE'S DOING WELL! A GO-BACK EVER CLEVER? NEVER!
LISTEN TO SUNTOP!
ESPECIALLY YOU, STRONGBOW. YOU WANT TO BE RID OF WINNOWILL? WELL, YOU CAN'T DO IT BY DESTROYING HER BODY.
"SHE'S AN ELF! KILL HER AND HER SPIRIT WILL LIVE ON, FREE TO DO WHATEVER HARM SHE LIKES -- TO ANY OF US -- FOREVER!"
IT IS SO! WINNOWILL'S WEB OF POWER MUST BE CUT WHILE SHE LIVES, ONE THREAD AT A TIME!
THEN, PERHAPS, WE MIGHT EVEN BECOME FRIENDS WITH THE GLIDERS --
-- AND USE THEIR GIANT BIRDS TO VISIT THE SUN FOLK, OR THE GO-BACKS, OR OTHER TRIBES WE DON'T YET KNOW!
IT IS TIME TO STOP LIVING AFRAID -- BUT WHICH THREAD TO CUT FIRST? HMMM...
AH!

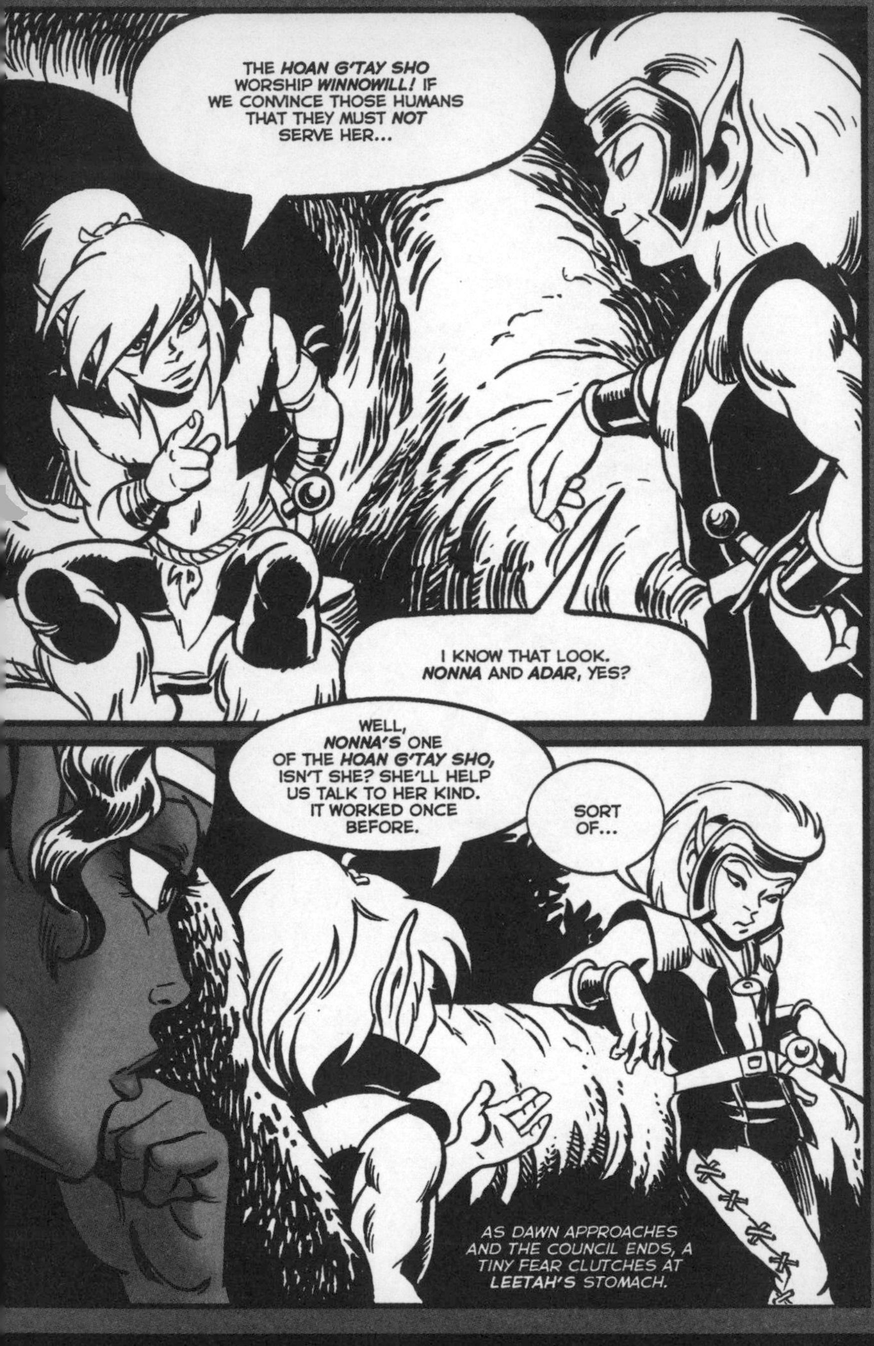

THE HOAN G'TAY SHO WORSHIP WINNOWILL! IF WE CONVINCE THOSE HUMANS THAT THEY MUST NOT SERVE HER...
I KNOW THAT LOOK. NONNA AND ADAR, YES?
WELL, NONNA'S ONE OF THE HOAN G'TAY SHO, ISN'T SHE? SHE'LL HELP US TALK TO HER KIND. IT WORKED ONCE BEFORE.
SORT OF...
AS DAWN APPROACHES AND THE COUNCIL ENDS, A TINY FEAR CLUTCHES AT LEETAH'S STOMACH.

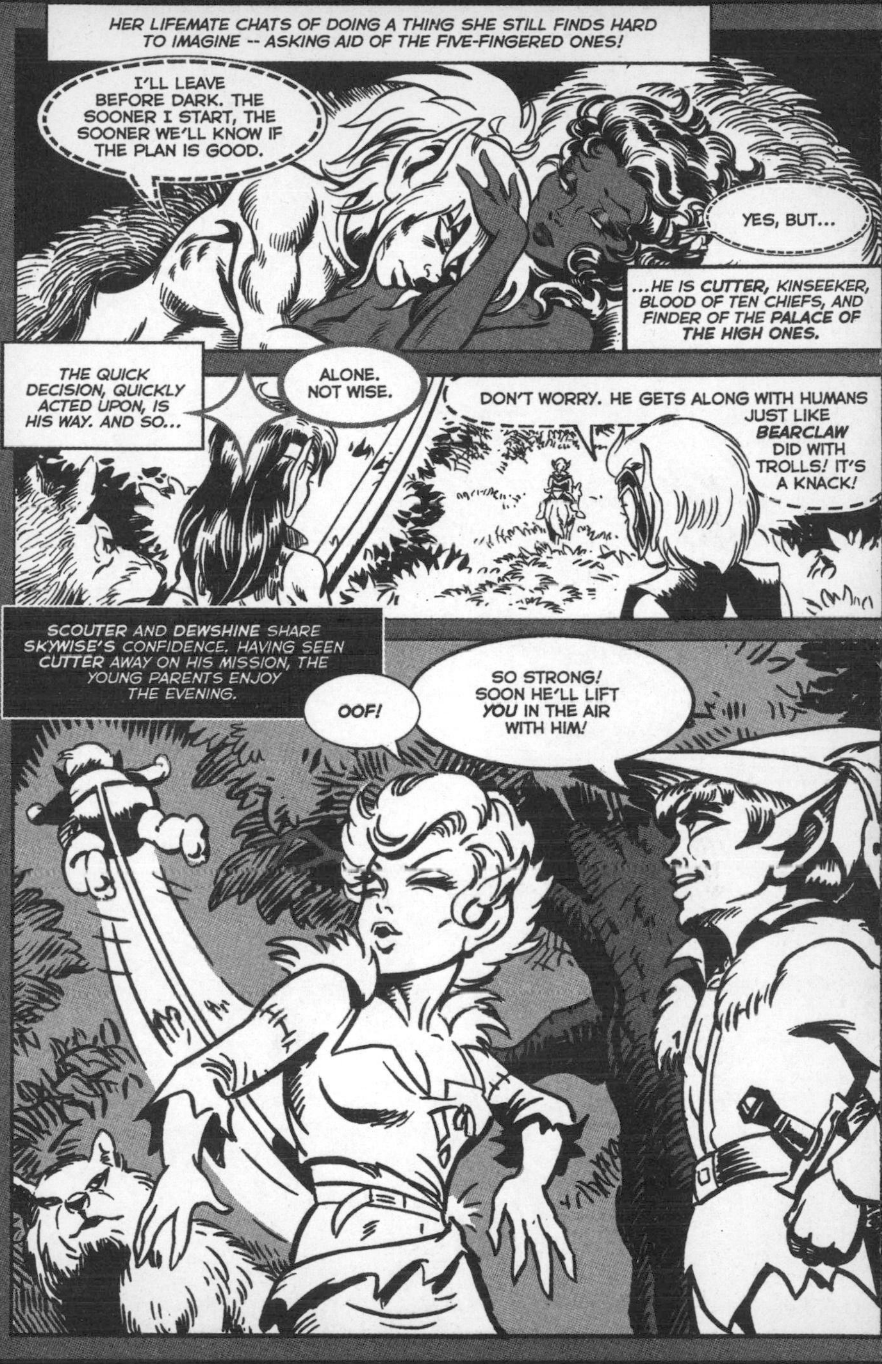
HER LIFEMATE CHATS OF DOING A THING SHE STILL FINDS HARD TO IMAGINE -- ASKING AID OF THE FIVE-FINGERED ONES!
I'LL LEAVE BEFORE DARK. THE SOONER I START, THE SOONER WE'LL KNOW IF THE PLAN IS GOOD.
YES, BUT...
...HE IS CUTTER, KINSEEKER, BLOOD OF TEN CHIEFS, AND FINDER OF THE PALACE OF THE HIGH ONES.
THE QUICK DECISION, QUICKLY ACTED UPON, IS HIS WAY. AND SO...
ALONE. NOT WISE.
DON'T WORRY. HE GETS ALONG WITH HUMANS JUST LIKE BEARCLAW DID WITH TROLLS! IT'S A KNACK!
SCOUTER AND DEWSHINE SHARE SKYWISE'S CONFIDENCE. HAVING SEEN CUTTER AWAY ON HIS MISSION, THE YOUNG PARENTS ENJOY THE EVENING.
OOF!
SO STRONG! SOON HE'LL LIFT YOU IN THE AIR WITH HIM!

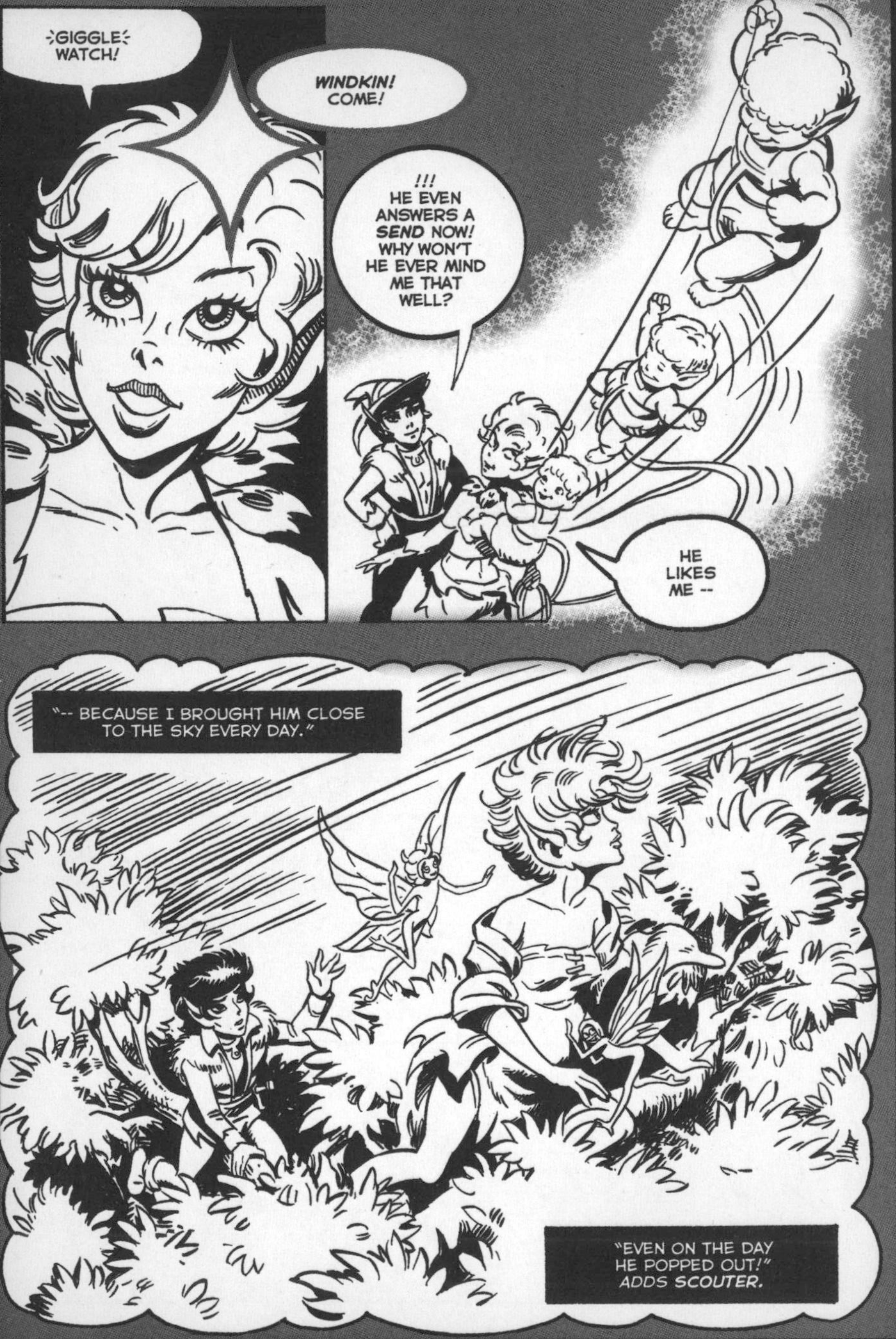

-:GIGGLE:- WATCH!
WINDKIN! COME!
!!! HE EVEN ANSWERS A SEND NOW! WHY WON'T HE EVER MIND ME THAT WELL?
HE LIKES ME --
"-- BECAUSE I BROUGHT HIM CLOSE TO THE SKY EVERY DAY."
"EVEN ON THE DAY HE POPPED OUT!" ADDS SCOUTER.

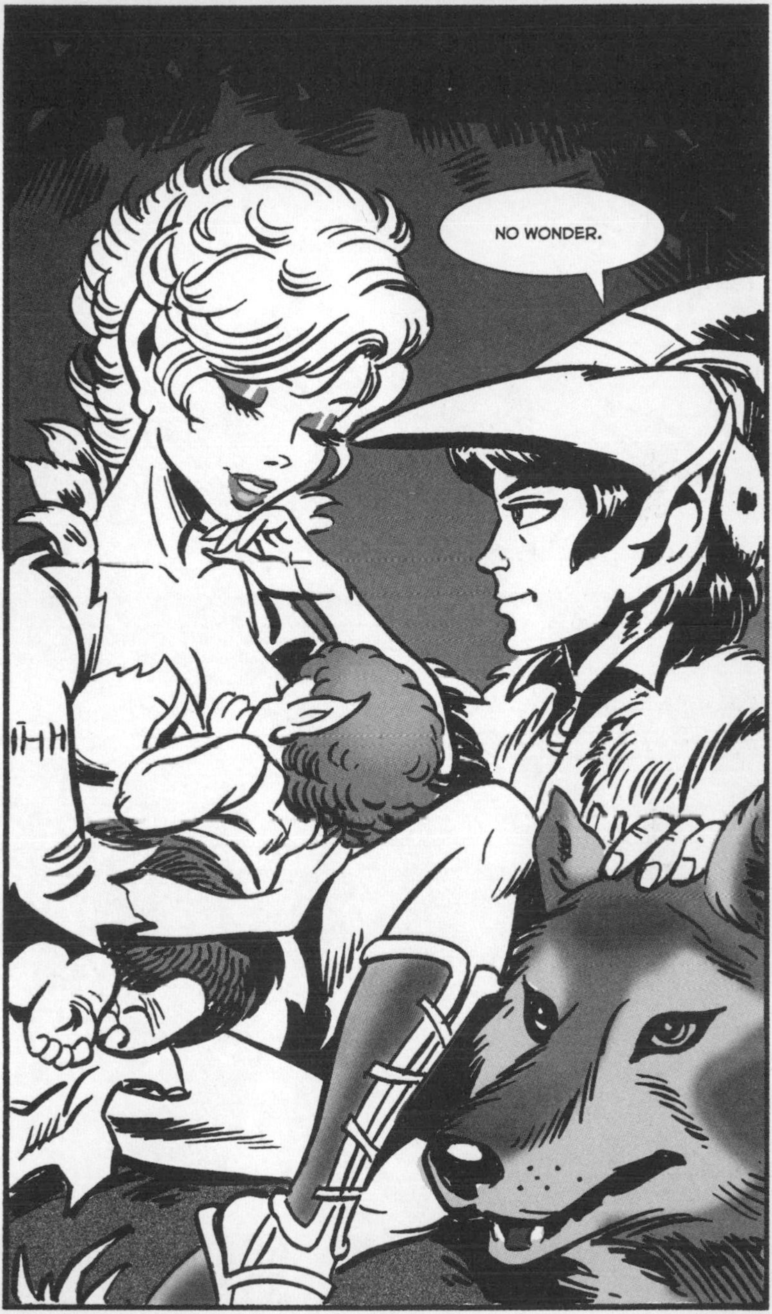
NO WONDER.

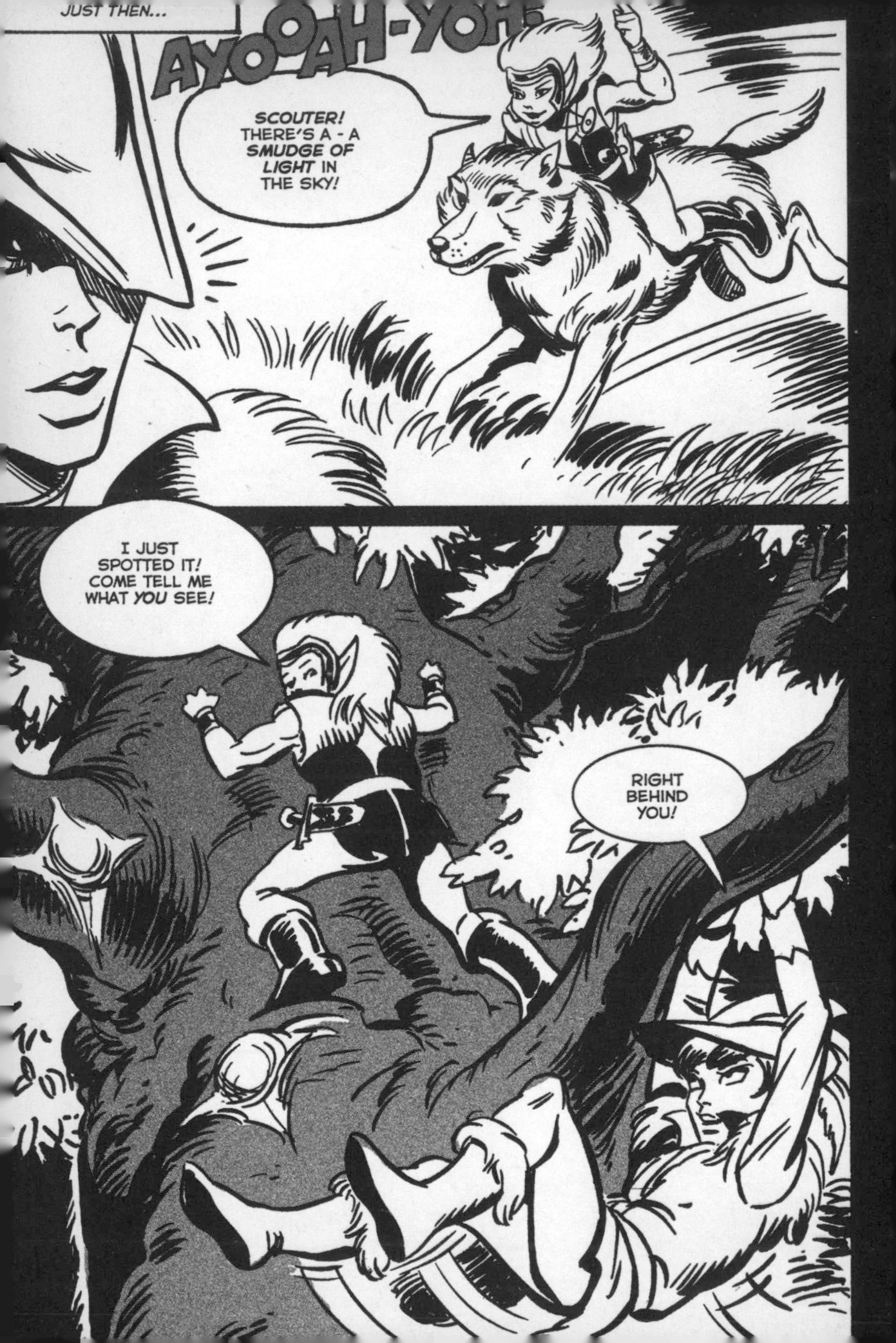
JUST THEN...
AYOOOAH-YOH!
SCOUTER! THERE'S A - A SMUDGE OF LIGHT IN THE SKY!
I JUST SPOTTED IT! COME TELL ME WHAT YOU SEE!
RIGHT BEHIND YOU!

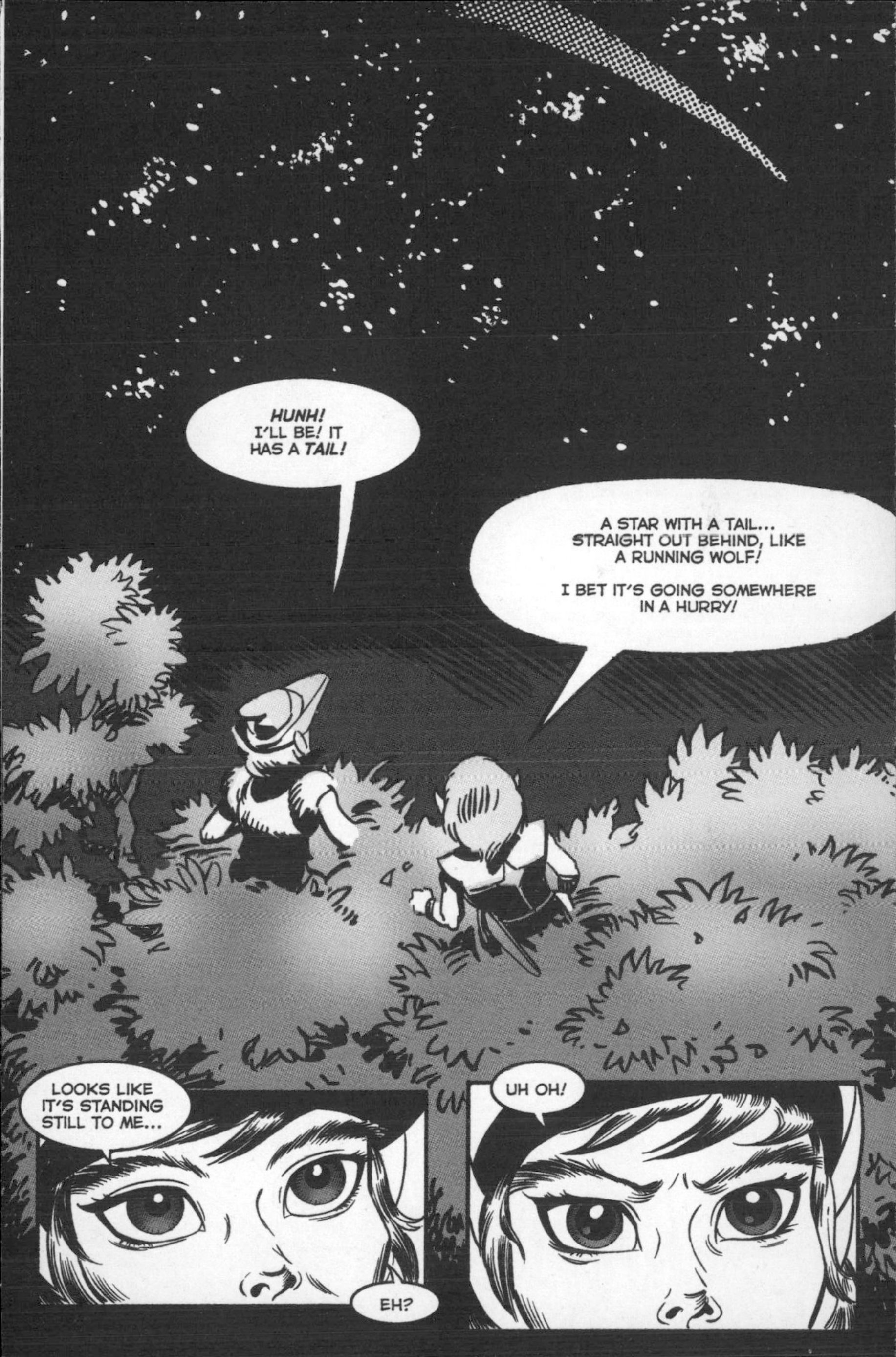

HUNH! I'LL BE! IT HAS A *TAIL!*
A STAR WITH A TAIL... STRAIGHT OUT BEHIND, LIKE A RUNNING WOLF!
I BET IT'S GOING SOMEWHERE IN A HURRY!
LOOKS LIKE IT'S STANDING STILL TO ME...
EH?
UH OH!

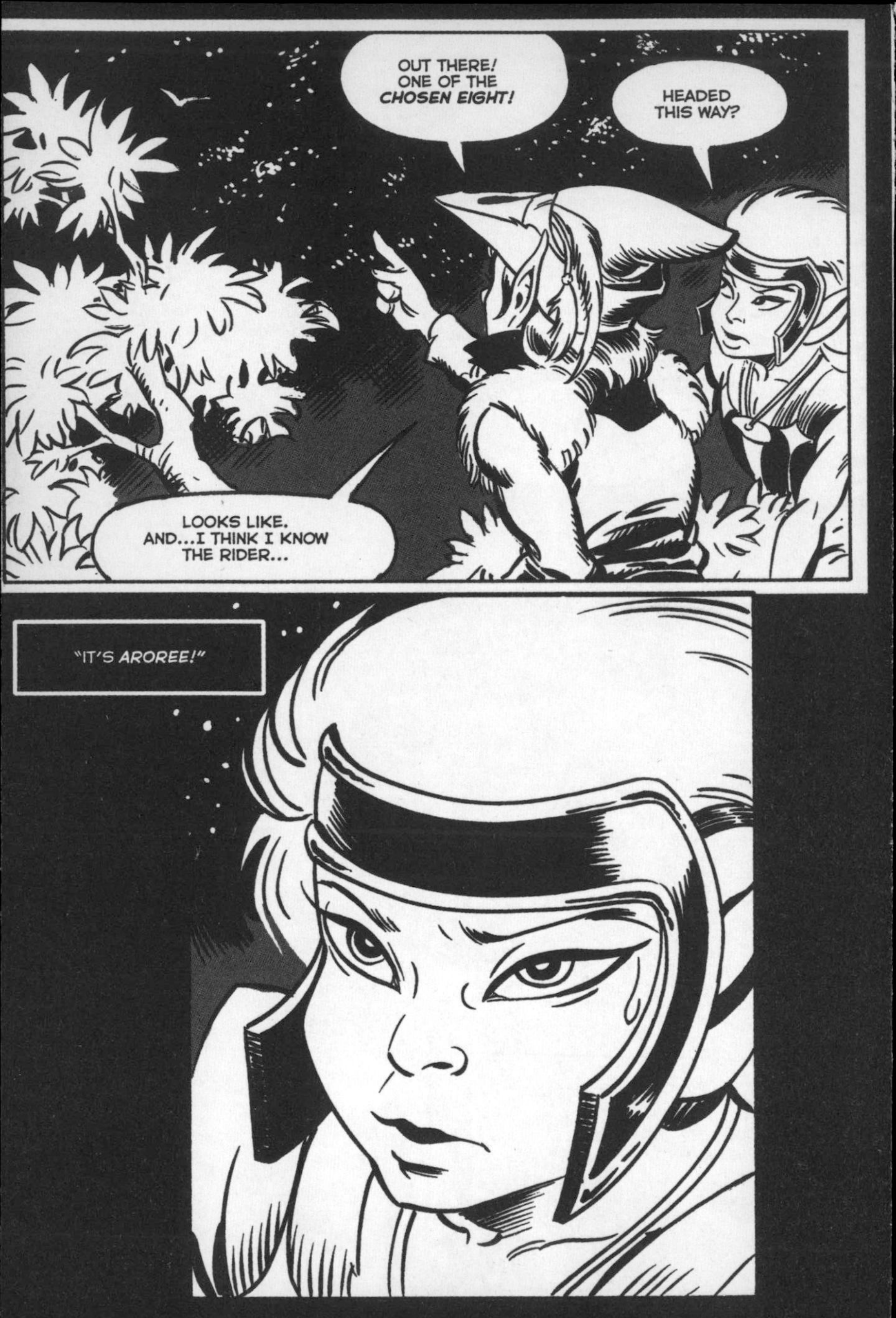
OUT THERE! ONE OF THE CHOSEN EIGHT!
HEADED THIS WAY?
LOOKS LIKE. AND...I THINK I KNOW THE RIDER...
"IT'S AROREE!"

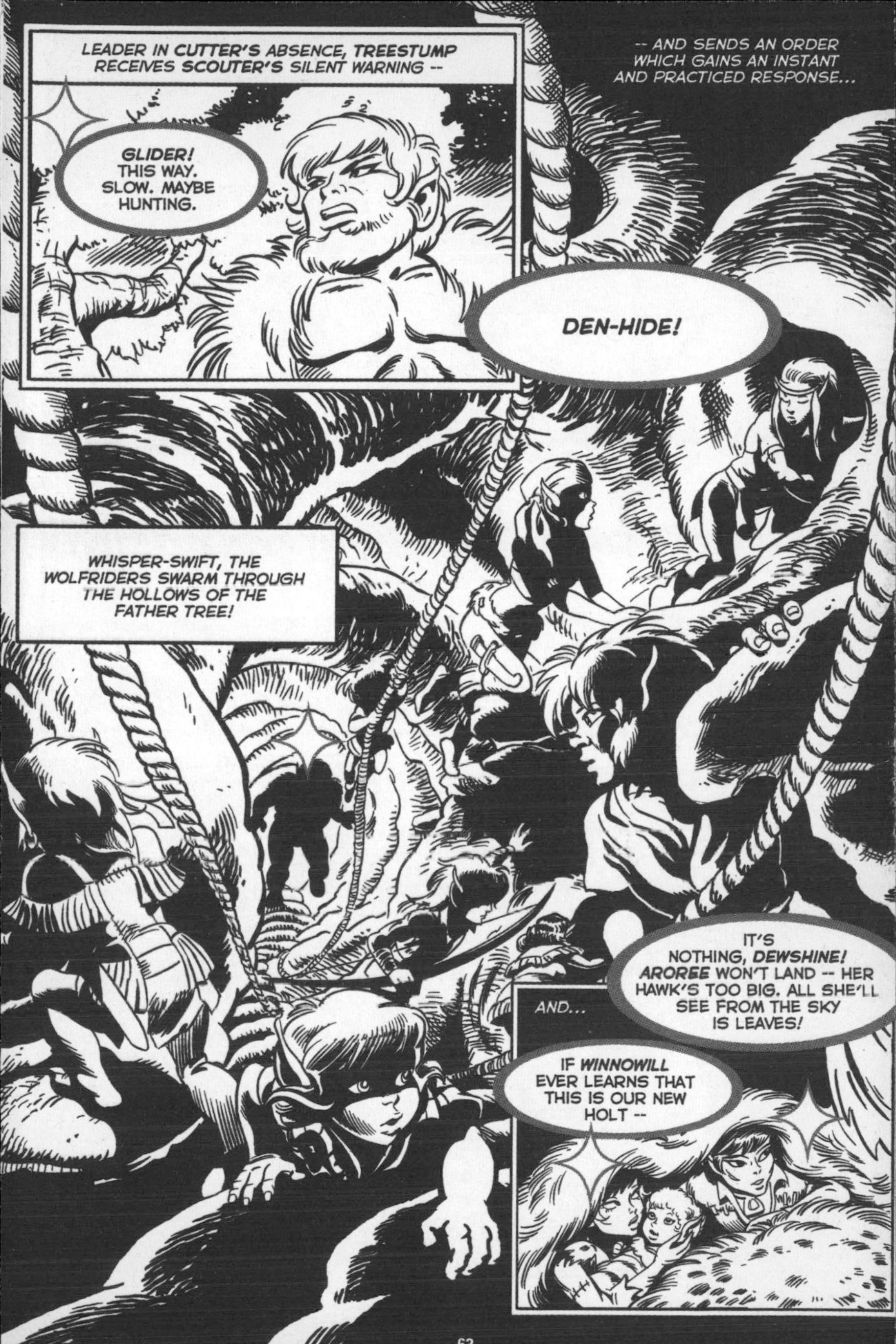

LEADER IN CUTTER'S ABSENCE, TREESTUMP RECEIVES SCOUTER'S SILENT WARNING --
GLIDER! THIS WAY. SLOW. MAYBE HUNTING.
-- AND SENDS AN ORDER WHICH GAINS AN INSTANT AND PRACTICED RESPONSE...
DEN-HIDE!
WHISPER-SWIFT, THE WOLFRIDERS SWARM THROUGH THE HOLLOWS OF THE FATHER TREE!
AND...
IT'S NOTHING, DEWSHINE! AROREE WON'T LAND -- HER HAWK'S TOO BIG. ALL SHE'LL SEE FROM THE SKY IS LEAVES!
IF WINNOWILL EVER LEARNS THAT THIS IS OUR NEW HOLT --

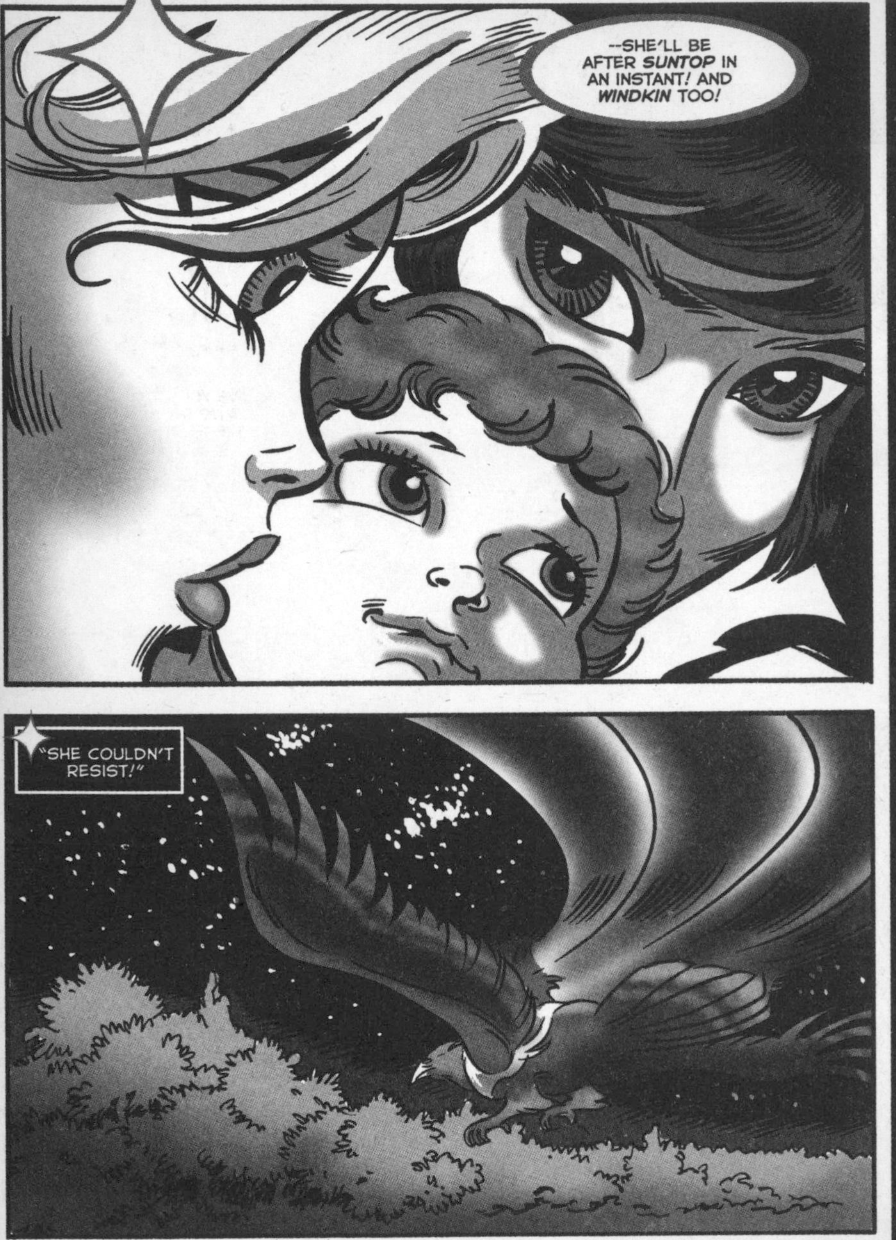
--SHE'LL BE AFTER SUNTOP IN AN INSTANT! AND WINDKIN TOO!
"SHE COULDN'T RESIST!"

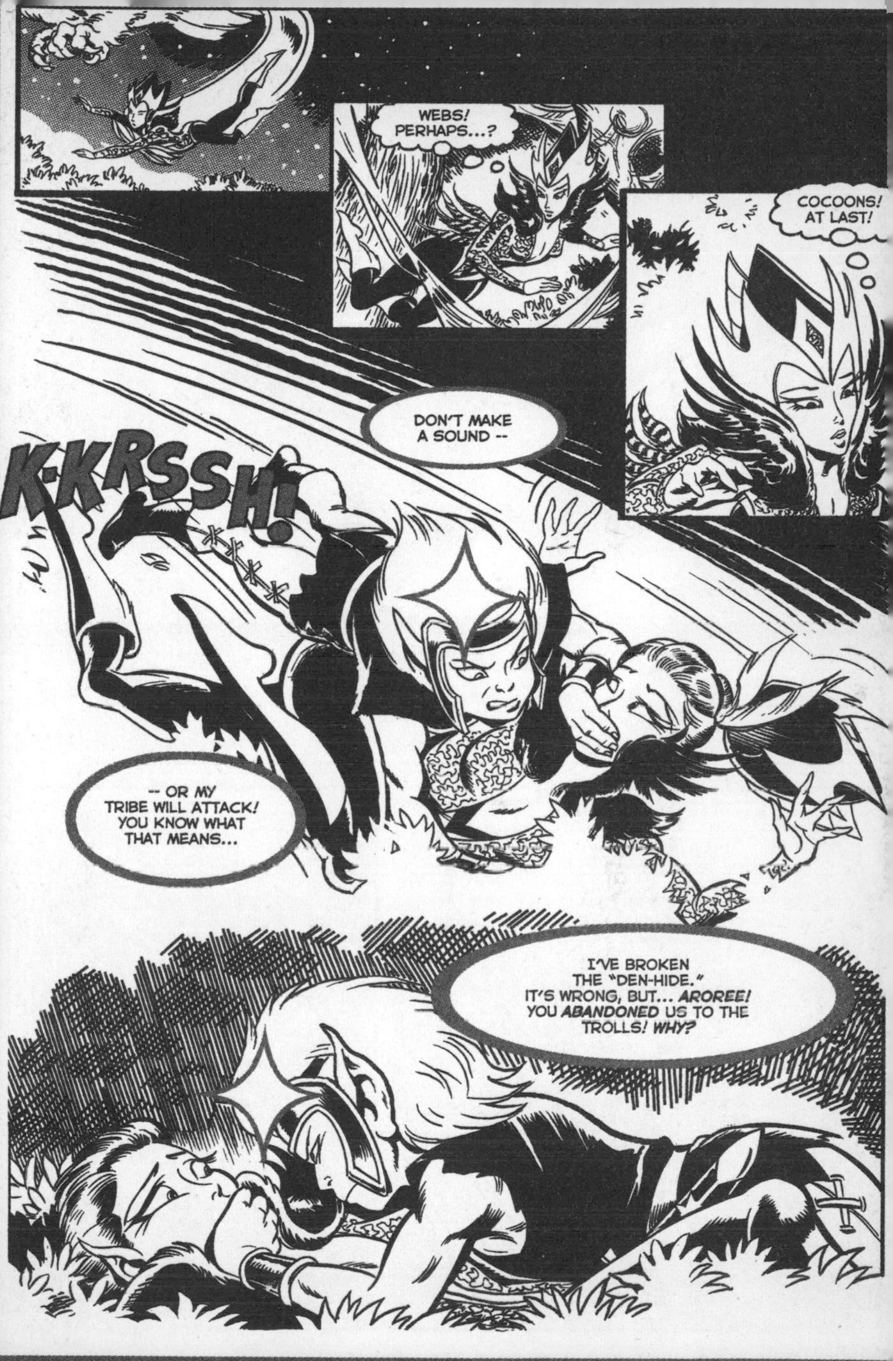
WEBS! PERHAPS...?
COCOONS! AT LAST!
DON'T MAKE A SOUND --
K-KRSSH!
-- OR MY TRIBE WILL ATTACK! YOU KNOW WHAT THAT MEANS...
I'VE BROKEN THE "DEN-HIDE." IT'S WRONG, BUT... *AROREE!* YOU *ABANDONED* US TO THE TROLLS! *WHY?*

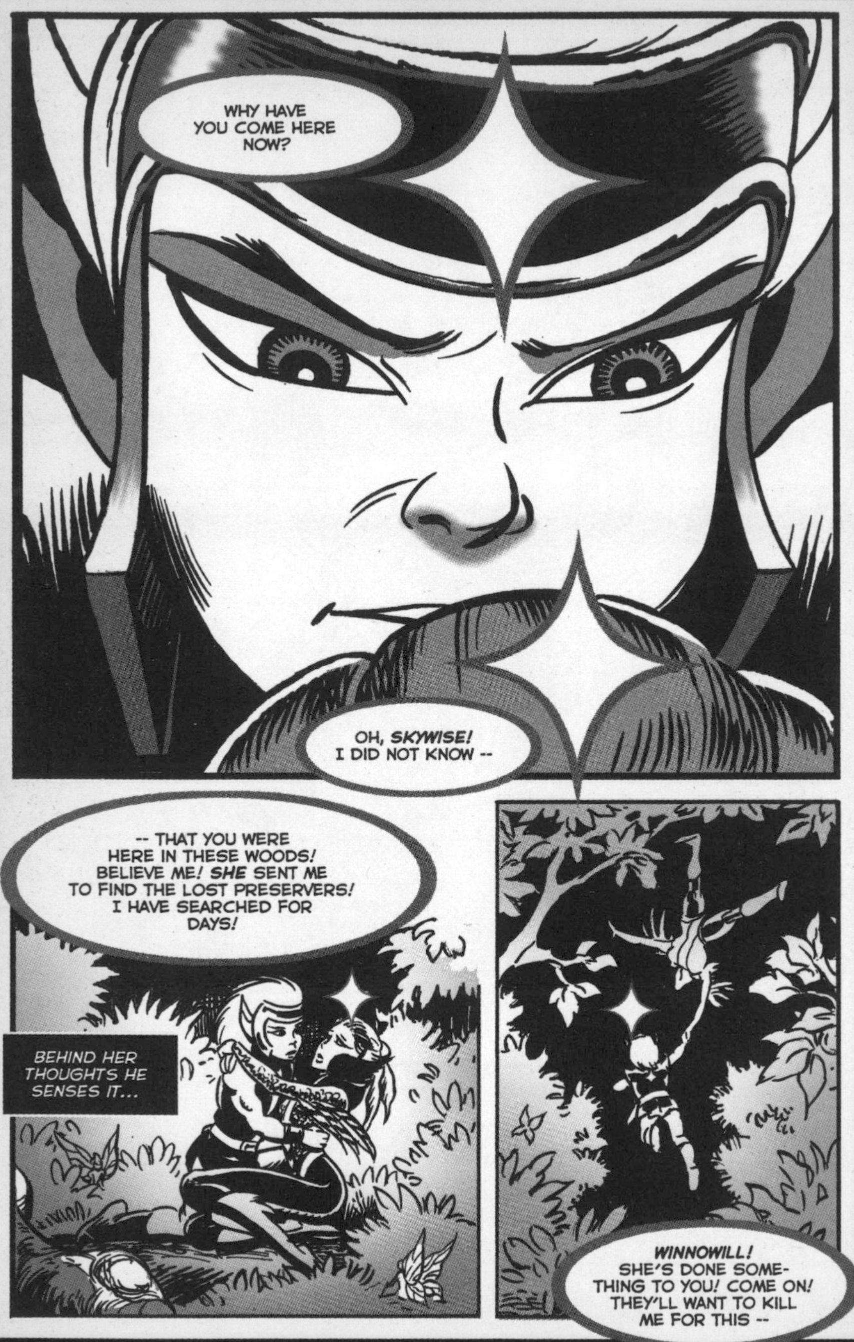
WHY HAVE YOU COME HERE NOW?
OH, SKYWISE! I DID NOT KNOW --
-- THAT YOU WERE HERE IN THESE WOODS! BELIEVE ME! SHE SENT ME TO FIND THE LOST PRESERVERS! I HAVE SEARCHED FOR DAYS!
BEHIND HER THOUGHTS HE SENSES IT...
WINNOWILL! SHE'S DONE SOME-THING TO YOU! COME ON! THEY'LL WANT TO KILL ME FOR THIS --

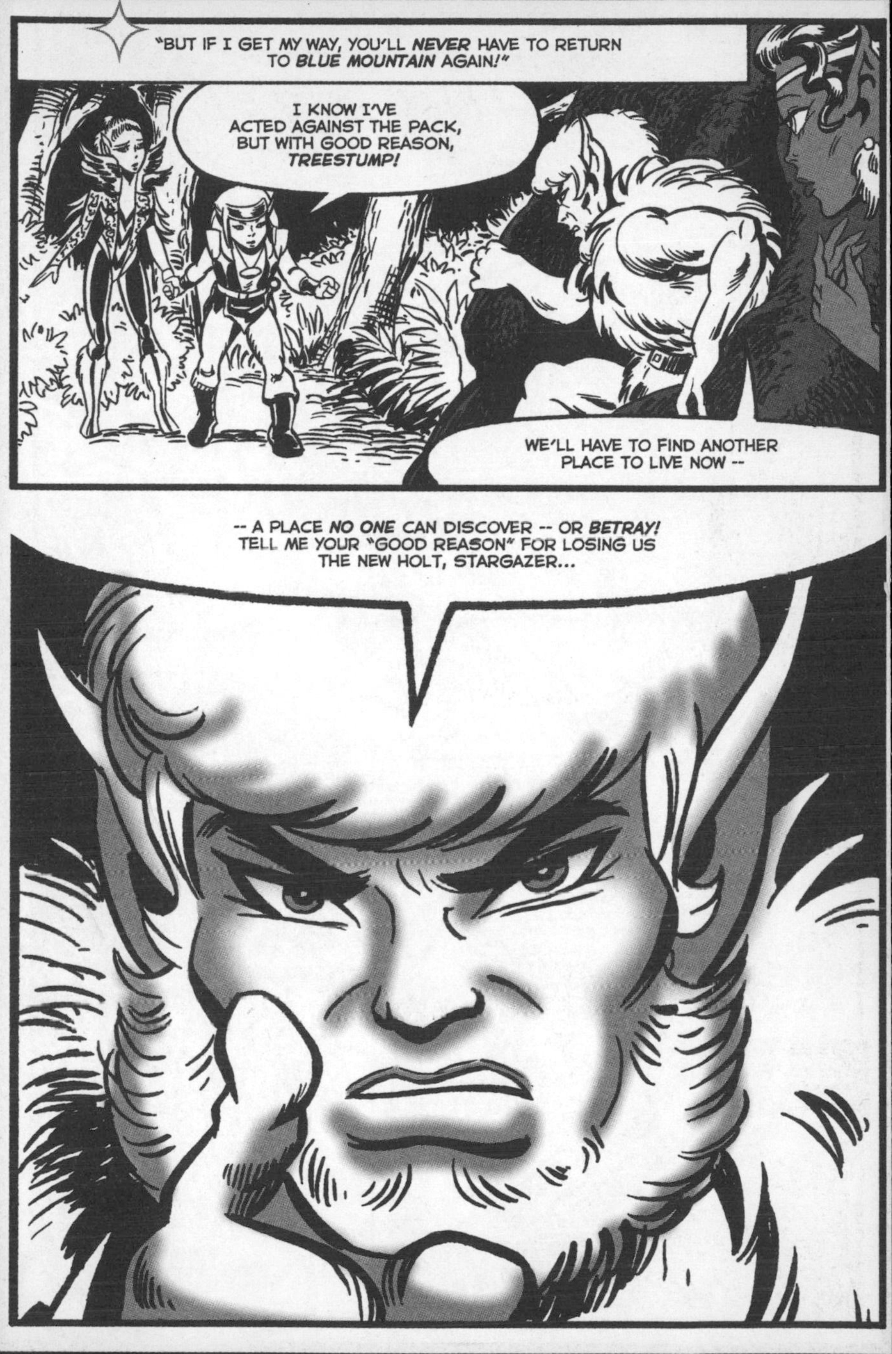
"BUT IF I GET MY WAY, YOU'LL NEVER HAVE TO RETURN TO BLUE MOUNTAIN AGAIN!"
I KNOW I'VE ACTED AGAINST THE PACK, BUT WITH GOOD REASON, TREESTUMP!
WE'LL HAVE TO FIND ANOTHER PLACE TO LIVE NOW --
-- A PLACE NO ONE CAN DISCOVER -- OR BETRAY! TELL ME YOUR "GOOD REASON" FOR LOSING US THE NEW HOLT, STARGAZER...

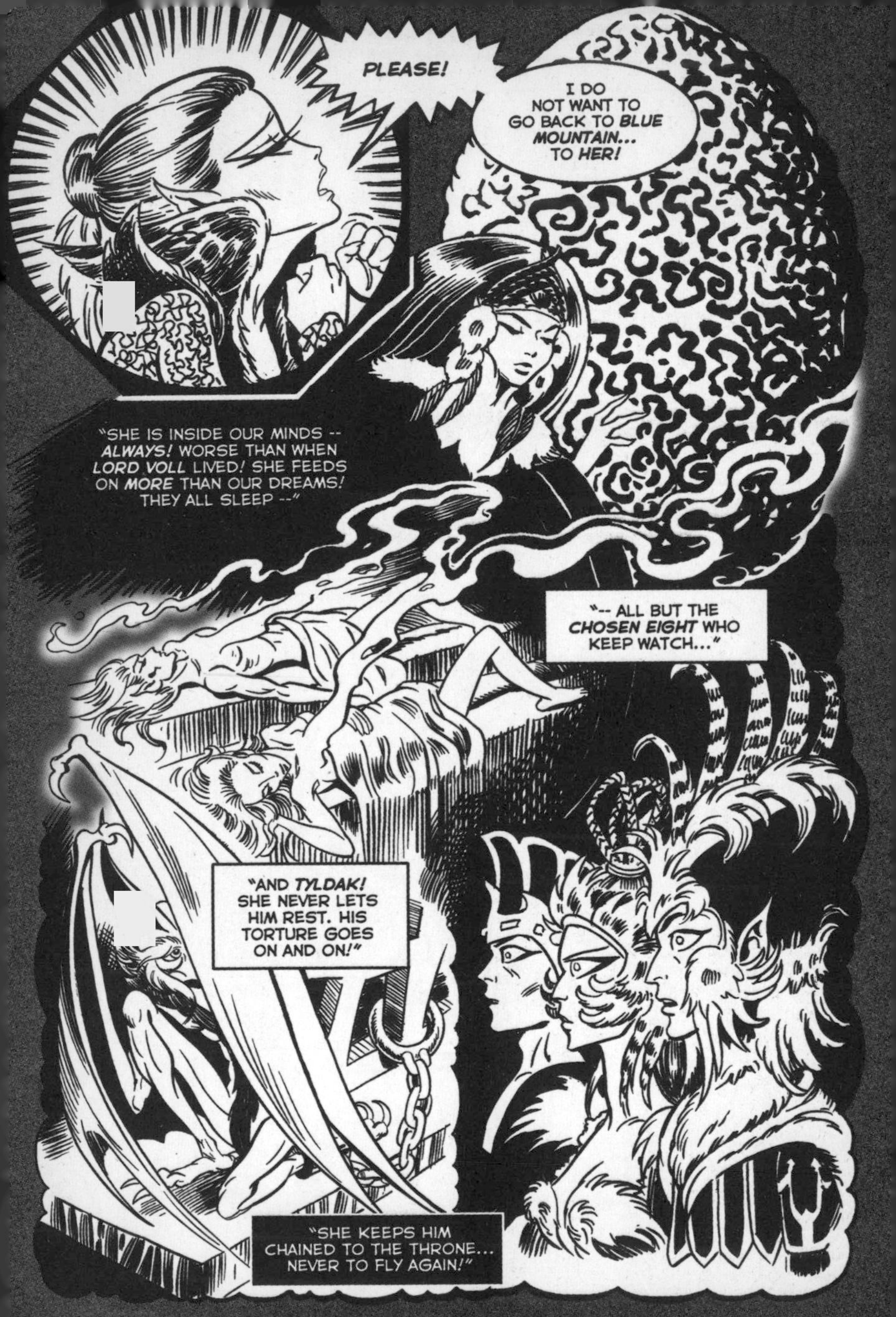
PLEASE!
I DO NOT WANT TO GO BACK TO *BLUE MOUNTAIN*... TO *HER!*
"SHE IS INSIDE OUR MINDS -- *ALWAYS!* WORSE THAN WHEN *LORD VOLL* LIVED! SHE FEEDS ON *MORE* THAN OUR DREAMS! THEY ALL SLEEP --"
"-- ALL BUT THE *CHOSEN EIGHT* WHO KEEP WATCH..."
"AND *TYLDAK!* SHE NEVER LETS HIM REST. HIS TORTURE GOES ON AND ON!"
"SHE KEEPS HIM CHAINED TO THE THRONE... NEVER TO FLY AGAIN!"

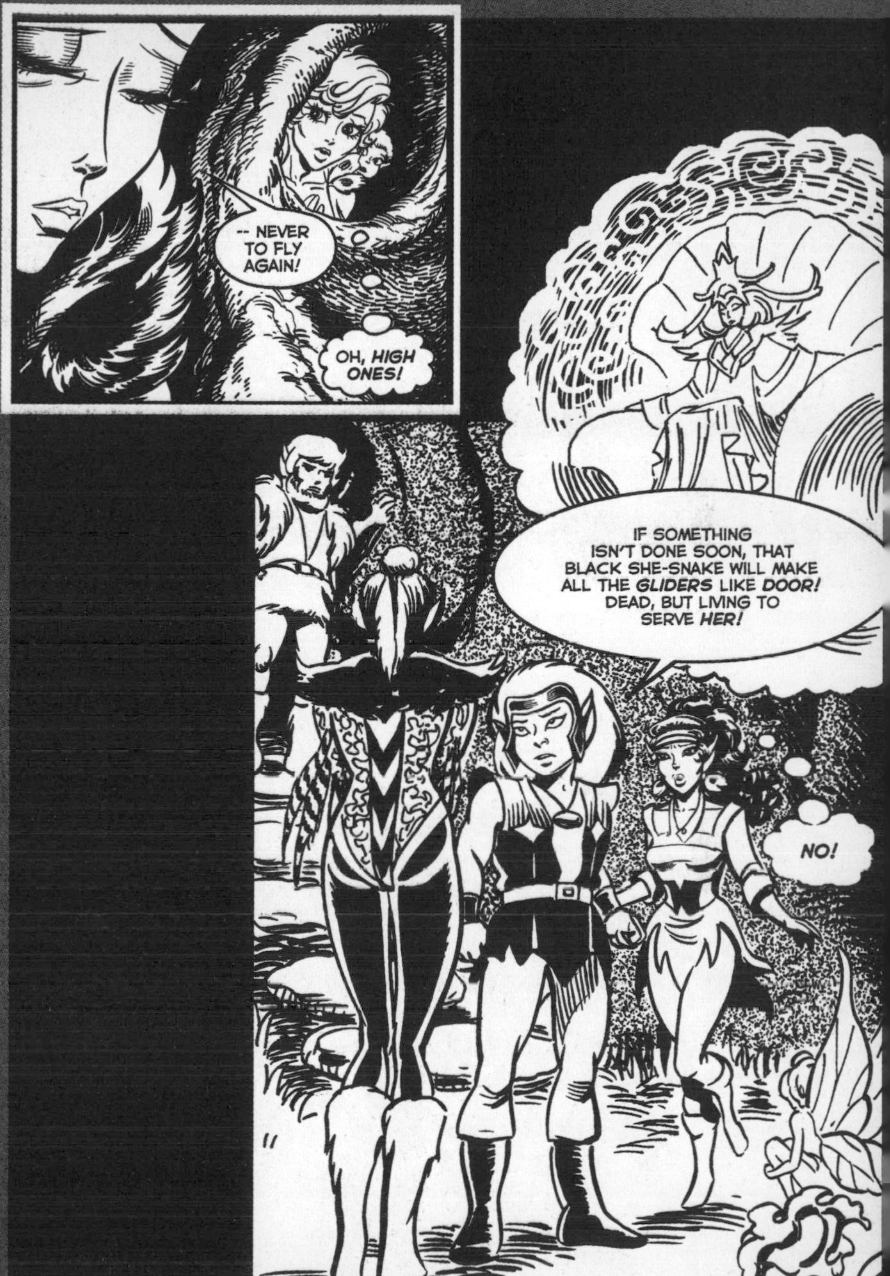
-- NEVER TO FLY AGAIN!
OH, HIGH ONES!
IF SOMETHING ISN'T DONE SOON, THAT BLACK SHE-SNAKE WILL MAKE ALL THE *GLIDERS* LIKE *DOOR!* DEAD, BUT LIVING TO SERVE *HER!*
NO!

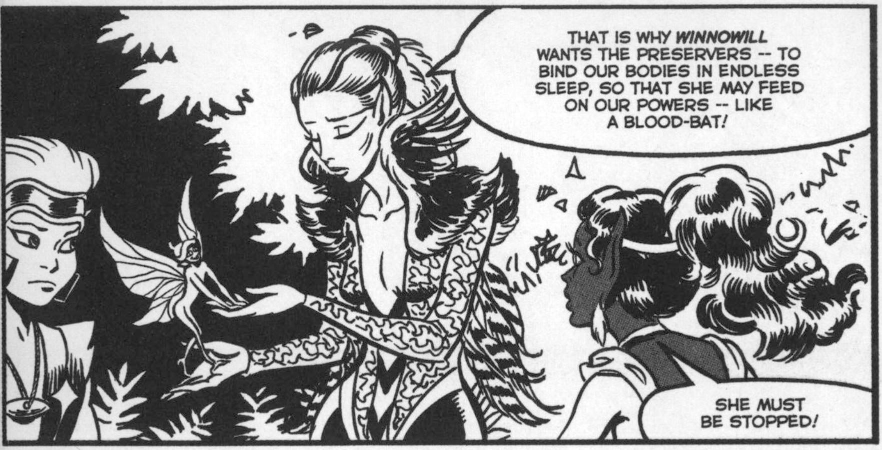
THAT IS WHY WINNOWILL WANTS THE PRESERVERS -- TO BIND OUR BODIES IN ENDLESS SLEEP, SO THAT SHE MAY FEED ON OUR POWERS -- LIKE A BLOOD-BAT!
SHE MUST BE STOPPED!

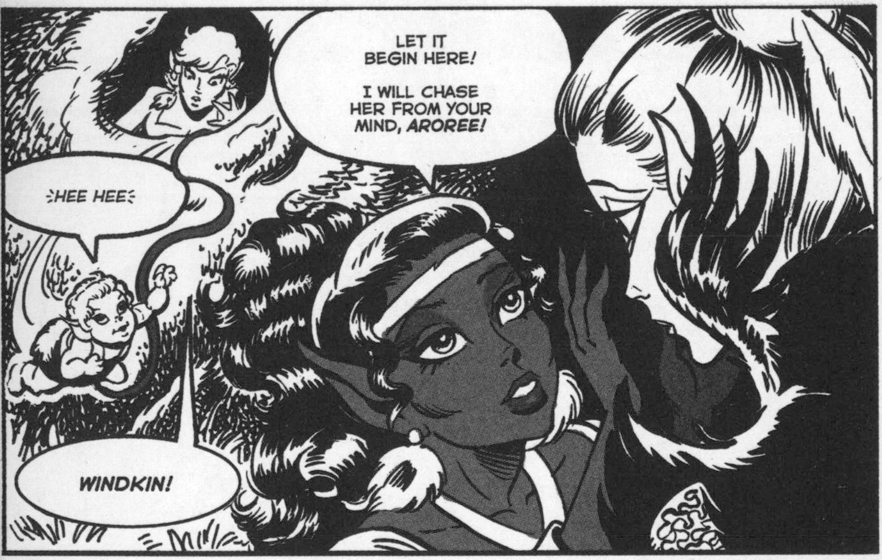
LET IT BEGIN HERE!
I WILL CHASE HER FROM YOUR MIND, AROREE!
HEE HEE
WINDKIN!

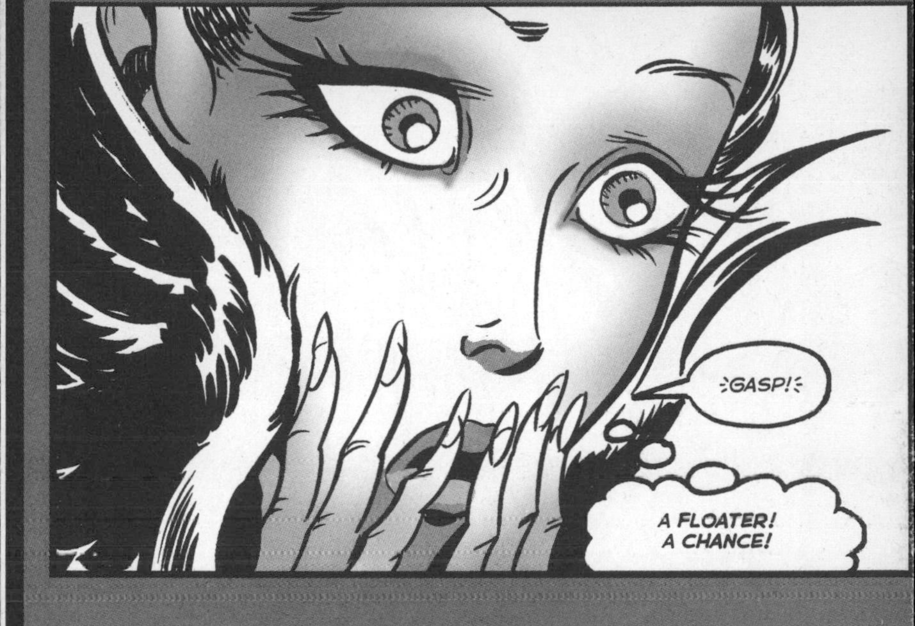
GASP!
A FLOATER!
A CHANCE!
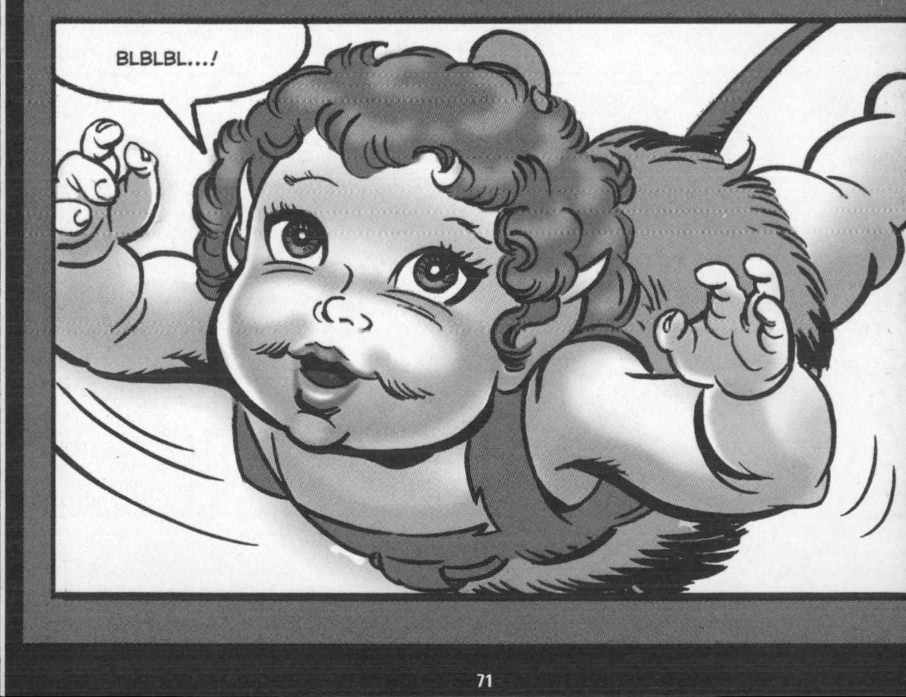
BLBLBL...!

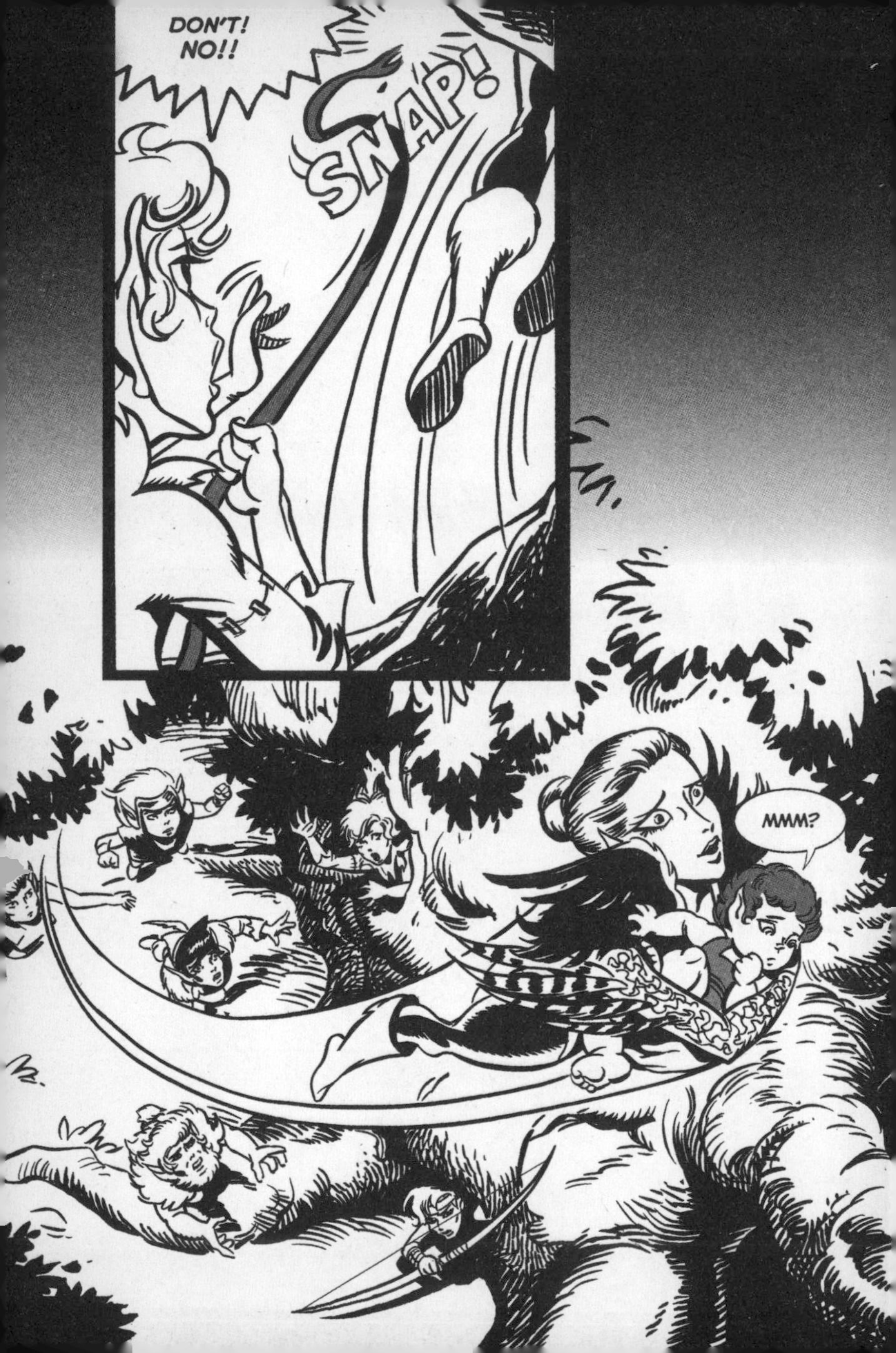

DON'T! NO!!
SNAP!
MMM?

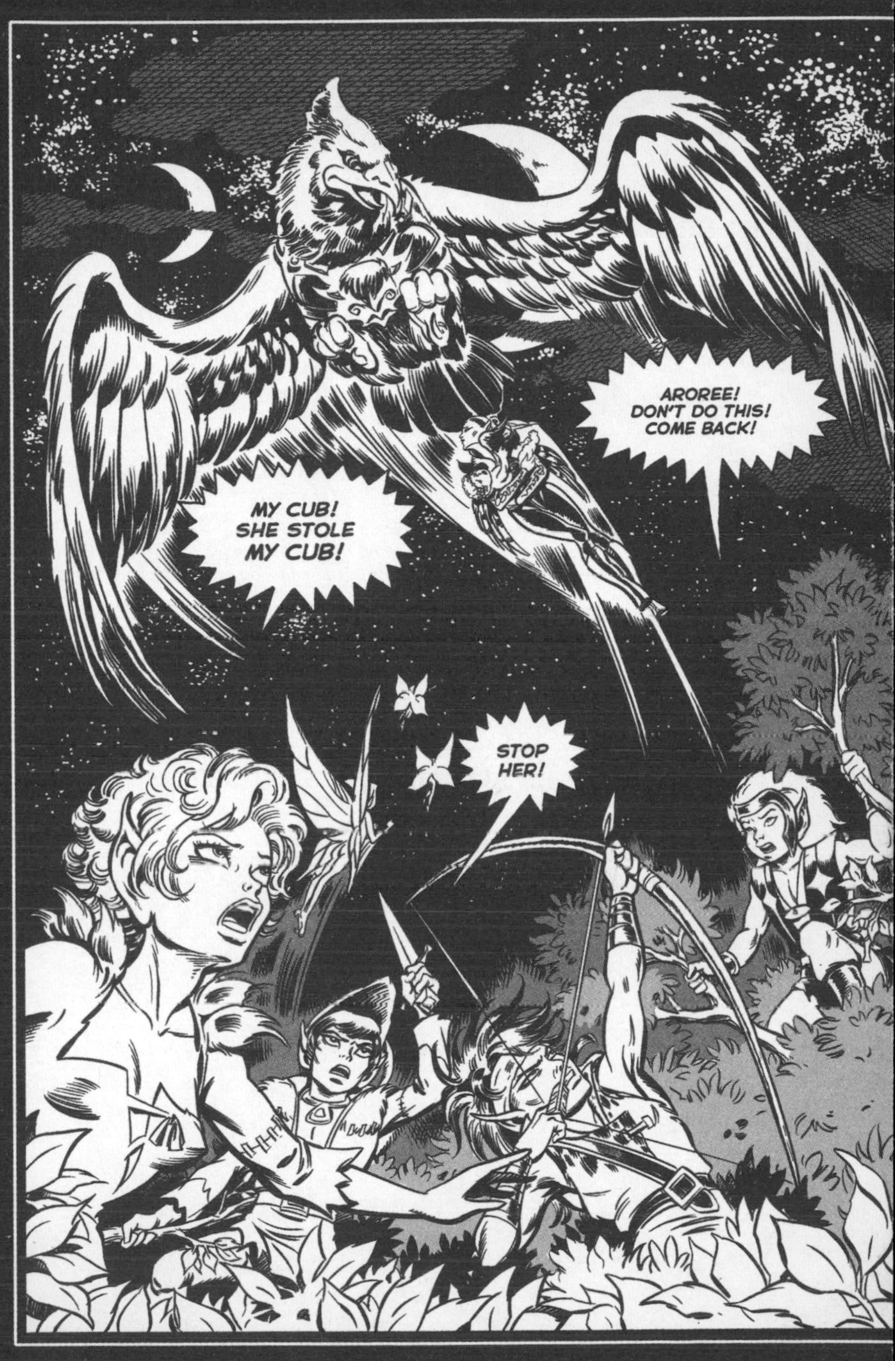
AROREE! DON'T DO THIS! COME BACK!
MY CUB! SHE STOLE MY CUB!
STOP HER!

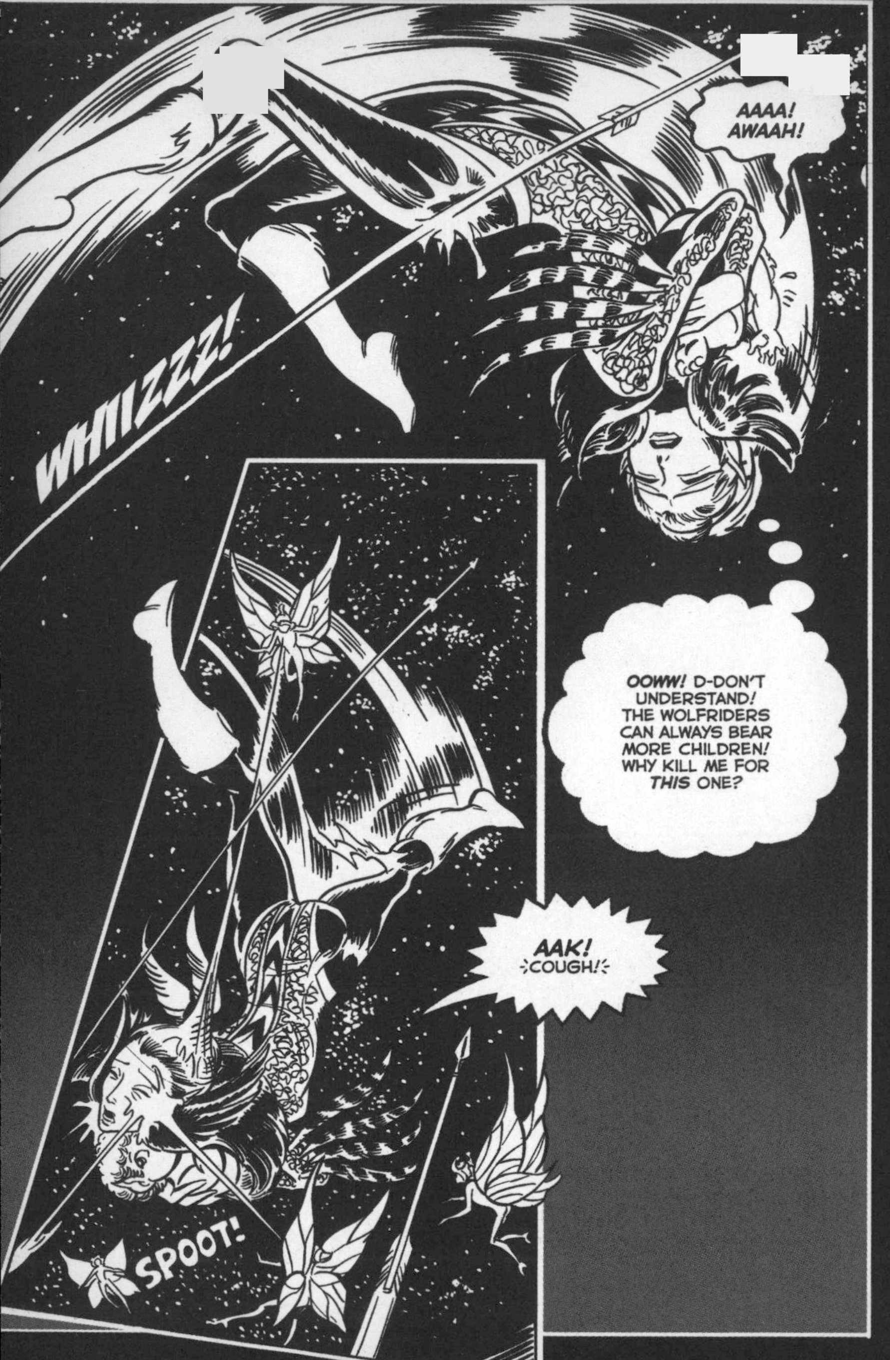
AAAA! AWAAH!
WHIIZZZ!
OOWW! D-DON'T UNDERSTAND! THE WOLFRIDERS CAN ALWAYS BEAR MORE CHILDREN! WHY KILL ME FOR THIS ONE?
AAK! -COUGH!-
SPOOT!

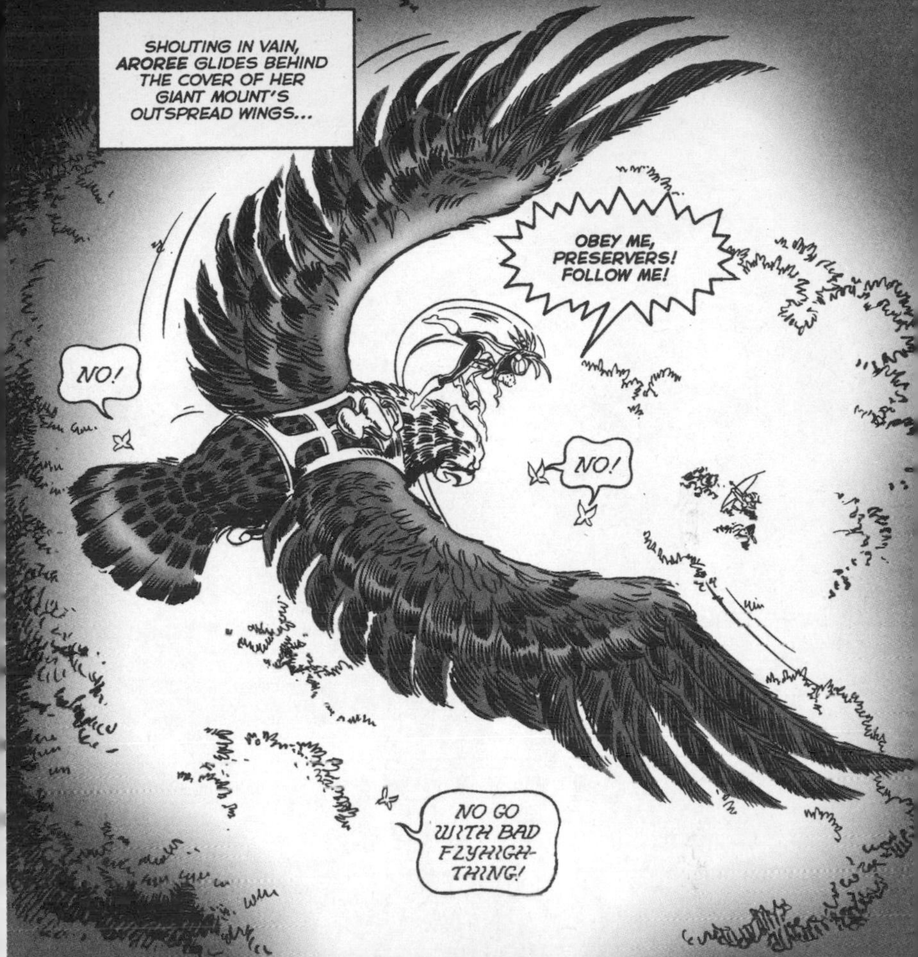
SHOUTING IN VAIN, AROREE GLIDES BEHIND THE COVER OF HER GIANT MOUNT'S OUTSPREAD WINGS...
OBEY ME, PRESERVERS! FOLLOW ME!
NO!
NO!
NO GO WITH BAD FLYHIGH-THING!

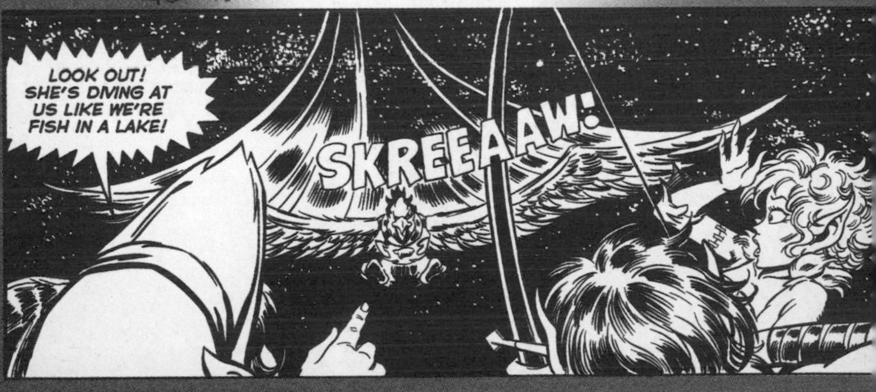
LOOK OUT! SHE'S DIVING AT US LIKE WE'RE FISH IN A LAKE!
SKREEAAW!

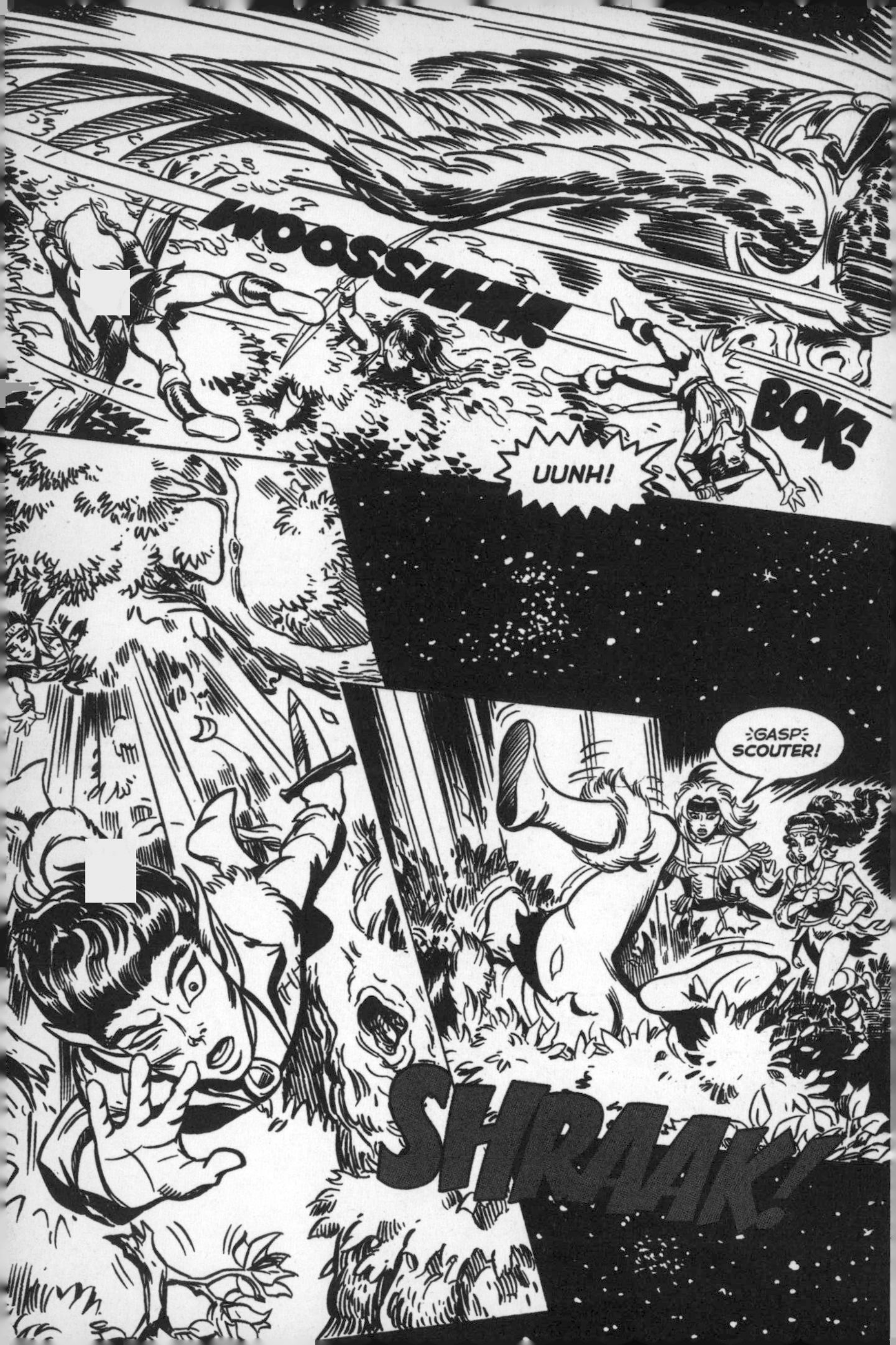
WOOSHHH!
BOK!
UUNH!
GASP
SCOUTER!
SHRAAK!

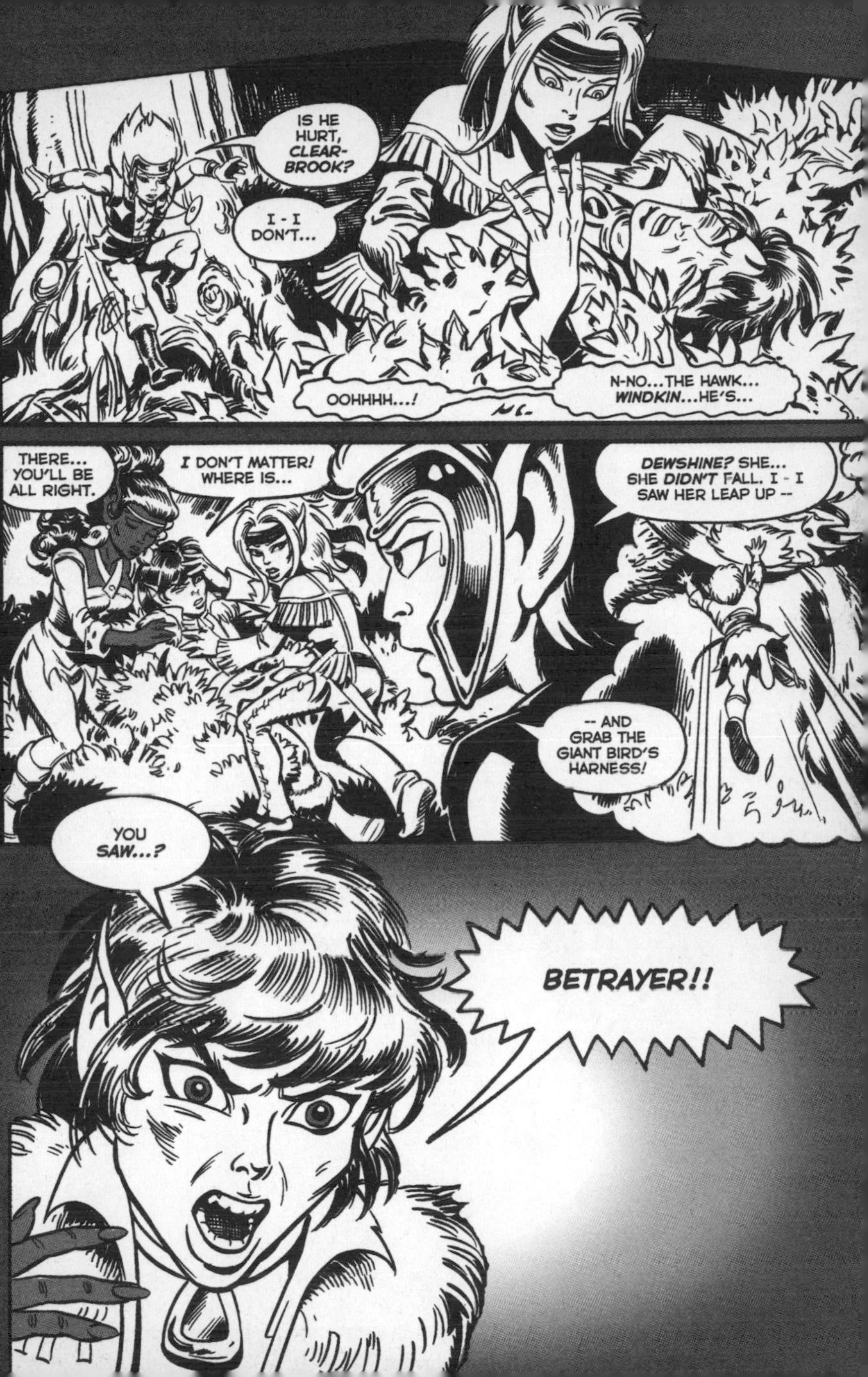

IS HE HURT, CLEAR-BROOK?
I - I DON'T...
OOHHHH...!
N-NO...THE HAWK... WINDKIN...HE'S...
THERE... YOU'LL BE ALL RIGHT.
I DON'T MATTER! WHERE IS...
DEWSHINE? SHE... SHE DIDN'T FALL. I - I SAW HER LEAP UP --
-- AND GRAB THE GIANT BIRD'S HARNESS!
YOU SAW...?
BETRAYER!!

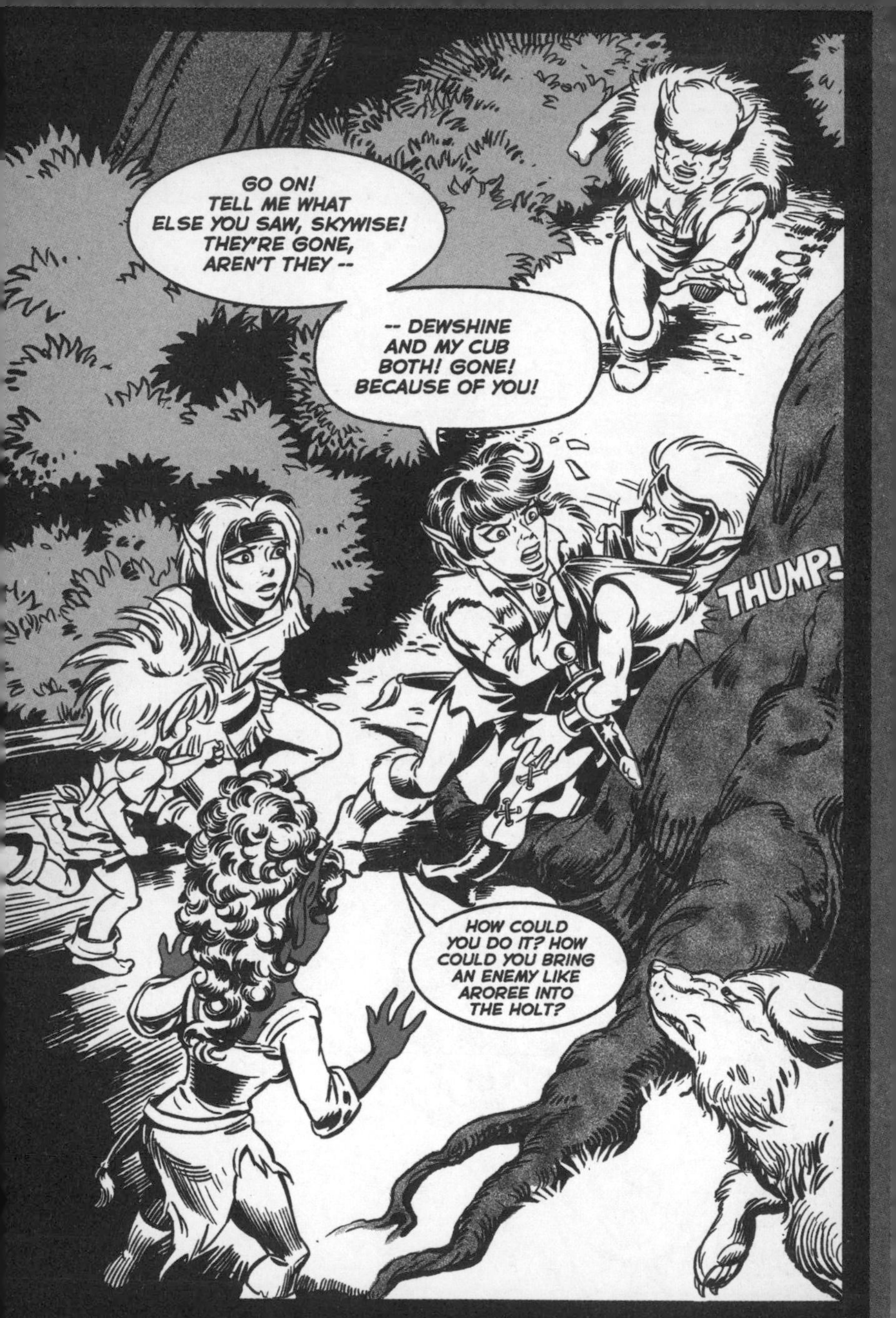
GO ON! TELL ME WHAT ELSE YOU SAW, SKYWISE! THEY'RE GONE, AREN'T THEY --
-- DEWSHINE AND MY CUB BOTH! GONE! BECAUSE OF YOU!
THUMP!
HOW COULD YOU DO IT? HOW COULD YOU BRING AN ENEMY LIKE AROREE INTO THE HOLT?

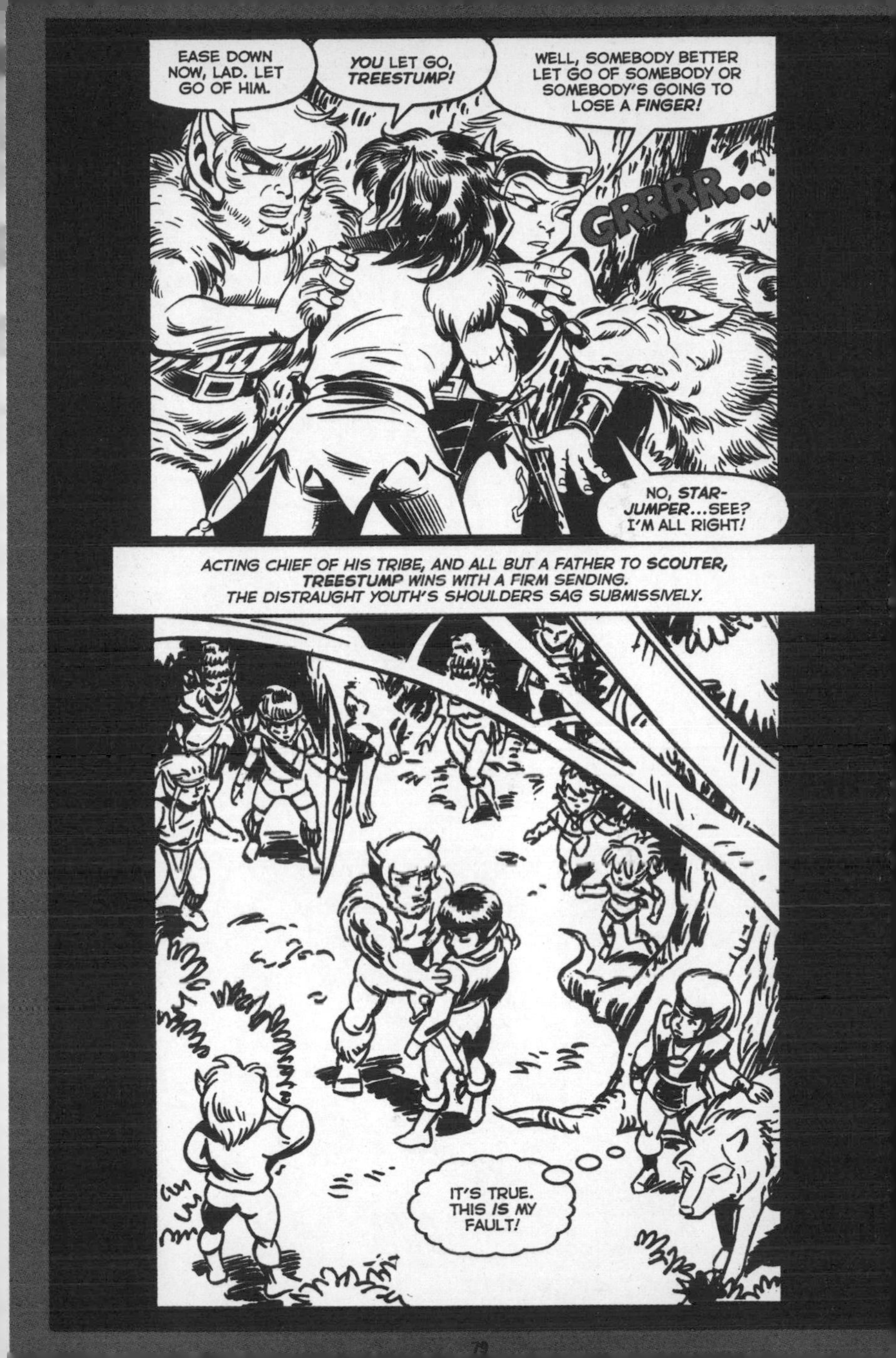

EASE DOWN NOW, LAD. LET GO OF HIM.
YOU LET GO, TREESTUMP!
WELL, SOMEBODY BETTER LET GO OF SOMEBODY OR SOMEBODY'S GOING TO LOSE A FINGER!
GRRRR...
NO, STAR-JUMPER...SEE? I'M ALL RIGHT!
ACTING CHIEF OF HIS TRIBE, AND ALL BUT A FATHER TO SCOUTER, TREESTUMP WINS WITH A FIRM SENDING. THE DISTRAUGHT YOUTH'S SHOULDERS SAG SUBMISSIVELY.
IT'S TRUE. THIS IS MY FAULT!

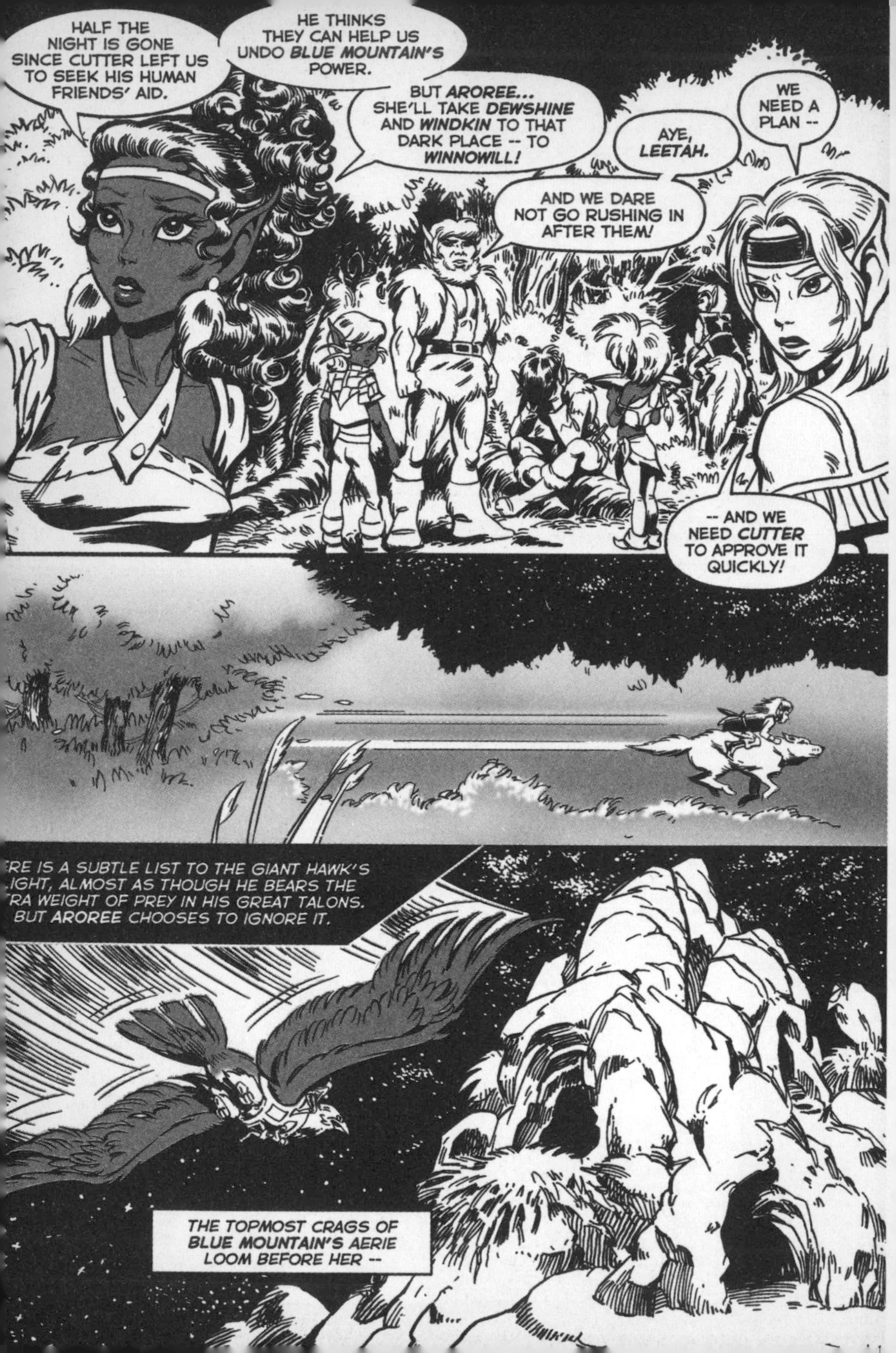
HALF THE NIGHT IS GONE SINCE CUTTER LEFT US TO SEEK HIS HUMAN FRIENDS' AID.
HE THINKS THEY CAN HELP US UNDO BLUE MOUNTAIN'S POWER.
BUT AROREE... SHE'LL TAKE DEWSHINE AND WINDKIN TO THAT DARK PLACE -- TO WINNOWILL!
AYE, LEETAH.
AND WE DARE NOT GO RUSHING IN AFTER THEM!
WE NEED A PLAN --
-- AND WE NEED CUTTER TO APPROVE IT QUICKLY!
RE IS A SUBTLE LIST TO THE GIANT HAWK'S IGHT, ALMOST AS THOUGH HE BEARS THE RA WEIGHT OF PREY IN HIS GREAT TALONS. BUT AROREE CHOOSES TO IGNORE IT.
THE TOPMOST CRAGS OF BLUE MOUNTAIN'S AERIE LOOM BEFORE HER --

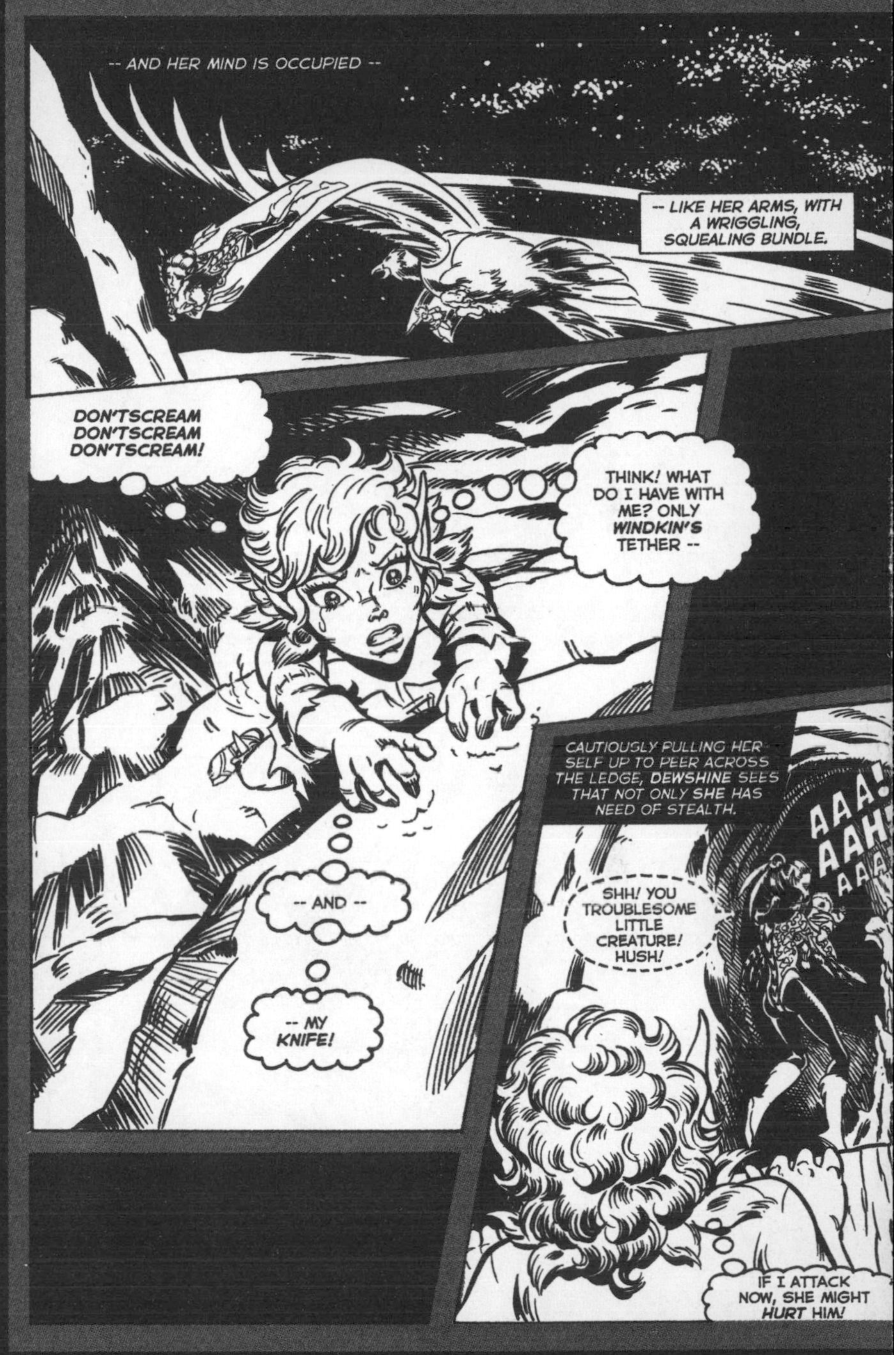
-- AND HER MIND IS OCCUPIED --
-- LIKE HER ARMS, WITH A WRIGGLING, SQUEALING BUNDLE.
DON'TSCREAM DON'TSCREAM DON'TSCREAM!
THINK! WHAT DO I HAVE WITH ME? ONLY WINDKIN'S TETHER --
-- AND --
-- MY KNIFE!
CAUTIOUSLY PULLING HERSELF UP TO PEER ACROSS THE LEDGE, DEWSHINE SEES THAT NOT ONLY SHE HAS NEED OF STEALTH.
AAA! AAH! AAA!
SHH! YOU TROUBLESOME LITTLE CREATURE! HUSH!
IF I ATTACK NOW, SHE MIGHT HURT HIM!

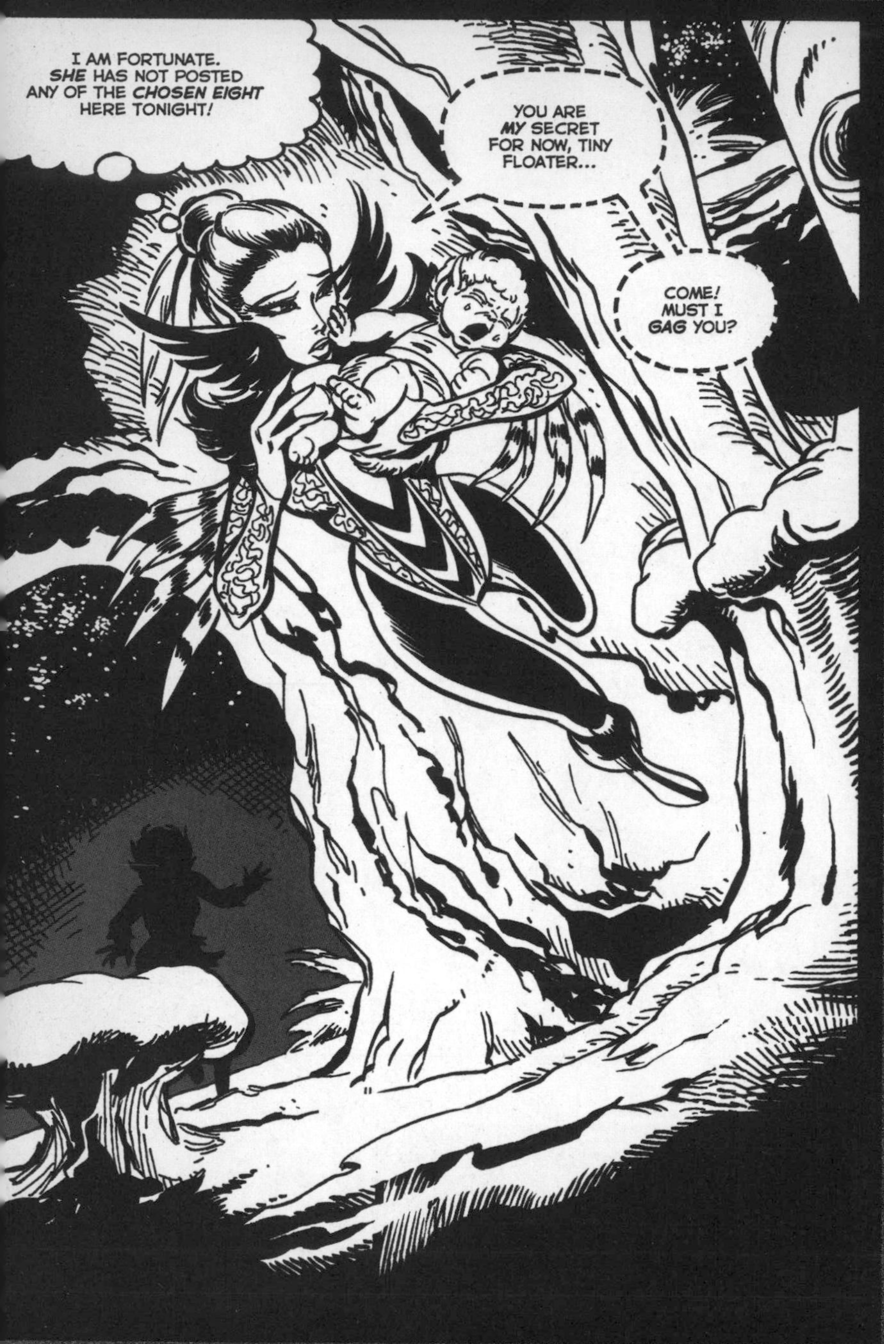
I AM FORTUNATE. *SHE* HAS NOT POSTED ANY OF THE *CHOSEN EIGHT* HERE TONIGHT!
YOU ARE *MY* SECRET FOR NOW, TINY FLOATER...
COME! MUST I *GAG* YOU?

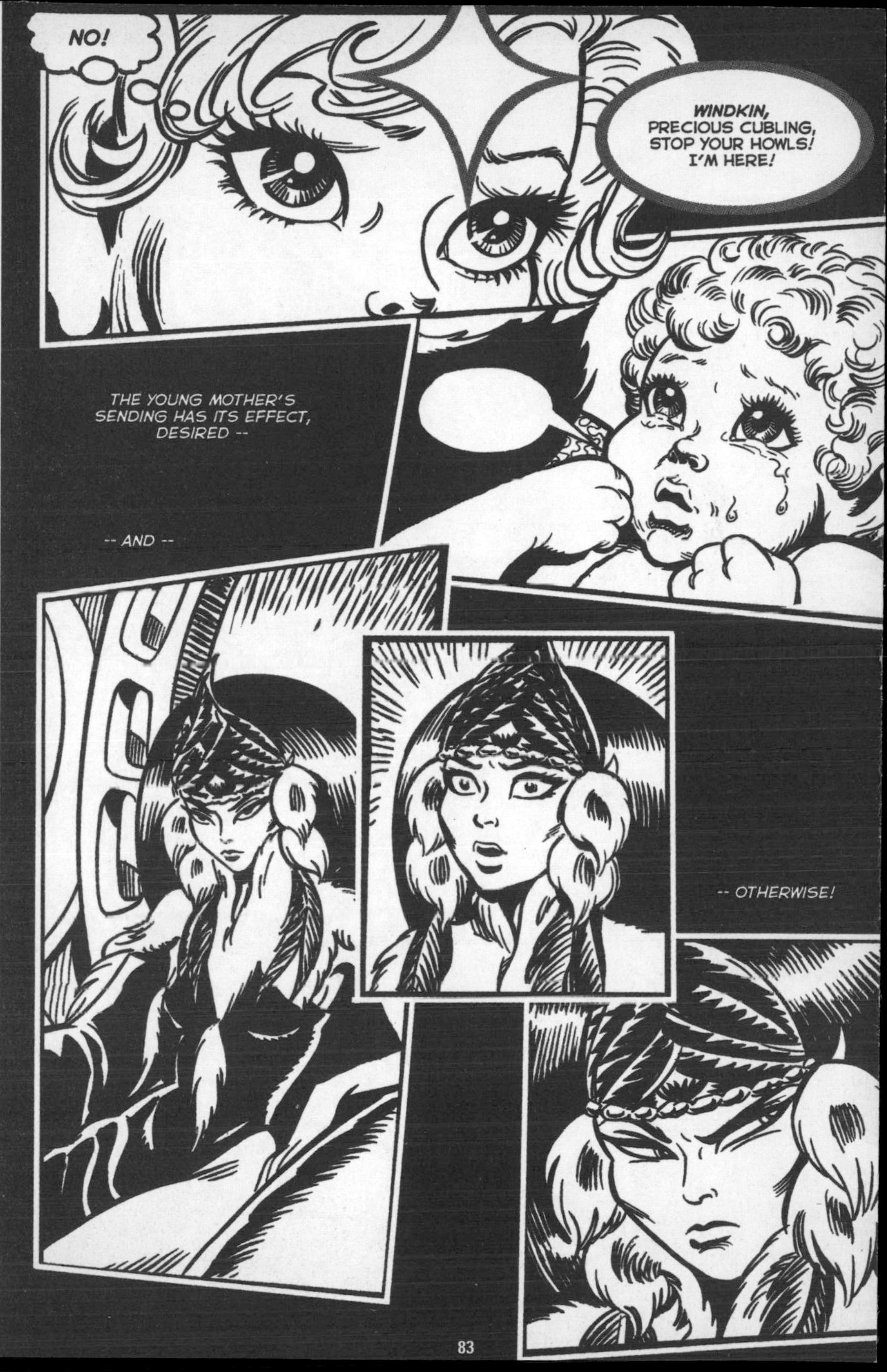
NO!
WINDKIN, PRECIOUS CUBLING, STOP YOUR HOWLS! I'M HERE!
THE YOUNG MOTHER'S SENDING HAS ITS EFFECT, DESIRED --
-- AND --
-- OTHERWISE!

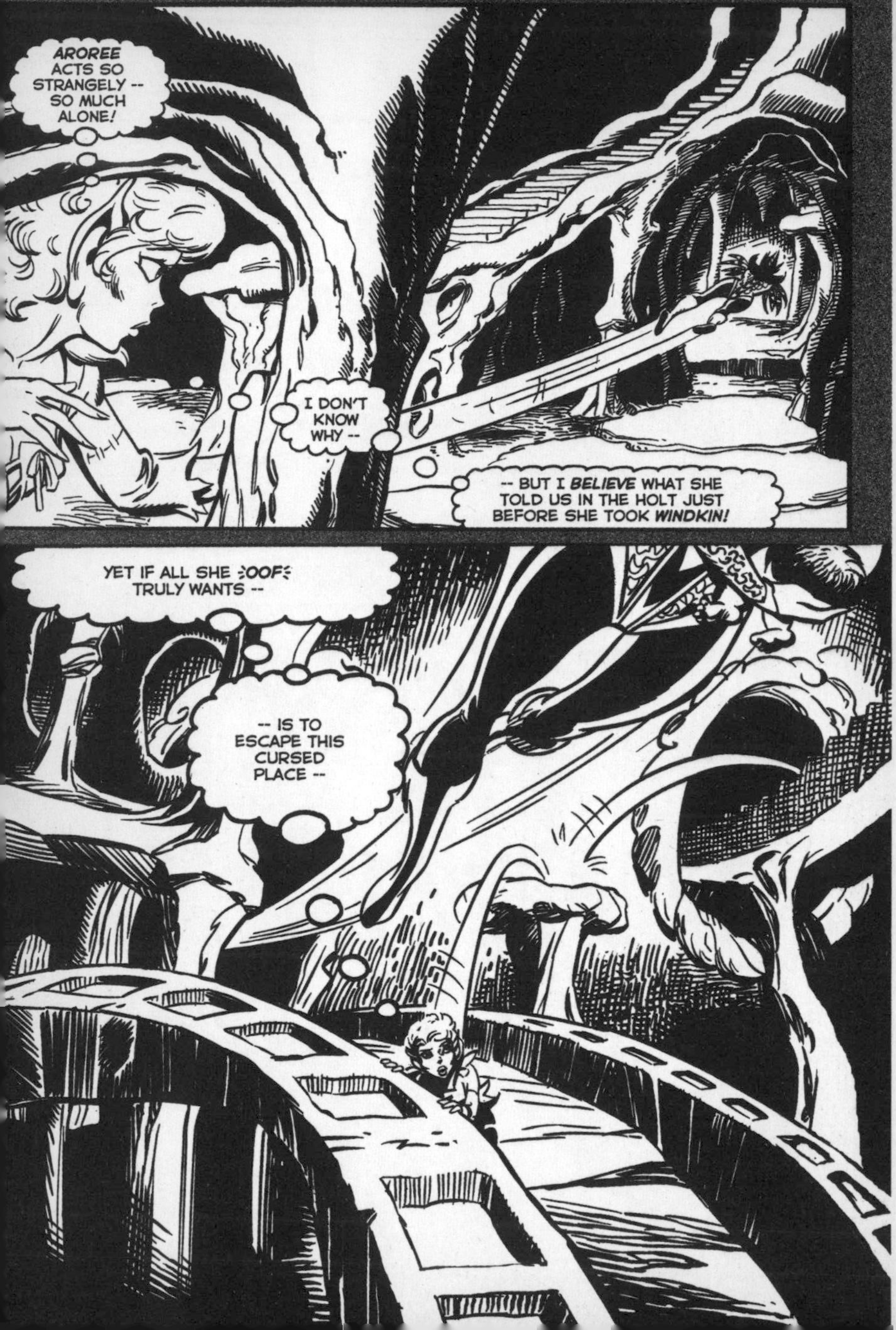
AROREE ACTS SO STRANGELY -- SO MUCH ALONE!
I DON'T KNOW WHY --
-- BUT I BELIEVE WHAT SHE TOLD US IN THE HOLT JUST BEFORE SHE TOOK WINDKIN!
YET IF ALL SHE -OOF- TRULY WANTS --
-- IS TO ESCAPE THIS CURSED PLACE --

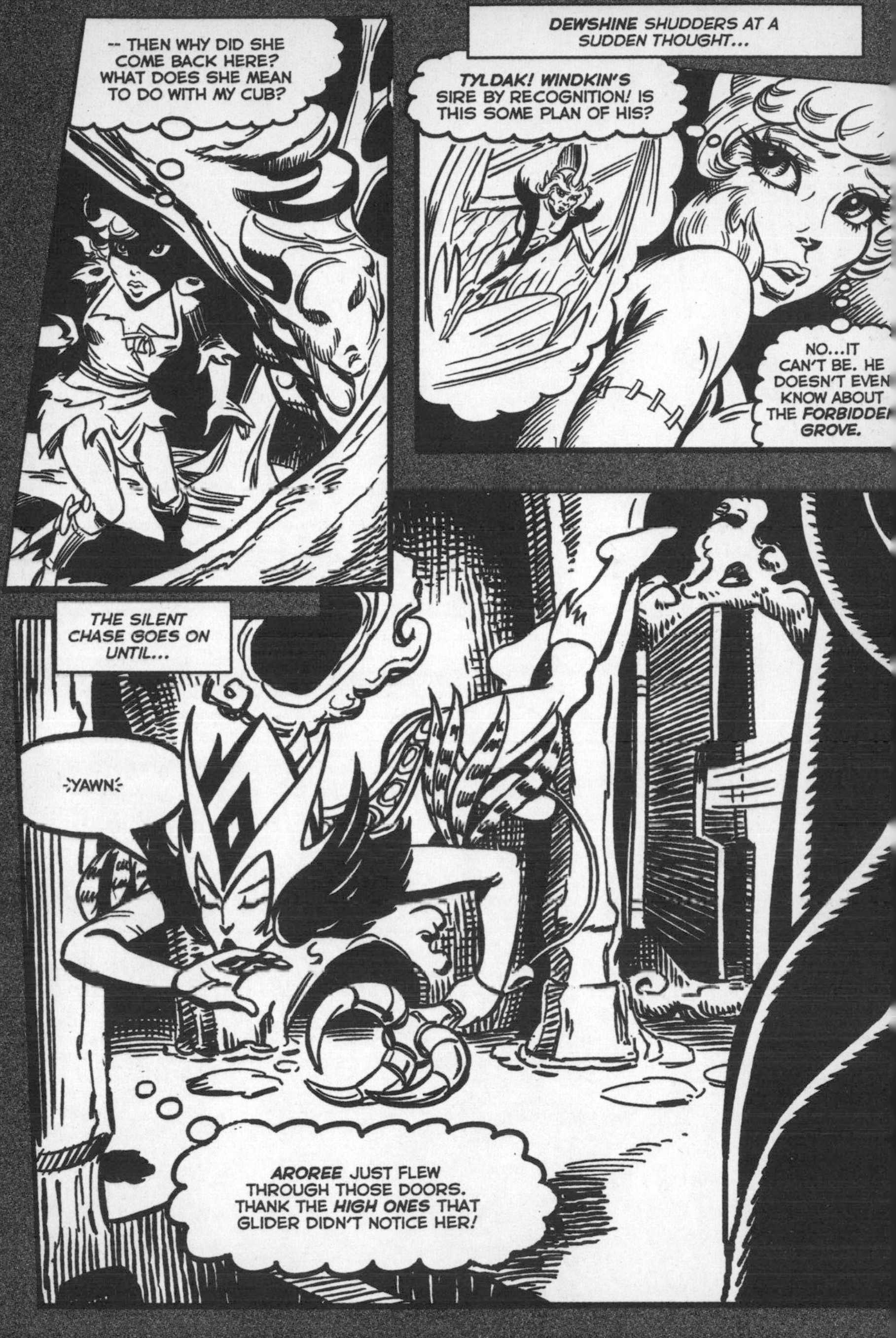

-- THEN WHY DID SHE COME BACK HERE? WHAT DOES SHE MEAN TO DO WITH MY CUB?
DEWSHINE SHUDDERS AT A SUDDEN THOUGHT...
TYLDAK! WINDKIN'S SIRE BY RECOGNITION! IS THIS SOME PLAN OF HIS?
NO...IT CAN'T BE. HE DOESN'T EVEN KNOW ABOUT THE FORBIDDEN GROVE.
THE SILENT CHASE GOES ON UNTIL...
YAWN
AROREE JUST FLEW THROUGH THOSE DOORS. THANK THE HIGH ONES THAT GLIDER DIDN'T NOTICE HER!

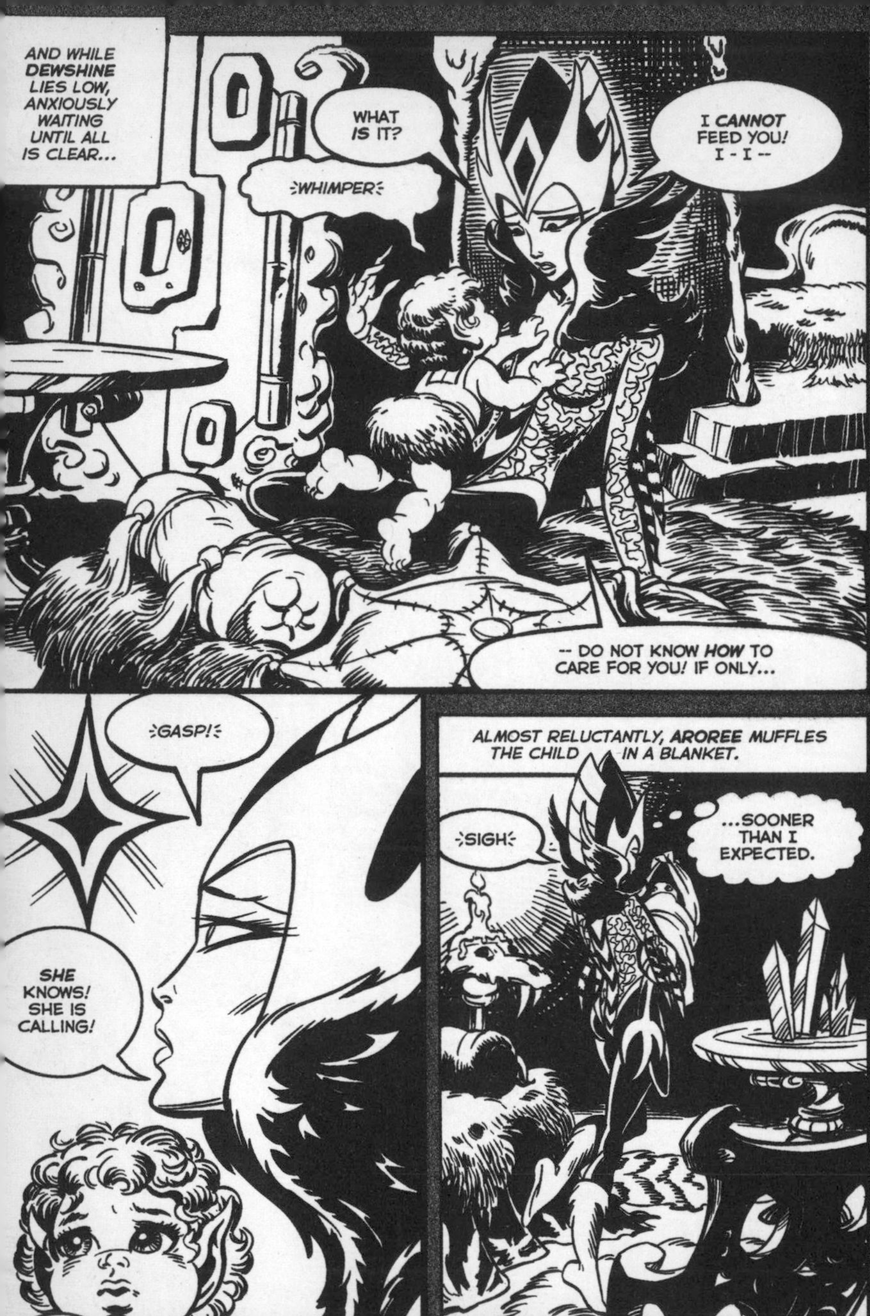
AND WHILE DEWSHINE LIES LOW, ANXIOUSLY WAITING UNTIL ALL IS CLEAR...
WHAT IS IT?
WHIMPER
I CANNOT FEED YOU! I - I --
-- DO NOT KNOW HOW TO CARE FOR YOU! IF ONLY...
GASP!
SHE KNOWS! SHE IS CALLING!
ALMOST RELUCTANTLY, AROREE MUFFLES THE CHILD IN A BLANKET.
SIGH
...SOONER THAN I EXPECTED.

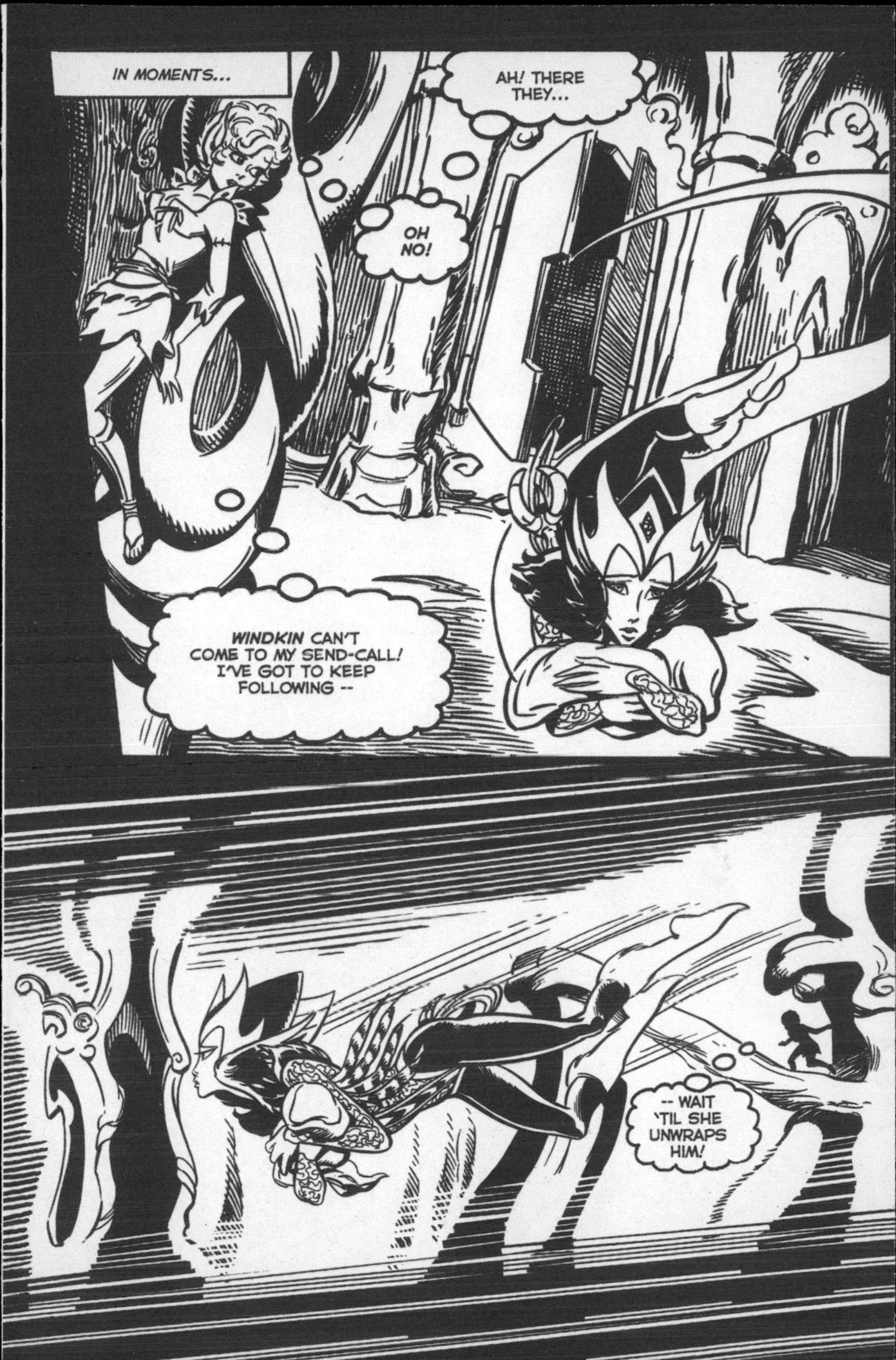
IN MOMENTS...
AH! THERE THEY...
OH NO!
WINDKIN CAN'T COME TO MY SEND-CALL! I'VE GOT TO KEEP FOLLOWING --
-- WAIT 'TIL SHE UNWRAPS HIM!

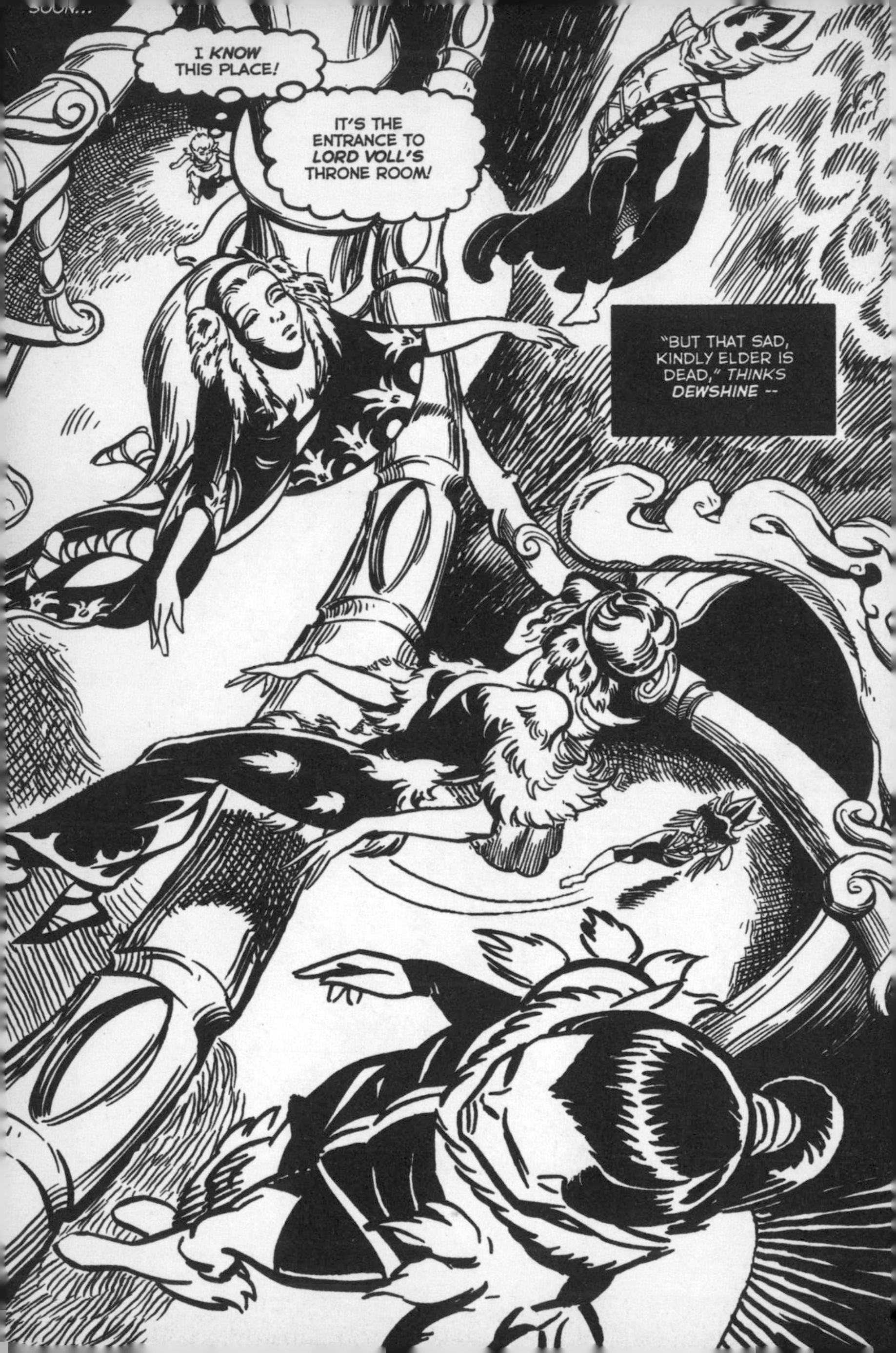
SOON...
I KNOW THIS PLACE!
IT'S THE ENTRANCE TO LORD VOLL'S THRONE ROOM!
"BUT THAT SAD, KINDLY ELDER IS DEAD," THINKS DEWSHINE --

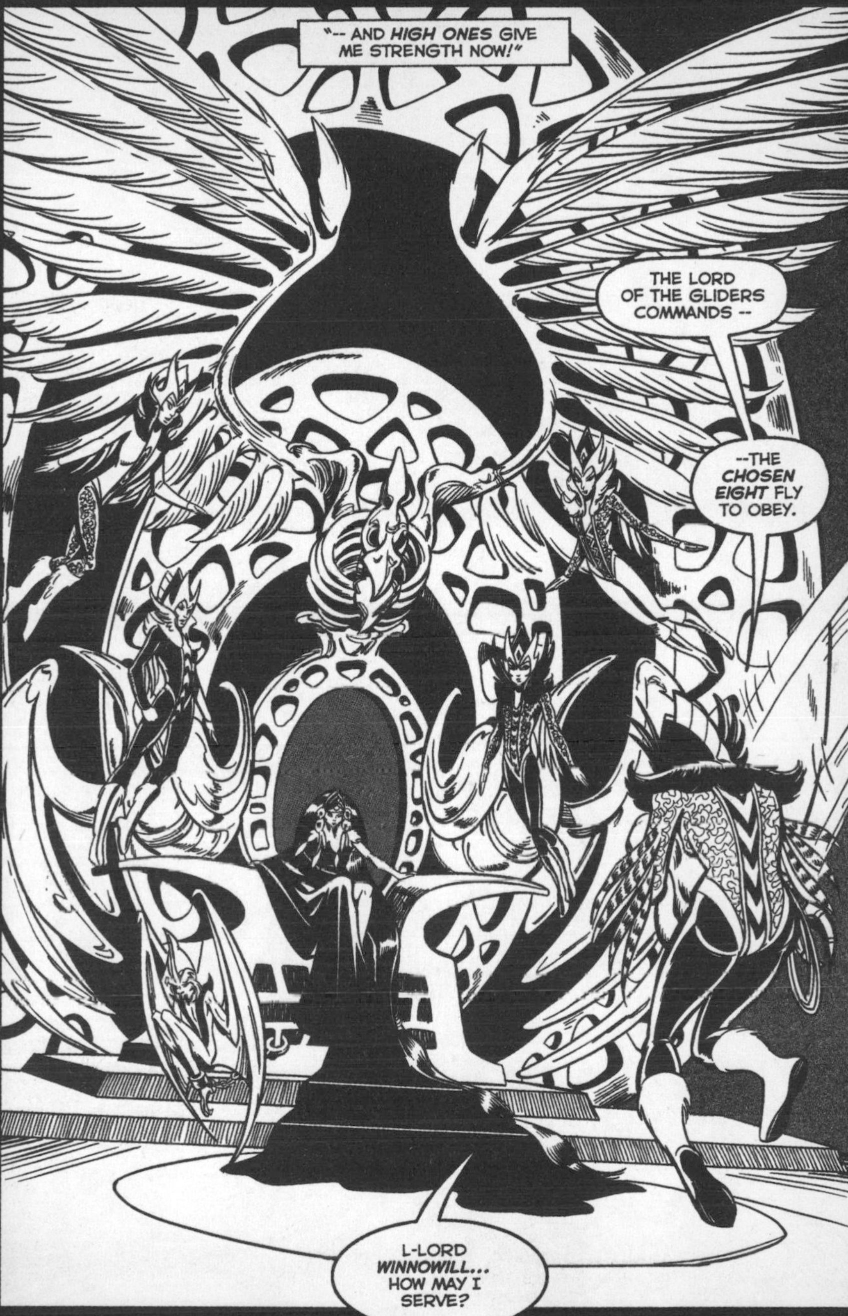
"-- AND HIGH ONES GIVE ME STRENGTH NOW!"
THE LORD OF THE GLIDERS COMMANDS --
--THE CHOSEN EIGHT FLY TO OBEY.
L-LORD WINNOWILL... HOW MAY I SERVE?

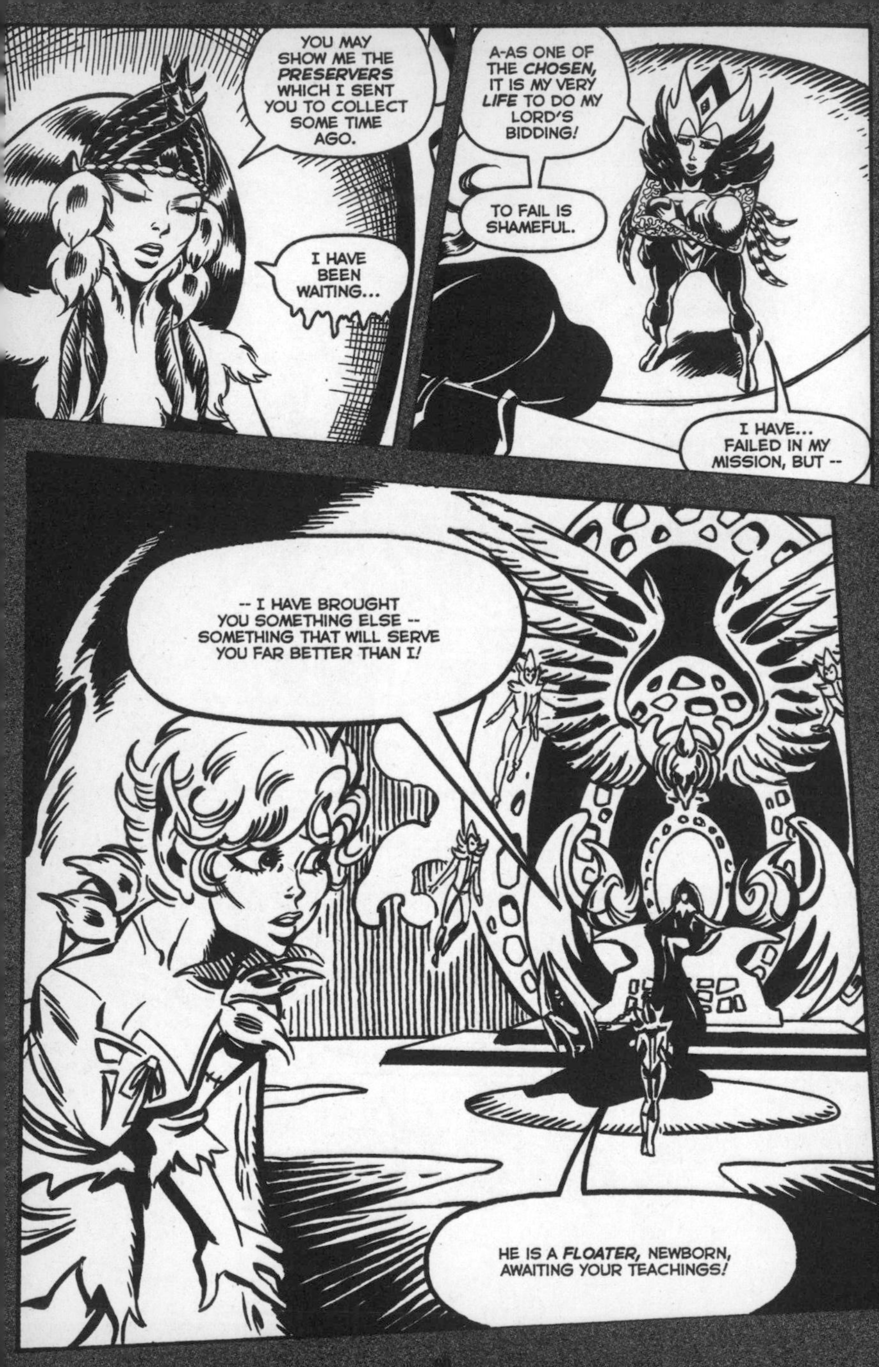
YOU MAY SHOW ME THE PRESERVERS WHICH I SENT YOU TO COLLECT SOME TIME AGO.
I HAVE BEEN WAITING...
A-AS ONE OF THE CHOSEN, IT IS MY VERY LIFE TO DO MY LORD'S BIDDING!
TO FAIL IS SHAMEFUL.
I HAVE... FAILED IN MY MISSION, BUT --
-- I HAVE BROUGHT YOU SOMETHING ELSE -- SOMETHING THAT WILL SERVE YOU FAR BETTER THAN I!
HE IS A FLOATER, NEWBORN, AWAITING YOUR TEACHINGS!

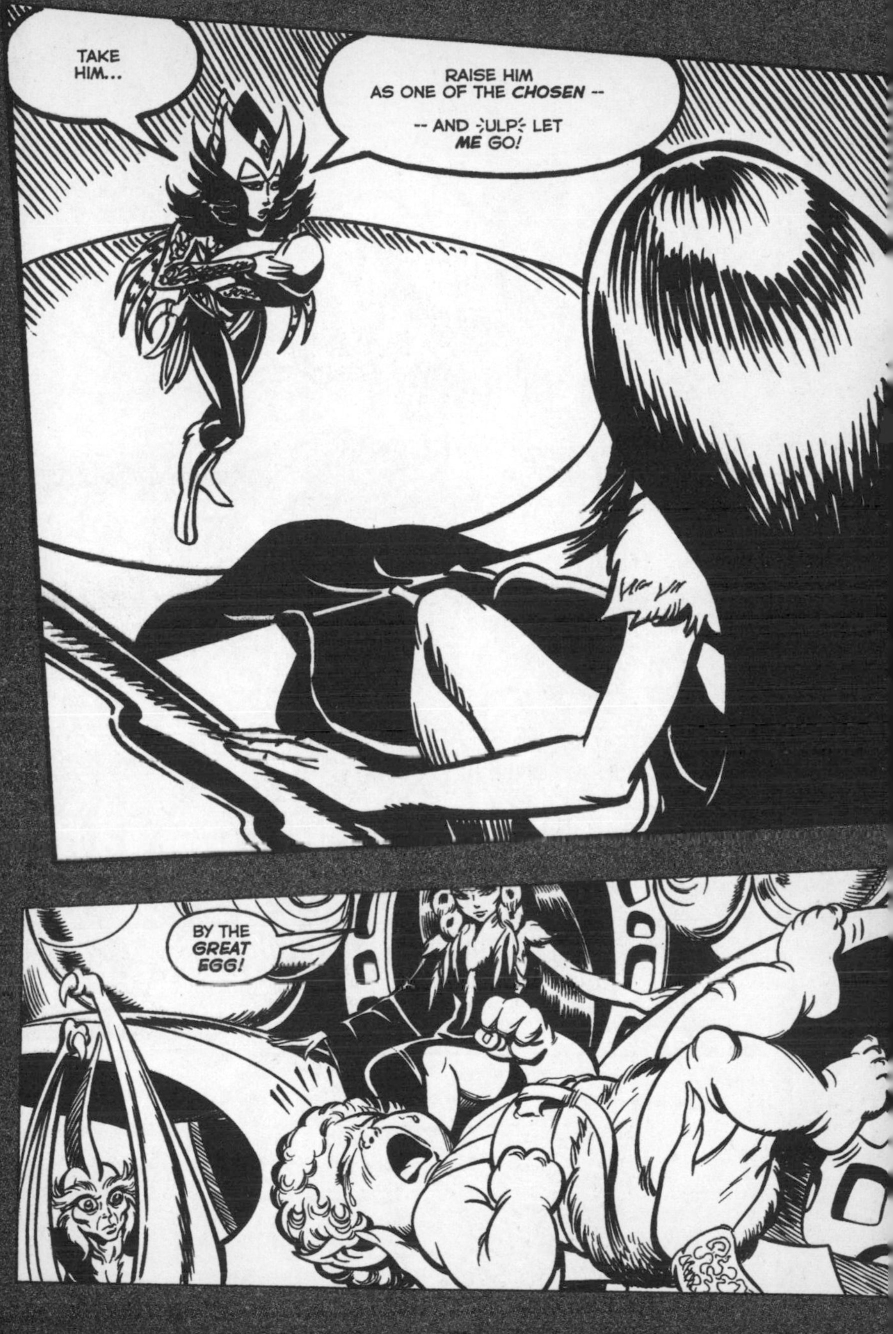
TAKE HIM...
RAISE HIM AS ONE OF THE *CHOSEN* --
-- AND ULP LET *ME* GO!
BY THE *GREAT EGG!*

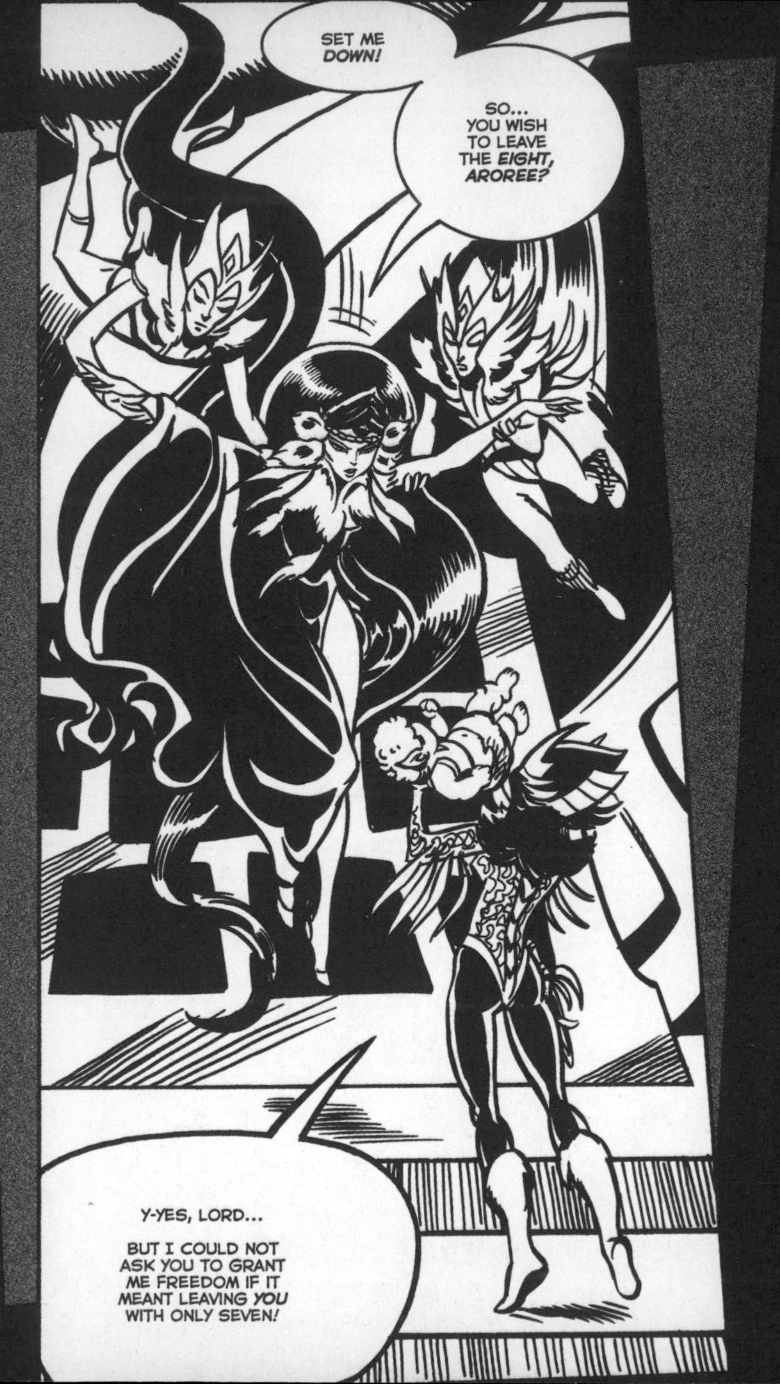
SET ME DOWN!
SO... YOU WISH TO LEAVE THE EIGHT, AROREE?
Y-YES, LORD...
BUT I COULD NOT ASK YOU TO GRANT ME FREEDOM IF IT MEANT LEAVING YOU WITH ONLY SEVEN!

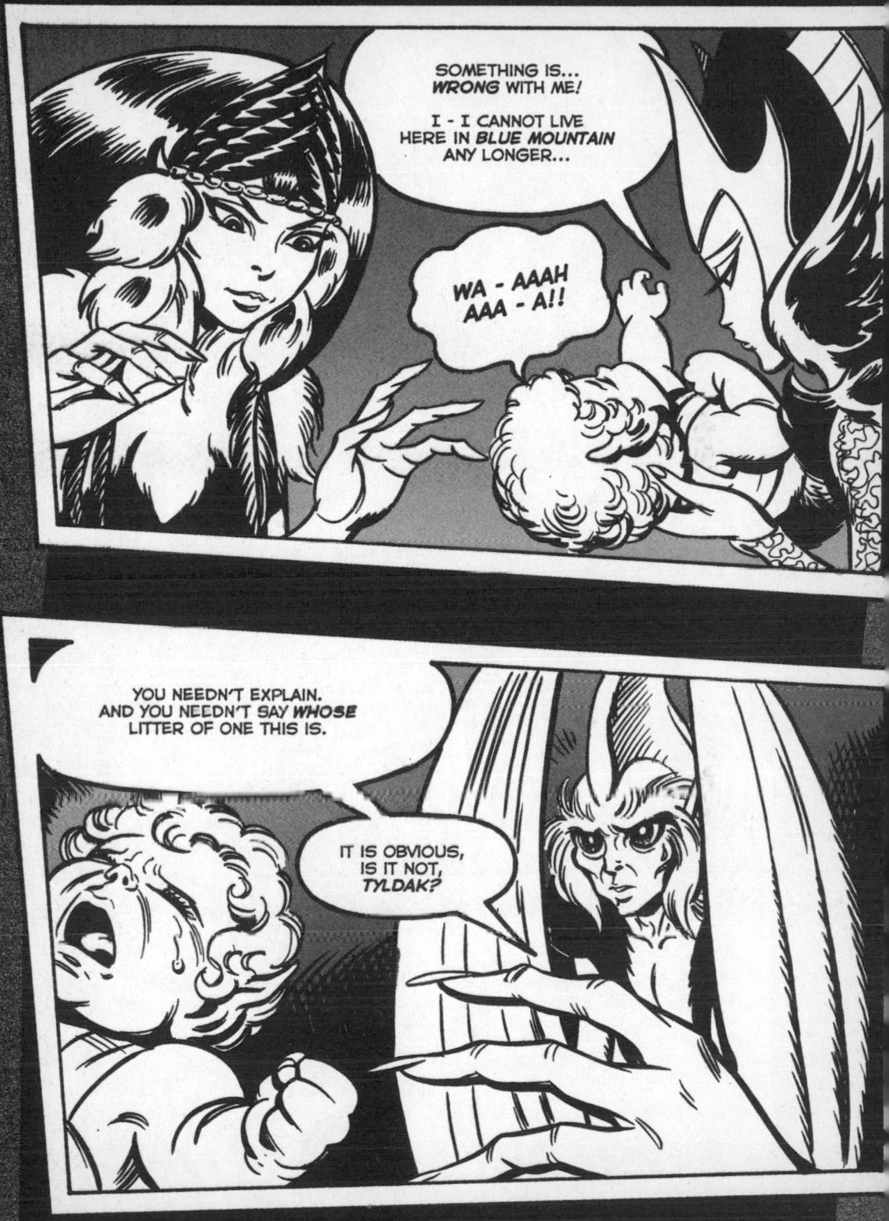
SOMETHING IS... *WRONG* WITH ME!
I - I CANNOT LIVE HERE IN *BLUE MOUNTAIN* ANY LONGER...
WA - AAAH AAA - A!!
YOU NEEDN'T EXPLAIN. AND YOU NEEDN'T SAY *WHOSE* LITTER OF ONE THIS IS.
IT IS OBVIOUS, IS IT NOT, *TYLDAK?*

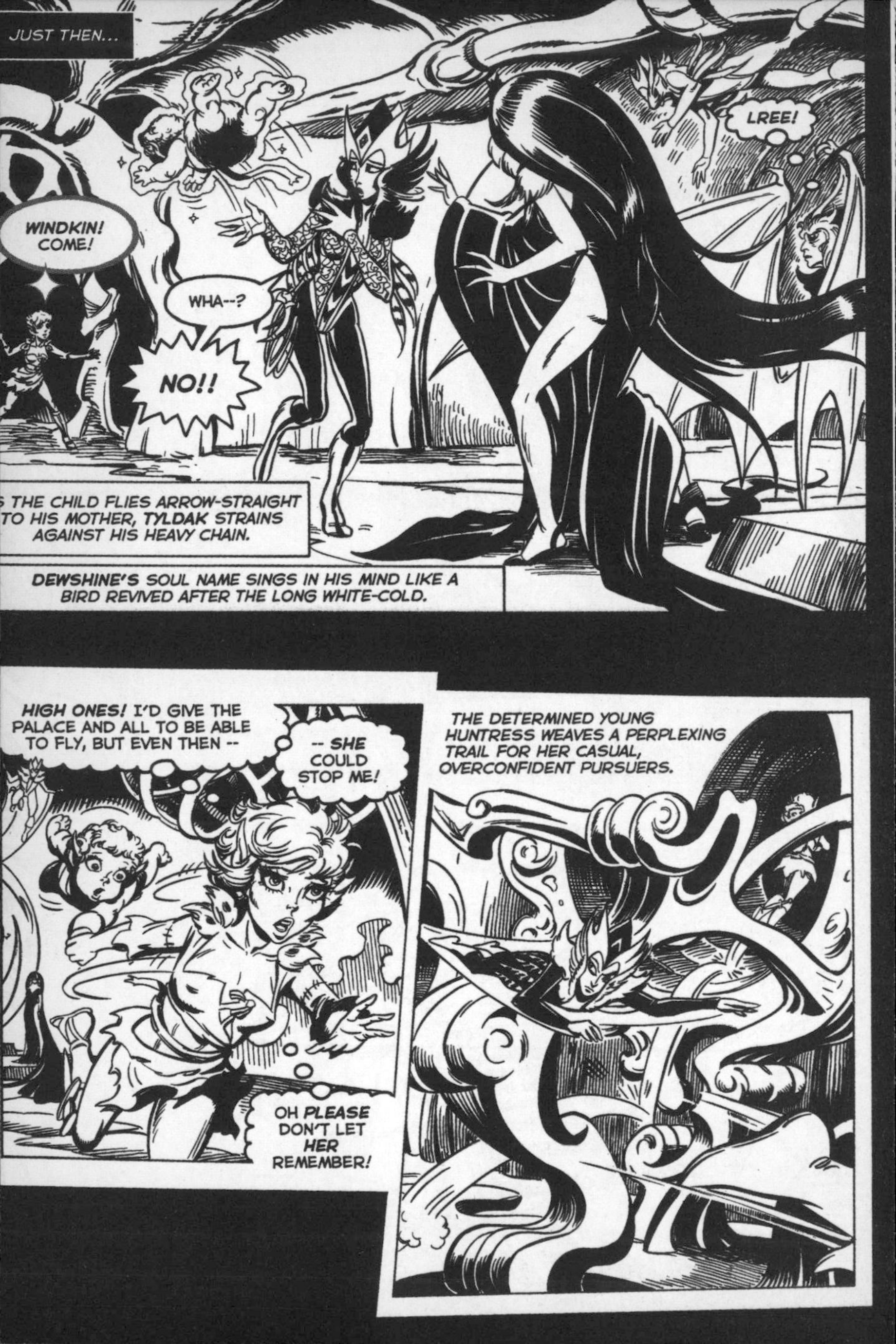
JUST THEN...
WINDKIN! COME!
WHA--?
NO!!
LREE!
S THE CHILD FLIES ARROW-STRAIGHT TO HIS MOTHER, TYLDAK STRAINS AGAINST HIS HEAVY CHAIN.
DEWSHINE'S SOUL NAME SINGS IN HIS MIND LIKE A BIRD REVIVED AFTER THE LONG WHITE-COLD.
HIGH ONES! I'D GIVE THE PALACE AND ALL TO BE ABLE TO FLY, BUT EVEN THEN --
-- SHE COULD STOP ME!
OH PLEASE DON'T LET HER REMEMBER!
THE DETERMINED YOUNG HUNTRESS WEAVES A PERPLEXING TRAIL FOR HER CASUAL, OVERCONFIDENT PURSUERS.

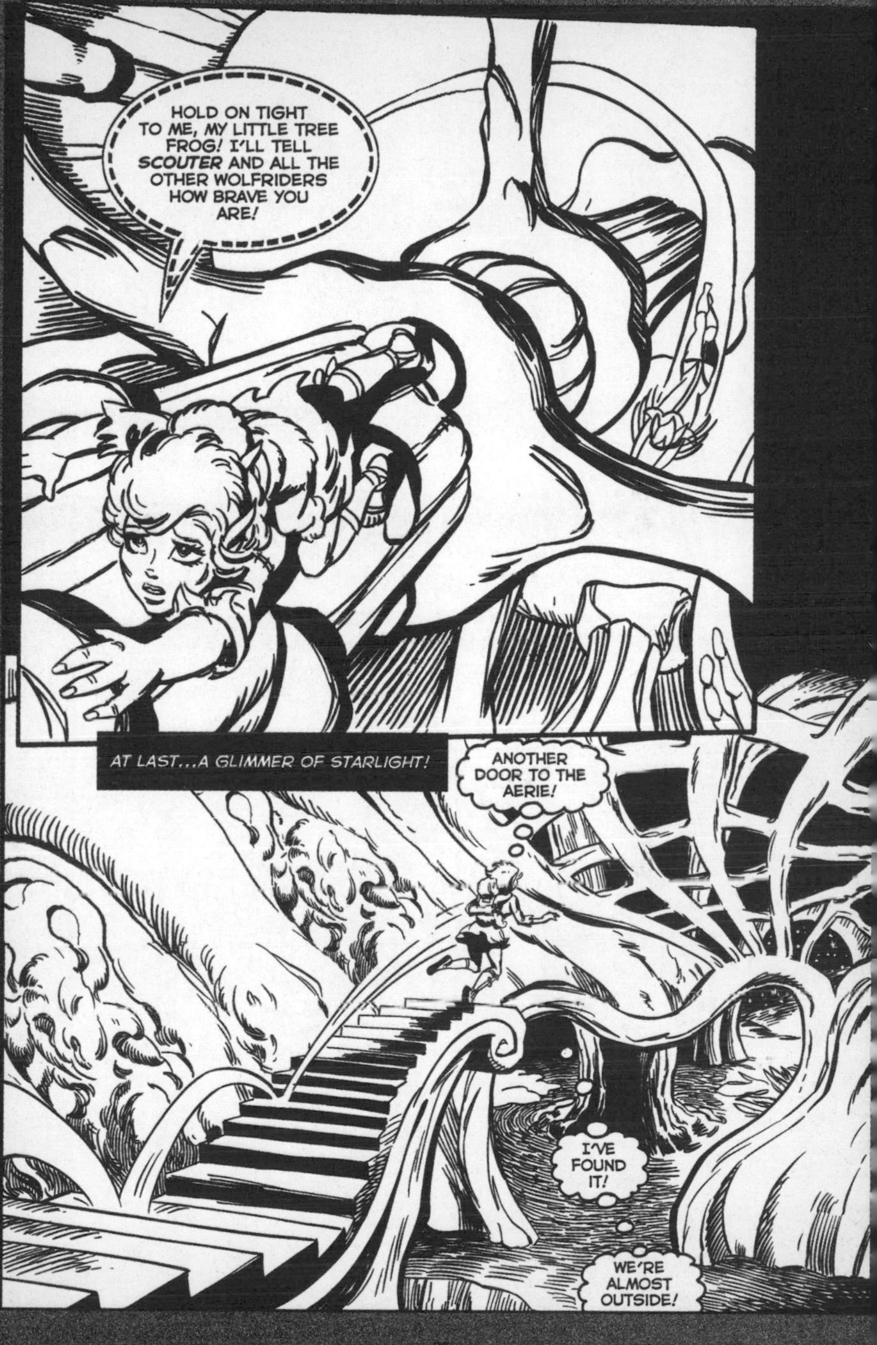
HOLD ON TIGHT TO ME, MY LITTLE TREE FROG! I'LL TELL SCOUTER AND ALL THE OTHER WOLFRIDERS HOW BRAVE YOU ARE!
AT LAST...A GLIMMER OF STARLIGHT!
ANOTHER DOOR TO THE AERIE!
I'VE FOUND IT!
WE'RE ALMOST OUTSIDE!

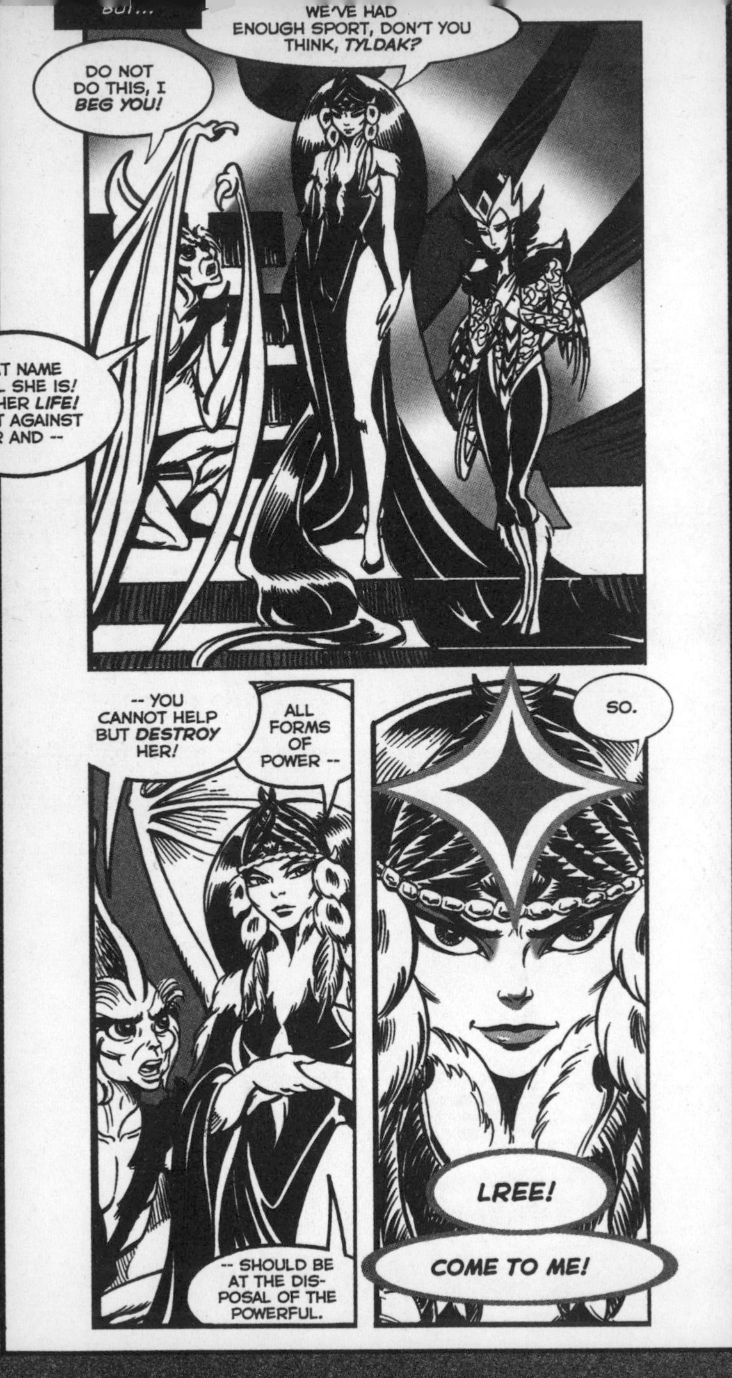
BUT...
WE'VE HAD ENOUGH SPORT, DON'T YOU THINK, *TYLDAK?*
DO NOT DO THIS, I *BEG YOU!*
THAT NAME IS ALL SHE IS! IT IS HER *LIFE!* USE IT AGAINST HER AND --
-- YOU CANNOT HELP BUT *DESTROY* HER!
ALL FORMS OF POWER --
-- SHOULD BE AT THE DISPOSAL OF THE POWERFUL.
SO.
LREE!
COME TO ME!

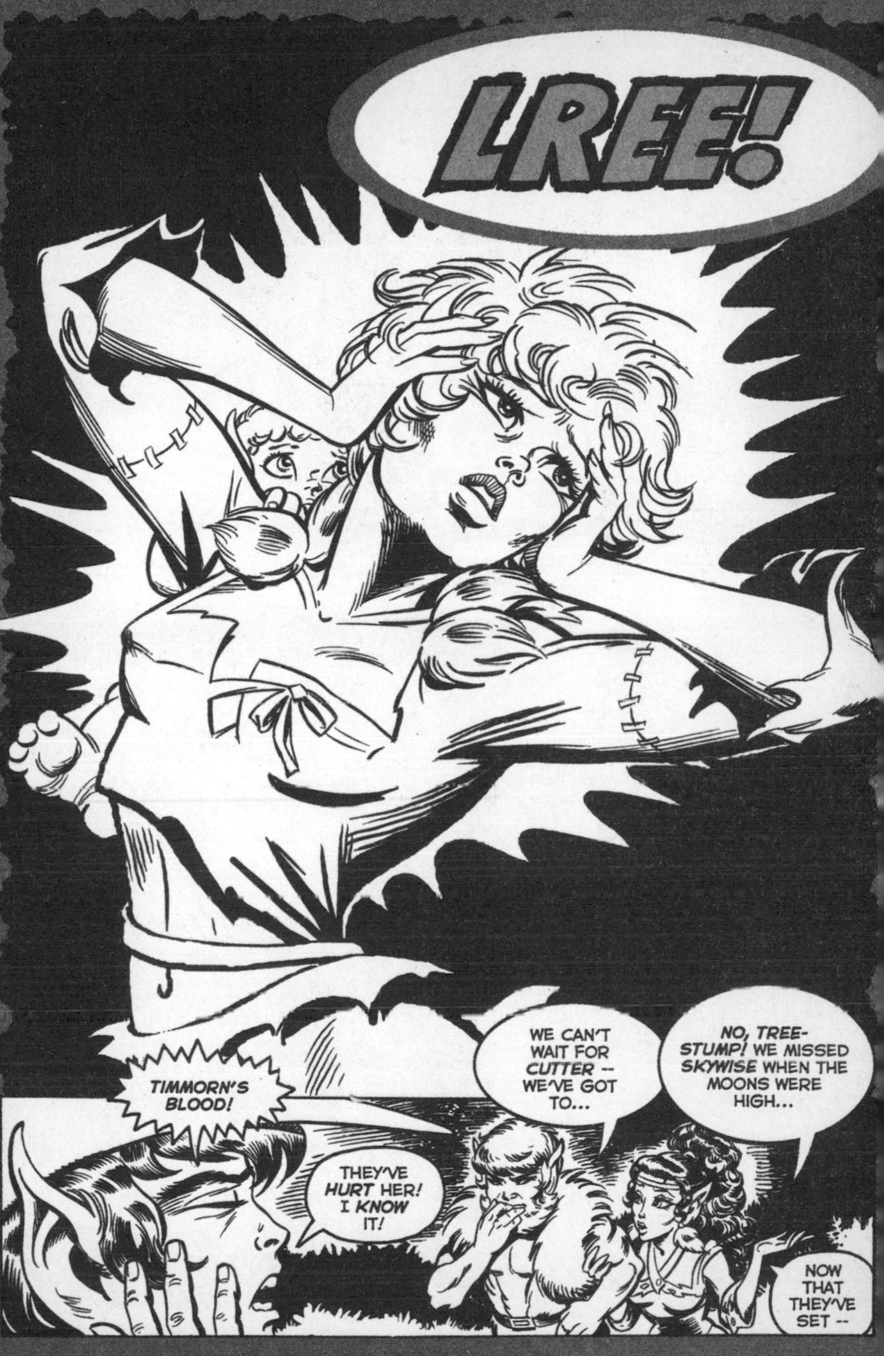
LREE!
TIMMORN'S BLOOD!
THEY'VE HURT HER! I KNOW IT!
WE CAN'T WAIT FOR CUTTER -- WE'VE GOT TO...
NO, TREE-STUMP! WE MISSED SKYWISE WHEN THE MOONS WERE HIGH...
NOW THAT THEY'VE SET --

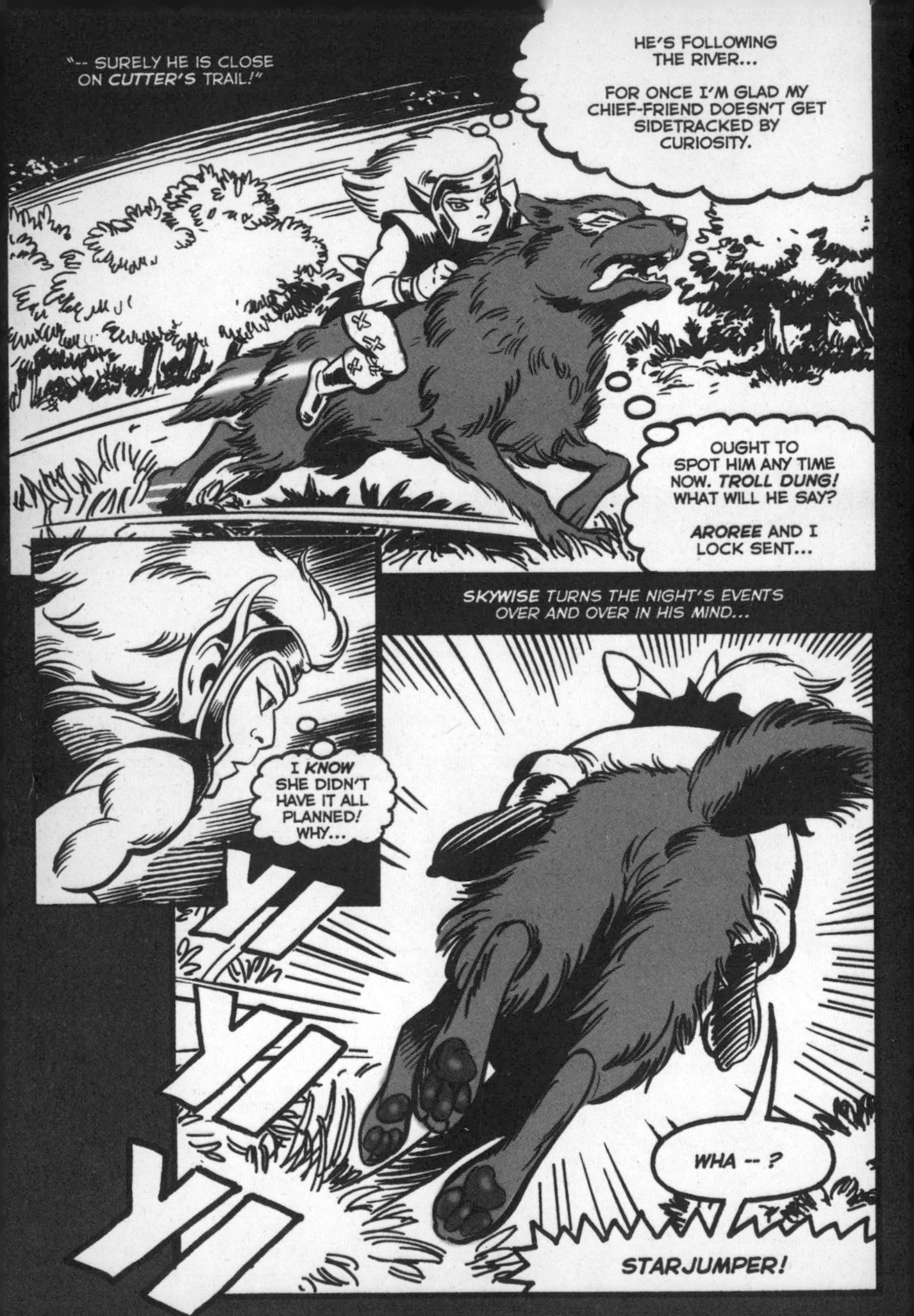
"-- SURELY HE IS CLOSE ON *CUTTER'S* TRAIL!"
HE'S FOLLOWING THE RIVER...
FOR ONCE I'M GLAD MY CHIEF-FRIEND DOESN'T GET SIDETRACKED BY CURIOSITY.
OUGHT TO SPOT HIM ANY TIME NOW. *TROLL DUNG!* WHAT WILL HE SAY?
AROREE AND I LOCK SENT...
SKYWISE TURNS THE NIGHT'S EVENTS OVER AND OVER IN HIS MIND...
I *KNOW* SHE DIDN'T HAVE IT ALL PLANNED! WHY...
WHA -- ?
STARJUMPER!

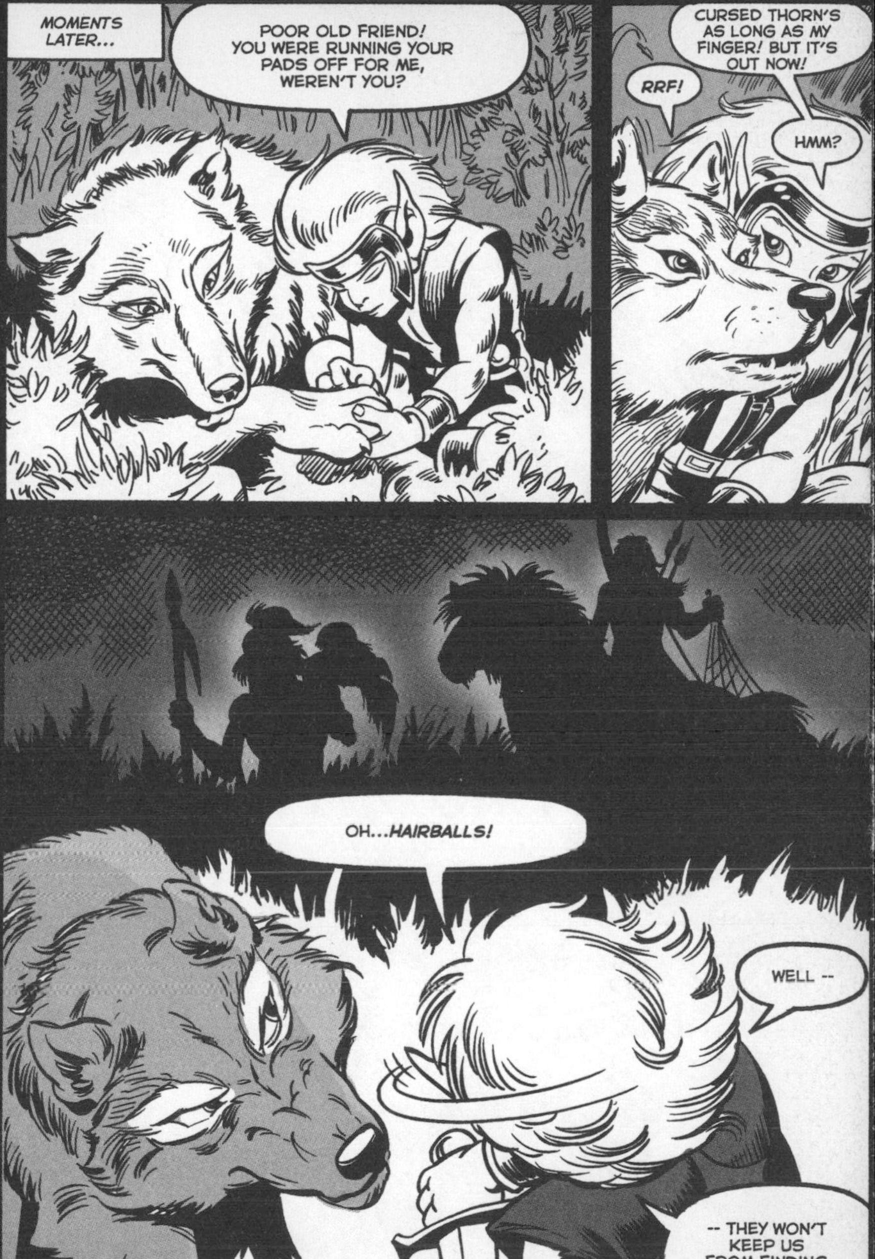
MOMENTS LATER...
POOR OLD FRIEND! YOU WERE RUNNING YOUR PADS OFF FOR ME, WEREN'T YOU?
CURSED THORN'S AS LONG AS MY FINGER! BUT IT'S OUT NOW!
RRF!
HMM?
OH...HAIRBALLS!
WELL --
-- THEY WON'T KEEP US FROM FINDING CUTTER!

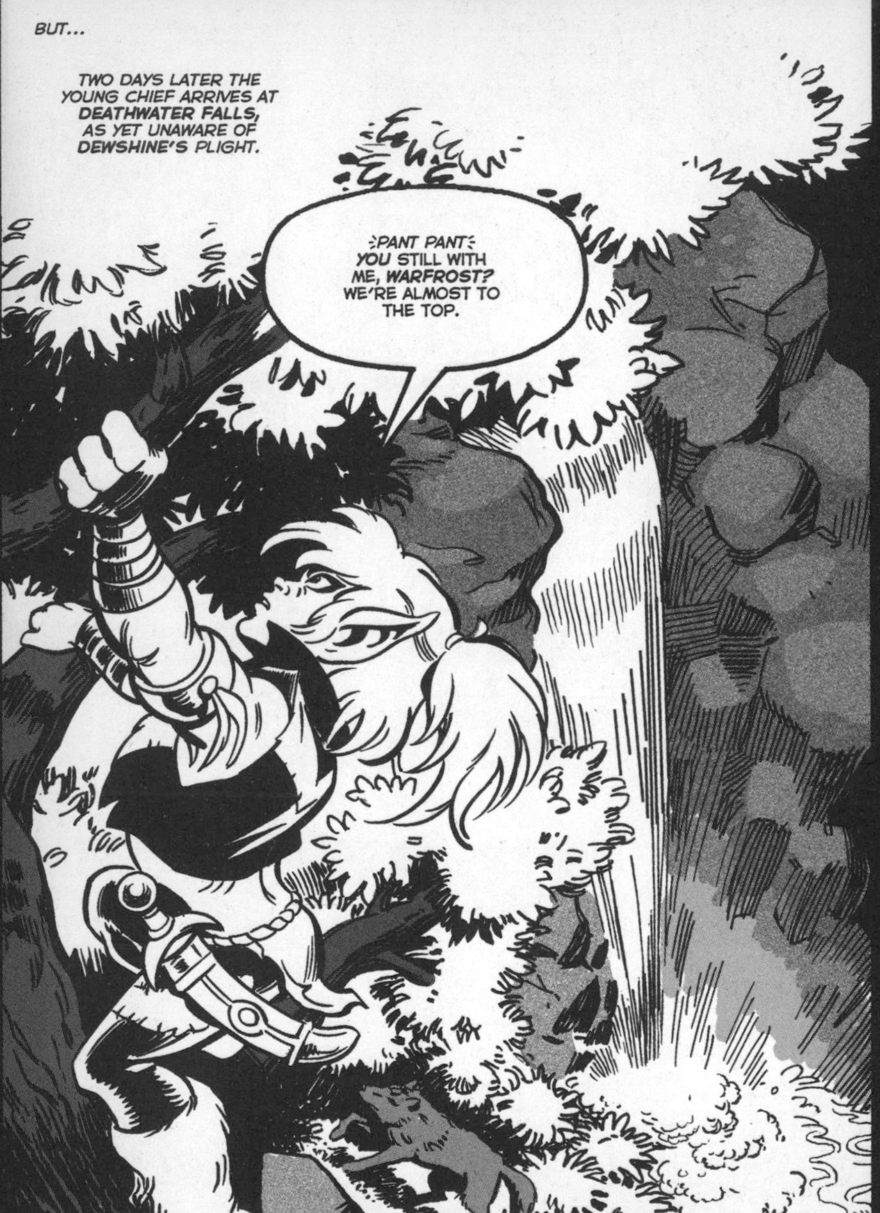
BUT...
TWO DAYS LATER THE YOUNG CHIEF ARRIVES AT DEATHWATER FALLS, AS YET UNAWARE OF DEWSHINE'S PLIGHT.
PANT PANT YOU STILL WITH ME, WARFROST? WE'RE ALMOST TO THE TOP.

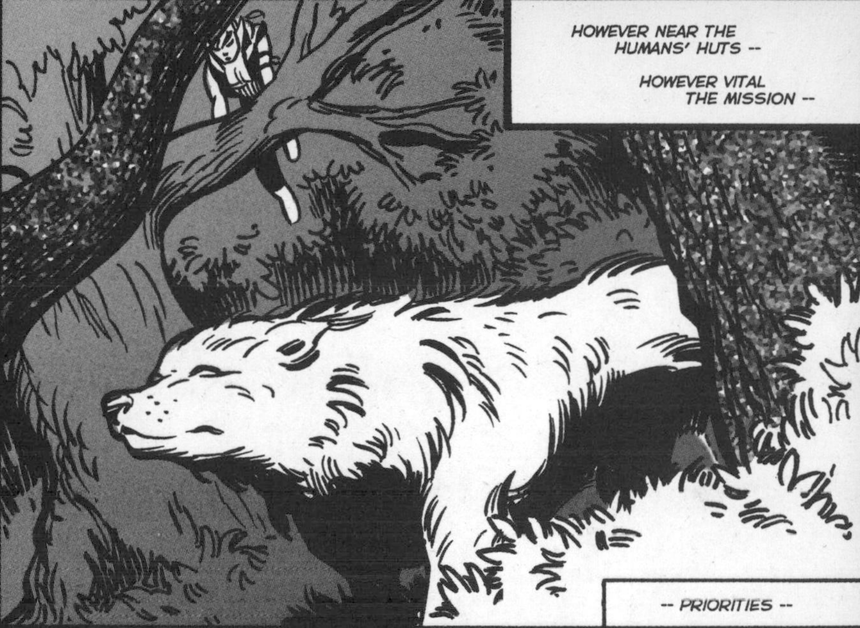
HOWEVER NEAR THE HUMANS' HUTS --
HOWEVER VITAL THE MISSION --
-- PRIORITIES --

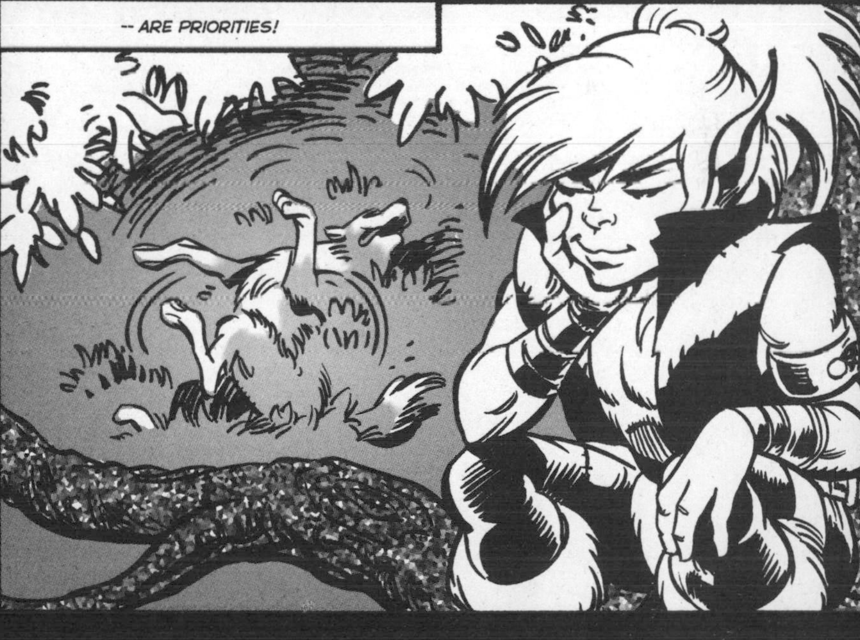
-- ARE PRIORITIES!

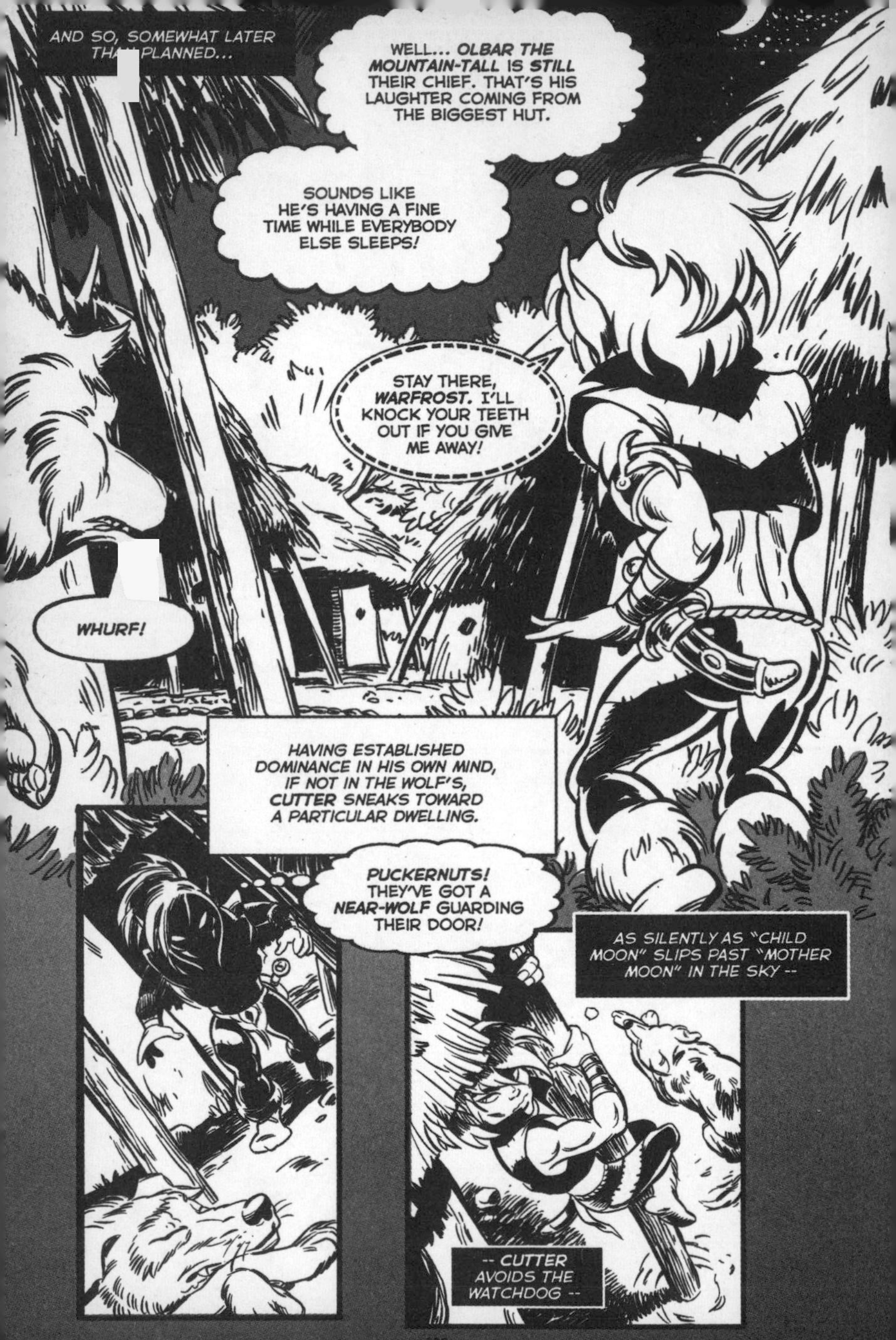
AND SO, SOMEWHAT LATER THAN PLANNED...
WELL... OLBAR THE MOUNTAIN-TALL IS STILL THEIR CHIEF. THAT'S HIS LAUGHTER COMING FROM THE BIGGEST HUT.
SOUNDS LIKE HE'S HAVING A FINE TIME WHILE EVERYBODY ELSE SLEEPS!
STAY THERE, WARFROST. I'LL KNOCK YOUR TEETH OUT IF YOU GIVE ME AWAY!
WHURF!
HAVING ESTABLISHED DOMINANCE IN HIS OWN MIND, IF NOT IN THE WOLF'S, CUTTER SNEAKS TOWARD A PARTICULAR DWELLING.
PUCKERNUTS! THEY'VE GOT A NEAR-WOLF GUARDING THEIR DOOR!
AS SILENTLY AS "CHILD MOON" SLIPS PAST "MOTHER MOON" IN THE SKY --
-- CUTTER AVOIDS THE WATCHDOG --

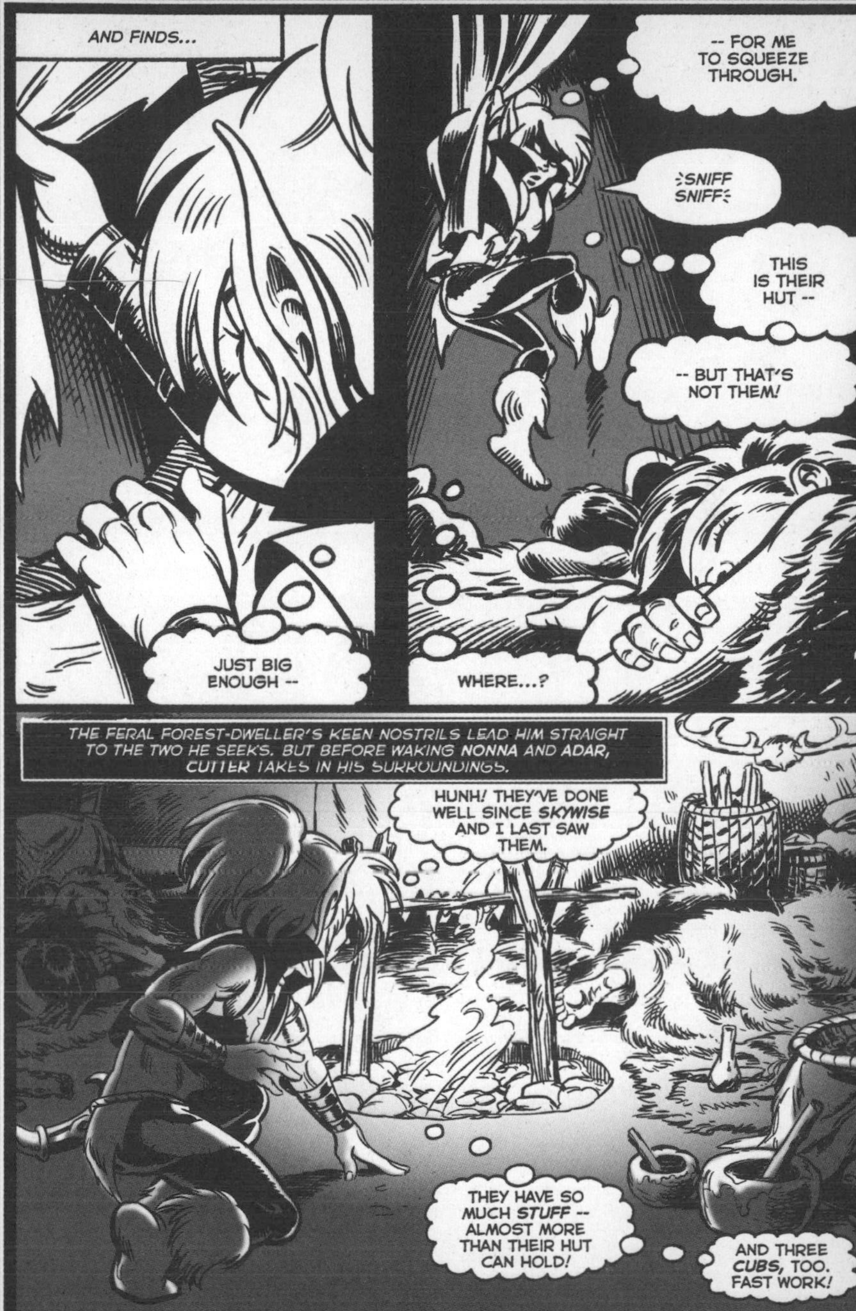
AND FINDS...
JUST BIG ENOUGH --
-- FOR ME TO SQUEEZE THROUGH.
SNIFF SNIFF
THIS IS THEIR HUT --
-- BUT THAT'S NOT THEM!
WHERE...?
THE FERAL FOREST-DWELLER'S KEEN NOSTRILS LEAD HIM STRAIGHT TO THE TWO HE SEEKS. BUT BEFORE WAKING NONNA AND ADAR, CUTTER TAKES IN HIS SURROUNDINGS.
HUNH! THEY'VE DONE WELL SINCE SKYWISE AND I LAST SAW THEM.
THEY HAVE SO MUCH STUFF -- ALMOST MORE THAN THEIR HUT CAN HOLD!
AND THREE CUBS, TOO. FAST WORK!

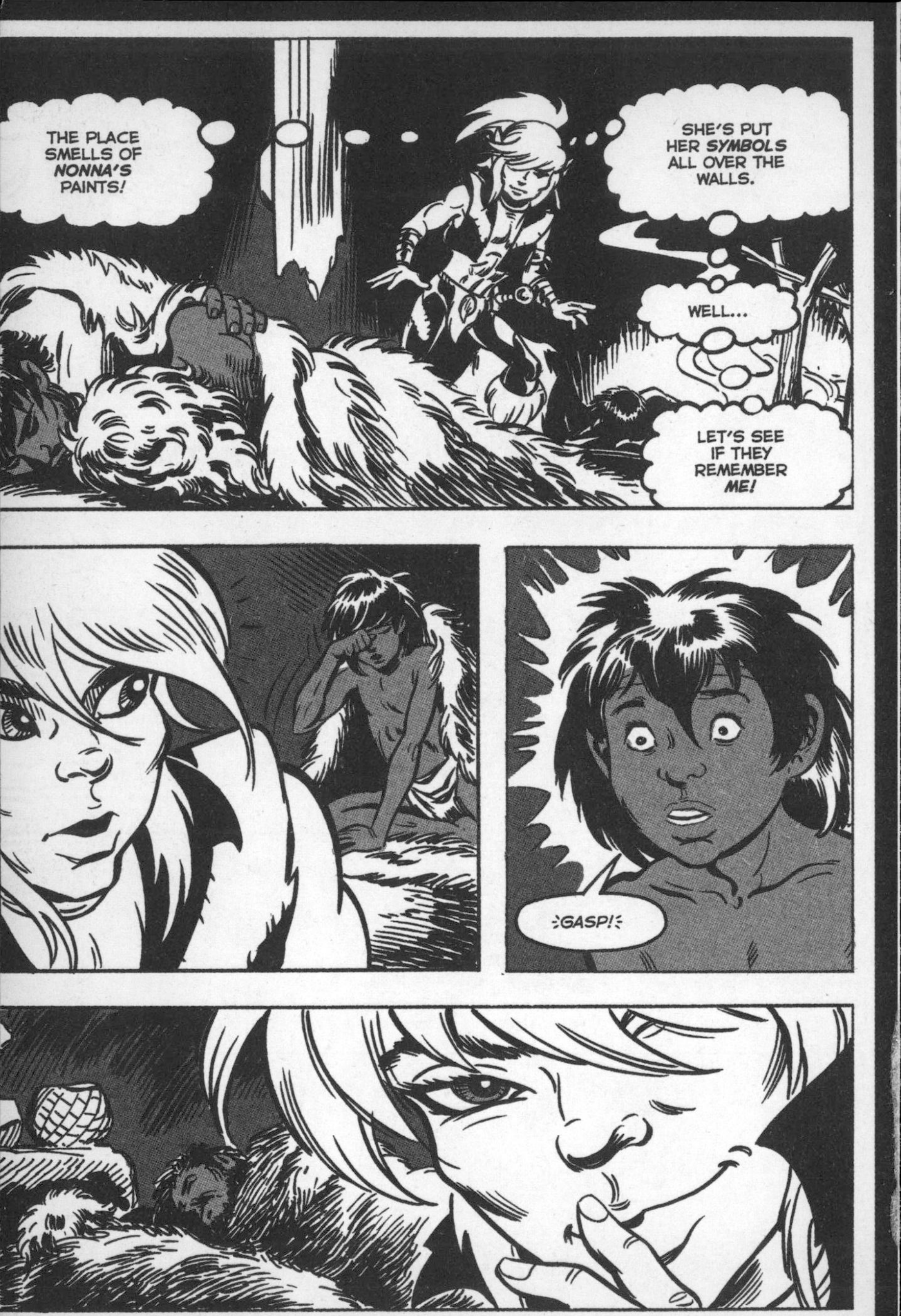
THE PLACE SMELLS OF NONNA'S PAINTS!
SHE'S PUT HER SYMBOLS ALL OVER THE WALLS.
WELL...
LET'S SEE IF THEY REMEMBER ME!
GASP!

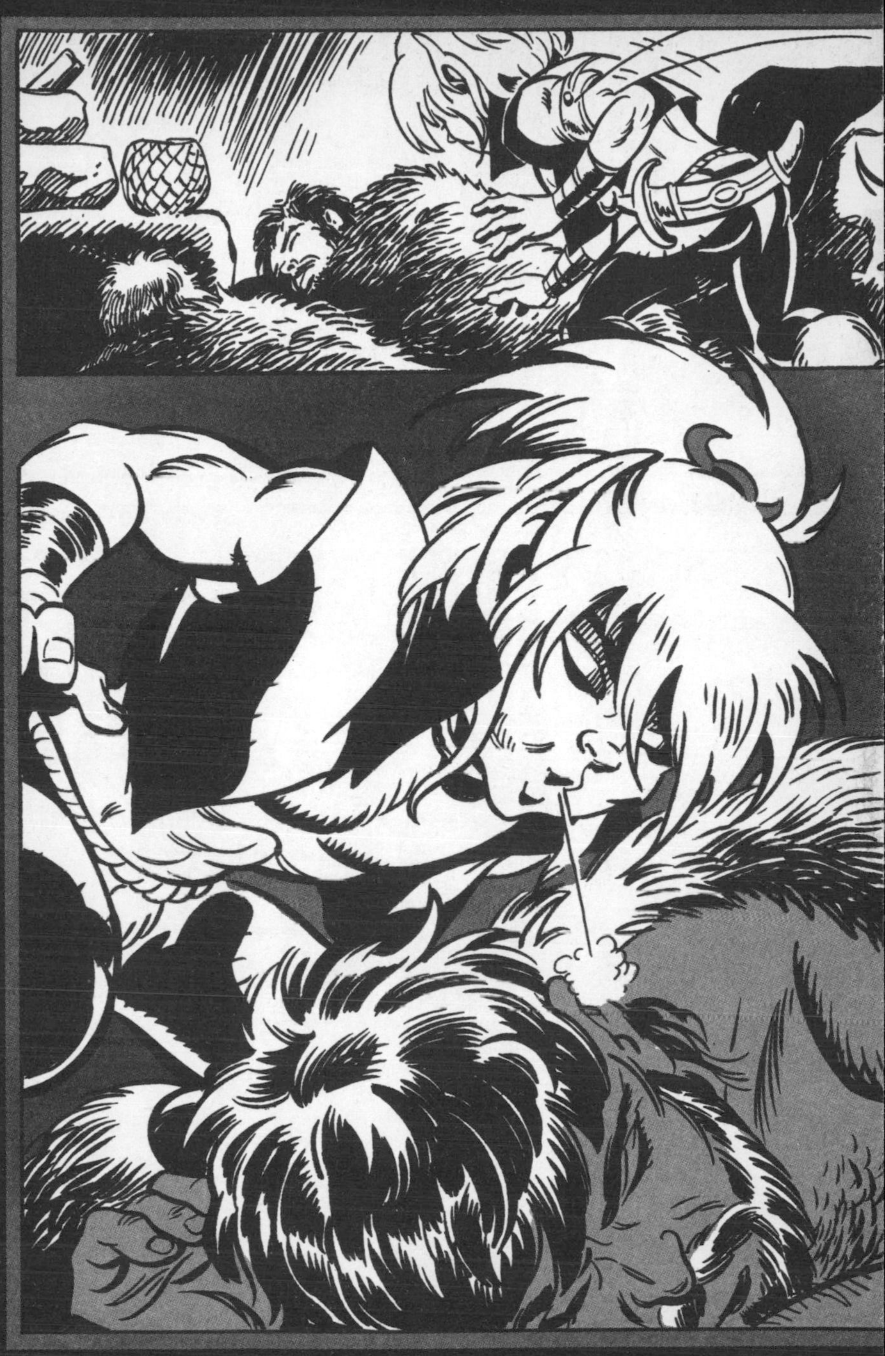

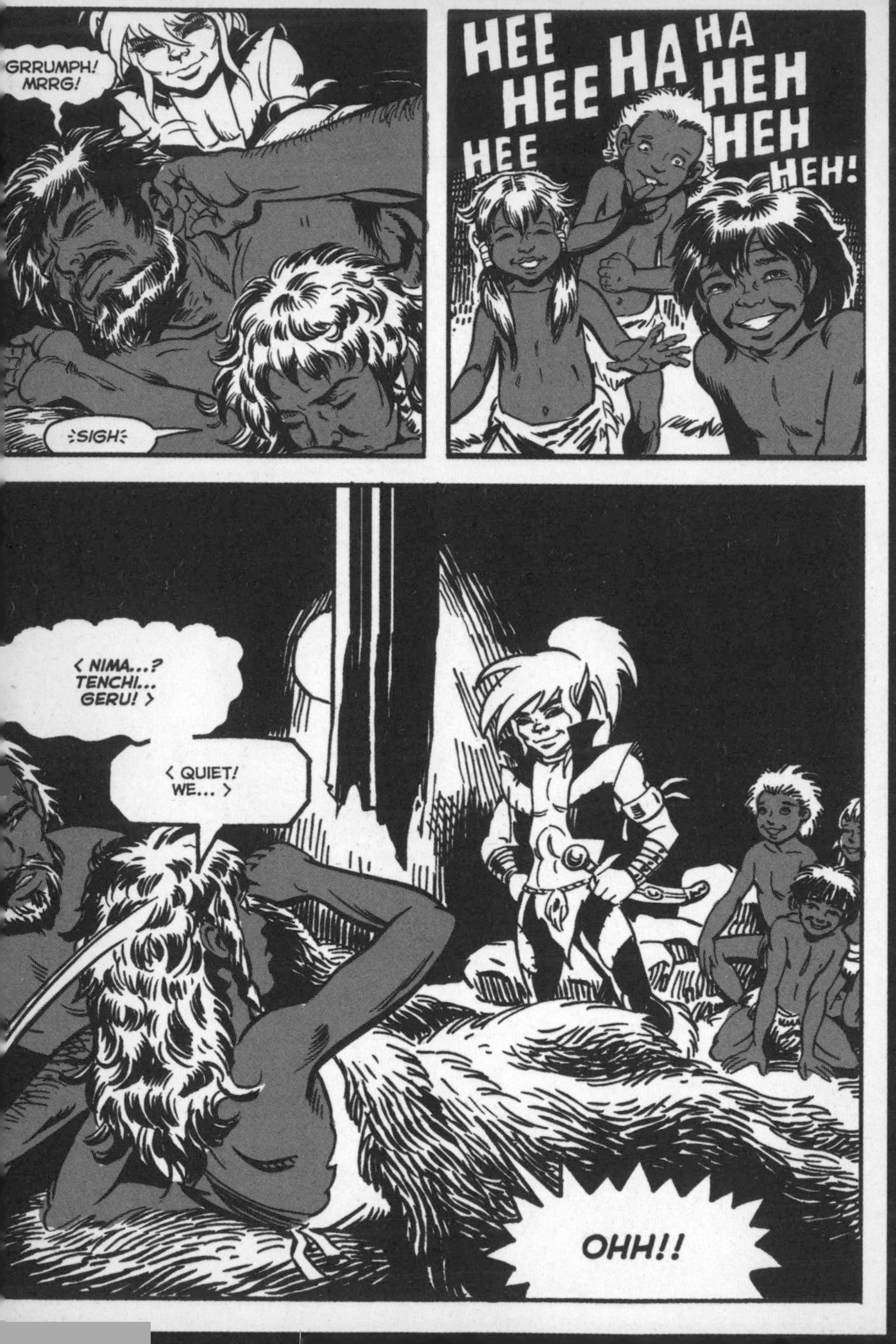
GRRUMPH! MRRG!
SIGH
HEE HEE HEE HA HA HEH HEH HEH!
< NIMA...? TENCHI... GERU! >
< QUIET! WE... >
OHH!!

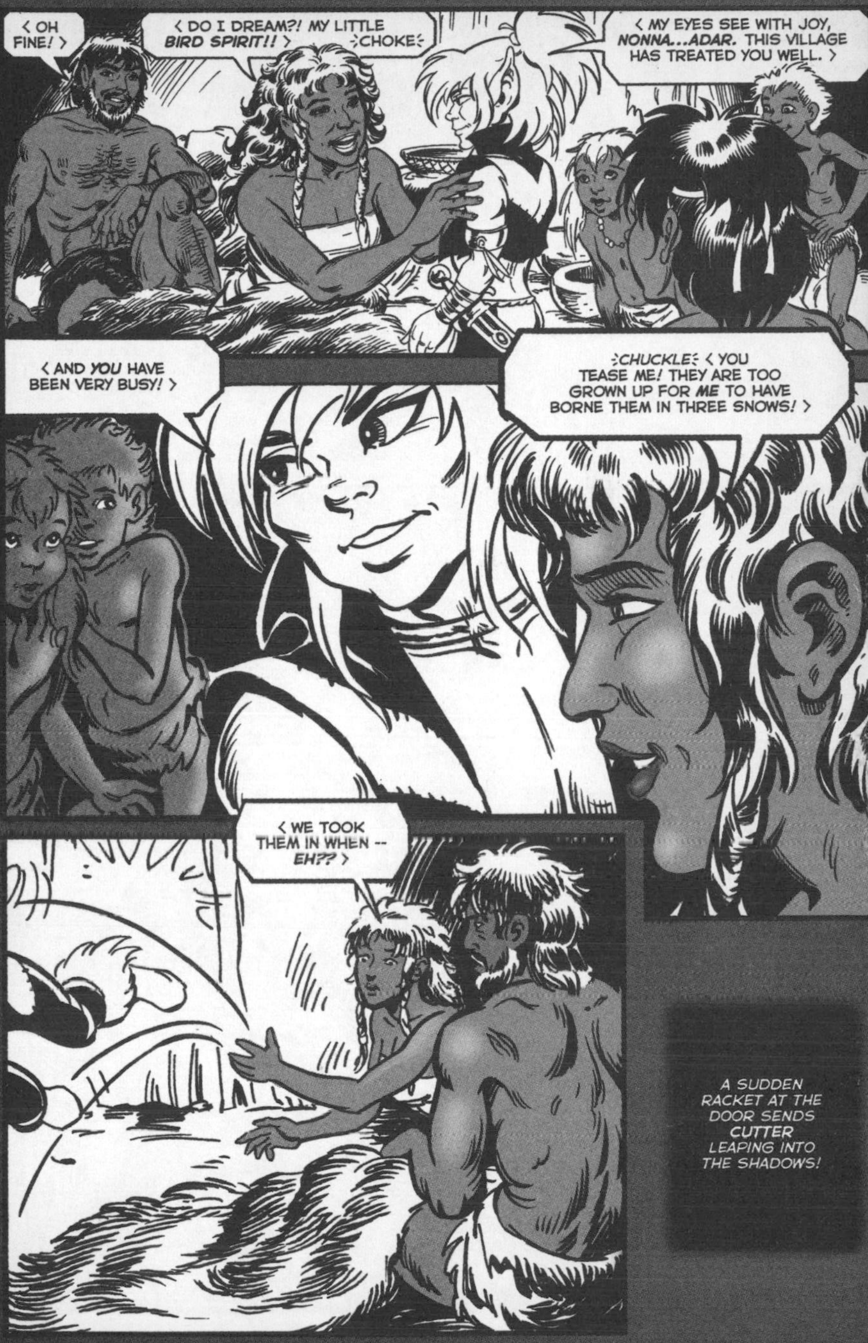
< OH FINE! >
< DO I DREAM?! MY LITTLE BIRD SPIRIT!! > ⁂CHOKE⁂
< MY EYES SEE WITH JOY, NONNA...ADAR. THIS VILLAGE HAS TREATED YOU WELL. >
< AND YOU HAVE BEEN VERY BUSY! >
⁂CHUCKLE⁂ < YOU TEASE ME! THEY ARE TOO GROWN UP FOR ME TO HAVE BORNE THEM IN THREE SNOWS! >
< WE TOOK THEM IN WHEN -- EH?? >
A SUDDEN RACKET AT THE DOOR SENDS CUTTER LEAPING INTO THE SHADOWS!

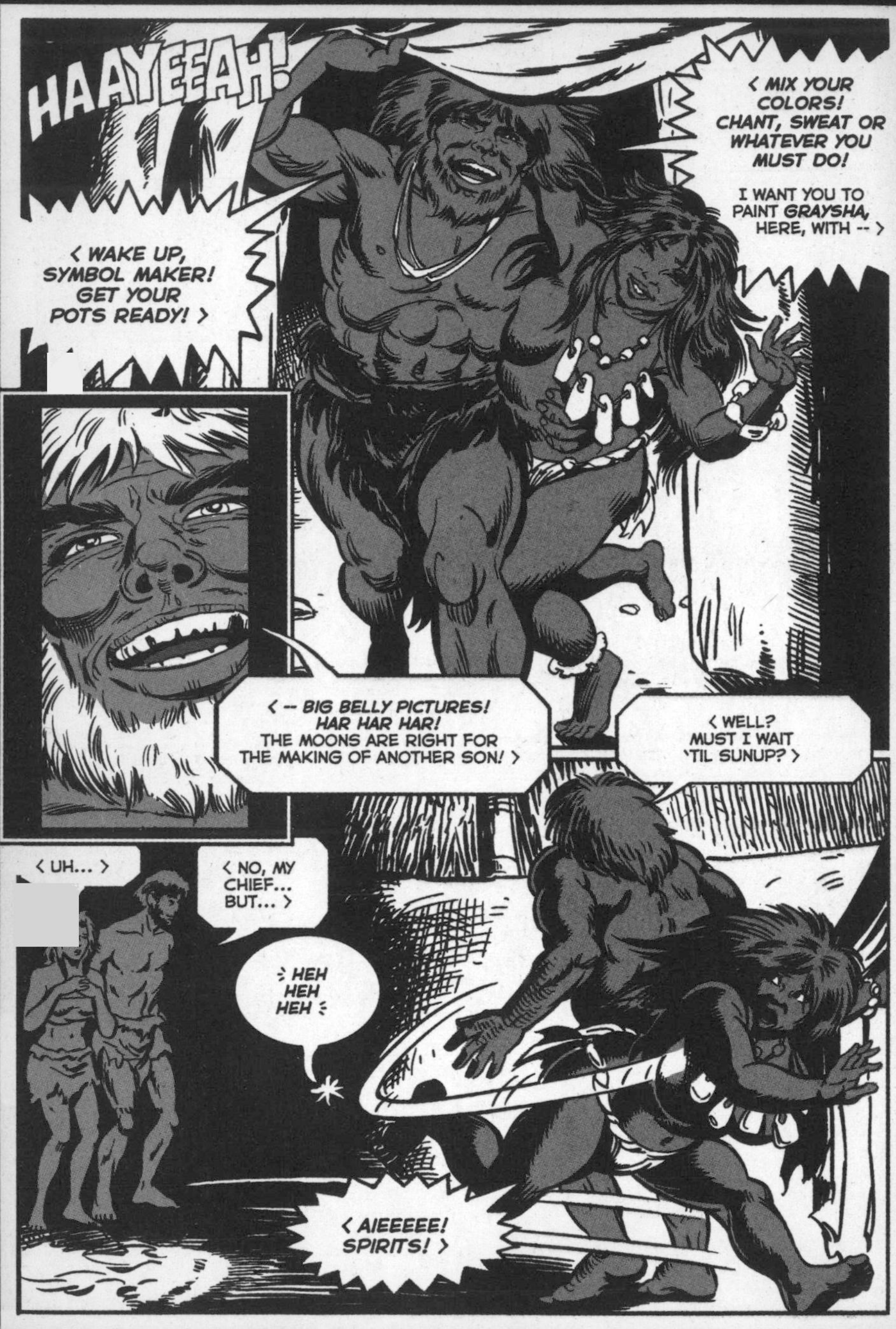
HAAYEEAH!
< MIX YOUR COLORS! CHANT, SWEAT OR WHATEVER YOU MUST DO!
I WANT YOU TO PAINT GRAYSHA, HERE, WITH -- >
< WAKE UP, SYMBOL MAKER! GET YOUR POTS READY! >
< -- BIG BELLY PICTURES! HAR HAR HAR! THE MOONS ARE RIGHT FOR THE MAKING OF ANOTHER SON! >
< WELL? MUST I WAIT 'TIL SUNUP? >
< UH... >
< NO, MY CHIEF... BUT... >
HEH HEH HEH
< AIEEEEE! SPIRITS! >

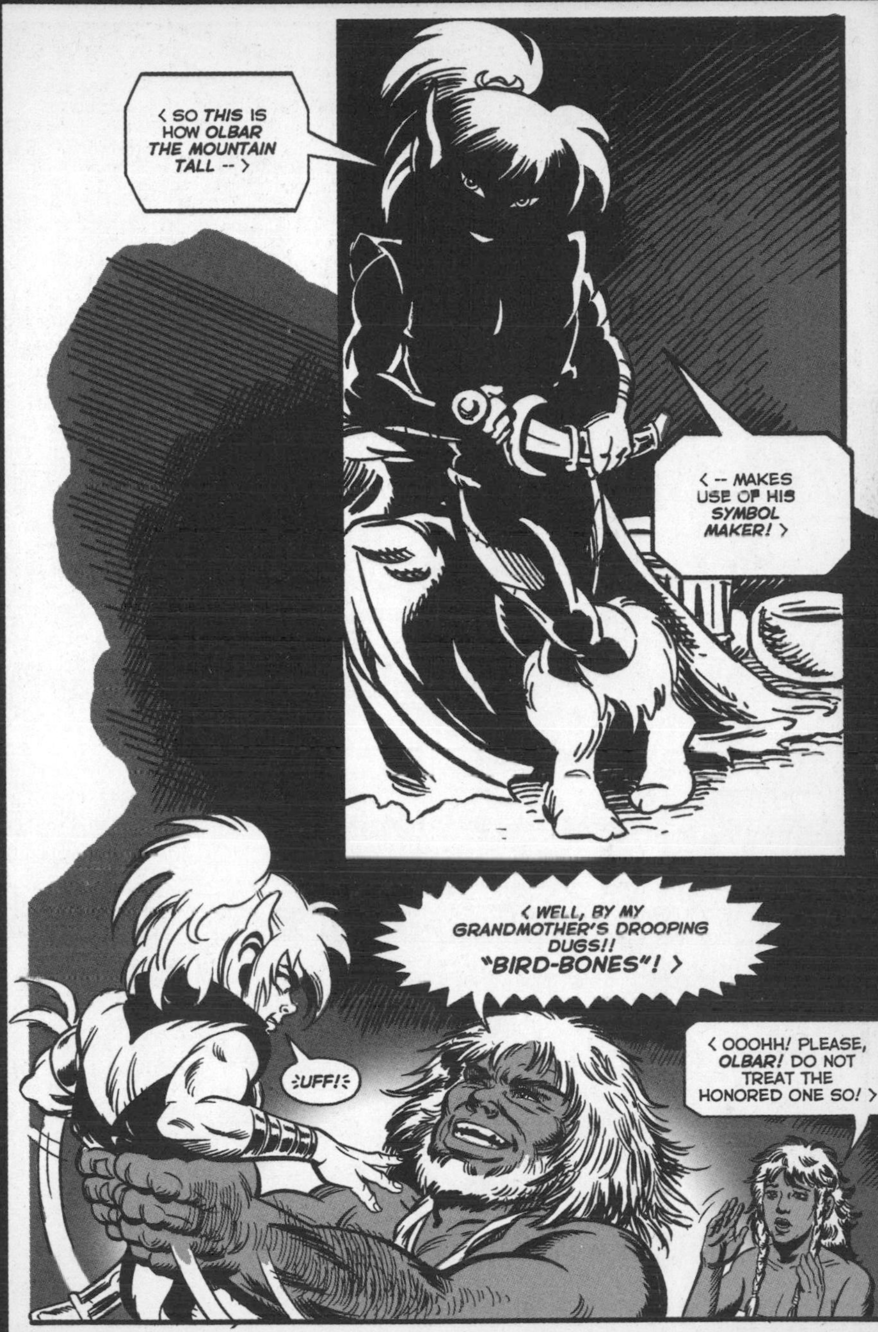
< SO THIS IS HOW OLBAR THE MOUNTAIN TALL -- >
< -- MAKES USE OF HIS SYMBOL MAKER! >
< WELL, BY MY GRANDMOTHER'S DROOPING DUGS!! "BIRD-BONES"! >
UFF!
< OOOHH! PLEASE, OLBAR! DO NOT TREAT THE HONORED ONE SO! >

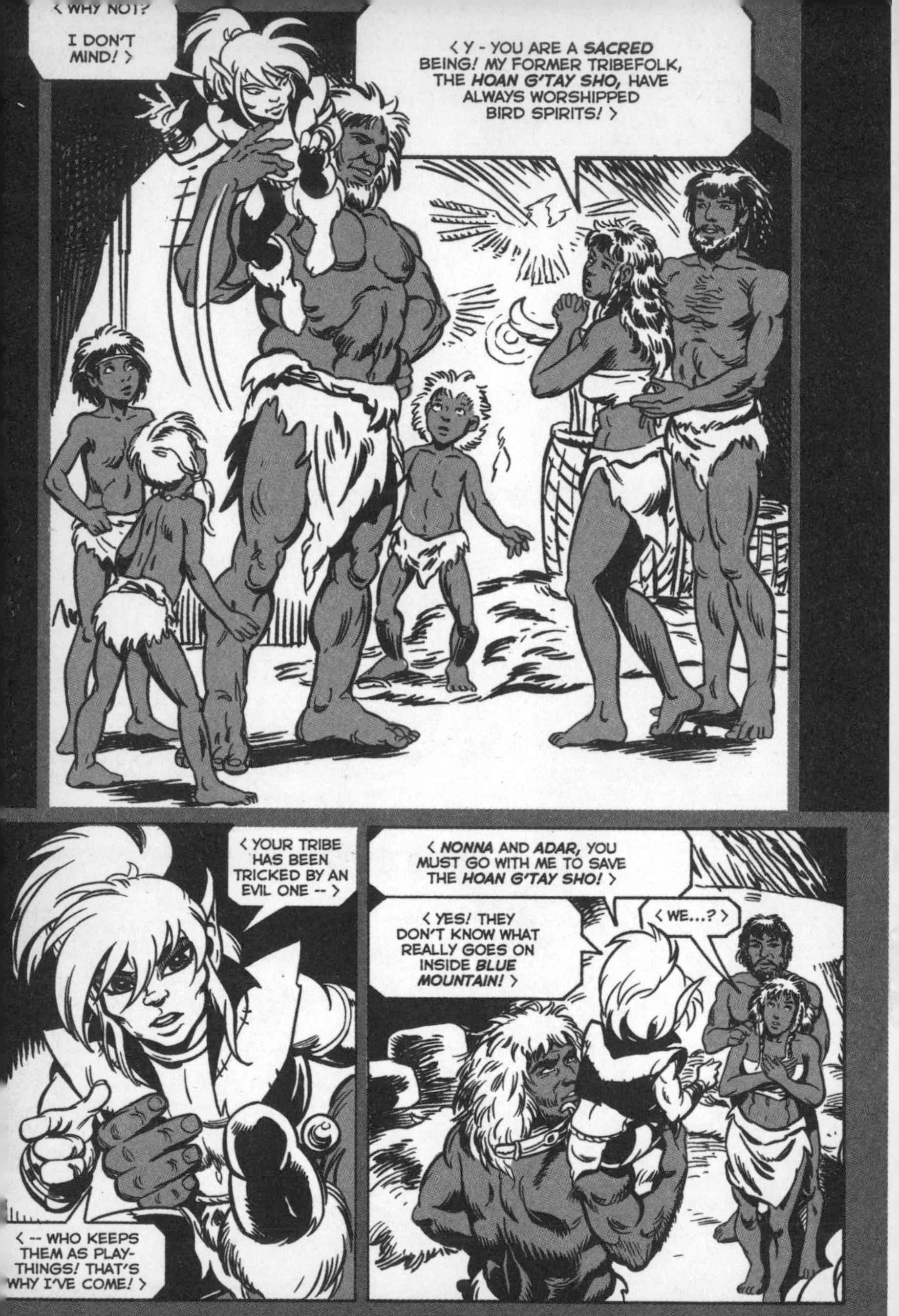

< WHY NOT? I DON'T MIND! >
< Y - YOU ARE A SACRED BEING! MY FORMER TRIBEFOLK, THE HOAN G'TAY SHO, HAVE ALWAYS WORSHIPPED BIRD SPIRITS! >
< YOUR TRIBE HAS BEEN TRICKED BY AN EVIL ONE -- >
< -- WHO KEEPS THEM AS PLAY-THINGS! THAT'S WHY I'VE COME! >
< NONNA AND ADAR, YOU MUST GO WITH ME TO SAVE THE HOAN G'TAY SHO! >
< YES! THEY DON'T KNOW WHAT REALLY GOES ON INSIDE BLUE MOUNTAIN! >
< WE...? >

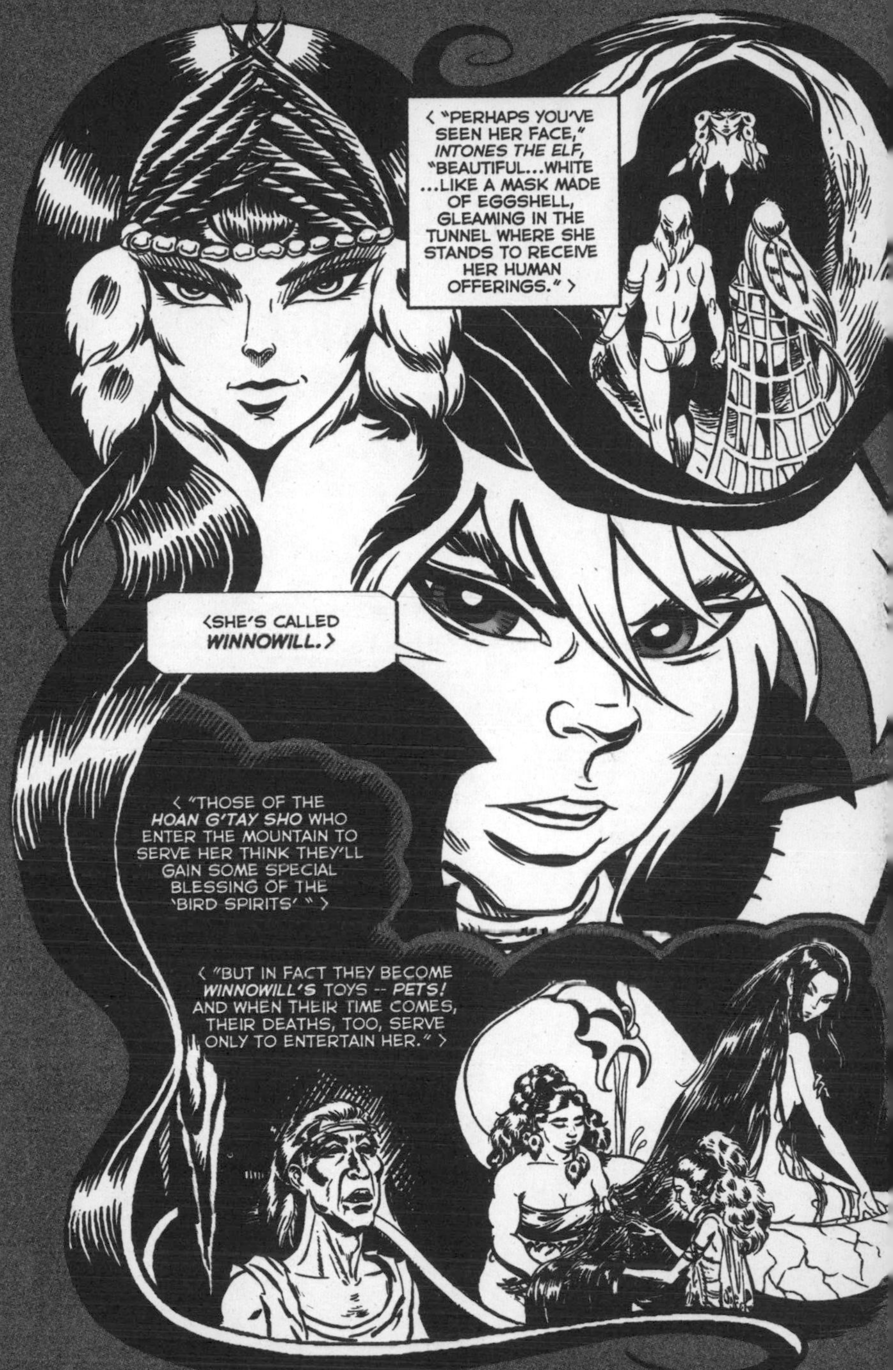

< "PERHAPS YOU'VE SEEN HER FACE," INTONES THE ELF, "BEAUTIFUL...WHITE ...LIKE A MASK MADE OF EGGSHELL, GLEAMING IN THE TUNNEL WHERE SHE STANDS TO RECEIVE HER HUMAN OFFERINGS." >
<SHE'S CALLED WINNOWILL.>
< "THOSE OF THE HOAN G'TAY SHO WHO ENTER THE MOUNTAIN TO SERVE HER THINK THEY'LL GAIN SOME SPECIAL BLESSING OF THE 'BIRD SPIRITS' " >
< "BUT IN FACT THEY BECOME WINNOWILL'S TOYS -- PETS! AND WHEN THEIR TIME COMES, THEIR DEATHS, TOO, SERVE ONLY TO ENTERTAIN HER." >

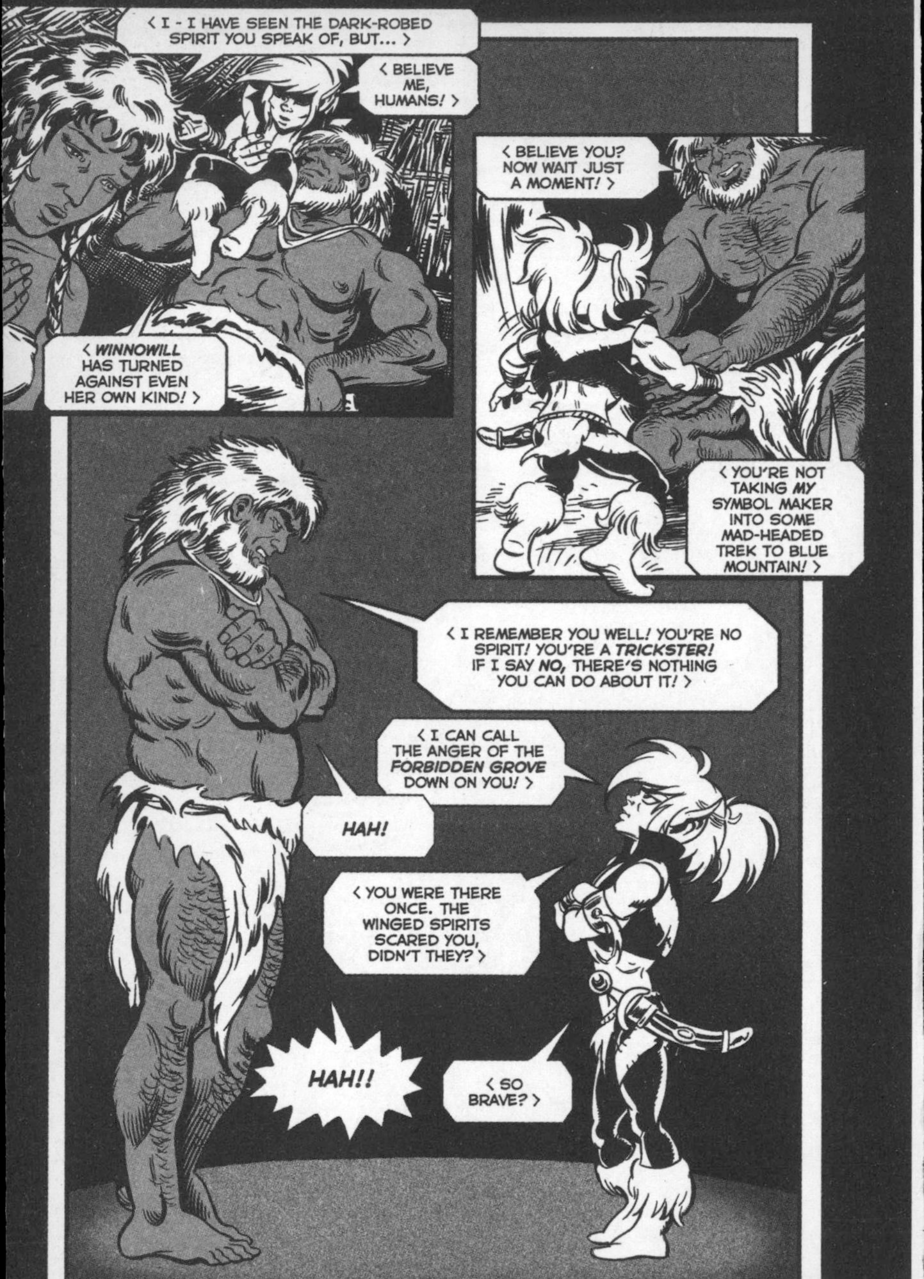
< I - I HAVE SEEN THE DARK-ROBED SPIRIT YOU SPEAK OF, BUT... >
< BELIEVE ME, HUMANS! >
< WINNOWILL HAS TURNED AGAINST EVEN HER OWN KIND! >
< BELIEVE YOU? NOW WAIT JUST A MOMENT! >
< YOU'RE NOT TAKING MY SYMBOL MAKER INTO SOME MAD-HEADED TREK TO BLUE MOUNTAIN! >
< I REMEMBER YOU WELL! YOU'RE NO SPIRIT! YOU'RE A TRICKSTER! IF I SAY NO, THERE'S NOTHING YOU CAN DO ABOUT IT! >
< I CAN CALL THE ANGER OF THE FORBIDDEN GROVE DOWN ON YOU! >
HAH!
< YOU WERE THERE ONCE. THE WINGED SPIRITS SCARED YOU, DIDN'T THEY? >
HAH!!
< SO BRAVE? >

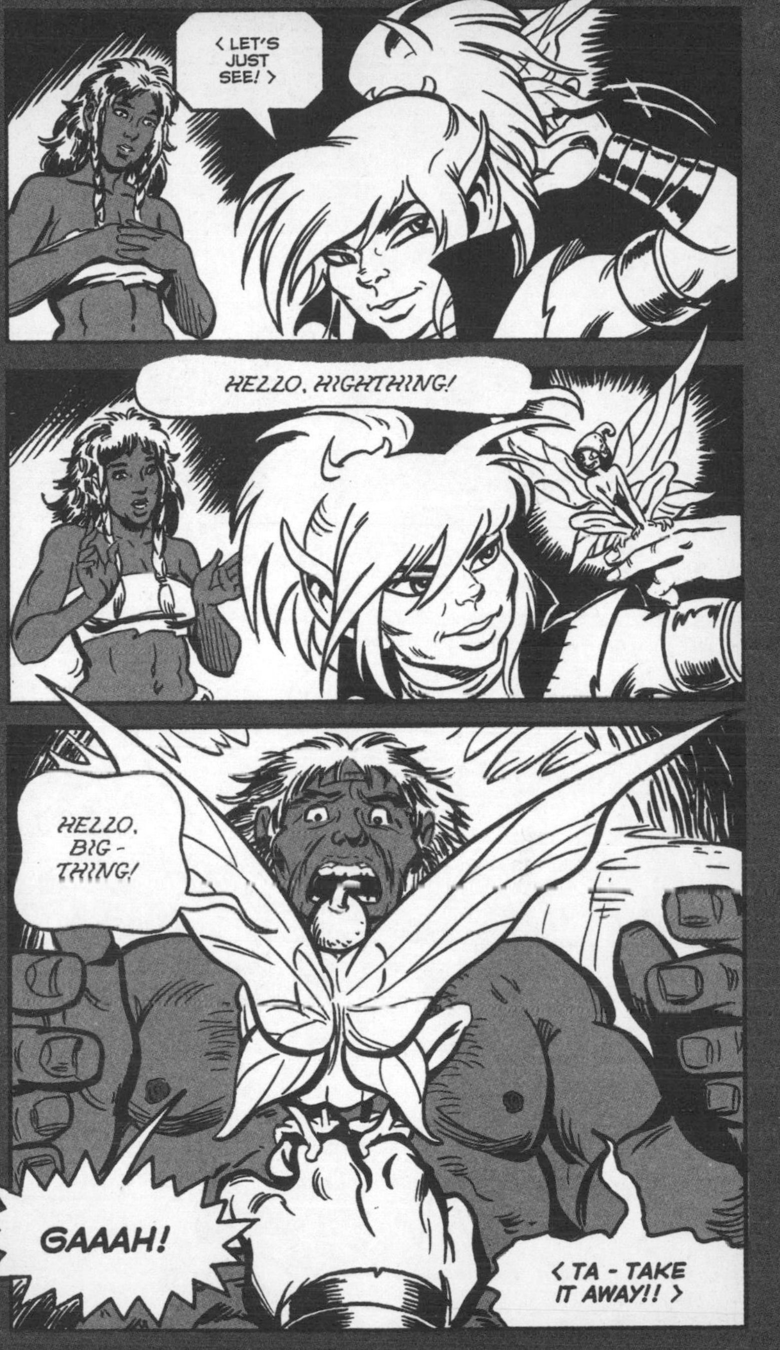

< LET'S JUST SEE! >
HELLO, HIGHTHING!
HELLO, BIG-THING!
GAAAH!
< TA - TAKE IT AWAY!! >

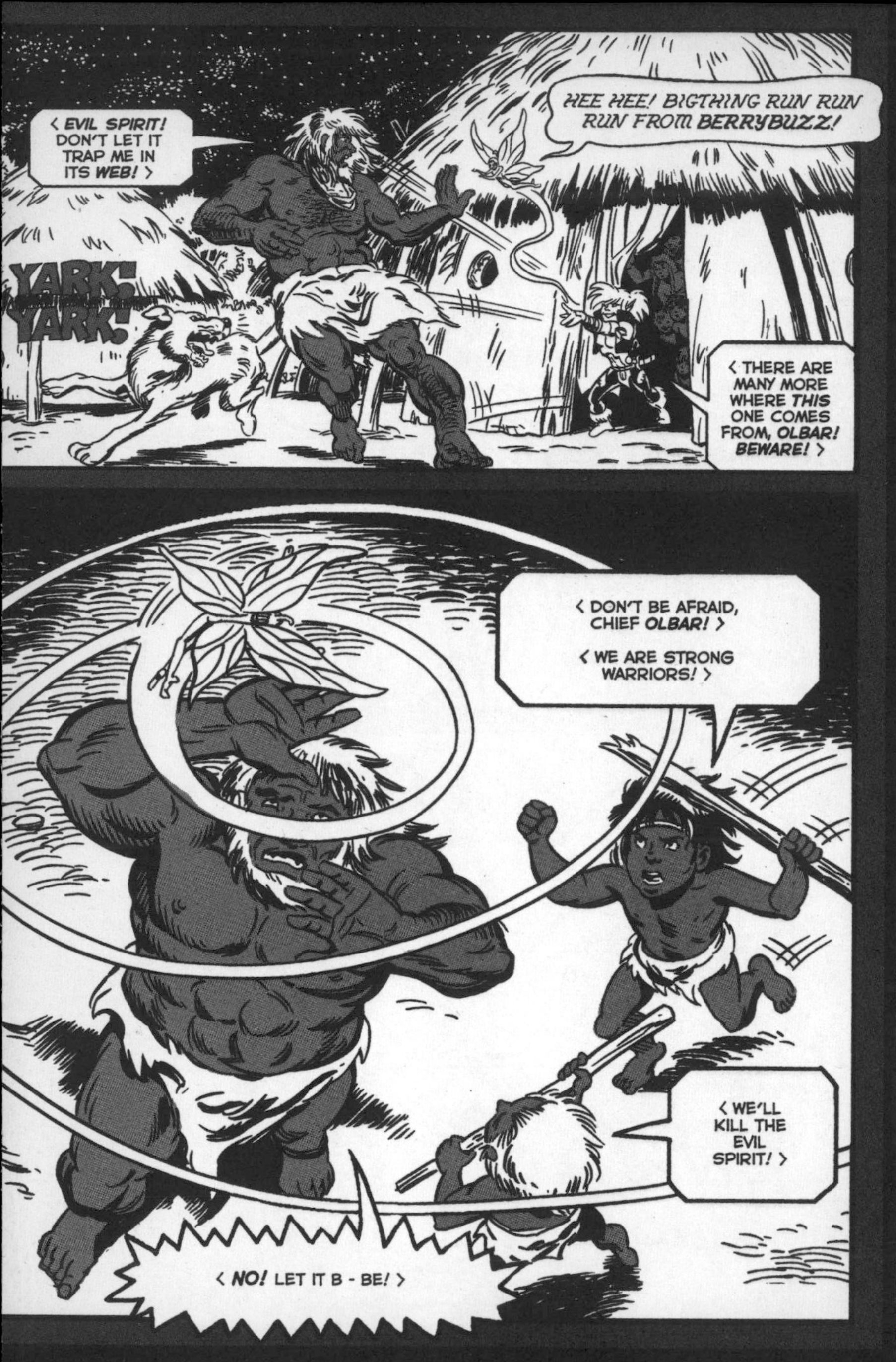

< EVIL SPIRIT! DON'T LET IT TRAP ME IN ITS WEB! >
HEE HEE! BIGTHING RUN RUN RUN FROM BERRYBUZZ!
YARK! YARK!
< THERE ARE MANY MORE WHERE THIS ONE COMES FROM, OLBAR! BEWARE! >
< DON'T BE AFRAID, CHIEF OLBAR! >
< WE ARE STRONG WARRIORS! >
< WE'LL KILL THE EVIL SPIRIT! >
< NO! LET IT B - BE! >

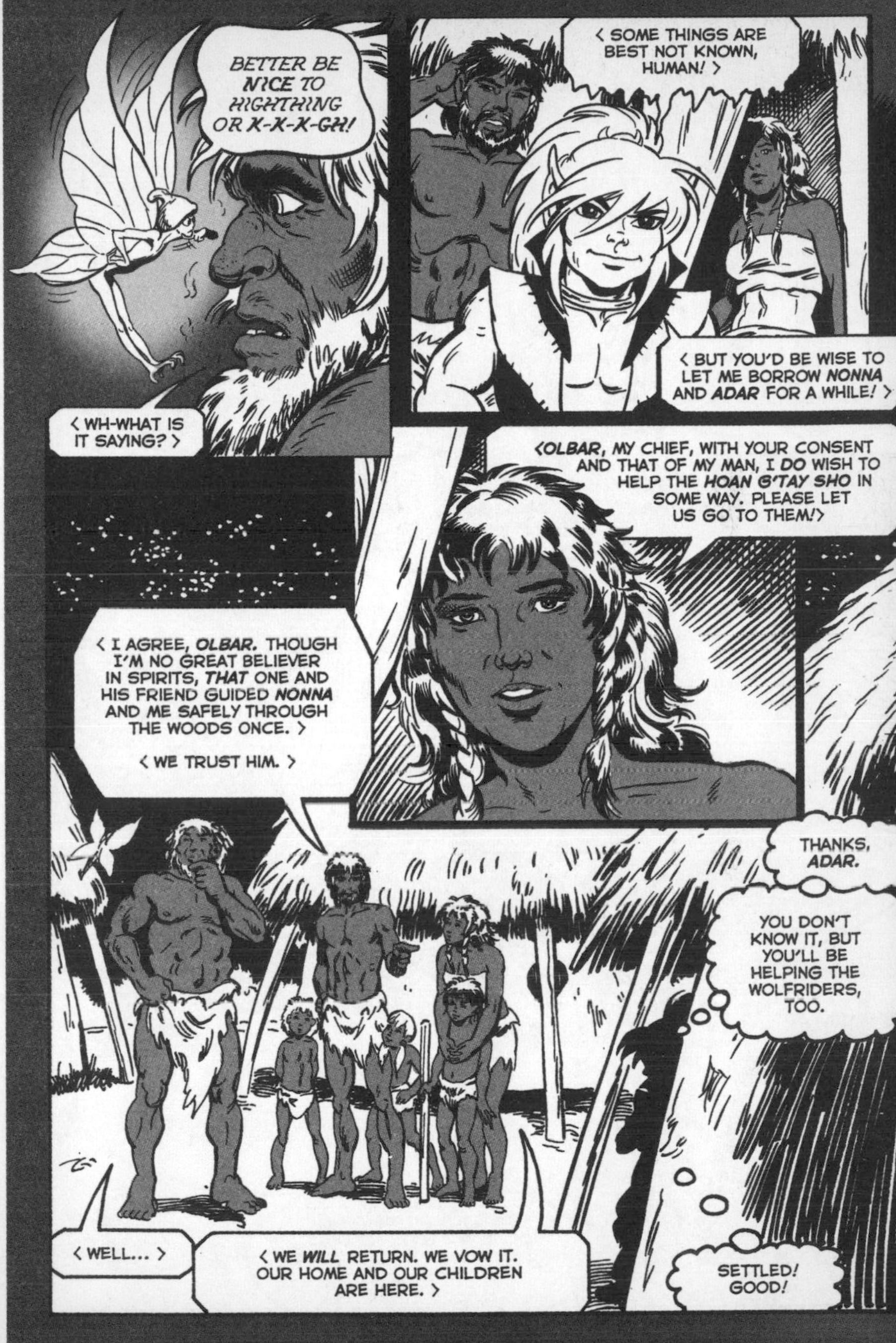
BETTER BE NICE TO HIGHTHING OR K-K-K-GH!
< WH-WHAT IS IT SAYING? >
< SOME THINGS ARE BEST NOT KNOWN, HUMAN! >
< BUT YOU'D BE WISE TO LET ME BORROW NONNA AND ADAR FOR A WHILE! >
<OLBAR, MY CHIEF, WITH YOUR CONSENT AND THAT OF MY MAN, I DO WISH TO HELP THE HOAN G'TAY SHO IN SOME WAY. PLEASE LET US GO TO THEM!>
< I AGREE, OLBAR. THOUGH I'M NO GREAT BELIEVER IN SPIRITS, THAT ONE AND HIS FRIEND GUIDED NONNA AND ME SAFELY THROUGH THE WOODS ONCE. >
< WE TRUST HIM. >
THANKS, ADAR.
YOU DON'T KNOW IT, BUT YOU'LL BE HELPING THE WOLFRIDERS, TOO.
< WELL... >
< WE WILL RETURN. WE VOW IT. OUR HOME AND OUR CHILDREN ARE HERE. >
SETTLED! GOOD!

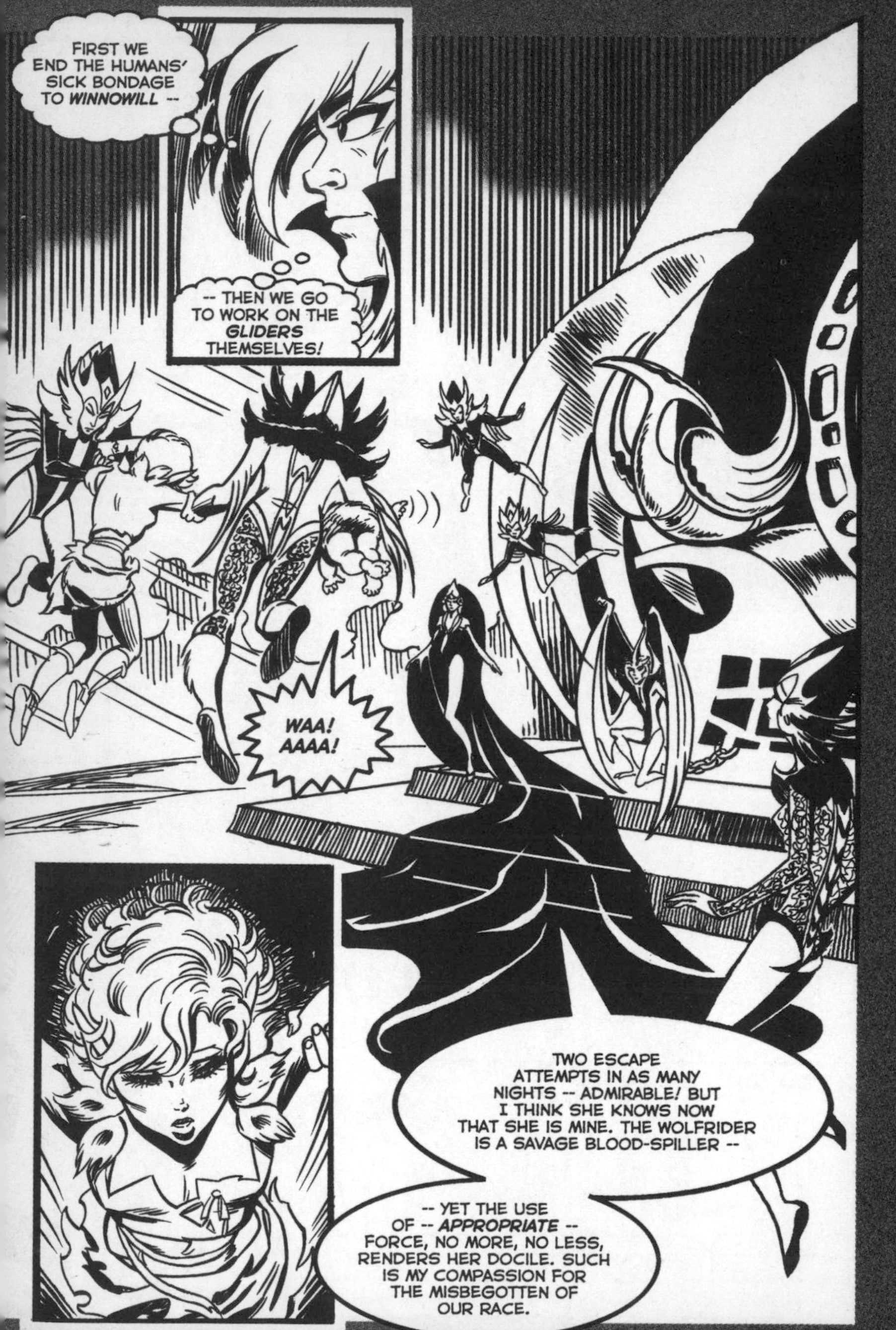

FIRST WE END THE HUMANS' SICK BONDAGE TO WINNOWILL --
-- THEN WE GO TO WORK ON THE GLIDERS THEMSELVES!
WAA! AAAA!
TWO ESCAPE ATTEMPTS IN AS MANY NIGHTS -- ADMIRABLE! BUT I THINK SHE KNOWS NOW THAT SHE IS MINE. THE WOLFRIDER IS A SAVAGE BLOOD-SPILLER --
-- YET THE USE OF -- APPROPRIATE -- FORCE, NO MORE, NO LESS, RENDERS HER DOCILE. SUCH IS MY COMPASSION FOR THE MISBEGOTTEN OF OUR RACE.

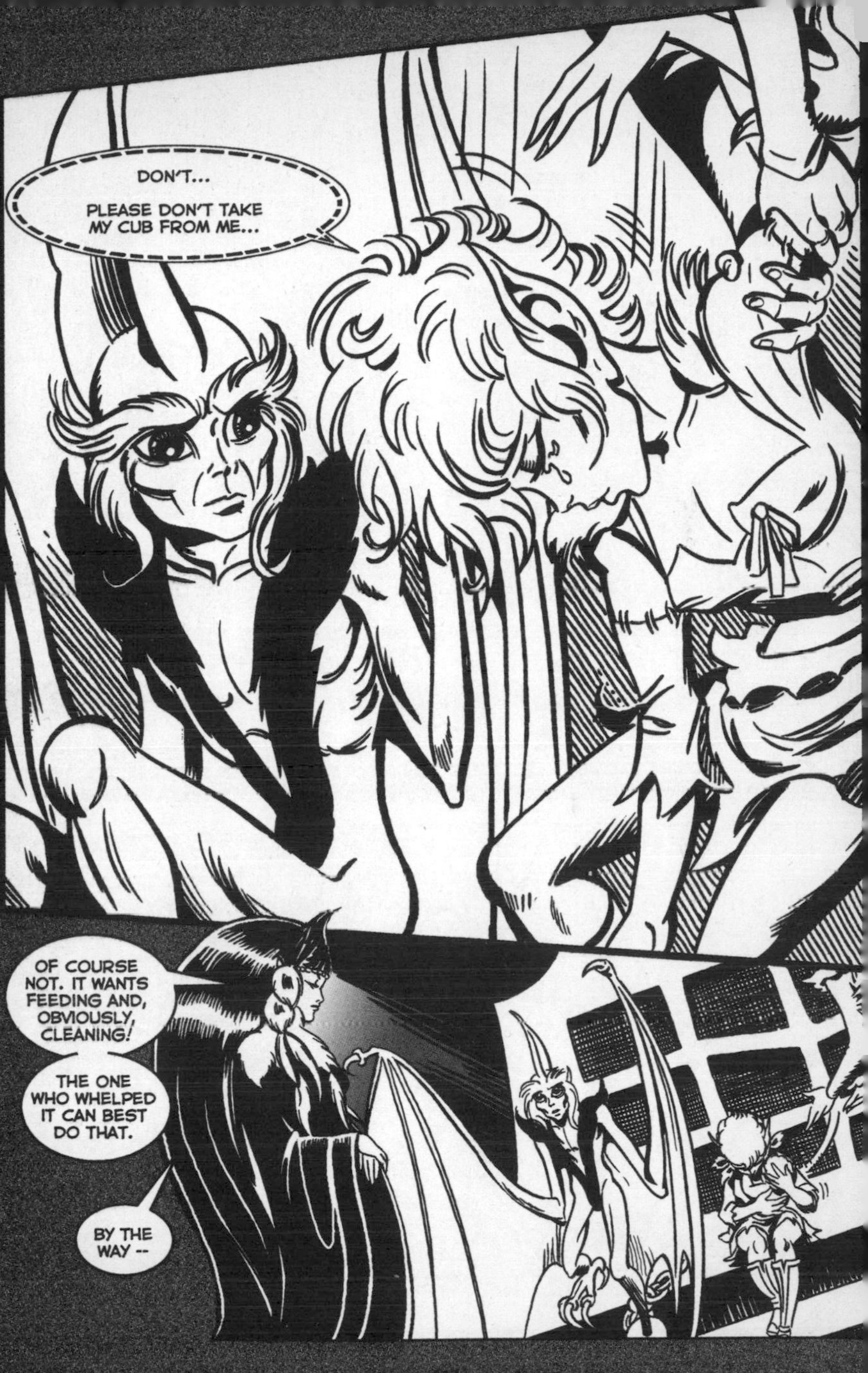

DON'T...
PLEASE DON'T TAKE MY CUB FROM ME...
OF COURSE NOT. IT WANTS FEEDING AND, OBVIOUSLY, CLEANING!
THE ONE WHO WHELPED IT CAN BEST DO THAT.
BY THE WAY --

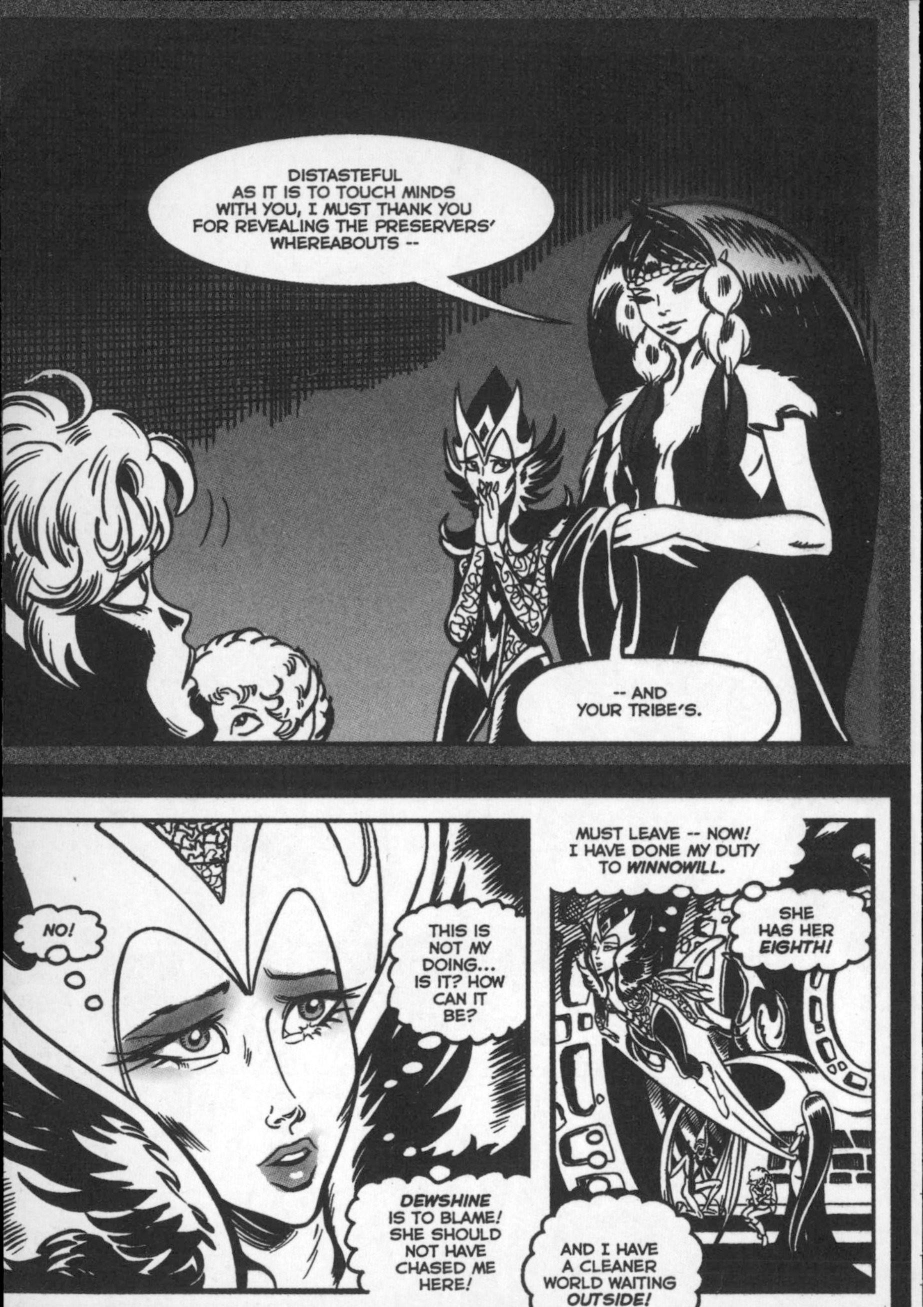
DISTASTEFUL AS IT IS TO TOUCH MINDS WITH YOU, I MUST THANK YOU FOR REVEALING THE PRESERVERS' WHEREABOUTS --
-- AND YOUR TRIBE'S.
NO!
THIS IS NOT MY DOING... IS IT? HOW CAN IT BE?
DEWSHINE IS TO BLAME! SHE SHOULD NOT HAVE CHASED ME HERE!
MUST LEAVE -- NOW! I HAVE DONE MY DUTY TO WINNOWILL.
SHE HAS HER EIGHTH!
AND I HAVE A CLEANER WORLD WAITING OUTSIDE!

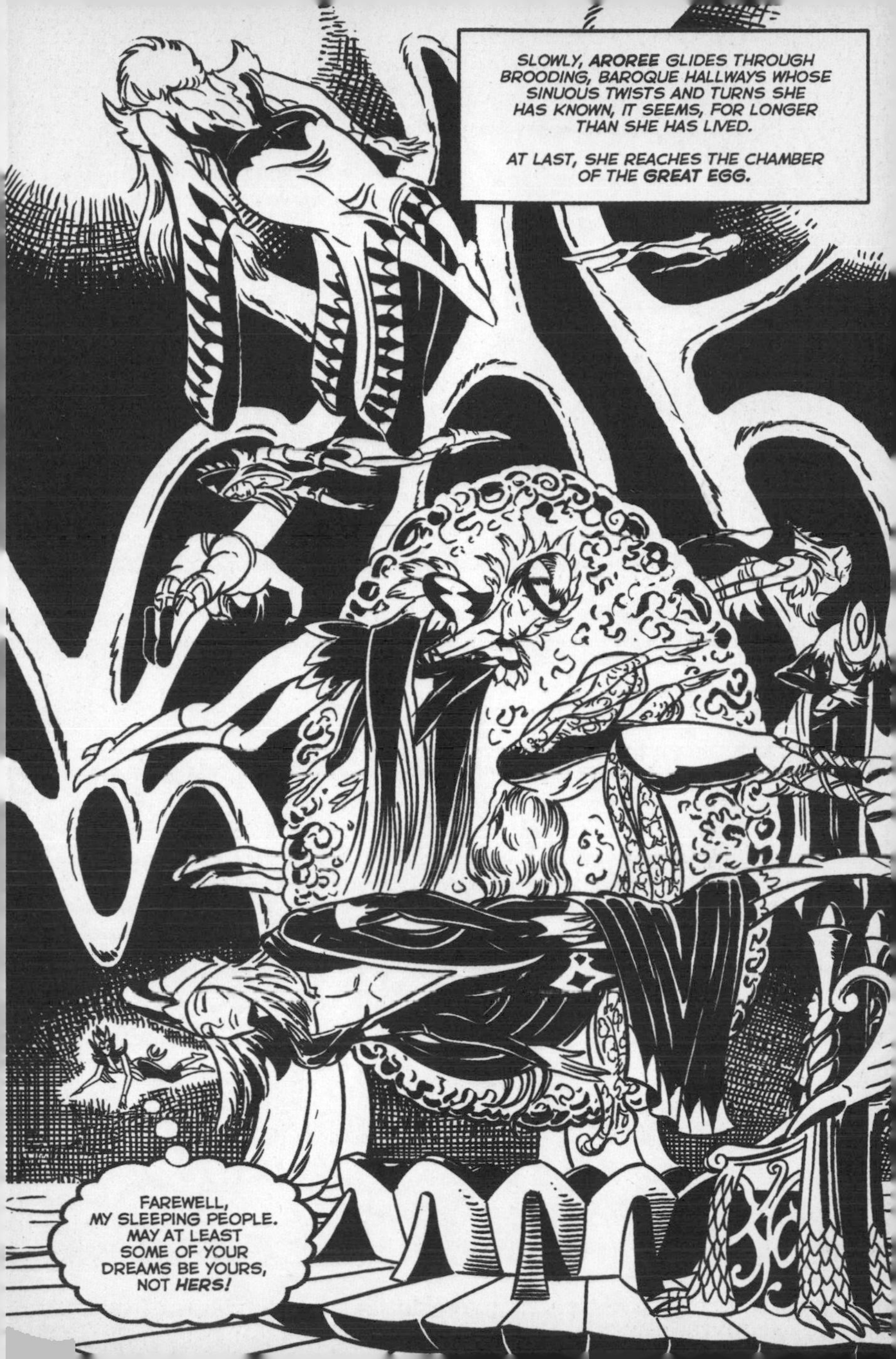
SLOWLY, AROREE GLIDES THROUGH BROODING, BAROQUE HALLWAYS WHOSE SINUOUS TWISTS AND TURNS SHE HAS KNOWN, IT SEEMS, FOR LONGER THAN SHE HAS LIVED.
AT LAST, SHE REACHES THE CHAMBER OF THE GREAT EGG.
FAREWELL, MY SLEEPING PEOPLE. MAY AT LEAST SOME OF YOUR DREAMS BE YOURS, NOT HERS!

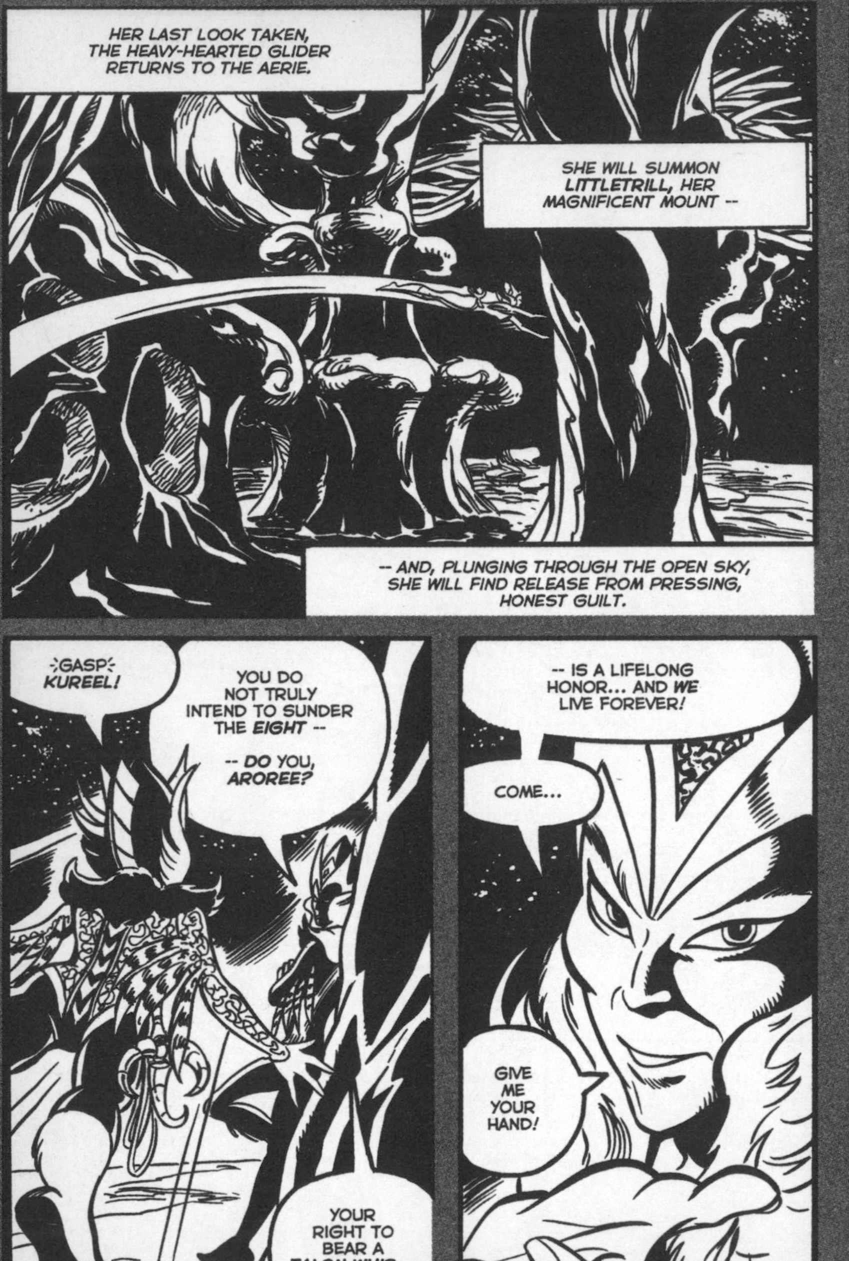
HER LAST LOOK TAKEN, THE HEAVY-HEARTED GLIDER RETURNS TO THE AERIE.
SHE WILL SUMMON *LITTLETRILL*, HER MAGNIFICENT MOUNT --
-- AND, PLUNGING THROUGH THE OPEN SKY, SHE WILL FIND RELEASE FROM PRESSING, HONEST GUILT.
GASP *KUREEL!*
YOU DO NOT TRULY INTEND TO SUNDER THE *EIGHT* --
-- *DO YOU, AROREE?*
YOUR RIGHT TO BEAR A *TALON-WHIP* --
-- IS A LIFELONG HONOR... AND *WE* LIVE FOREVER!
COME...
GIVE ME YOUR HAND!

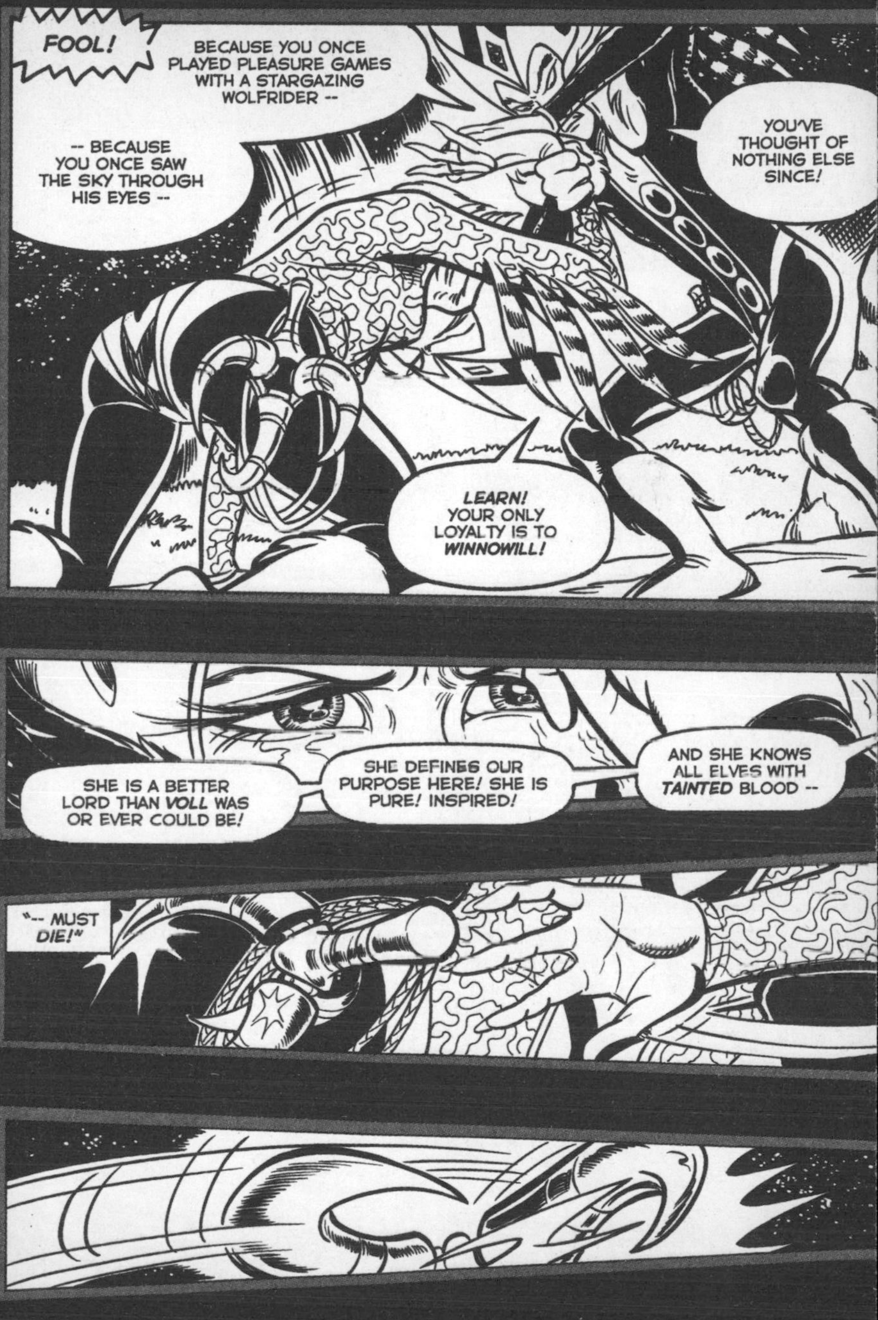
FOOL!
BECAUSE YOU ONCE PLAYED PLEASURE GAMES WITH A STARGAZING WOLFRIDER --
-- BECAUSE YOU ONCE SAW THE SKY THROUGH HIS EYES --
YOU'VE THOUGHT OF NOTHING ELSE SINCE!
LEARN! YOUR ONLY LOYALTY IS TO WINNOWILL!
SHE IS A BETTER LORD THAN VOLL WAS OR EVER COULD BE!
SHE DEFINES OUR PURPOSE HERE! SHE IS PURE! INSPIRED!
AND SHE KNOWS ALL ELVES WITH TAINTED BLOOD --
"-- MUST DIE!"

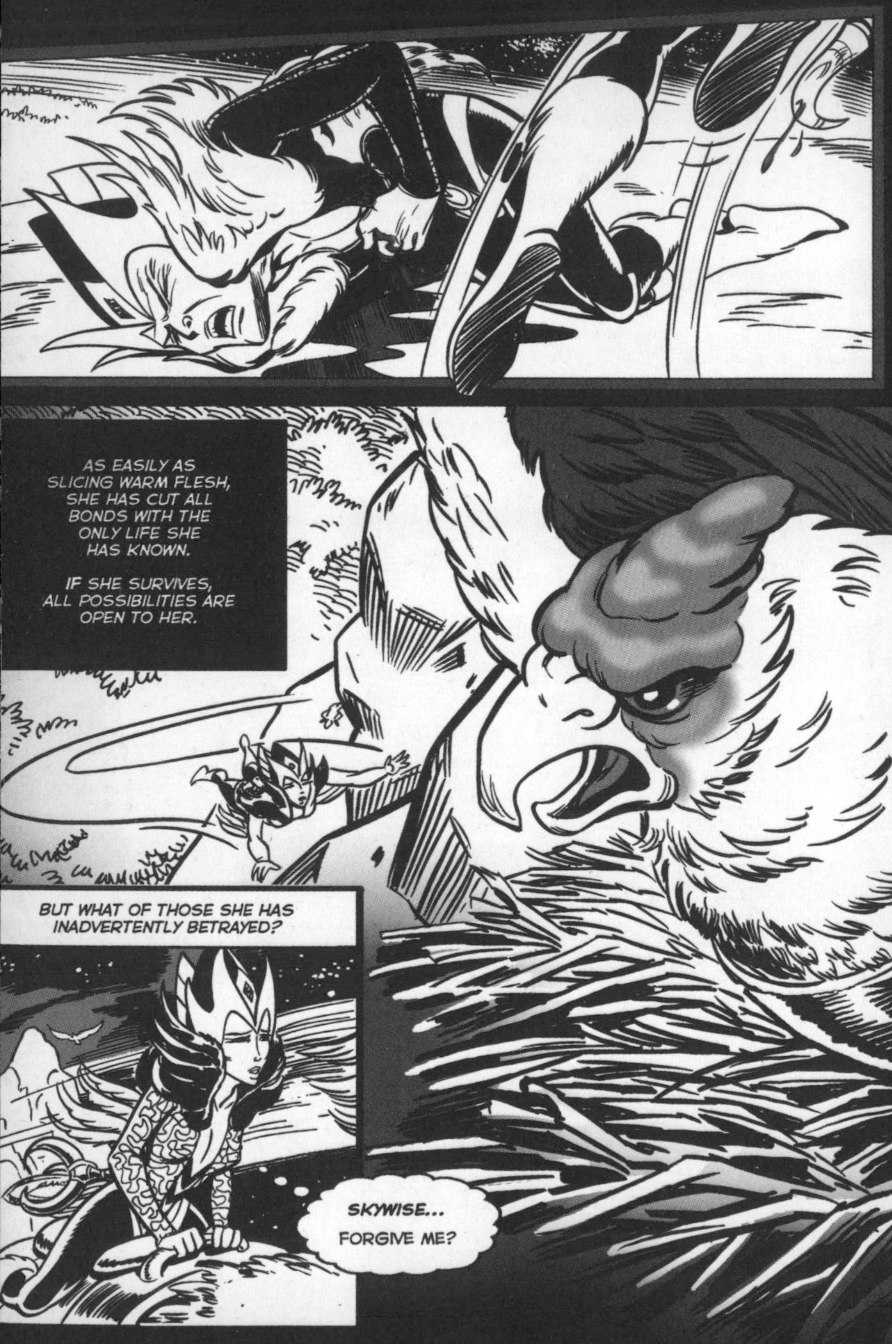
AS EASILY AS SLICING WARM FLESH, SHE HAS CUT ALL BONDS WITH THE ONLY LIFE SHE HAS KNOWN.
IF SHE SURVIVES, ALL POSSIBILITIES ARE OPEN TO HER.
BUT WHAT OF THOSE SHE HAS INADVERTENTLY BETRAYED?
SKYWISE... FORGIVE ME?

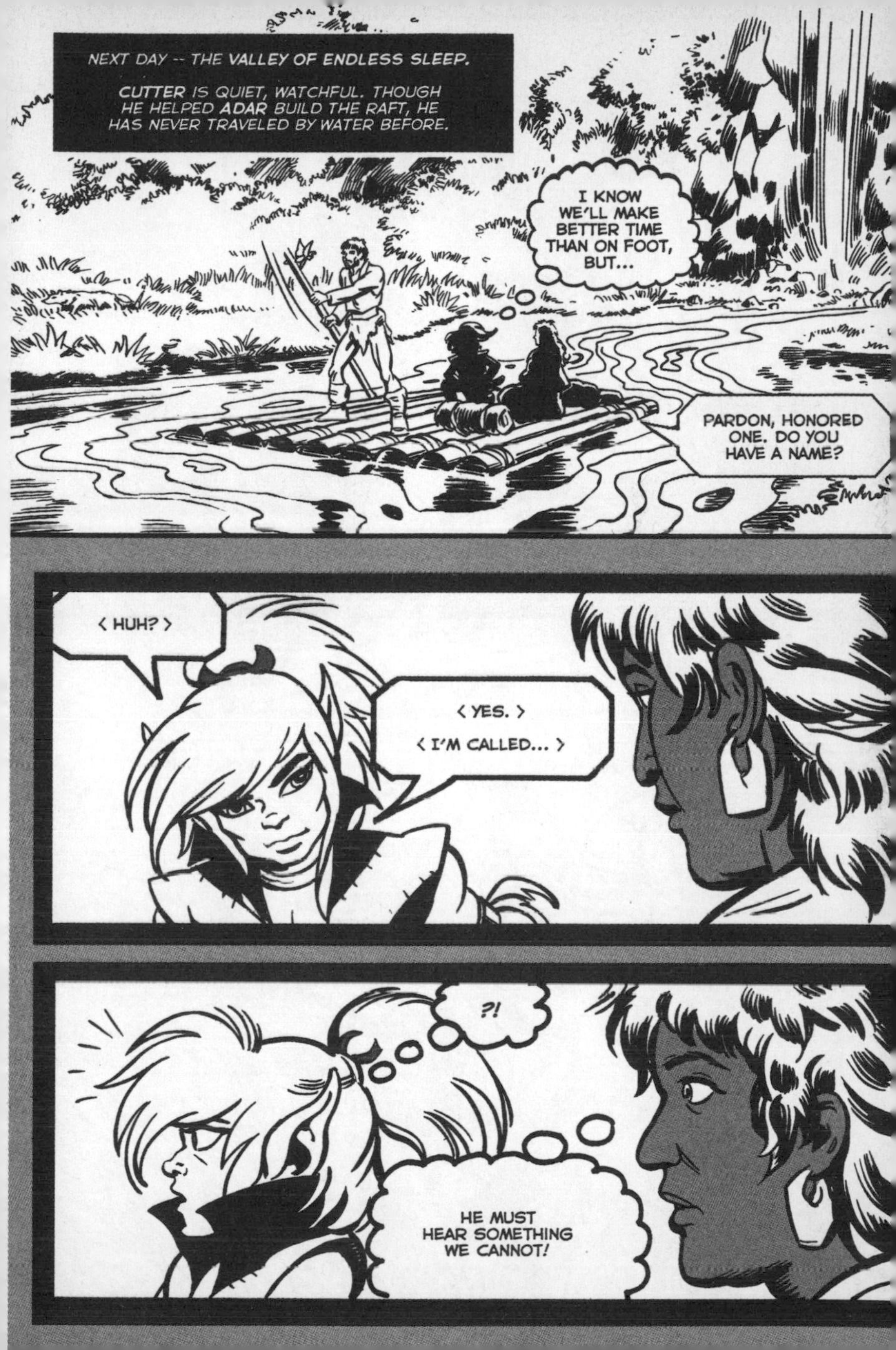
NEXT DAY -- THE VALLEY OF ENDLESS SLEEP.
CUTTER IS QUIET, WATCHFUL. THOUGH HE HELPED ADAR BUILD THE RAFT, HE HAS NEVER TRAVELED BY WATER BEFORE.
I KNOW WE'LL MAKE BETTER TIME THAN ON FOOT, BUT...
PARDON, HONORED ONE. DO YOU HAVE A NAME?
‹ HUH? ›
‹ YES. ›
‹ I'M CALLED... ›
?!
HE MUST HEAR SOMETHING WE CANNOT!

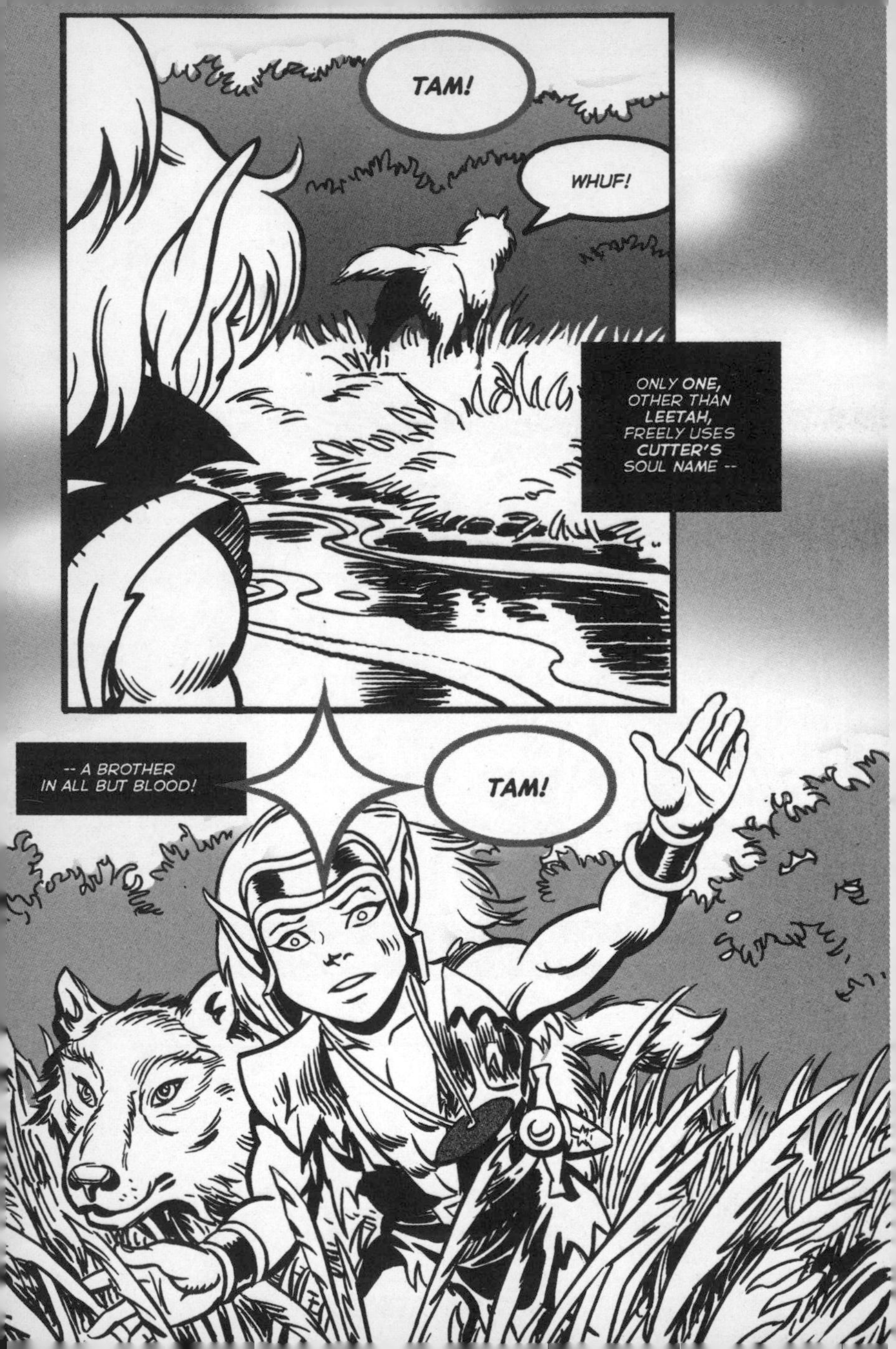
TAM!
WHUF!
ONLY ONE, OTHER THAN LEETAH, FREELY USES CUTTER'S SOUL NAME --
-- A BROTHER IN ALL BUT BLOOD!
TAM!

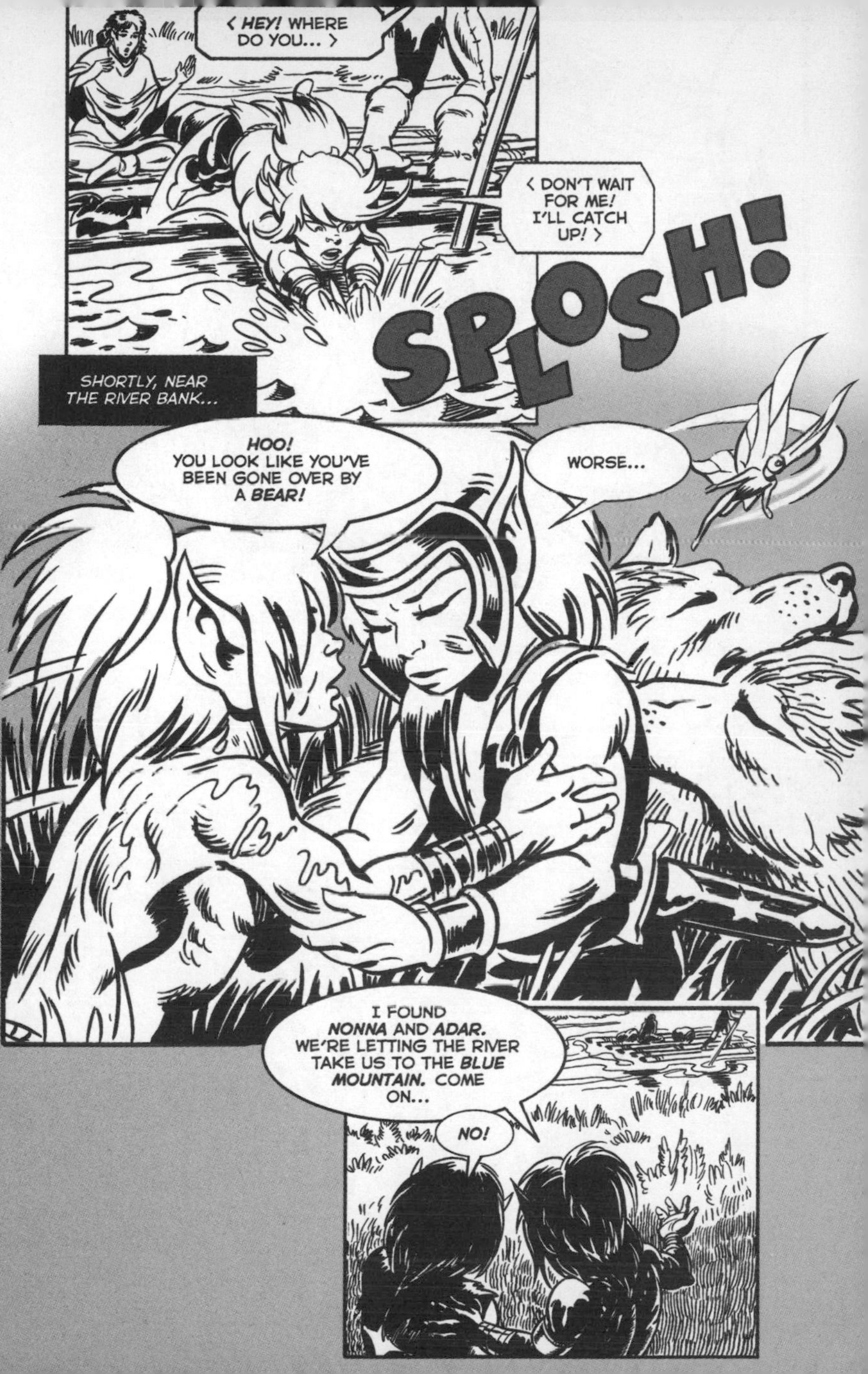

< HEY! WHERE DO YOU... >
< DON'T WAIT FOR ME! I'LL CATCH UP! >
SPLOSH!
SHORTLY, NEAR THE RIVER BANK...
HOO! YOU LOOK LIKE YOU'VE BEEN GONE OVER BY A BEAR!
WORSE...
I FOUND NONNA AND ADAR. WE'RE LETTING THE RIVER TAKE US TO THE BLUE MOUNTAIN. COME ON...
NO!

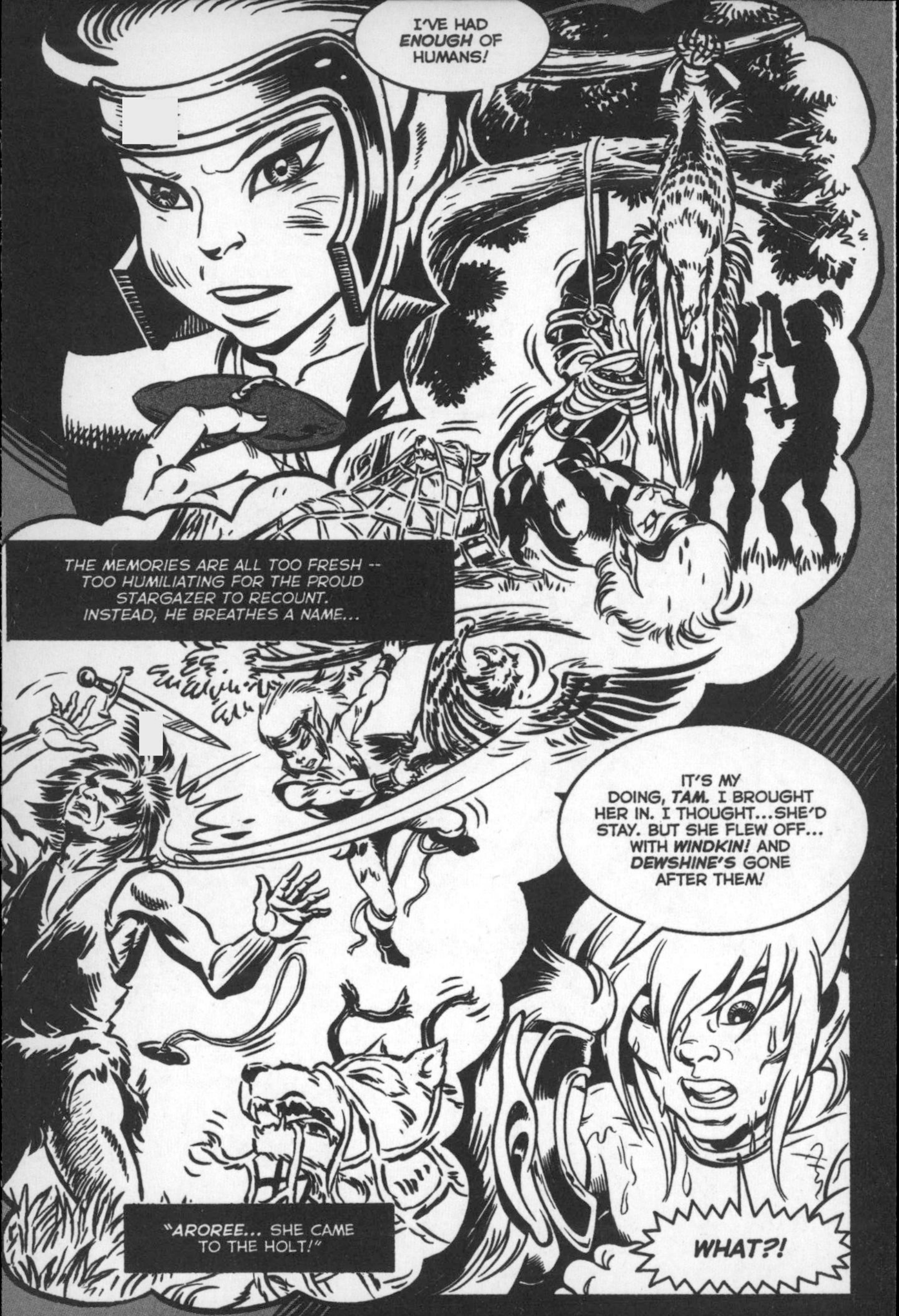
I'VE HAD ENOUGH OF HUMANS!
THE MEMORIES ARE ALL TOO FRESH -- TOO HUMILIATING FOR THE PROUD STARGAZER TO RECOUNT. INSTEAD, HE BREATHES A NAME...
"AROREE... SHE CAME TO THE HOLT!"
IT'S MY DOING, TAM. I BROUGHT HER IN. I THOUGHT...SHE'D STAY. BUT SHE FLEW OFF... WITH WINDKIN! AND DEWSHINE'S GONE AFTER THEM!
WHAT?!

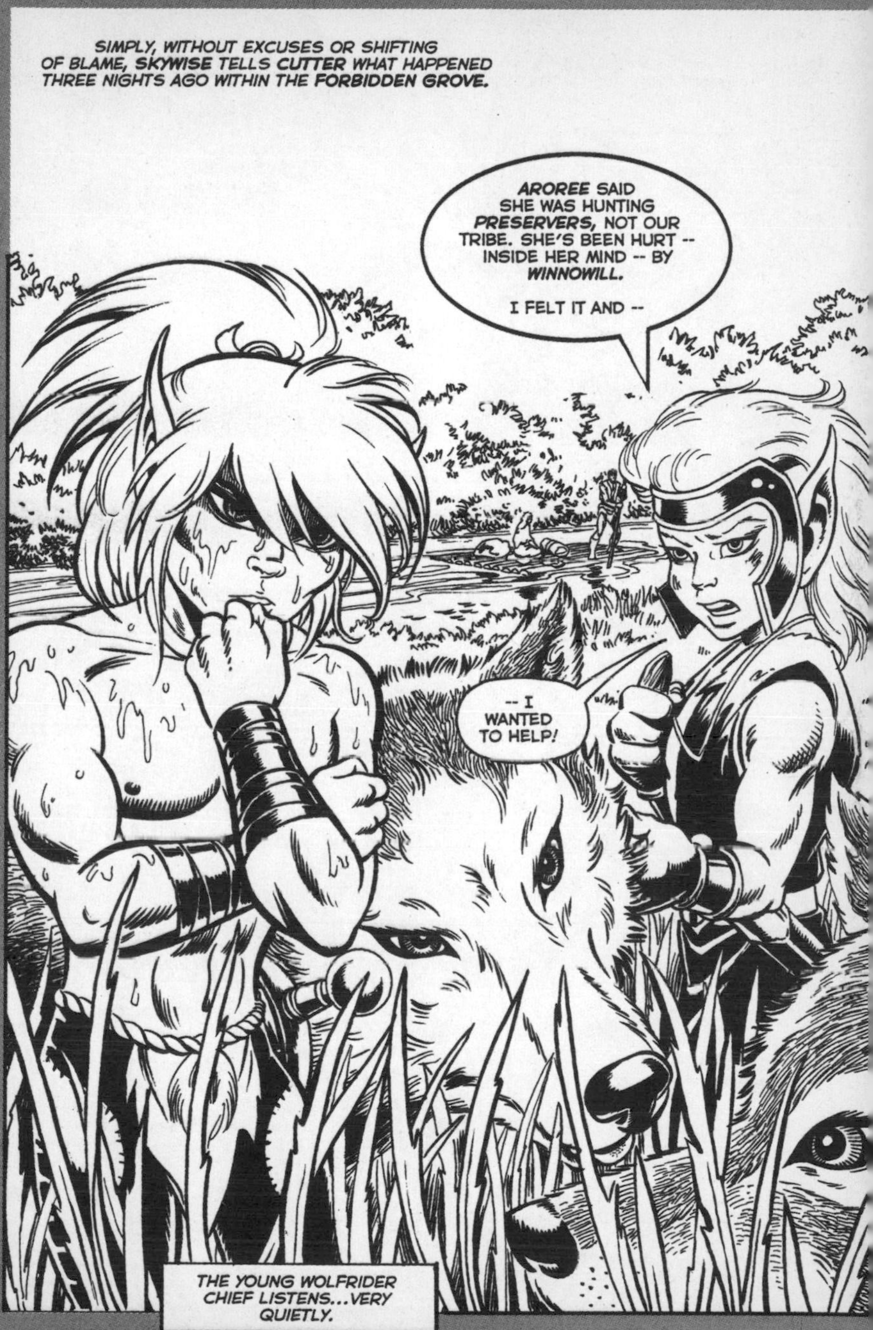

SIMPLY, WITHOUT EXCUSES OR SHIFTING OF BLAME, SKYWISE TELLS CUTTER WHAT HAPPENED THREE NIGHTS AGO WITHIN THE FORBIDDEN GROVE.
AROREE SAID SHE WAS HUNTING PRESERVERS, NOT OUR TRIBE. SHE'S BEEN HURT -- INSIDE HER MIND -- BY WINNOWILL.
I FELT IT AND --
-- I WANTED TO HELP!
THE YOUNG WOLFRIDER CHIEF LISTENS...VERY QUIETLY.

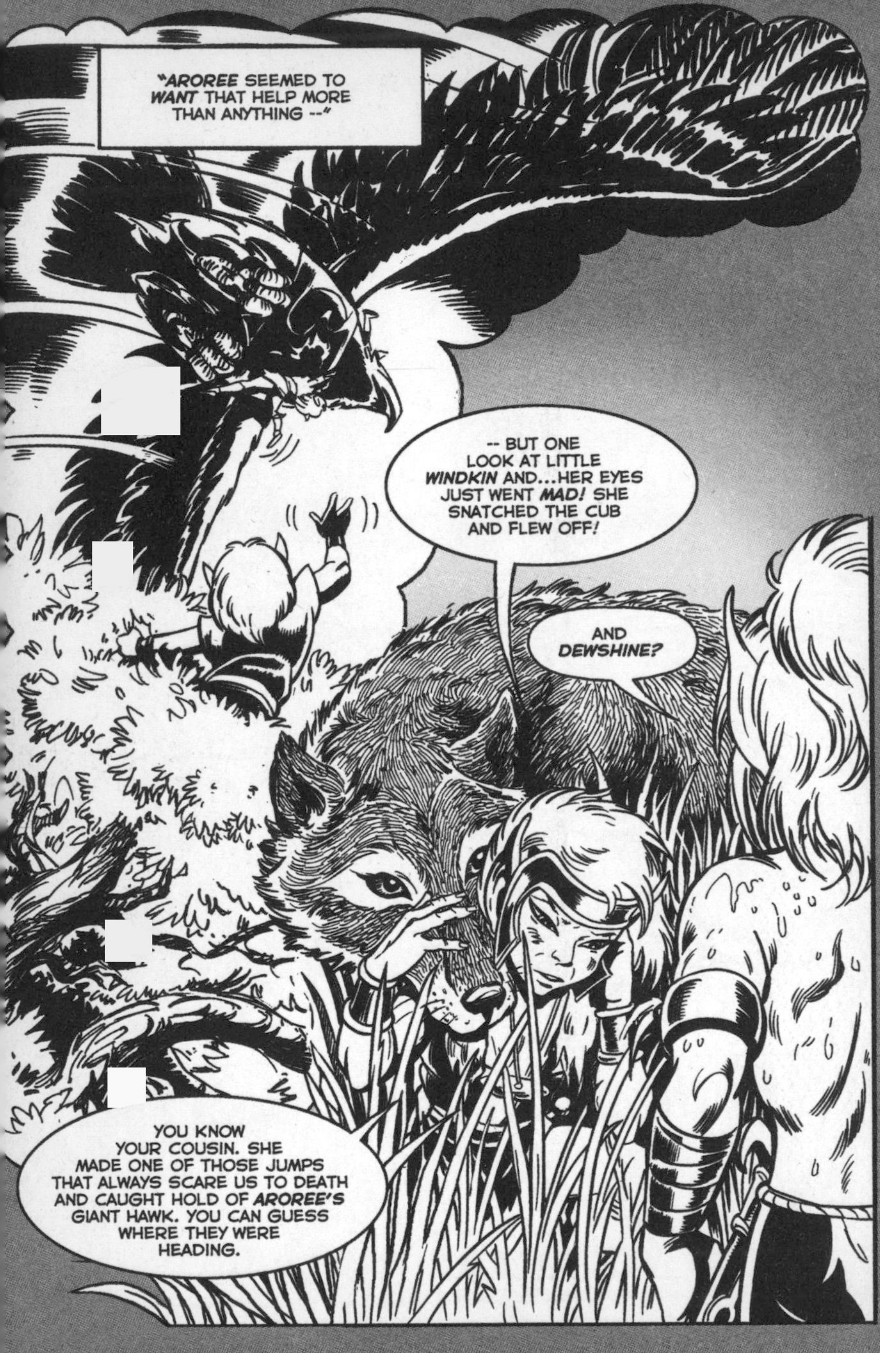
"AROREE SEEMED TO WANT THAT HELP MORE THAN ANYTHING --"
-- BUT ONE LOOK AT LITTLE WINDKIN AND...HER EYES JUST WENT MAD! SHE SNATCHED THE CUB AND FLEW OFF!
AND DEWSHINE?
YOU KNOW YOUR COUSIN. SHE MADE ONE OF THOSE JUMPS THAT ALWAYS SCARE US TO DEATH AND CAUGHT HOLD OF AROREE'S GIANT HAWK. YOU CAN GUESS WHERE THEY WERE HEADING.

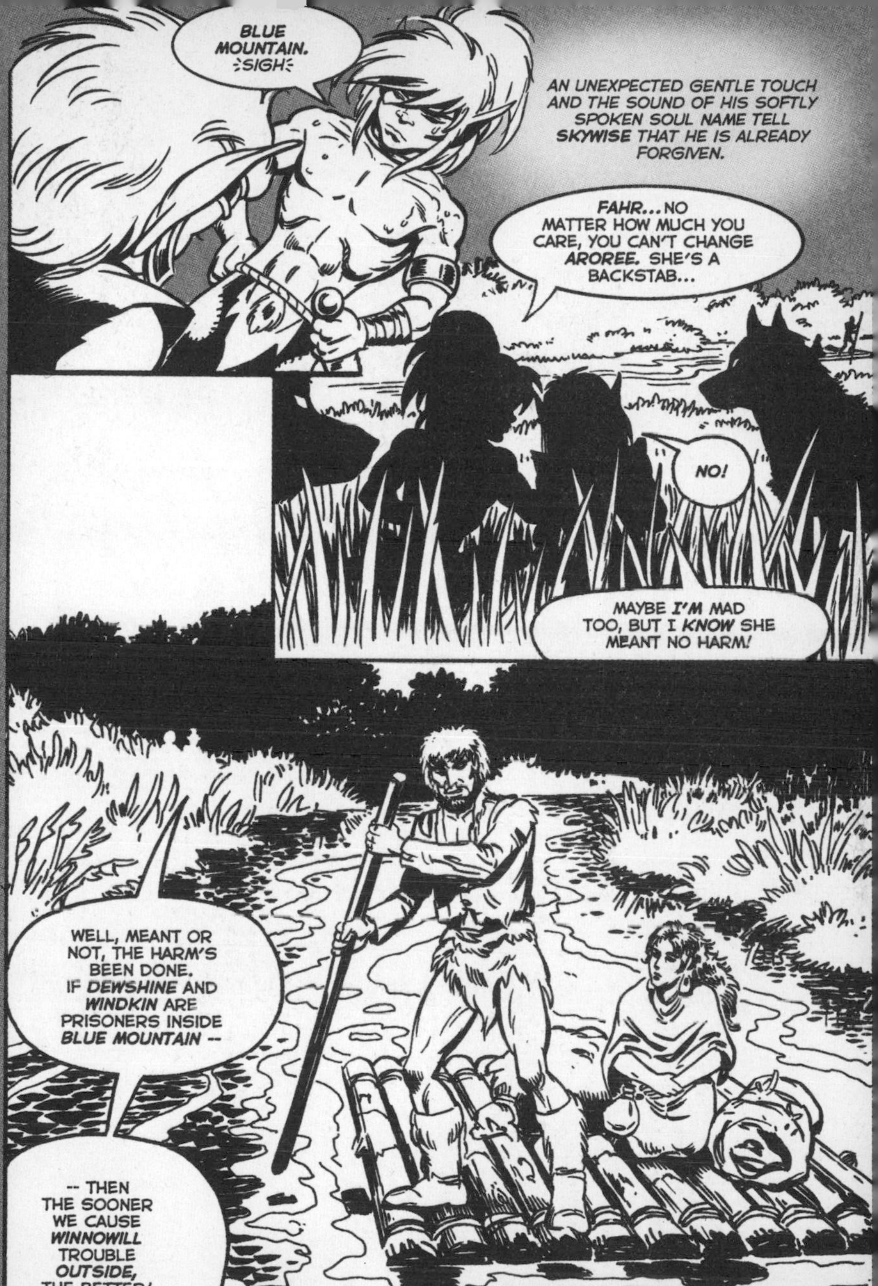
BLUE MOUNTAIN. ⁝SIGH⁝
AN UNEXPECTED GENTLE TOUCH AND THE SOUND OF HIS SOFTLY SPOKEN SOUL NAME TELL SKYWISE THAT HE IS ALREADY FORGIVEN.
FAHR... NO MATTER HOW MUCH YOU CARE, YOU CAN'T CHANGE AROREE. SHE'S A BACKSTAB...
NO!
MAYBE I'M MAD TOO, BUT I KNOW SHE MEANT NO HARM!
WELL, MEANT OR NOT, THE HARM'S BEEN DONE. IF DEWSHINE AND WINDKIN ARE PRISONERS INSIDE BLUE MOUNTAIN --
-- THEN THE SOONER WE CAUSE WINNOWILL TROUBLE OUTSIDE, THE BETTER!

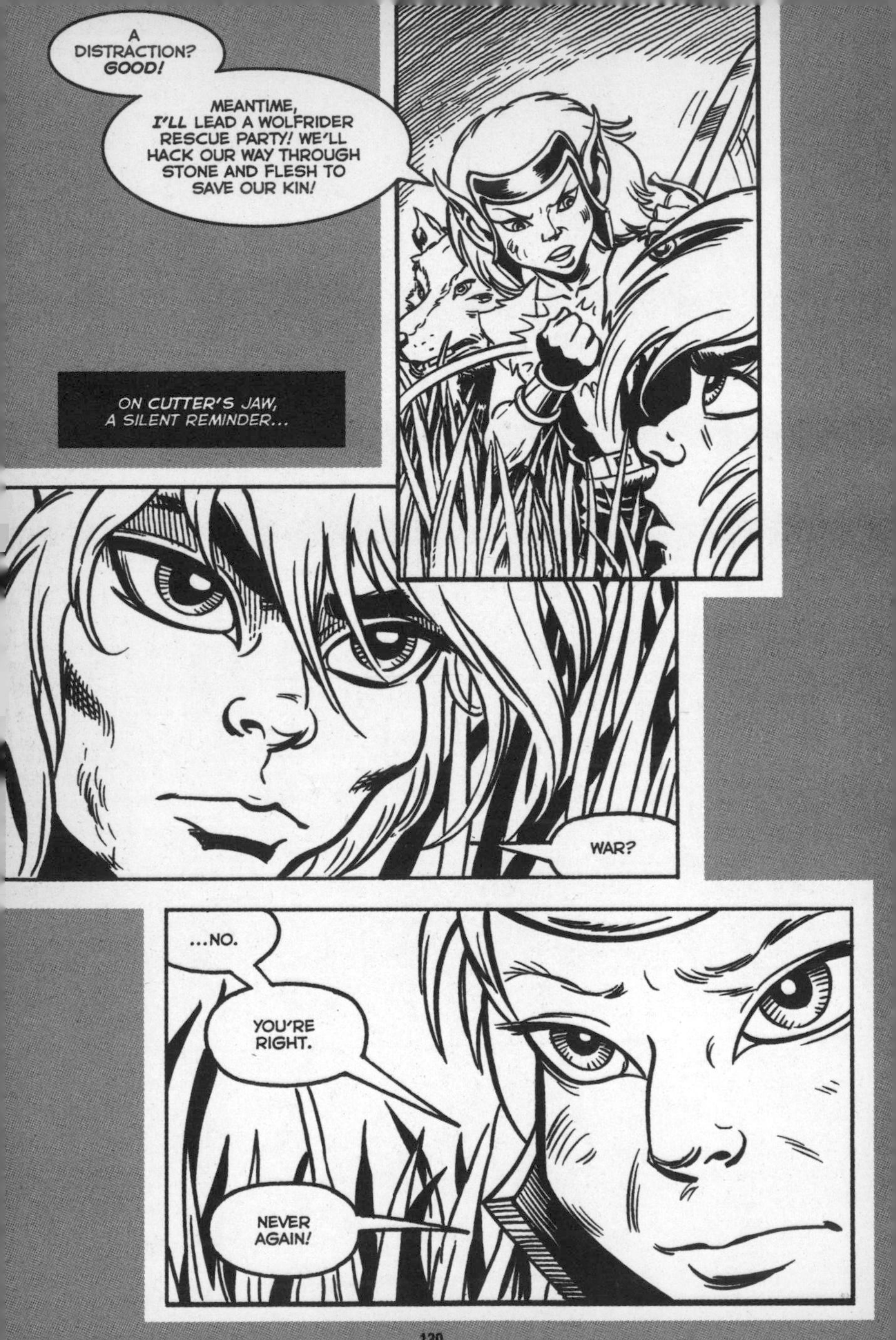
A DISTRACTION? GOOD!
MEANTIME, I'LL LEAD A WOLFRIDER RESCUE PARTY! WE'LL HACK OUR WAY THROUGH STONE AND FLESH TO SAVE OUR KIN!
ON CUTTER'S JAW, A SILENT REMINDER...
WAR?
...NO.
YOU'RE RIGHT.
NEVER AGAIN!

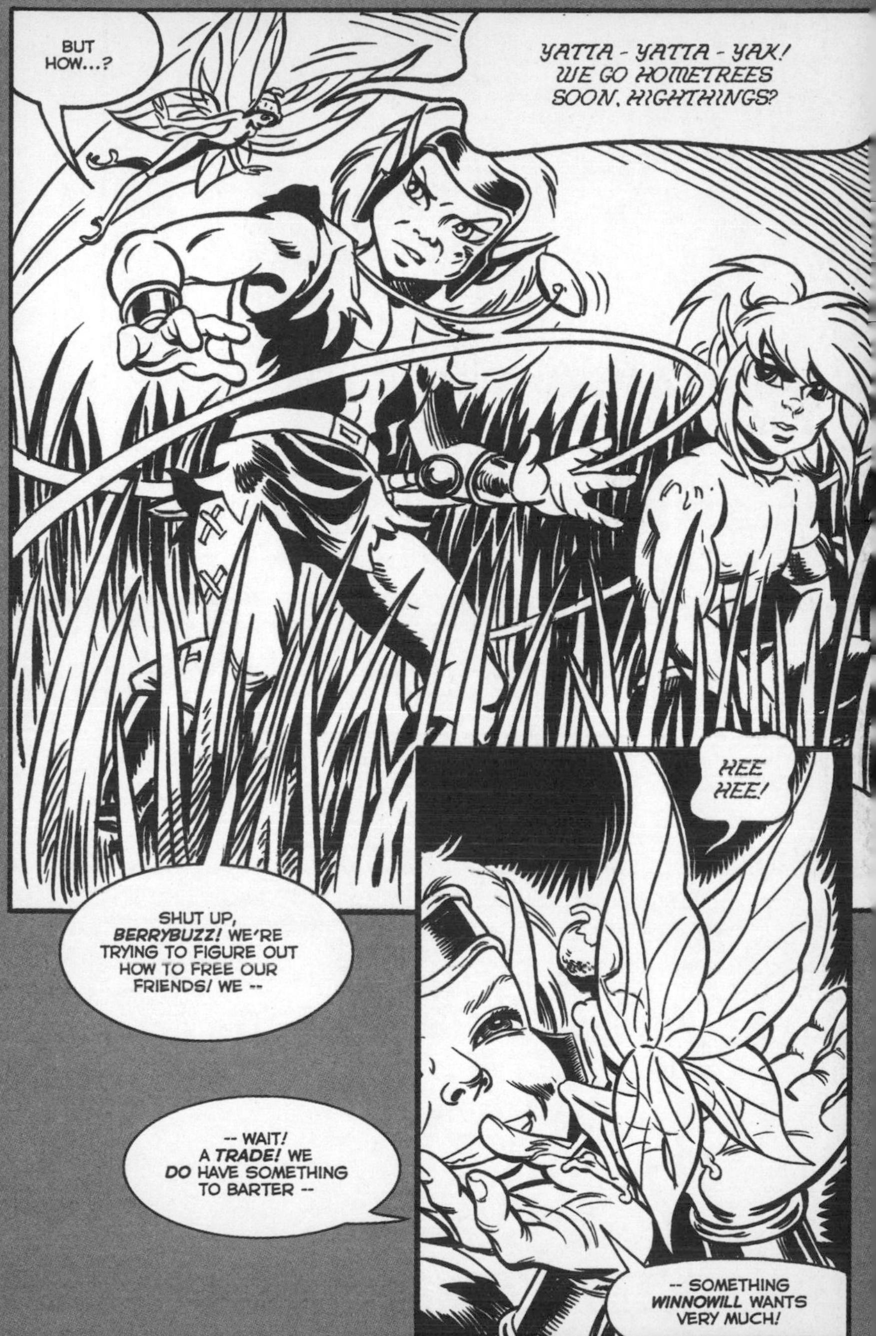
BUT HOW...?
YATTA - YATTA - YAK! WE GO HOMETREES SOON, HIGHTHINGS?
SHUT UP, *BERRYBUZZ!* WE'RE TRYING TO FIGURE OUT HOW TO FREE OUR FRIENDS! WE --
HEE HEE!
-- WAIT! A *TRADE!* WE *DO* HAVE SOMETHING TO BARTER --
-- SOMETHING *WINNOWILL* WANTS VERY MUCH!

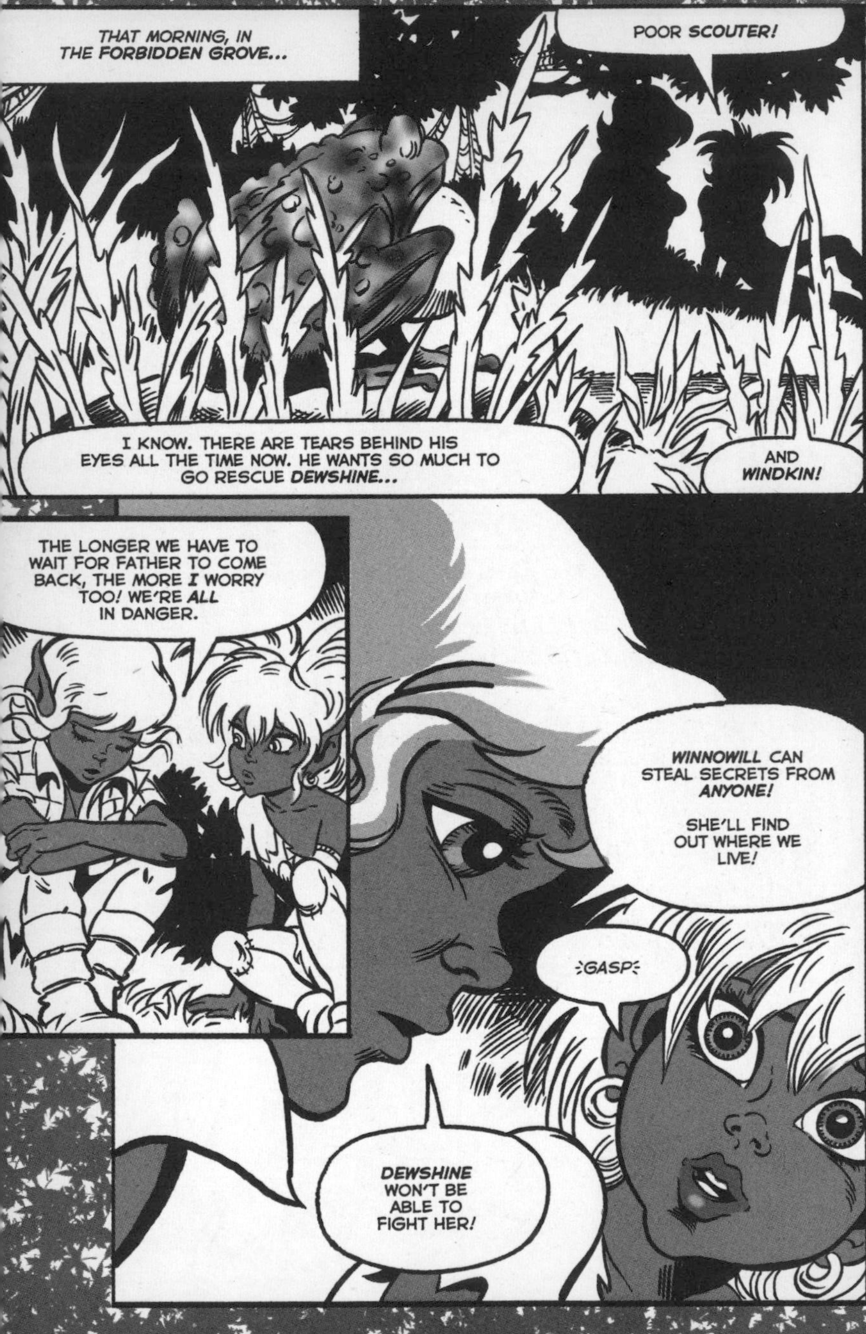
THAT MORNING, IN THE FORBIDDEN GROVE...
POOR SCOUTER!
I KNOW. THERE ARE TEARS BEHIND HIS EYES ALL THE TIME NOW. HE WANTS SO MUCH TO GO RESCUE DEWSHINE...
AND WINDKIN!
THE LONGER WE HAVE TO WAIT FOR FATHER TO COME BACK, THE MORE I WORRY TOO! WE'RE ALL IN DANGER.
WINNOWILL CAN STEAL SECRETS FROM ANYONE!
SHE'LL FIND OUT WHERE WE LIVE!
GASP
DEWSHINE WON'T BE ABLE TO FIGHT HER!

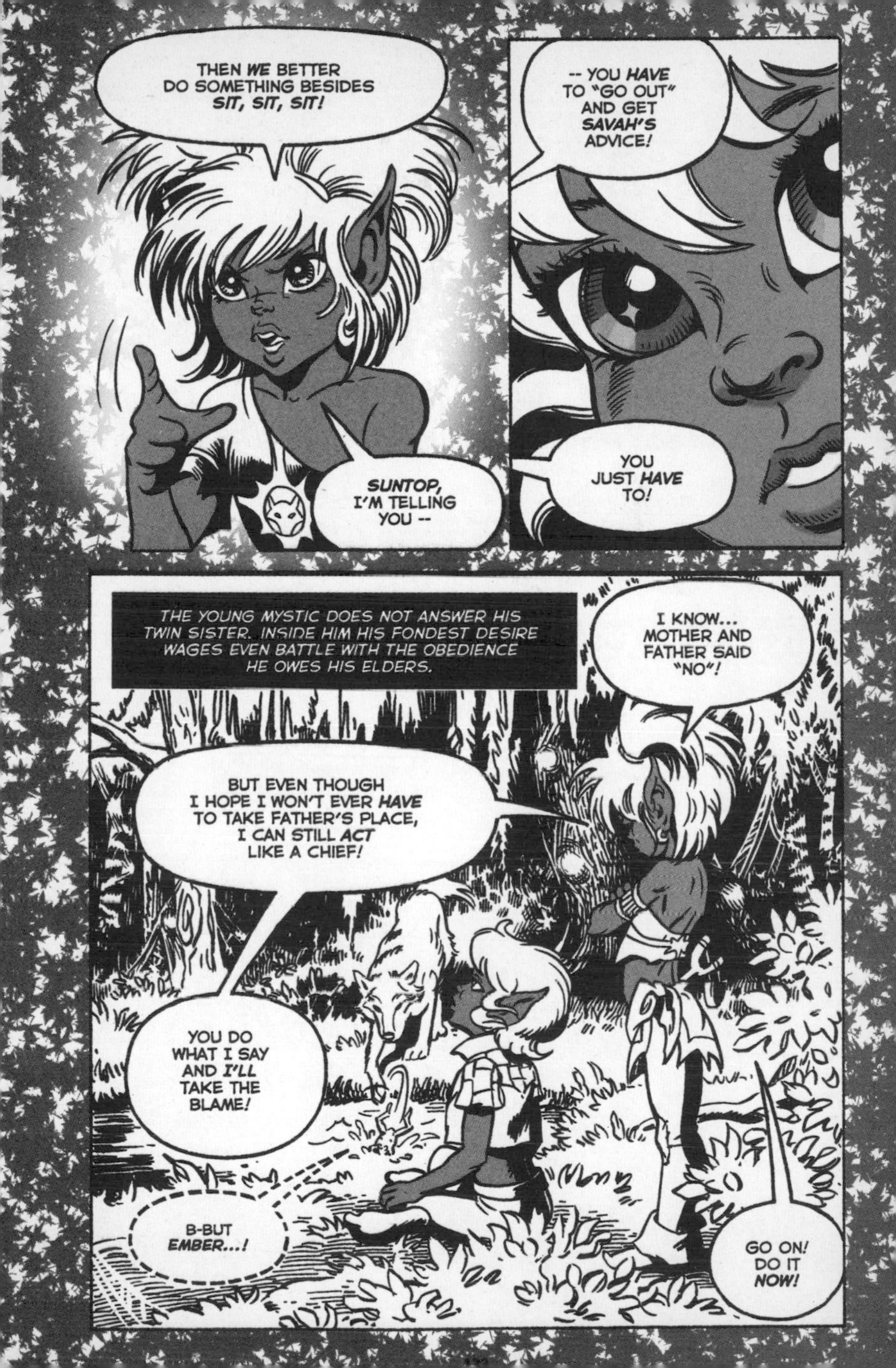
THEN WE BETTER DO SOMETHING BESIDES SIT, SIT, SIT!
SUNTOP, I'M TELLING YOU --
-- YOU HAVE TO "GO OUT" AND GET SAVAH'S ADVICE!
YOU JUST HAVE TO!
THE YOUNG MYSTIC DOES NOT ANSWER HIS TWIN SISTER. INSIDE HIM HIS FONDEST DESIRE WAGES EVEN BATTLE WITH THE OBEDIENCE HE OWES HIS ELDERS.
I KNOW... MOTHER AND FATHER SAID "NO"!
BUT EVEN THOUGH I HOPE I WON'T EVER HAVE TO TAKE FATHER'S PLACE, I CAN STILL ACT LIKE A CHIEF!
YOU DO WHAT I SAY AND I'LL TAKE THE BLAME!
B-BUT EMBER...!
GO ON! DO IT NOW!

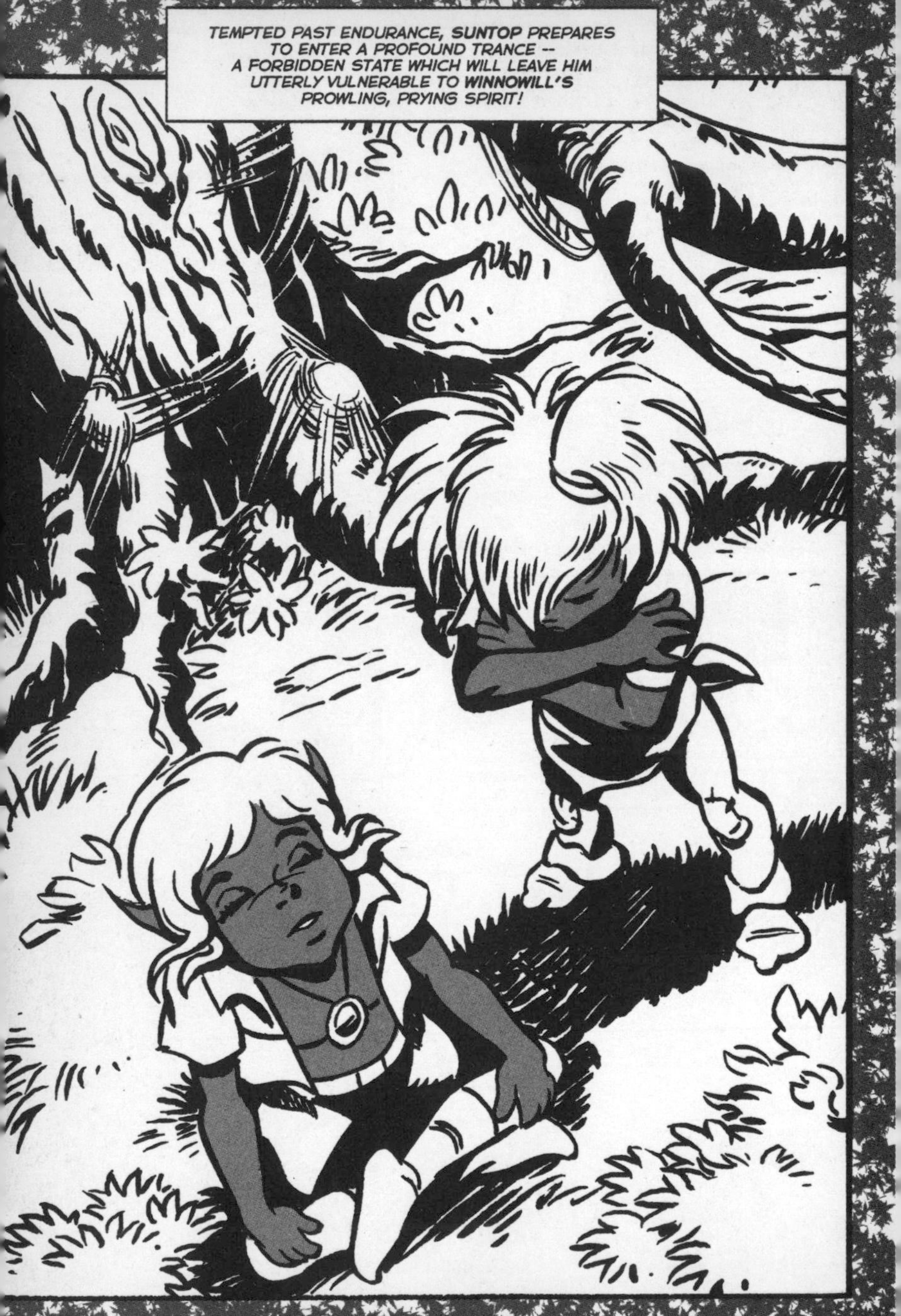
TEMPTED PAST ENDURANCE, SUNTOP PREPARES TO ENTER A PROFOUND TRANCE -- A FORBIDDEN STATE WHICH WILL LEAVE HIM UTTERLY VULNERABLE TO WINNOWILL'S PROWLING, PRYING SPIRIT!

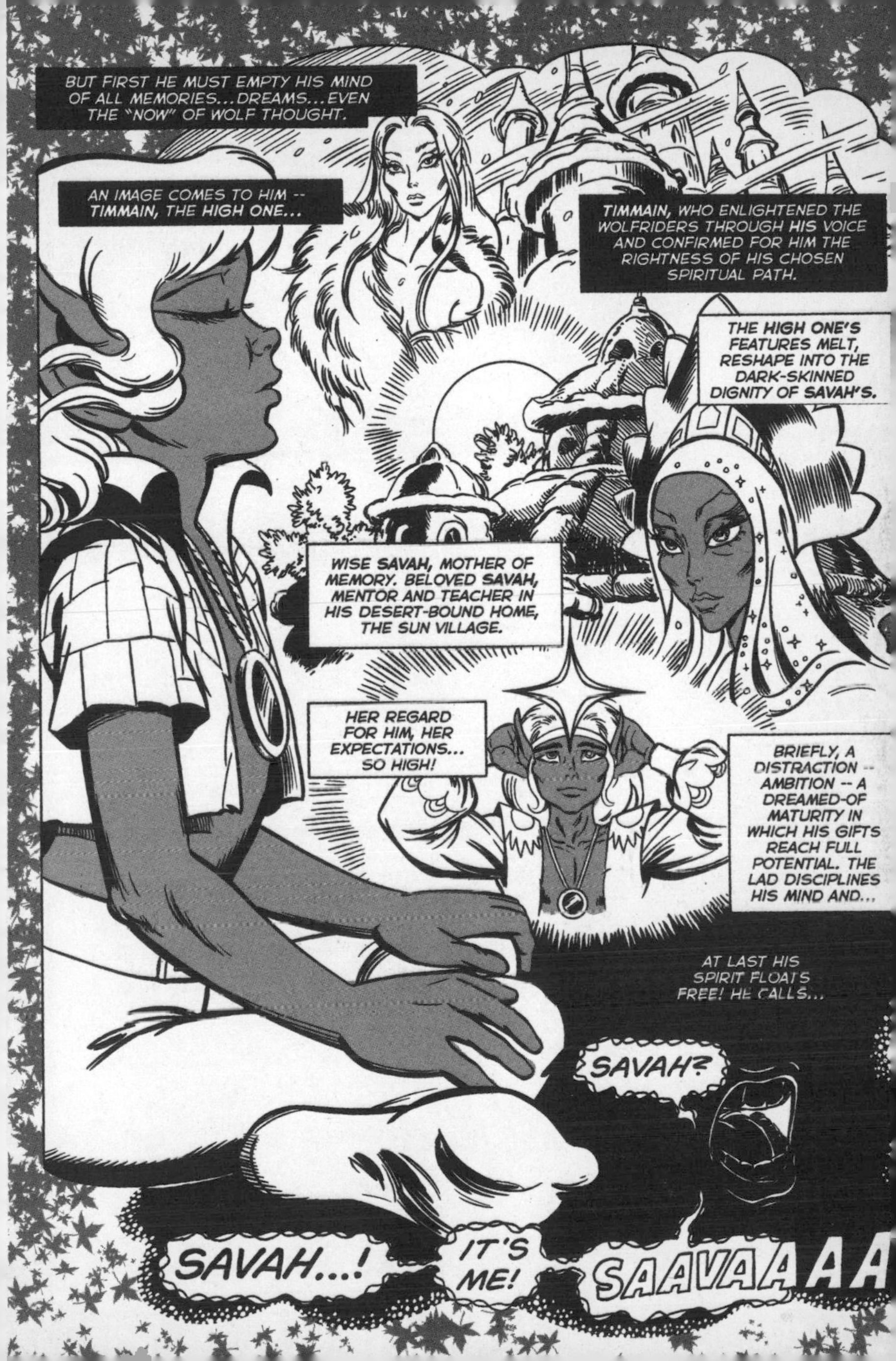
BUT FIRST HE MUST EMPTY HIS MIND OF ALL MEMORIES... DREAMS... EVEN THE "NOW" OF WOLF THOUGHT.
AN IMAGE COMES TO HIM -- TIMMAIN, THE HIGH ONE...
TIMMAIN, WHO ENLIGHTENED THE WOLFRIDERS THROUGH HIS VOICE AND CONFIRMED FOR HIM THE RIGHTNESS OF HIS CHOSEN SPIRITUAL PATH.
THE HIGH ONE'S FEATURES MELT, RESHAPE INTO THE DARK-SKINNED DIGNITY OF SAVAH'S.
WISE SAVAH, MOTHER OF MEMORY. BELOVED SAVAH, MENTOR AND TEACHER IN HIS DESERT-BOUND HOME, THE SUN VILLAGE.
HER REGARD FOR HIM, HER EXPECTATIONS... SO HIGH!
BRIEFLY, A DISTRACTION -- AMBITION -- A DREAMED-OF MATURITY IN WHICH HIS GIFTS REACH FULL POTENTIAL. THE LAD DISCIPLINES HIS MIND AND...
AT LAST HIS SPIRIT FLOATS FREE! HE CALLS...
SAVAH?
SAVAH...!
IT'S ME!
SAAVAAAAA

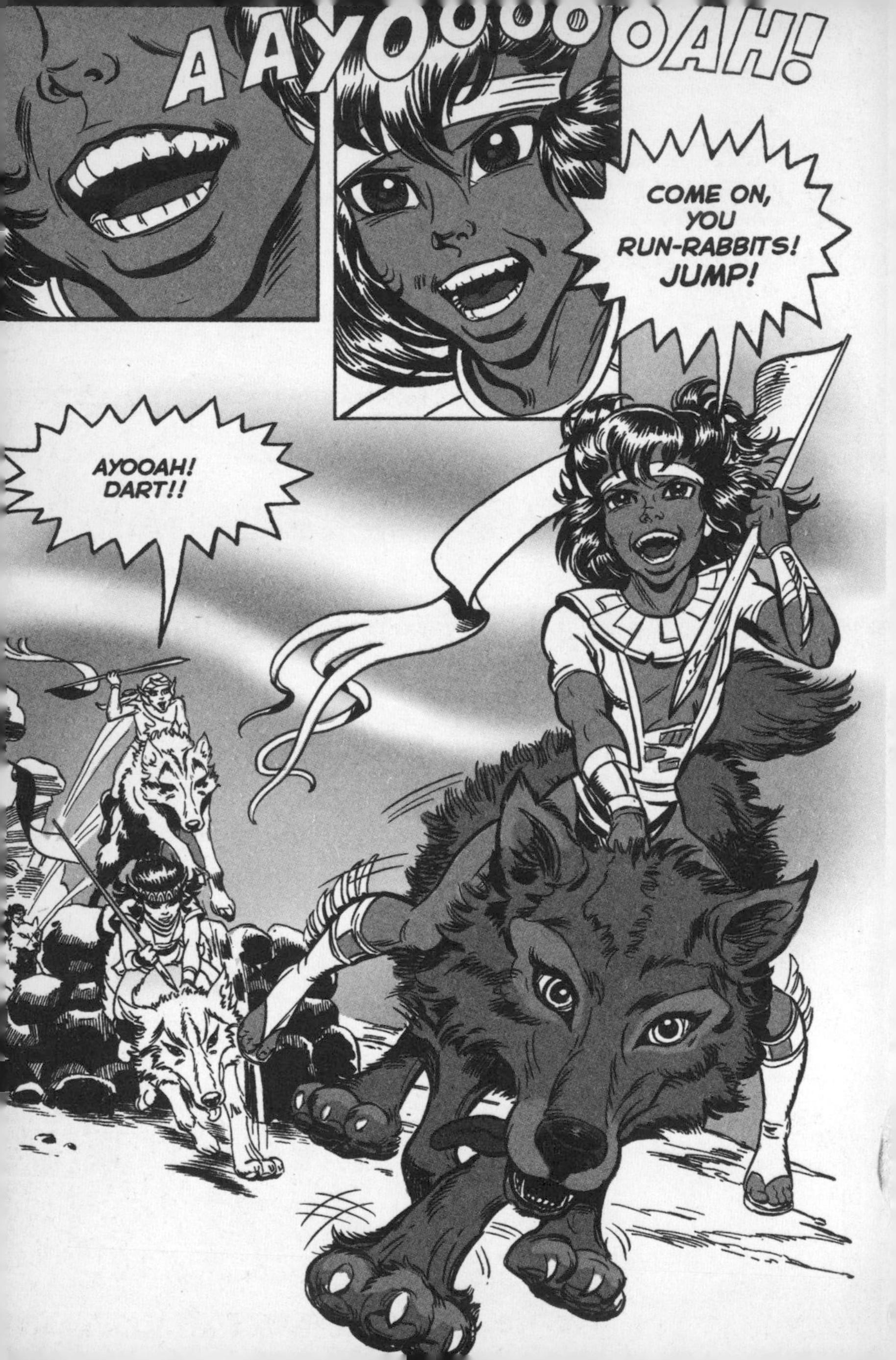
A AYOOOOOOAH!
COME ON, YOU RUN-RABBITS! JUMP!
AYOOAH! DART!!

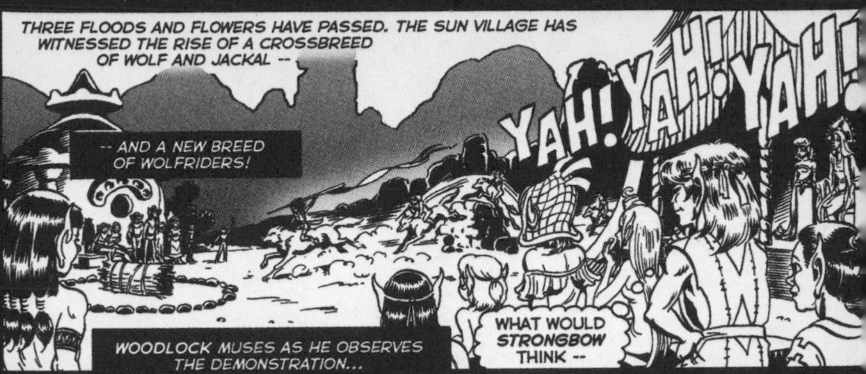
THREE FLOODS AND FLOWERS HAVE PASSED. THE SUN VILLAGE HAS WITNESSED THE RISE OF A CROSSBREED OF WOLF AND JACKAL --
-- AND A NEW BREED OF WOLFRIDERS!
YAH! YAH! YAH!
WOODLOCK MUSES AS HE OBSERVES THE DEMONSTRATION...
WHAT WOULD STRONGBOW THINK --

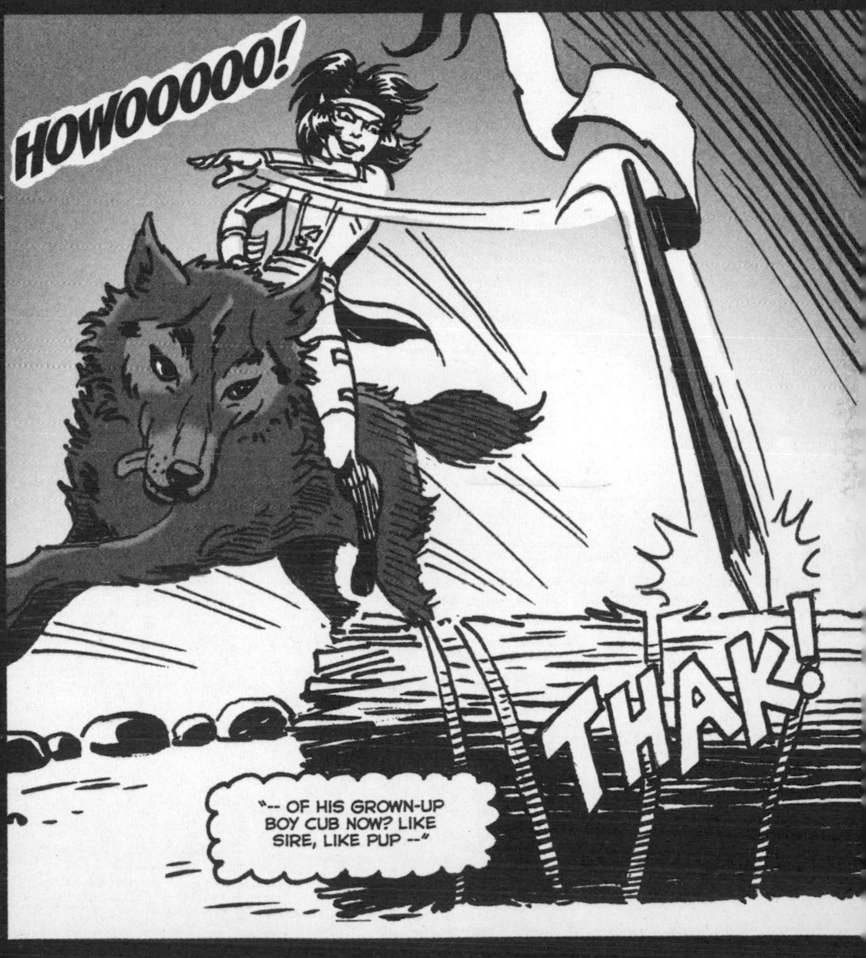
HOWOOOOO!
THAK!
"-- OF HIS GROWN-UP BOY CUB NOW? LIKE SIRE, LIKE PUP --"

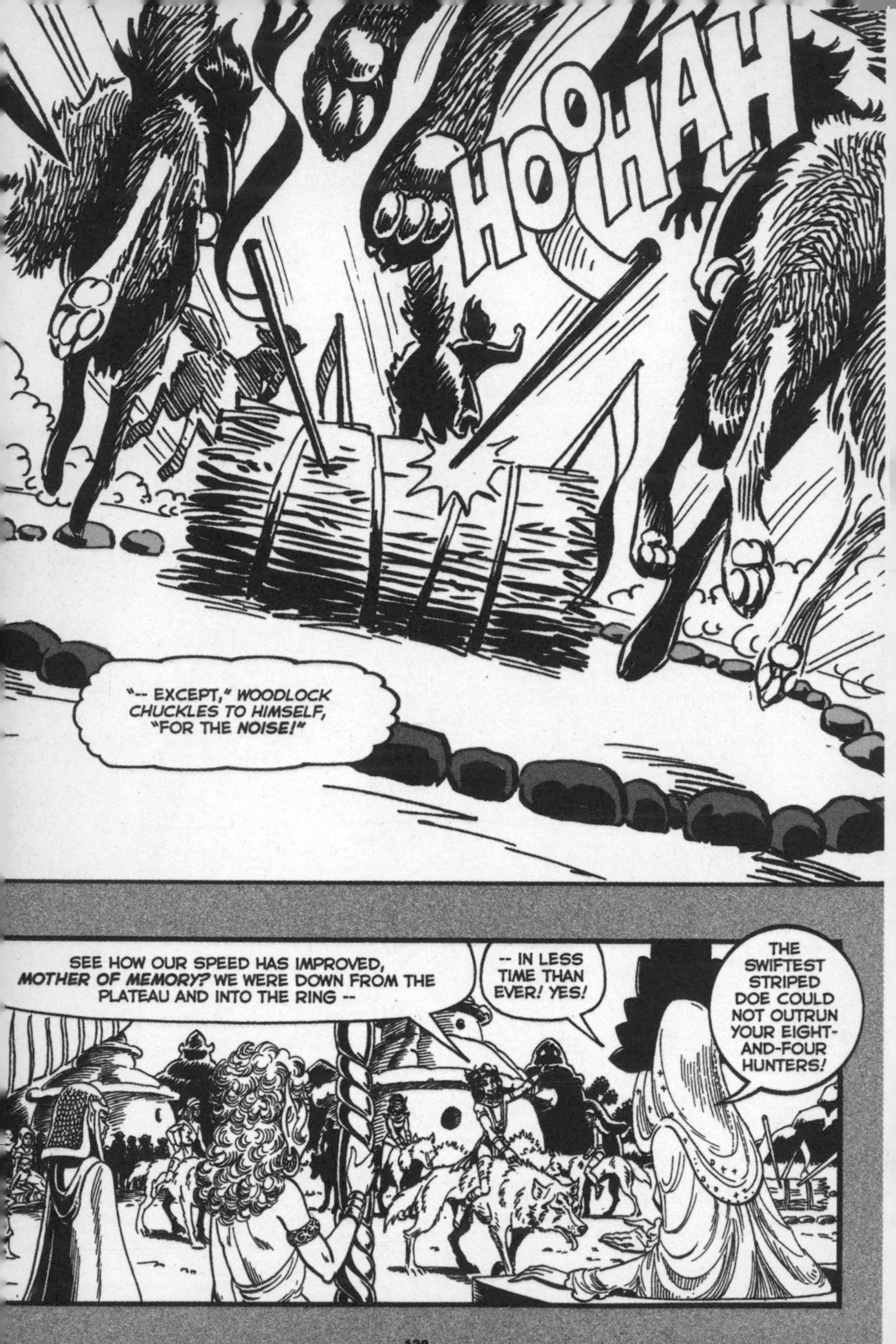
HOOHAH
"-- EXCEPT," WOODLOCK CHUCKLES TO HIMSELF, "FOR THE NOISE!"
SEE HOW OUR SPEED HAS IMPROVED, MOTHER OF MEMORY? WE WERE DOWN FROM THE PLATEAU AND INTO THE RING --
-- IN LESS TIME THAN EVER! YES!
THE SWIFTEST STRIPED DOE COULD NOT OUTRUN YOUR EIGHT-AND-FOUR HUNTERS!

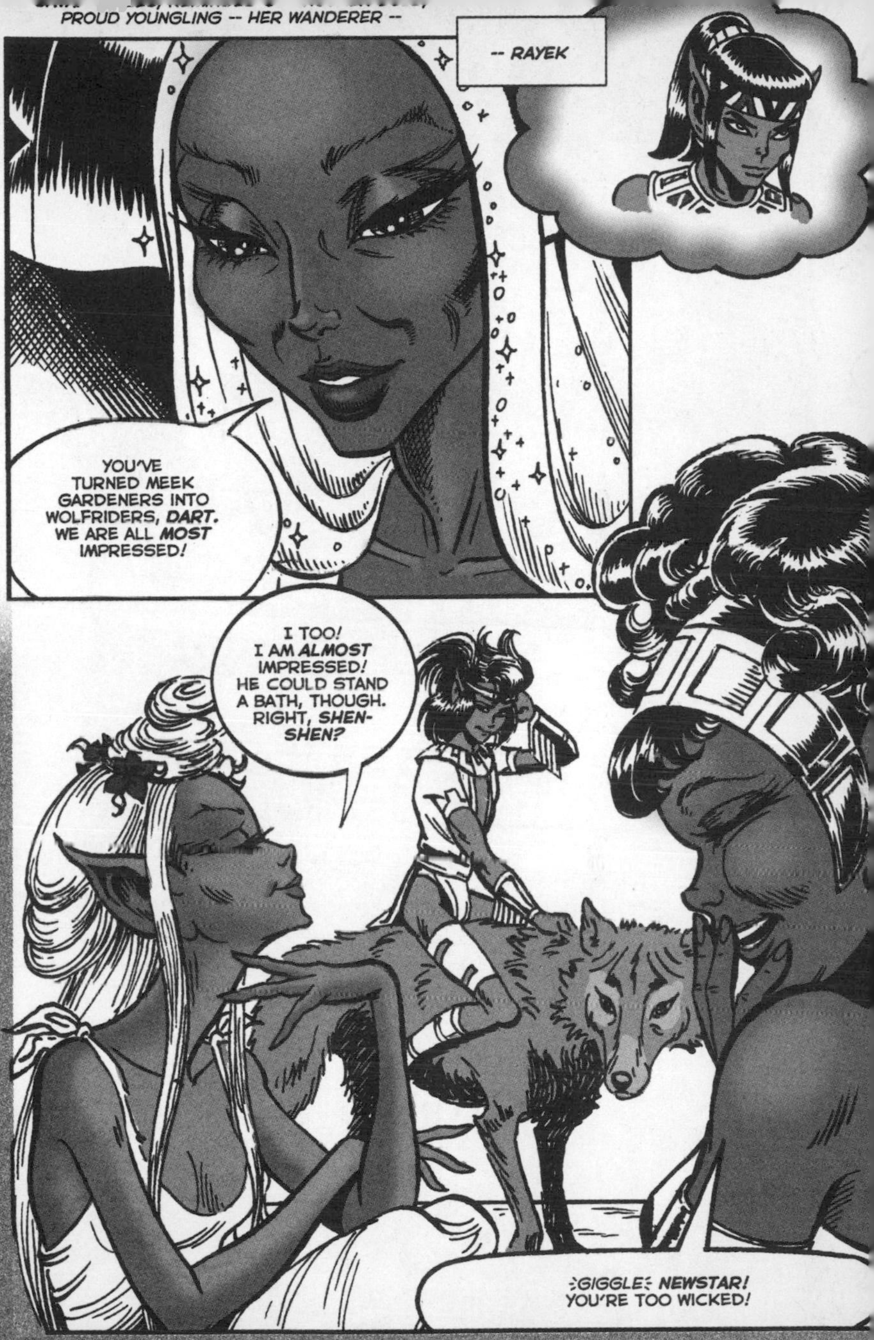
PROUD YOUNGLING -- HER WANDERER --
-- RAYEK
YOU'VE TURNED MEEK GARDENERS INTO WOLFRIDERS, DART. WE ARE ALL MOST IMPRESSED!
I TOO! I AM ALMOST IMPRESSED! HE COULD STAND A BATH, THOUGH. RIGHT, SHEN-SHEN?
:GIGGLE: NEWSTAR! YOU'RE TOO WICKED!

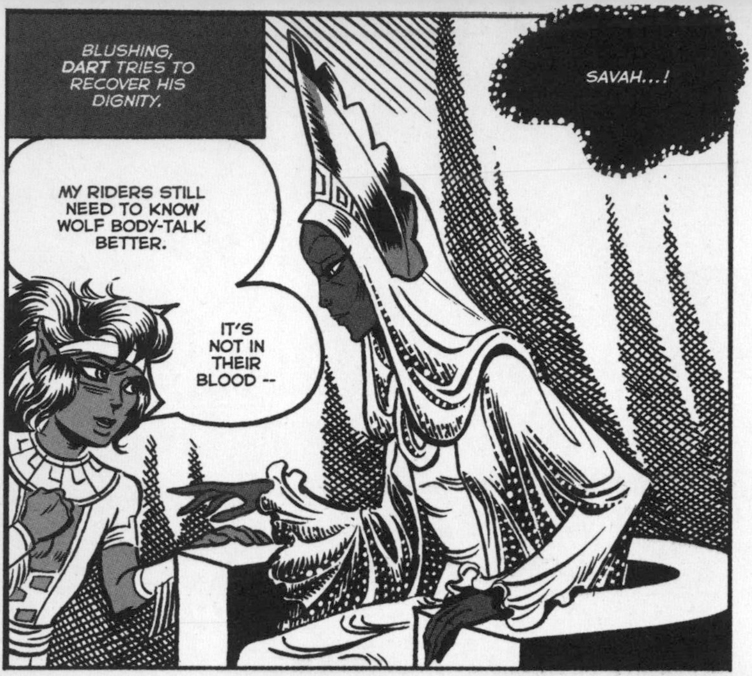
BLUSHING, DART TRIES TO RECOVER HIS DIGNITY.
SAVAH...!
MY RIDERS STILL NEED TO KNOW WOLF BODY-TALK BETTER.
IT'S NOT IN THEIR BLOOD --

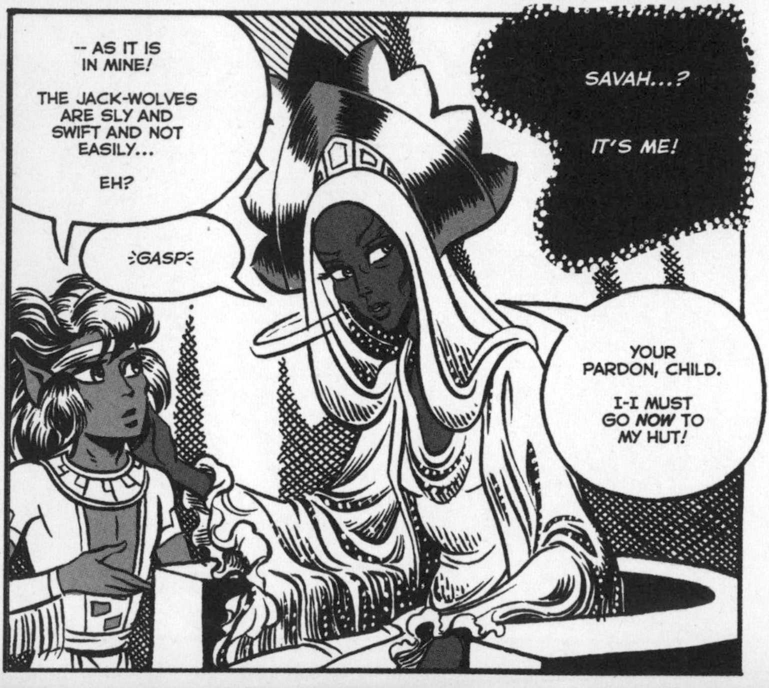
-- AS IT IS IN MINE!
THE JACK-WOLVES ARE SLY AND SWIFT AND NOT EASILY...
EH?
SAVAH...?
IT'S ME!
GASP
YOUR PARDON, CHILD.
I-I MUST GO NOW TO MY HUT!

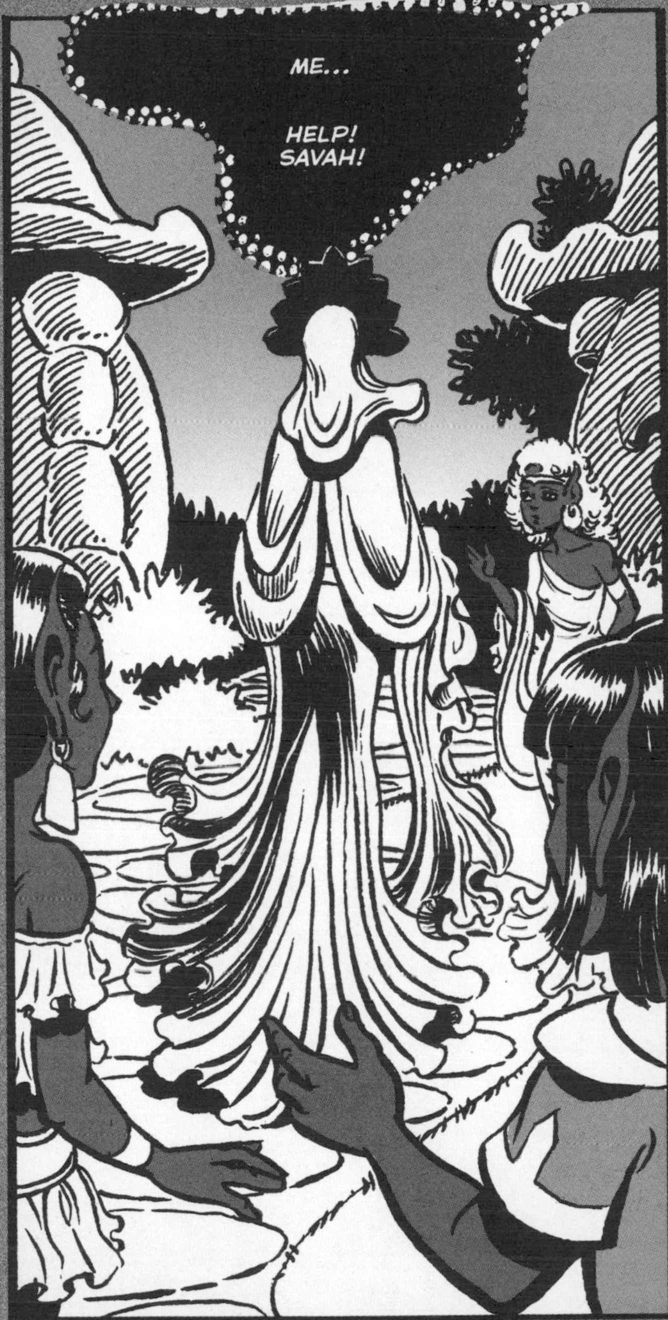
ME...
HELP! SAVAH!

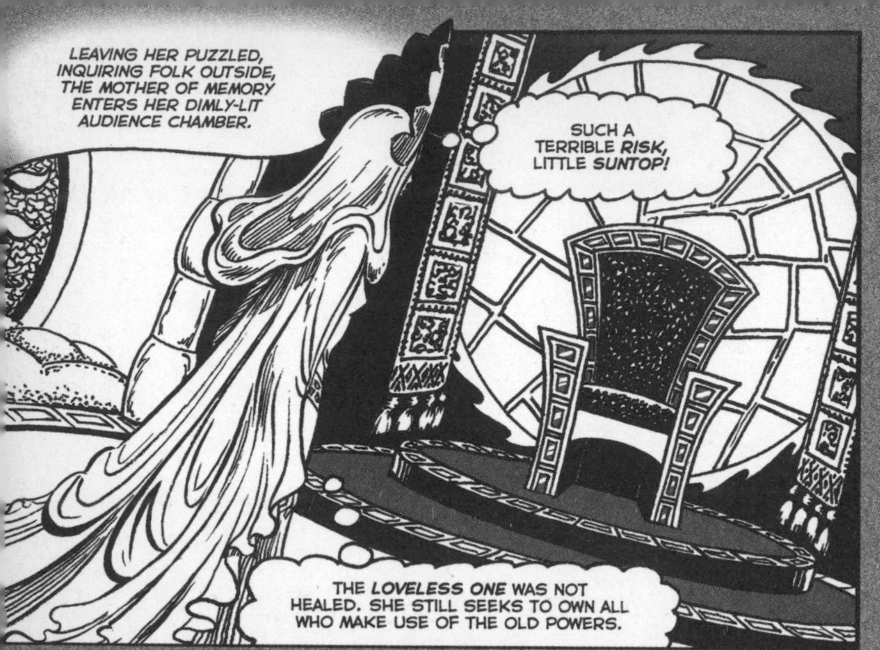
LEAVING HER PUZZLED, INQUIRING FOLK OUTSIDE, THE MOTHER OF MEMORY ENTERS HER DIMLY-LIT AUDIENCE CHAMBER.
SUCH A TERRIBLE *RISK*, LITTLE *SUNTOP!*
THE *LOVELESS ONE* WAS NOT HEALED. SHE STILL SEEKS TO OWN ALL WHO MAKE USE OF THE OLD POWERS.

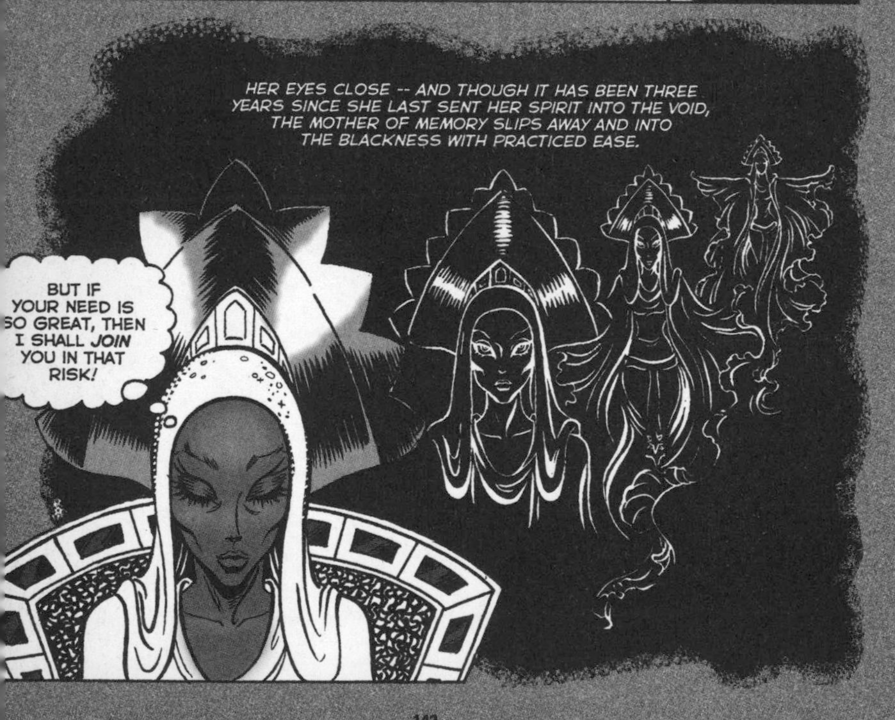
HER EYES CLOSE -- AND THOUGH IT HAS BEEN THREE YEARS SINCE SHE LAST SENT HER SPIRIT INTO THE VOID, THE MOTHER OF MEMORY SLIPS AWAY AND INTO THE BLACKNESS WITH PRACTICED EASE.
BUT IF YOUR NEED IS SO GREAT, THEN I SHALL *JOIN* YOU IN THAT RISK!

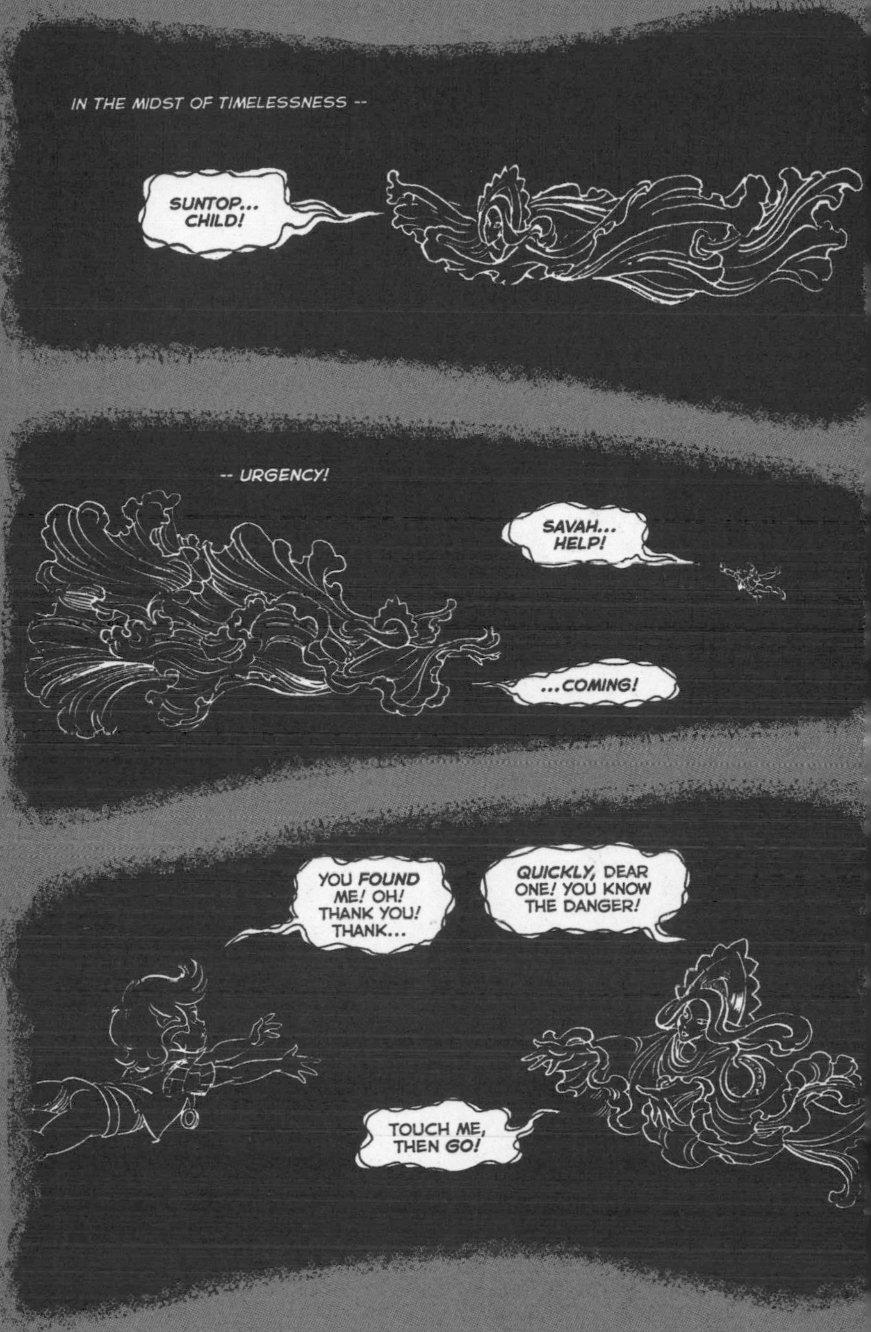
IN THE MIDST OF TIMELESSNESS --
SUNTOP... CHILD!
-- URGENCY!
SAVAH... HELP!
...COMING!
YOU FOUND ME! OH! THANK YOU! THANK...
QUICKLY, DEAR ONE! YOU KNOW THE DANGER!
TOUCH ME, THEN GO!

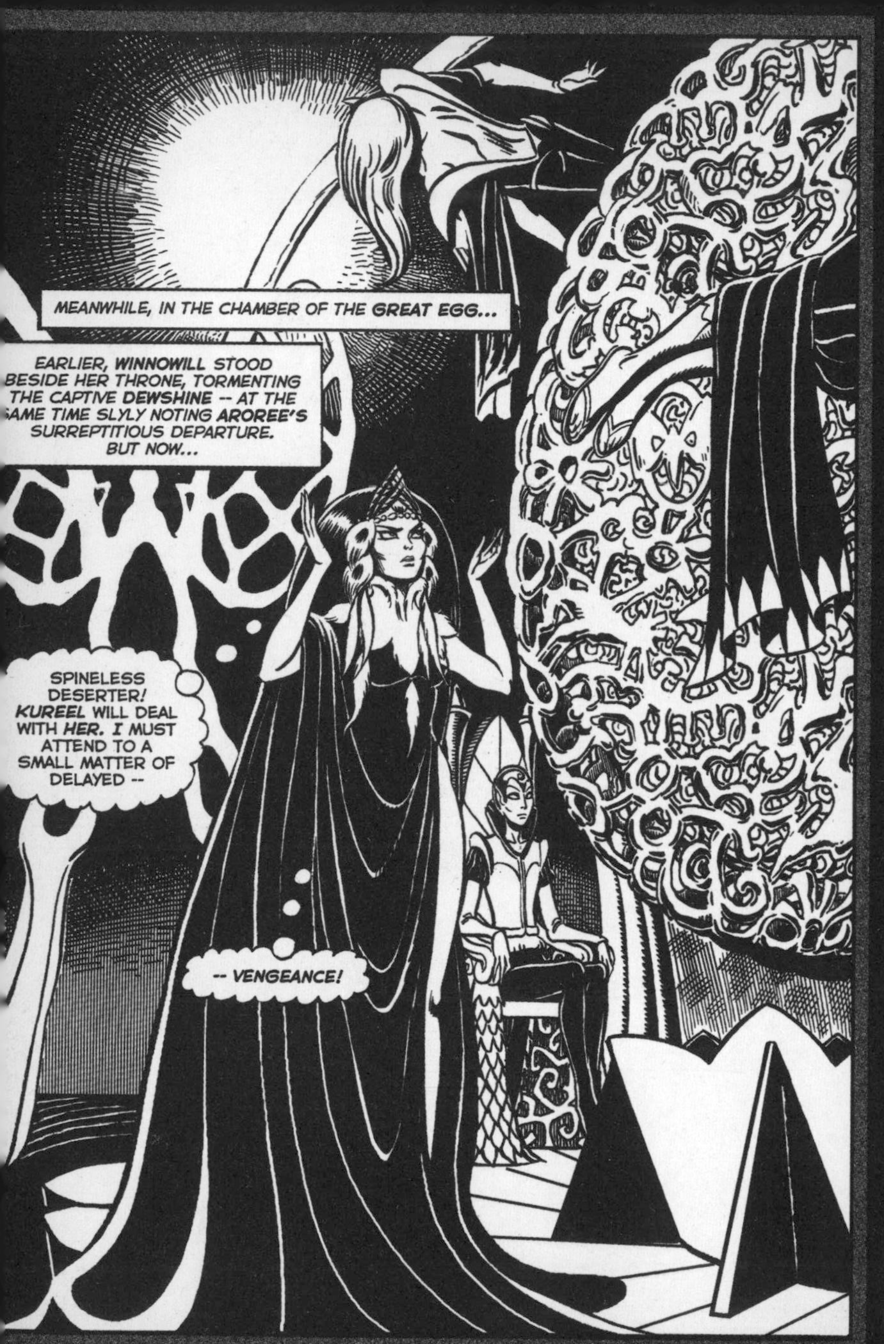
MEANWHILE, IN THE CHAMBER OF THE GREAT EGG...
EARLIER, WINNOWILL STOOD BESIDE HER THRONE, TORMENTING THE CAPTIVE DEWSHINE -- AT THE SAME TIME SLYLY NOTING AROREE'S SURREPTITIOUS DEPARTURE. BUT NOW...
SPINELESS DESERTER! KUREEL WILL DEAL WITH HER. I MUST ATTEND TO A SMALL MATTER OF DELAYED --
-- VENGEANCE!

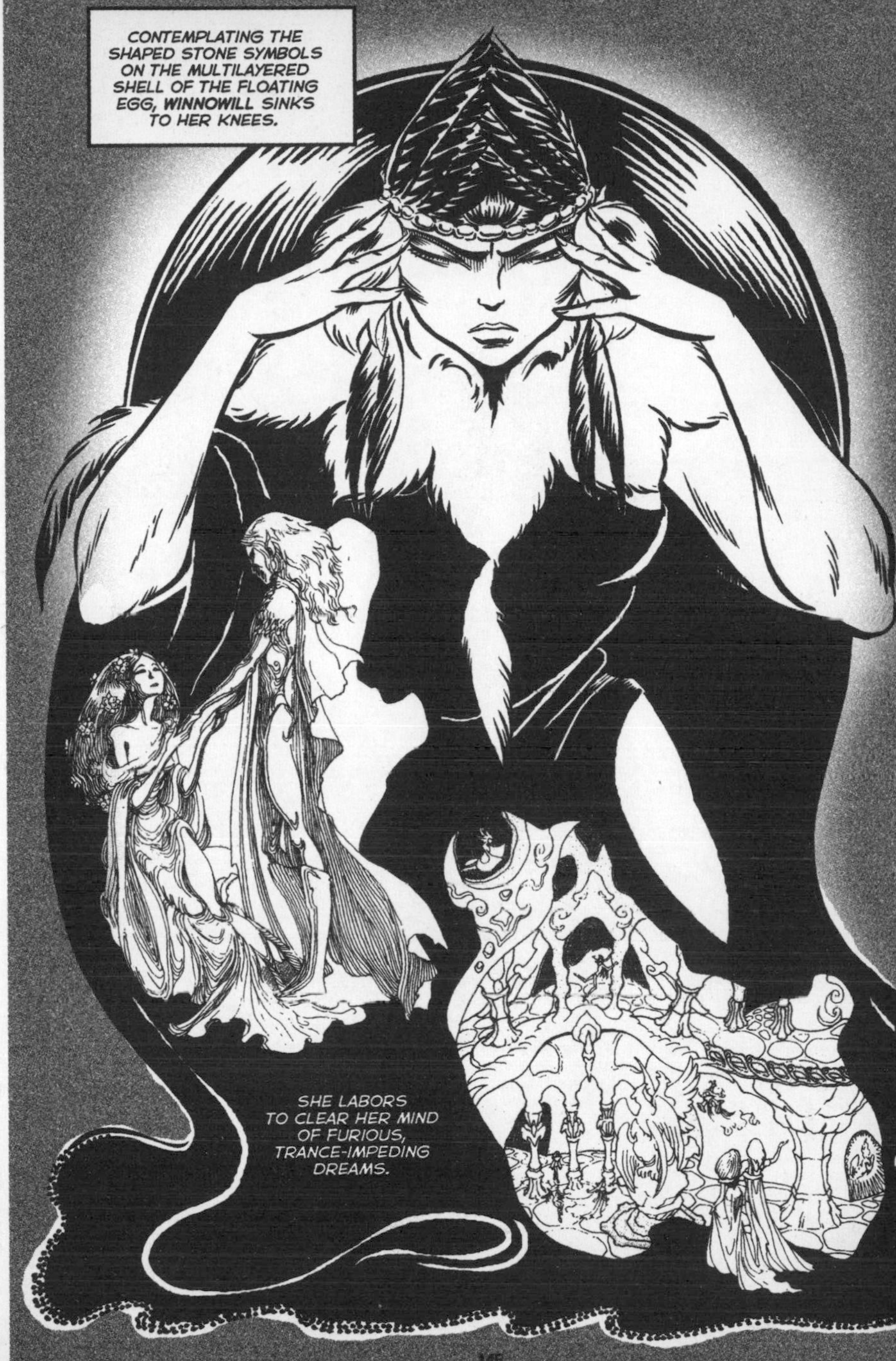
CONTEMPLATING THE SHAPED STONE SYMBOLS ON THE MULTILAYERED SHELL OF THE FLOATING EGG, WINNOWILL SINKS TO HER KNEES.
SHE LABORS TO CLEAR HER MIND OF FURIOUS, TRANCE-IMPEDING DREAMS.

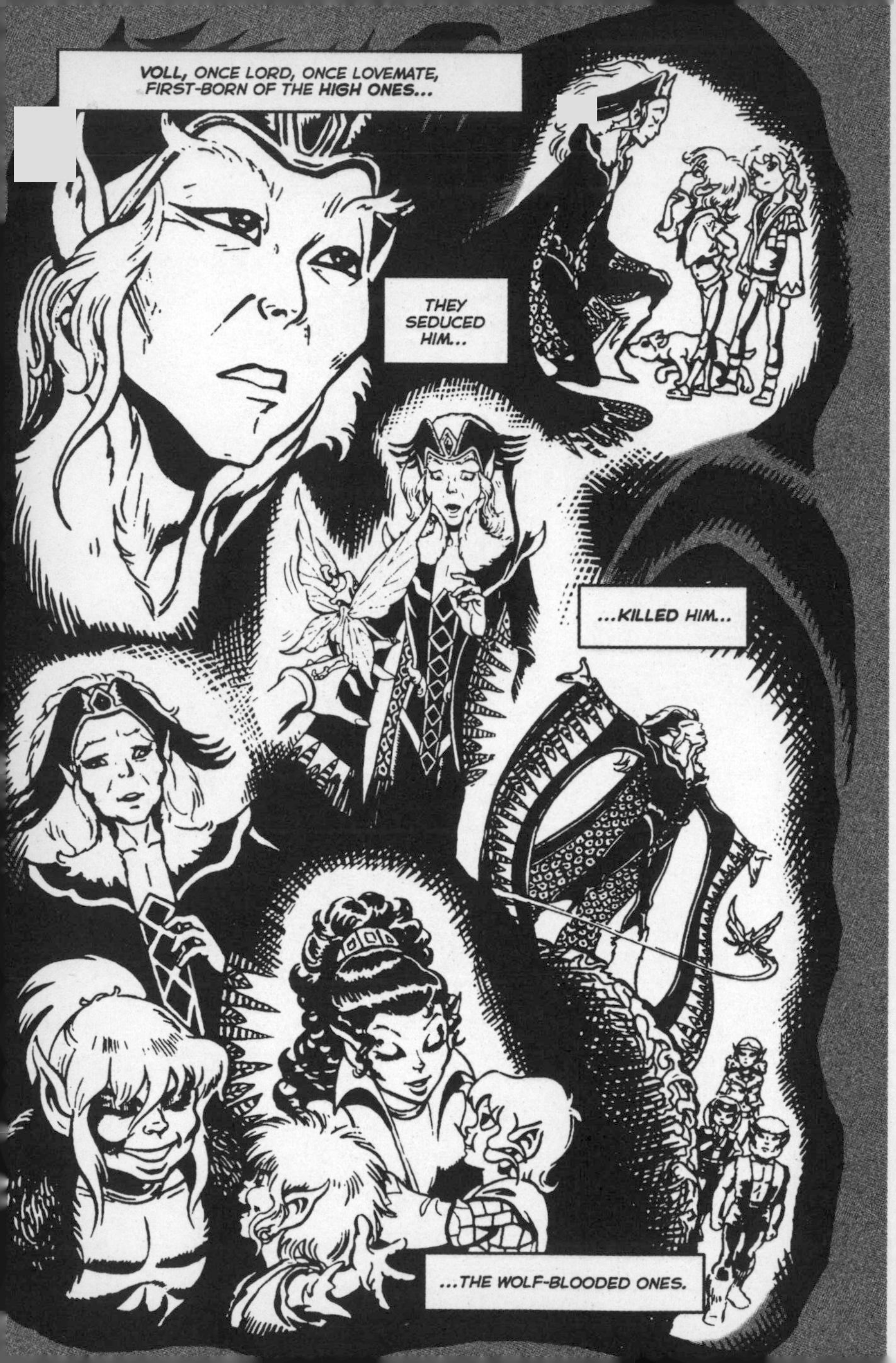
VOLL, ONCE LORD, ONCE LOVEMATE, FIRST-BORN OF THE HIGH ONES...
THEY SEDUCED HIM...
...KILLED HIM...
...THE WOLF-BLOODED ONES.

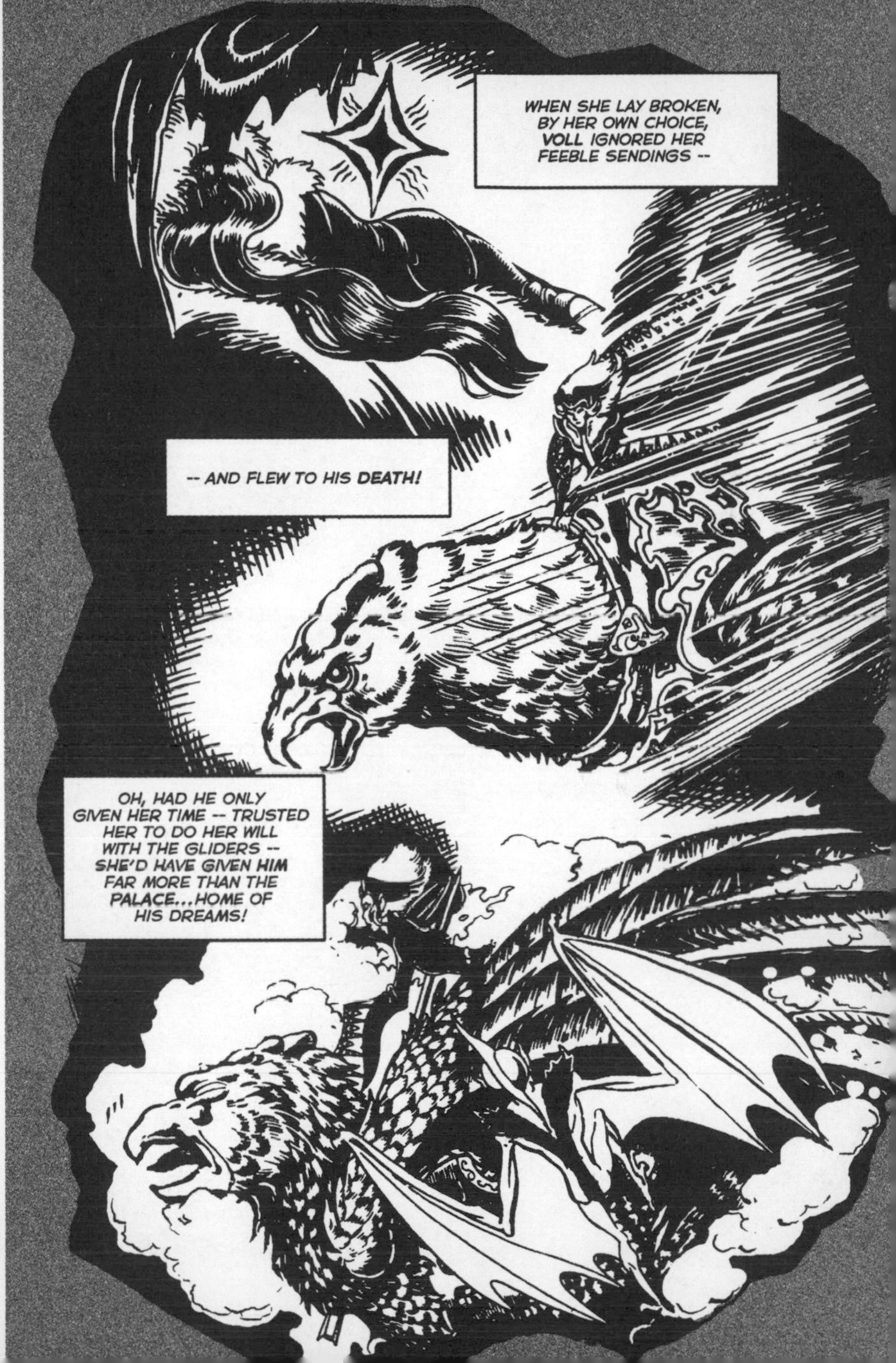
WHEN SHE LAY BROKEN, BY HER OWN CHOICE, VOLL IGNORED HER FEEBLE SENDINGS --
-- AND FLEW TO HIS DEATH!
OH, HAD HE ONLY GIVEN HER TIME -- TRUSTED HER TO DO HER WILL WITH THE GLIDERS -- SHE'D HAVE GIVEN HIM FAR MORE THAN THE PALACE...HOME OF HIS DREAMS!

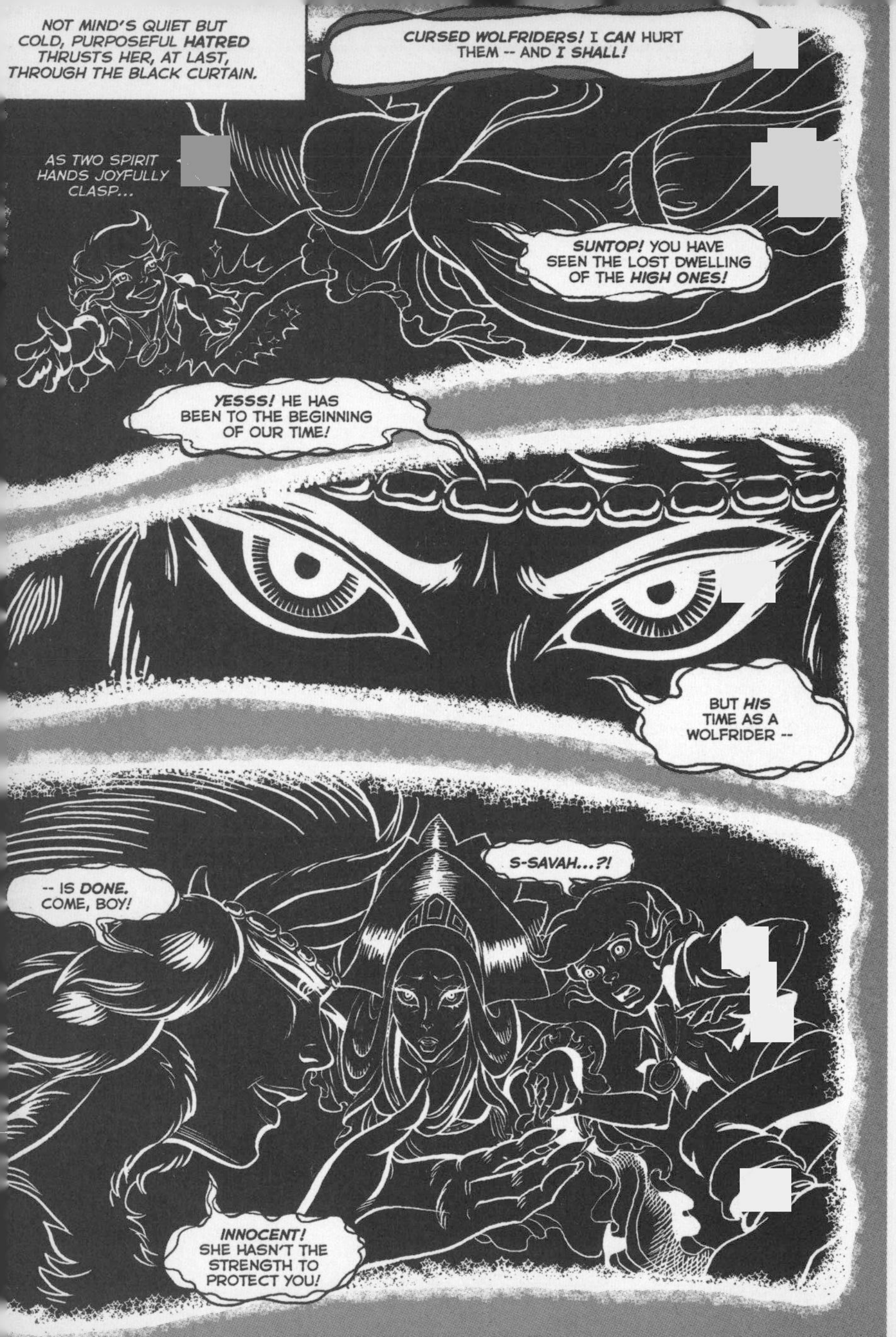
NOT MIND'S QUIET BUT COLD, PURPOSEFUL HATRED THRUSTS HER, AT LAST, THROUGH THE BLACK CURTAIN.
CURSED WOLFRIDERS! I CAN HURT THEM -- AND I SHALL!
AS TWO SPIRIT HANDS JOYFULLY CLASP...
SUNTOP! YOU HAVE SEEN THE LOST DWELLING OF THE HIGH ONES!
YESSS! HE HAS BEEN TO THE BEGINNING OF OUR TIME!
BUT HIS TIME AS A WOLFRIDER --
-- IS DONE. COME, BOY!
S-SAVAH...?!
INNOCENT! SHE HASN'T THE STRENGTH TO PROTECT YOU!

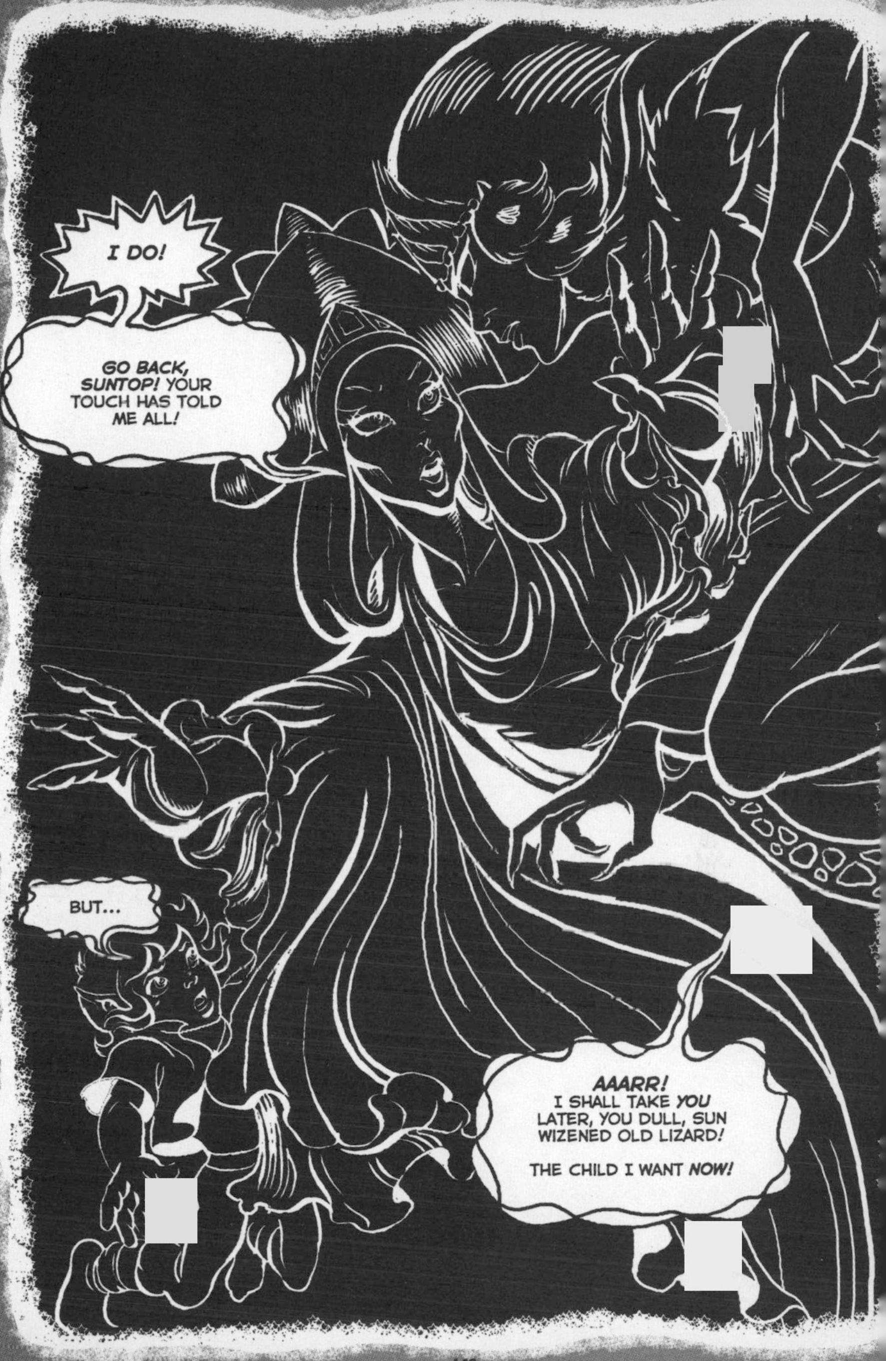
I DO!
GO BACK, SUNTOP! YOUR TOUCH HAS TOLD ME ALL!
BUT...
AAARR! I SHALL TAKE YOU LATER, YOU DULL, SUN WIZENED OLD LIZARD!
THE CHILD I WANT NOW!

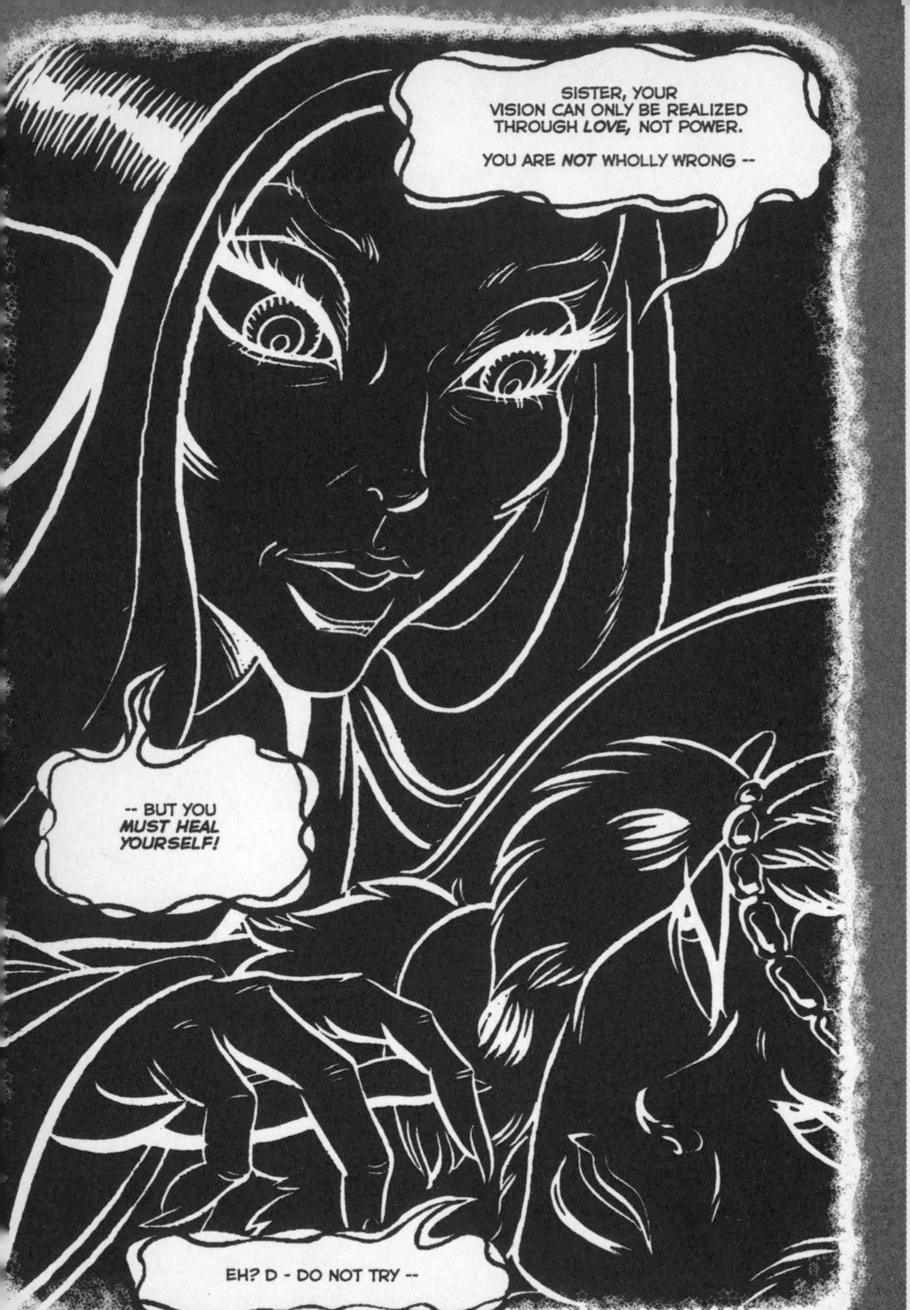

SISTER, YOUR VISION CAN ONLY BE REALIZED THROUGH *LOVE,* NOT POWER.
YOU ARE ***NOT*** WHOLLY WRONG --
-- BUT YOU ***MUST HEAL YOURSELF!***
EH? D - DO NOT TRY --

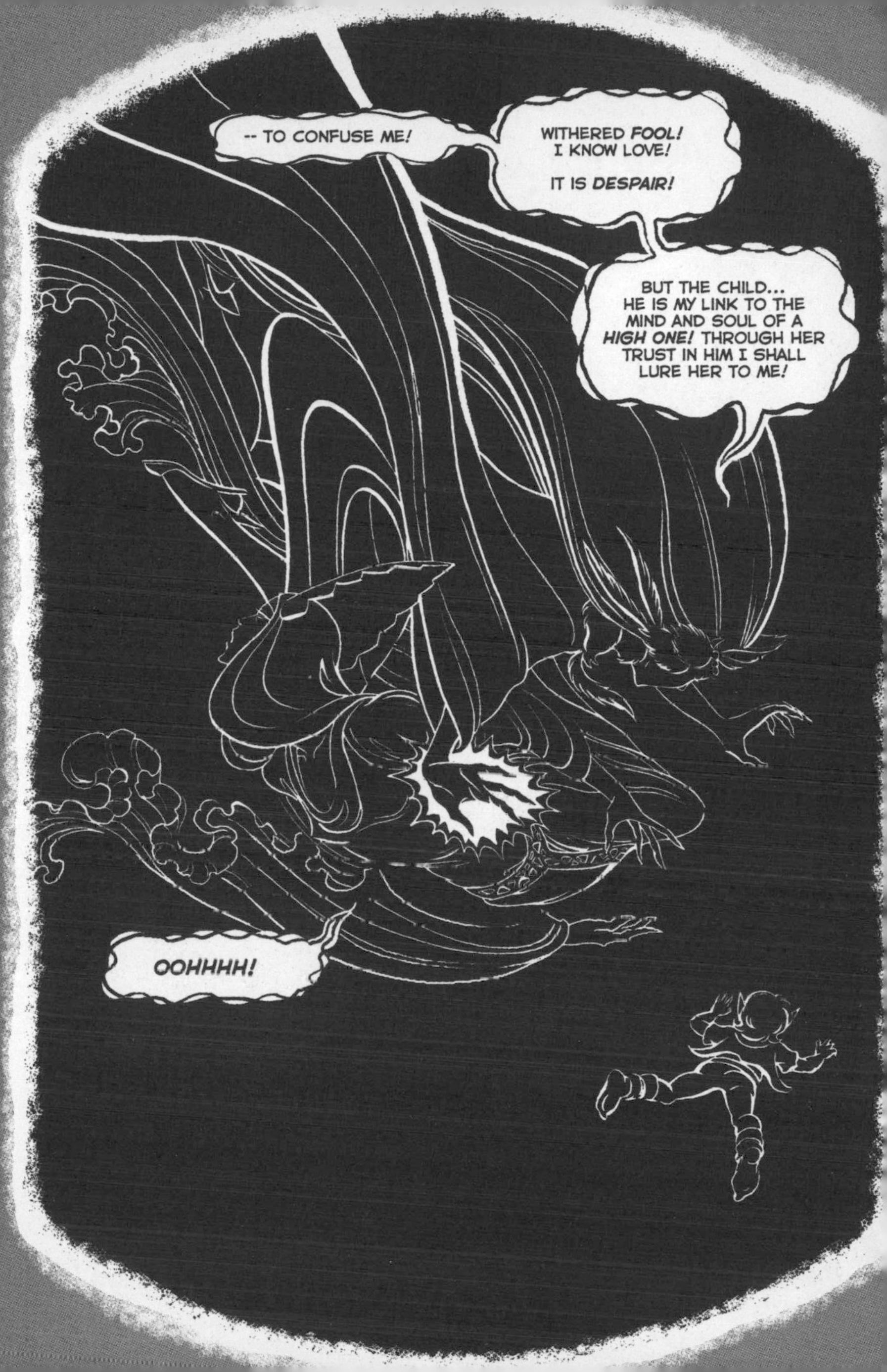
-- TO CONFUSE ME!
WITHERED FOOL! I KNOW LOVE! IT IS DESPAIR!
BUT THE CHILD... HE IS MY LINK TO THE MIND AND SOUL OF A HIGH ONE! THROUGH HER TRUST IN HIM I SHALL LURE HER TO ME!
OOHHHH!

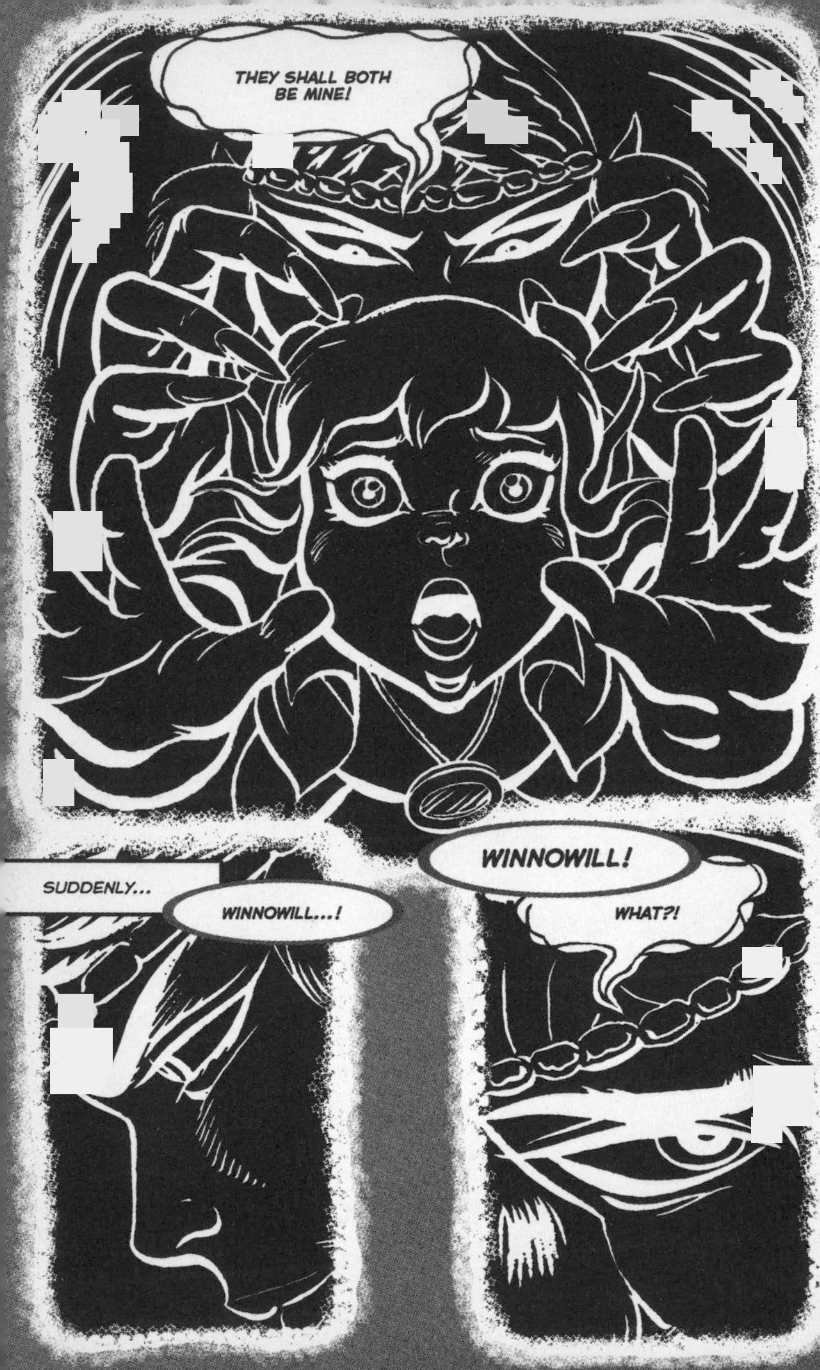
THEY SHALL BOTH BE MINE!
SUDDENLY...
WINNOWILL...!
WINNOWILL!
WHAT?!

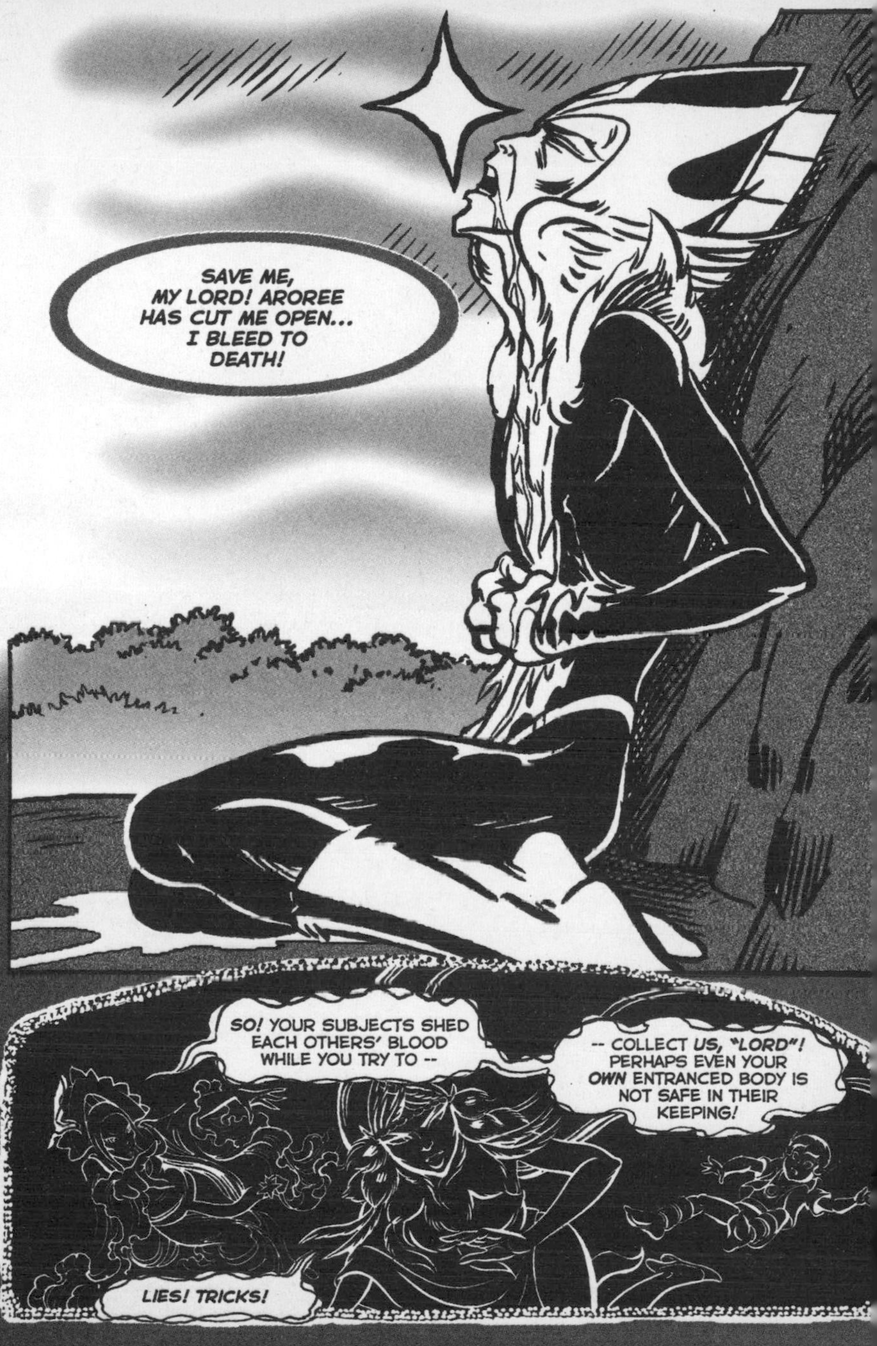
SAVE ME, MY LORD! AROREE HAS CUT ME OPEN... I BLEED TO DEATH!
SO! YOUR SUBJECTS SHED EACH OTHERS' BLOOD WHILE YOU TRY TO --
-- COLLECT US, "LORD"! PERHAPS EVEN YOUR OWN ENTRANCED BODY IS NOT SAFE IN THEIR KEEPING!
LIES! TRICKS!

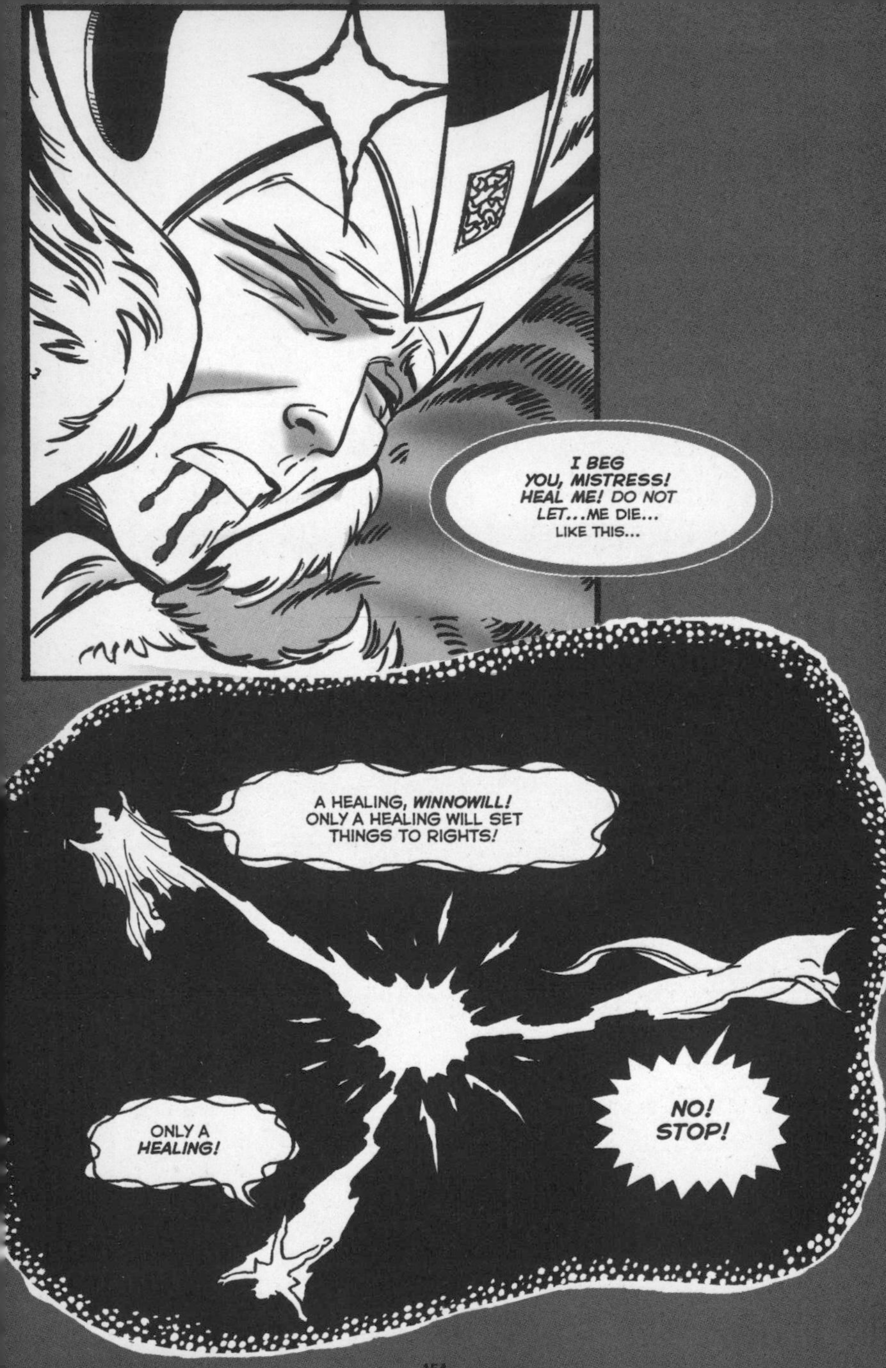
I BEG YOU, MISTRESS! HEAL ME! DO NOT LET...ME DIE... LIKE THIS...
A HEALING, WINNOWILL! ONLY A HEALING WILL SET THINGS TO RIGHTS!
ONLY A HEALING!
NO! STOP!

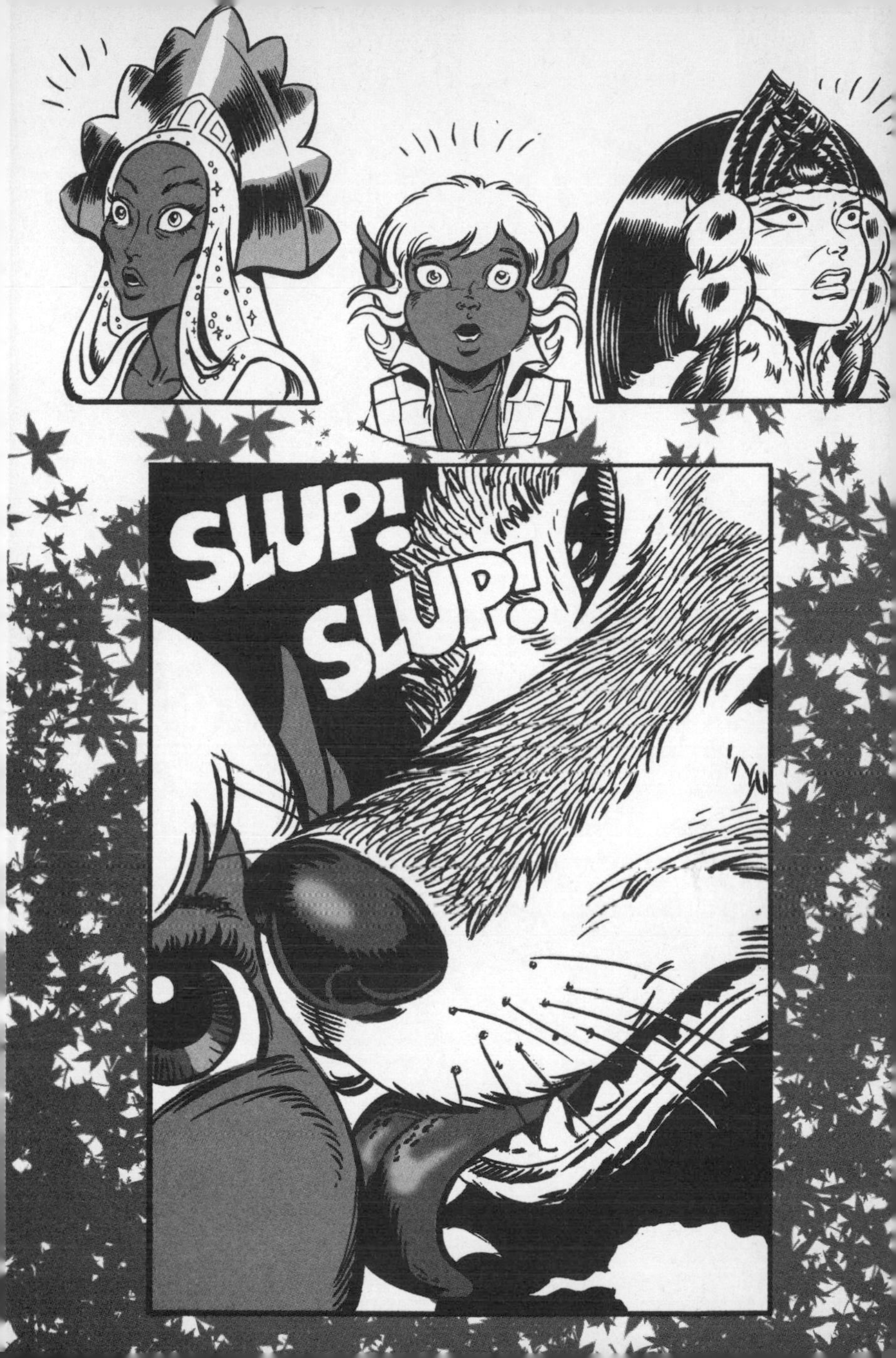
SLUP!
SLUP!

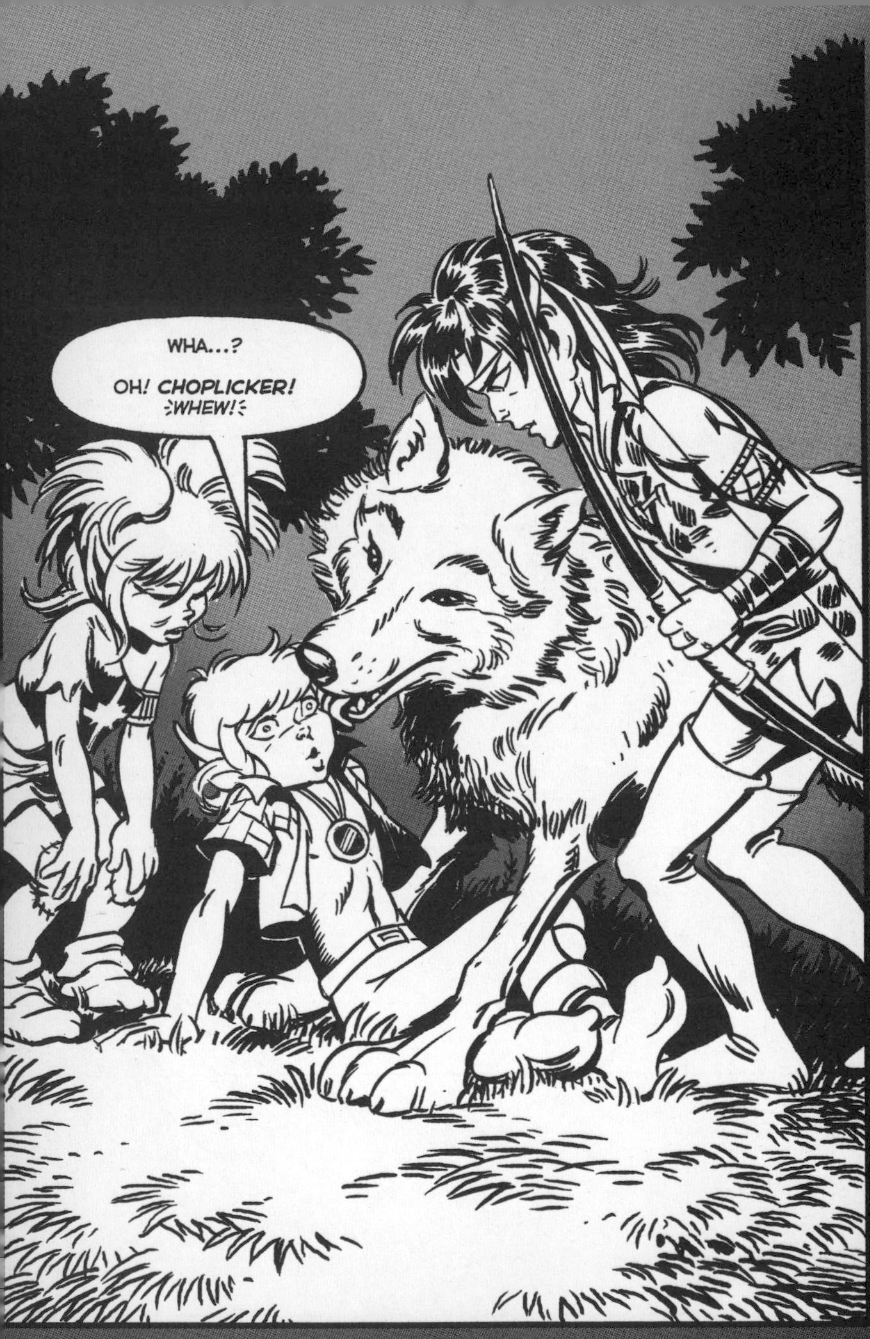
WHA...?
OH! CHOPLICKER!
WHEW!

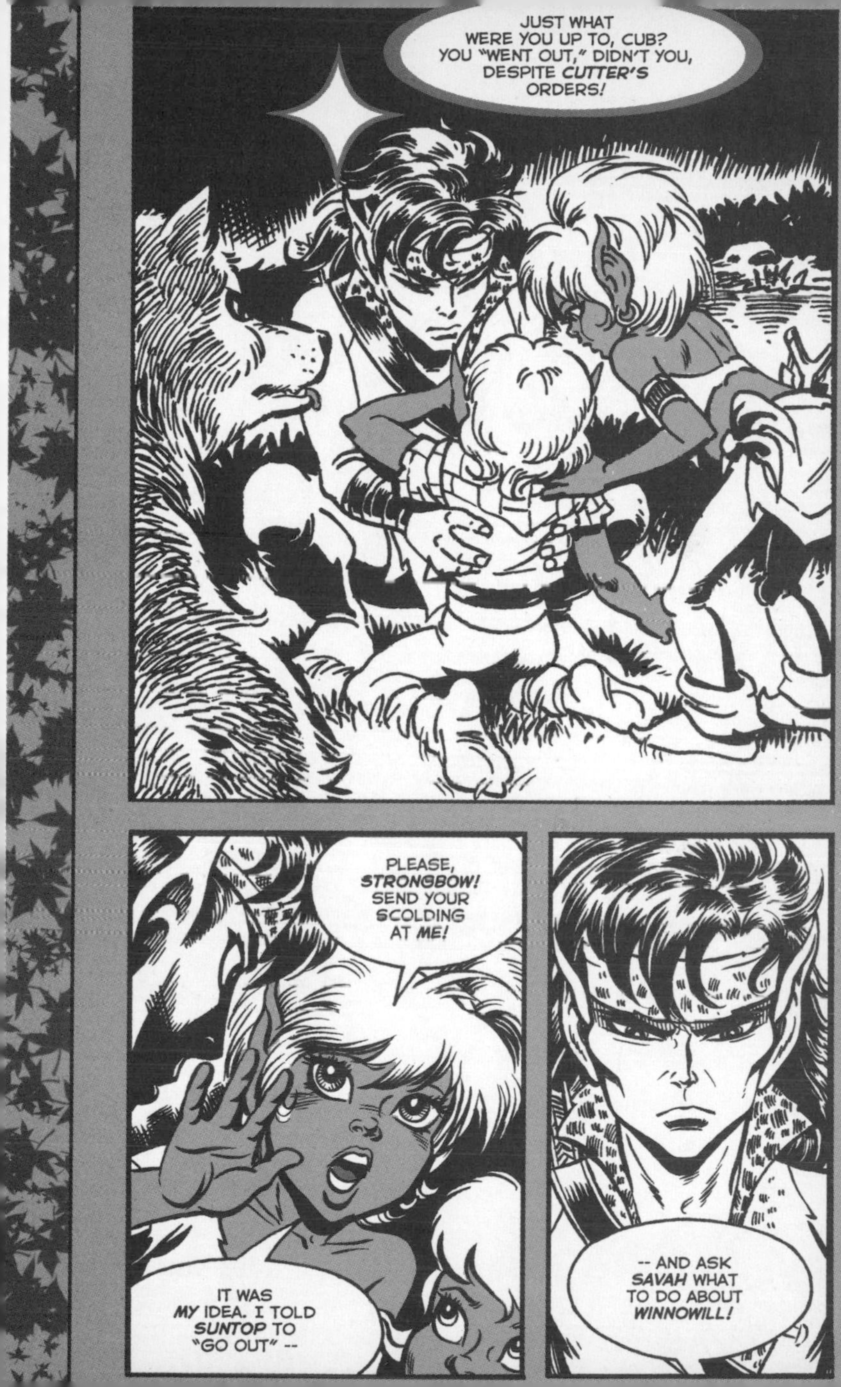
JUST WHAT WERE YOU UP TO, CUB? YOU "WENT OUT," DIDN'T YOU, DESPITE *CUTTER'S* ORDERS!
PLEASE, *STRONGBOW!* SEND YOUR SCOLDING AT *ME!*
IT WAS *MY* IDEA. I TOLD *SUNTOP* TO "GO OUT" --
-- AND ASK *SAVAH* WHAT TO DO ABOUT *WINNOWILL!*

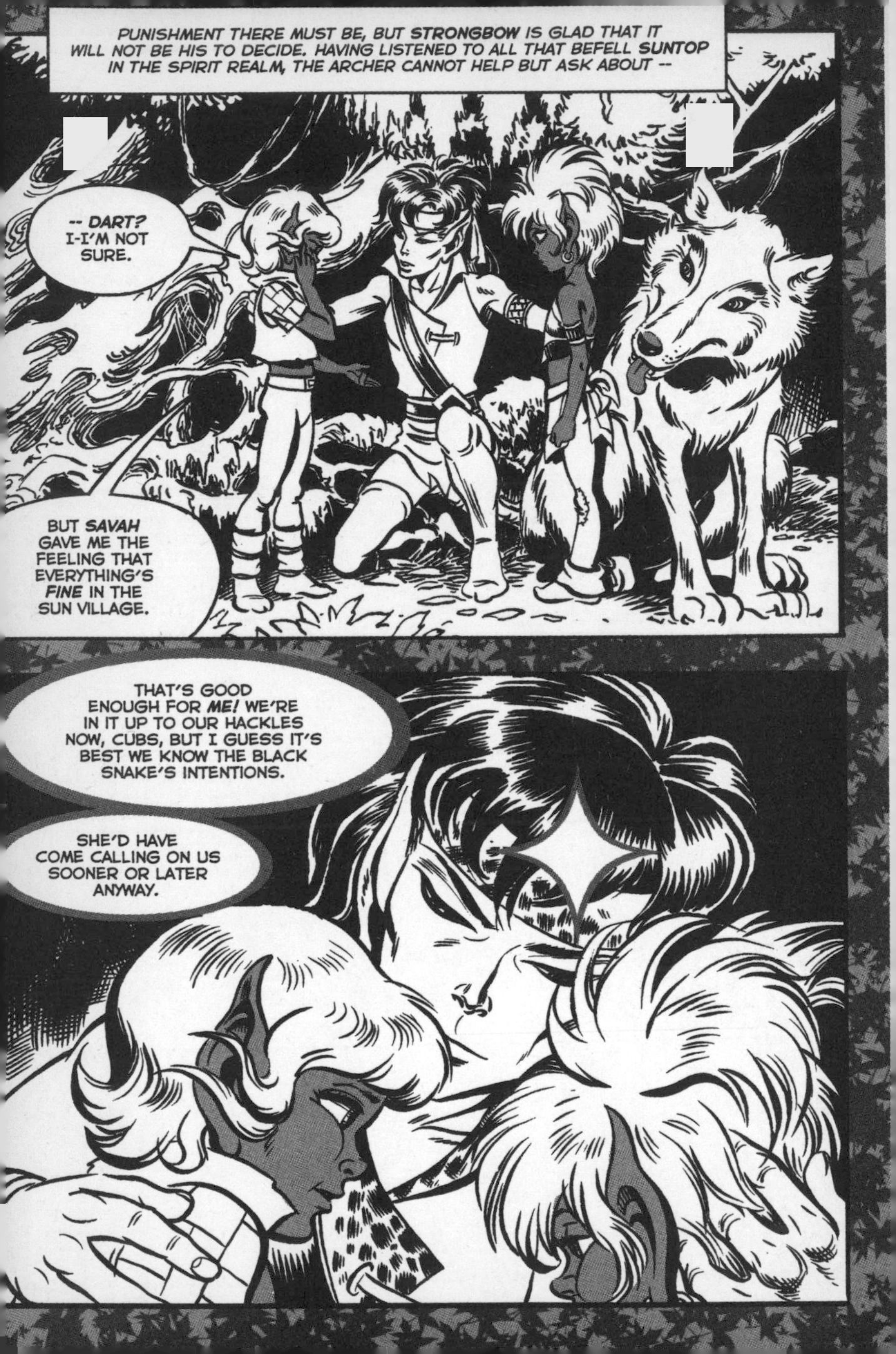
PUNISHMENT THERE MUST BE, BUT STRONGBOW IS GLAD THAT IT WILL NOT BE HIS TO DECIDE. HAVING LISTENED TO ALL THAT BEFELL SUNTOP IN THE SPIRIT REALM, THE ARCHER CANNOT HELP BUT ASK ABOUT --
-- DART? I-I'M NOT SURE.
BUT SAVAH GAVE ME THE FEELING THAT EVERYTHING'S FINE IN THE SUN VILLAGE.
THAT'S GOOD ENOUGH FOR ME! WE'RE IN IT UP TO OUR HACKLES NOW, CUBS, BUT I GUESS IT'S BEST WE KNOW THE BLACK SNAKE'S INTENTIONS.
SHE'D HAVE COME CALLING ON US SOONER OR LATER ANYWAY.

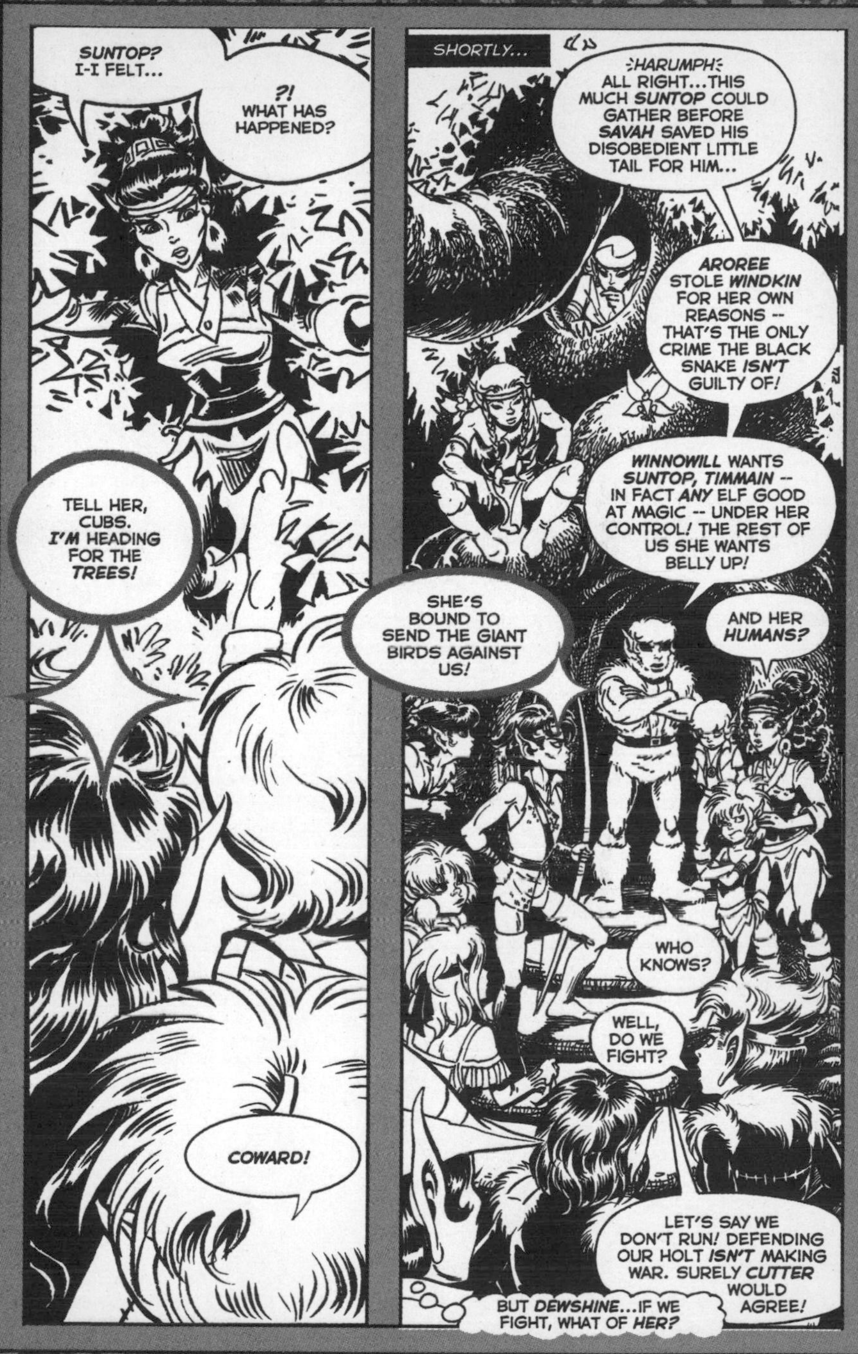
SUNTOP? I-I FELT...
?! WHAT HAS HAPPENED?
TELL HER, CUBS. I'M HEADING FOR THE TREES!
COWARD!
SHORTLY...
HARUMPH ALL RIGHT...THIS MUCH SUNTOP COULD GATHER BEFORE SAVAH SAVED HIS DISOBEDIENT LITTLE TAIL FOR HIM...
AROREE STOLE WINDKIN FOR HER OWN REASONS -- THAT'S THE ONLY CRIME THE BLACK SNAKE ISN'T GUILTY OF!
WINNOWILL WANTS SUNTOP, TIMMAIN -- IN FACT ANY ELF GOOD AT MAGIC -- UNDER HER CONTROL! THE REST OF US SHE WANTS BELLY UP!
SHE'S BOUND TO SEND THE GIANT BIRDS AGAINST US!
AND HER HUMANS?
WHO KNOWS?
WELL, DO WE FIGHT?
LET'S SAY WE DON'T RUN! DEFENDING OUR HOLT ISN'T MAKING WAR. SURELY CUTTER WOULD AGREE!
BUT DEWSHINE...IF WE FIGHT, WHAT OF HER?

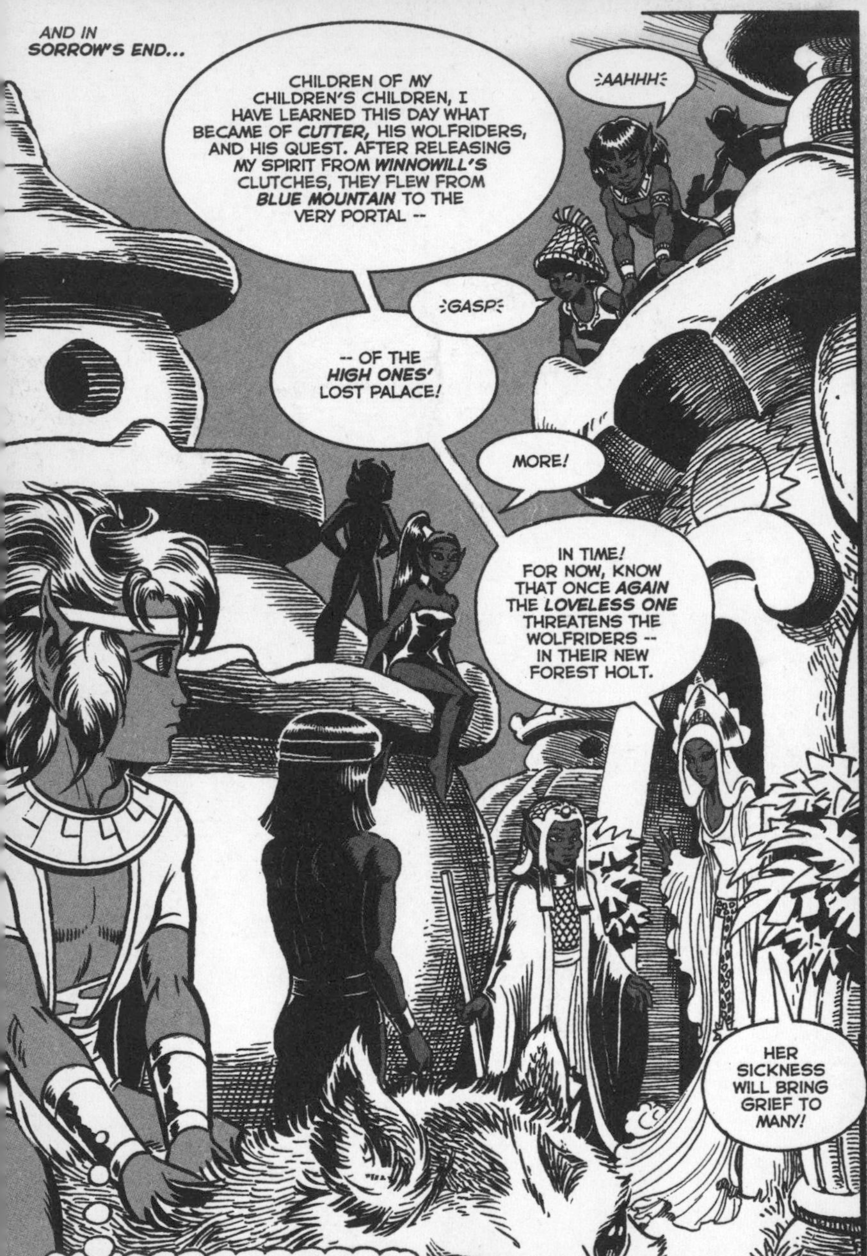
AND IN SORROW'S END...
CHILDREN OF MY CHILDREN'S CHILDREN, I HAVE LEARNED THIS DAY WHAT BECAME OF *CUTTER,* HIS WOLFRIDERS, AND HIS QUEST. AFTER RELEASING *MY* SPIRIT FROM *WINNOWILL'S* CLUTCHES, THEY FLEW FROM *BLUE MOUNTAIN* TO THE VERY PORTAL --
AAHHH
GASP
-- OF THE *HIGH ONES'* LOST PALACE!
MORE!
IN TIME! FOR NOW, KNOW THAT ONCE *AGAIN* THE *LOVELESS ONE* THREATENS THE WOLFRIDERS -- IN THEIR NEW FOREST HOLT.
HER SICKNESS WILL BRING GRIEF TO MANY!
MOTHER...FATHER...SO FAR AWAY! IS THERE SOME WAY I CAN HELP THEM?

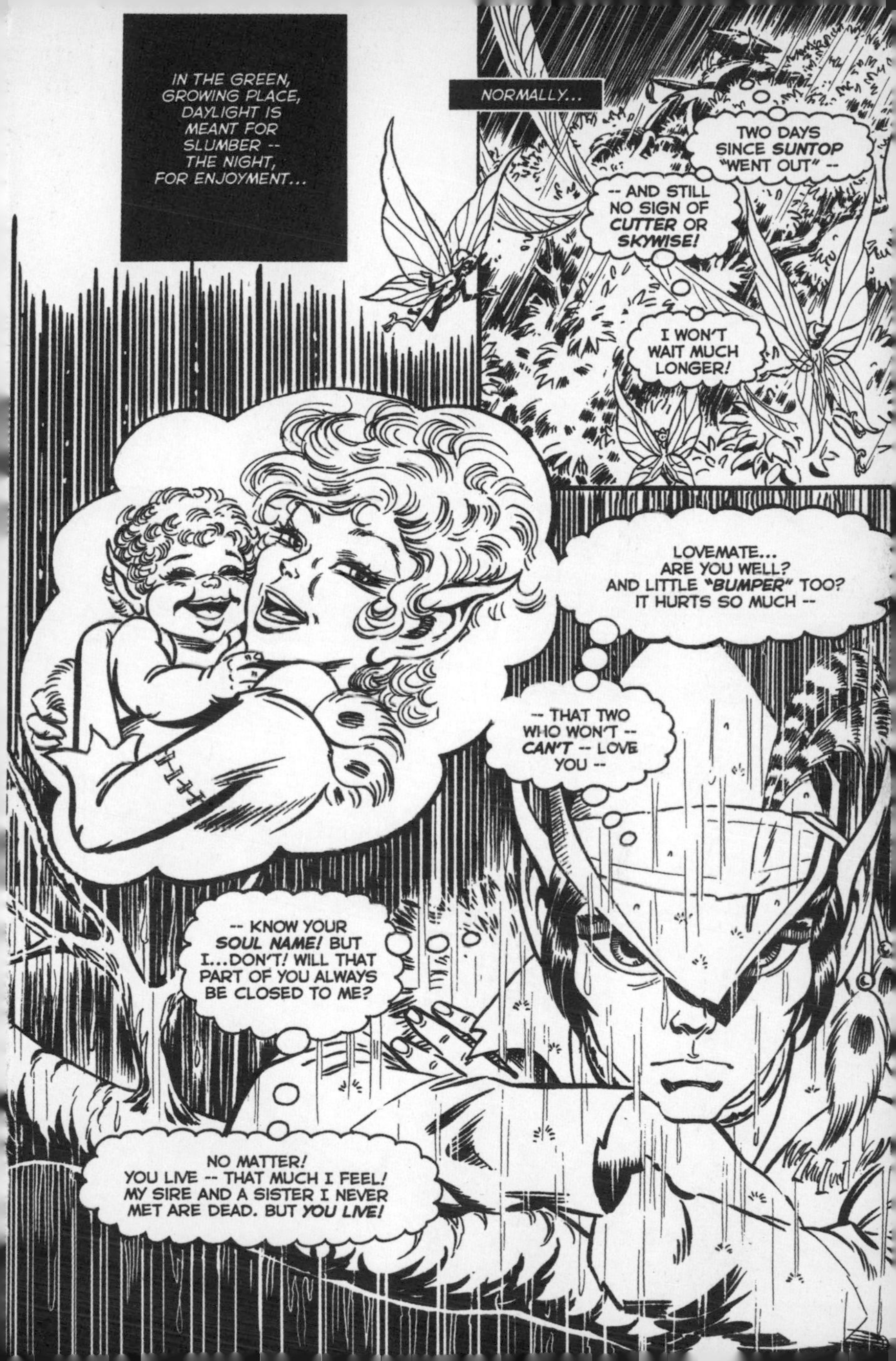
IN THE GREEN, GROWING PLACE, DAYLIGHT IS MEANT FOR SLUMBER -- THE NIGHT, FOR ENJOYMENT...
NORMALLY...
TWO DAYS SINCE SUNTOP "WENT OUT" --
-- AND STILL NO SIGN OF CUTTER OR SKYWISE!
I WON'T WAIT MUCH LONGER!
LOVEMATE... ARE YOU WELL? AND LITTLE "BUMPER" TOO? IT HURTS SO MUCH --
-- THAT TWO WHO WON'T -- CAN'T -- LOVE YOU --
-- KNOW YOUR SOUL NAME! BUT I...DON'T! WILL THAT PART OF YOU ALWAYS BE CLOSED TO ME?
NO MATTER! YOU LIVE -- THAT MUCH I FEEL! MY SIRE AND A SISTER I NEVER MET ARE DEAD. BUT YOU LIVE!

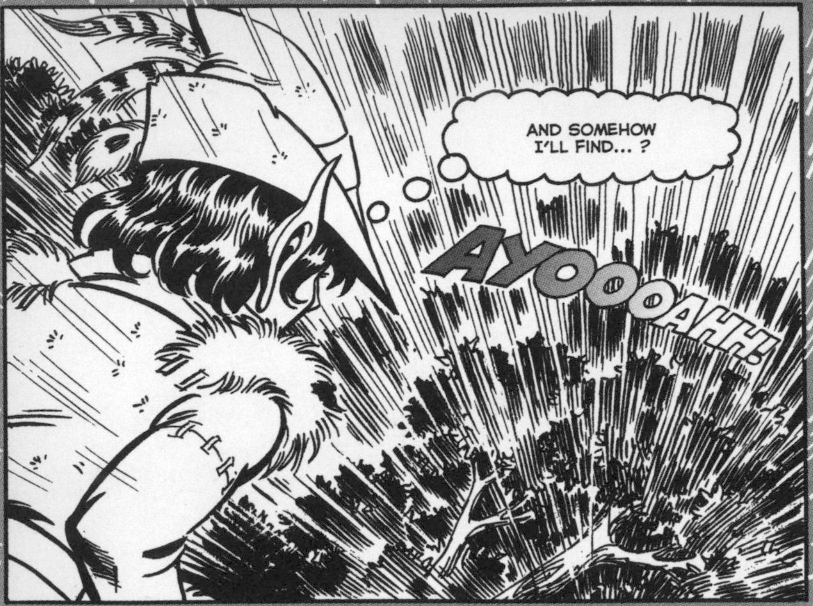
AND SOMEHOW I'LL FIND... ?
AYOOOAHH!

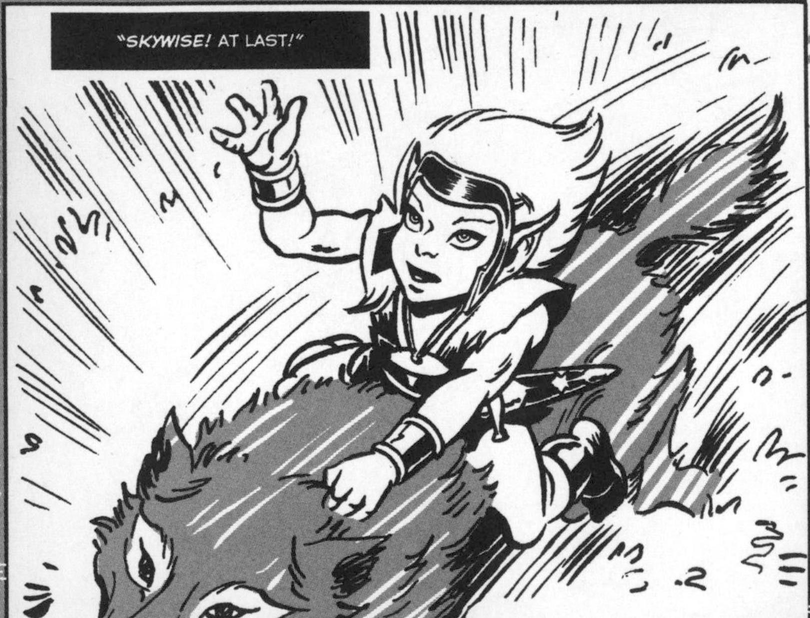
"SKYWISE! AT LAST!"

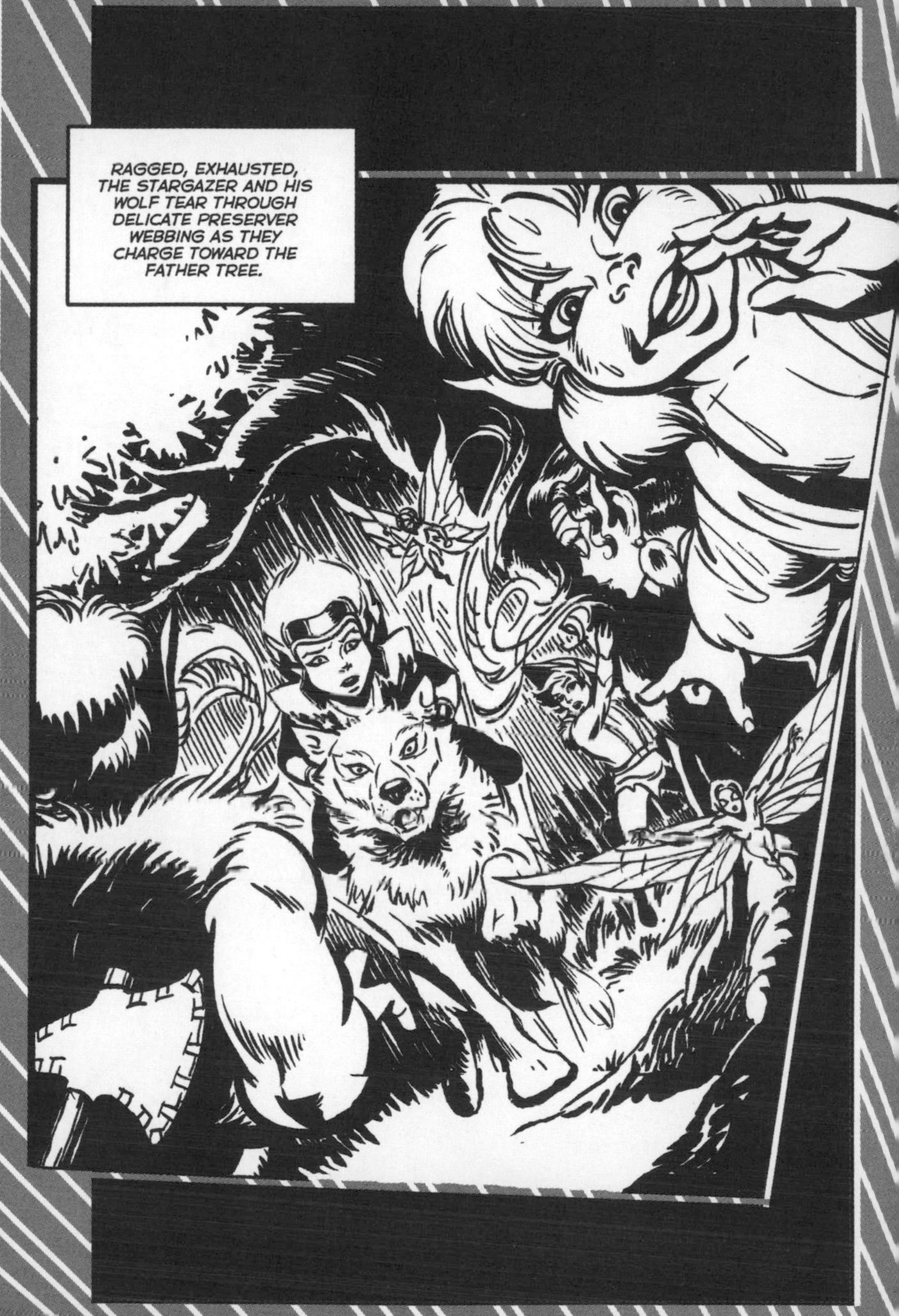
RAGGED, EXHAUSTED, THE STARGAZER AND HIS WOLF TEAR THROUGH DELICATE PRESERVER WEBBING AS THEY CHARGE TOWARD THE FATHER TREE.

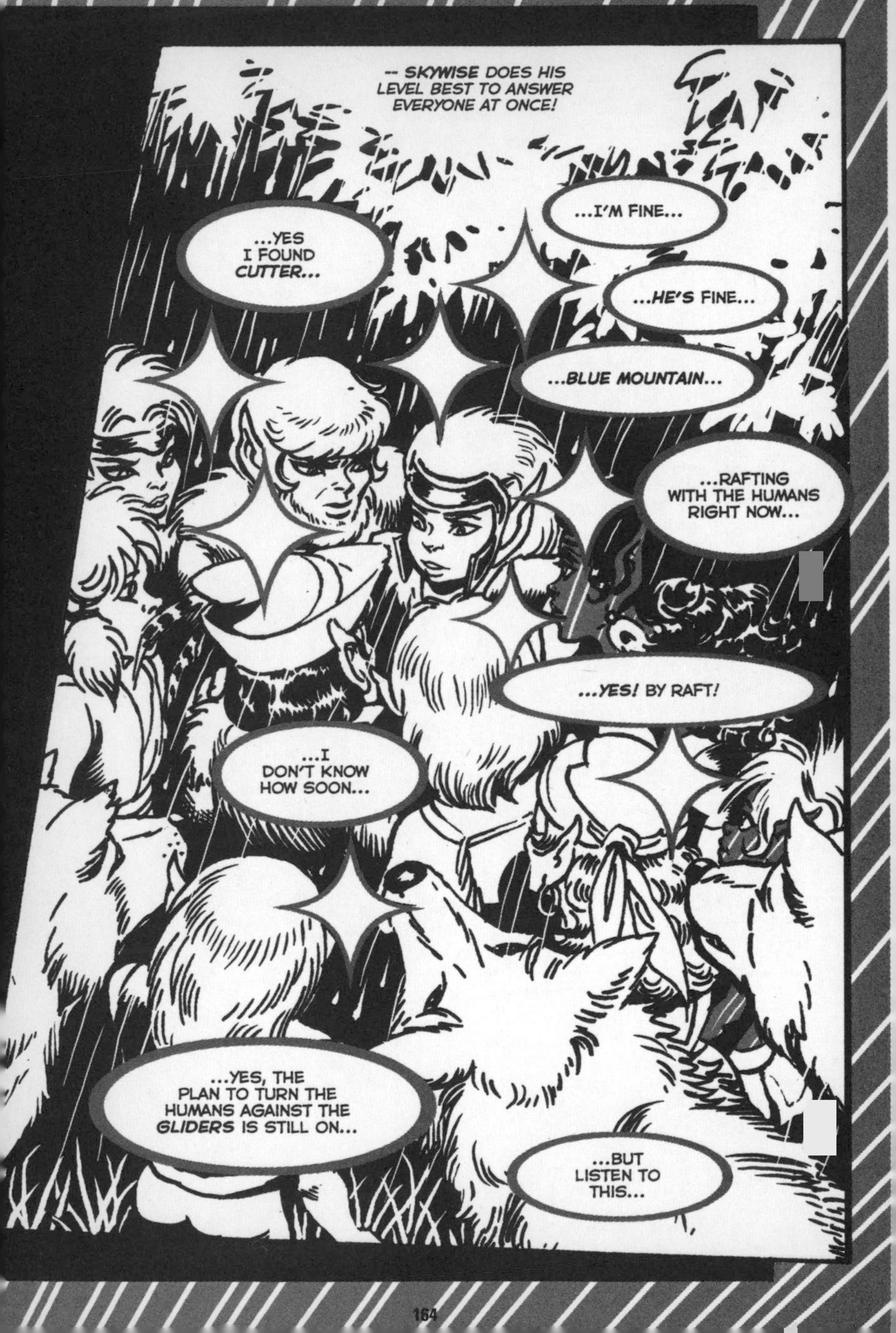
-- SKYWISE DOES HIS LEVEL BEST TO ANSWER EVERYONE AT ONCE!
...YES I FOUND CUTTER...
...I'M FINE...
...HE'S FINE...
...BLUE MOUNTAIN...
...RAFTING WITH THE HUMANS RIGHT NOW...
...YES! BY RAFT!
...I DON'T KNOW HOW SOON...
...YES, THE PLAN TO TURN THE HUMANS AGAINST THE GLIDERS IS STILL ON...
...BUT LISTEN TO THIS...

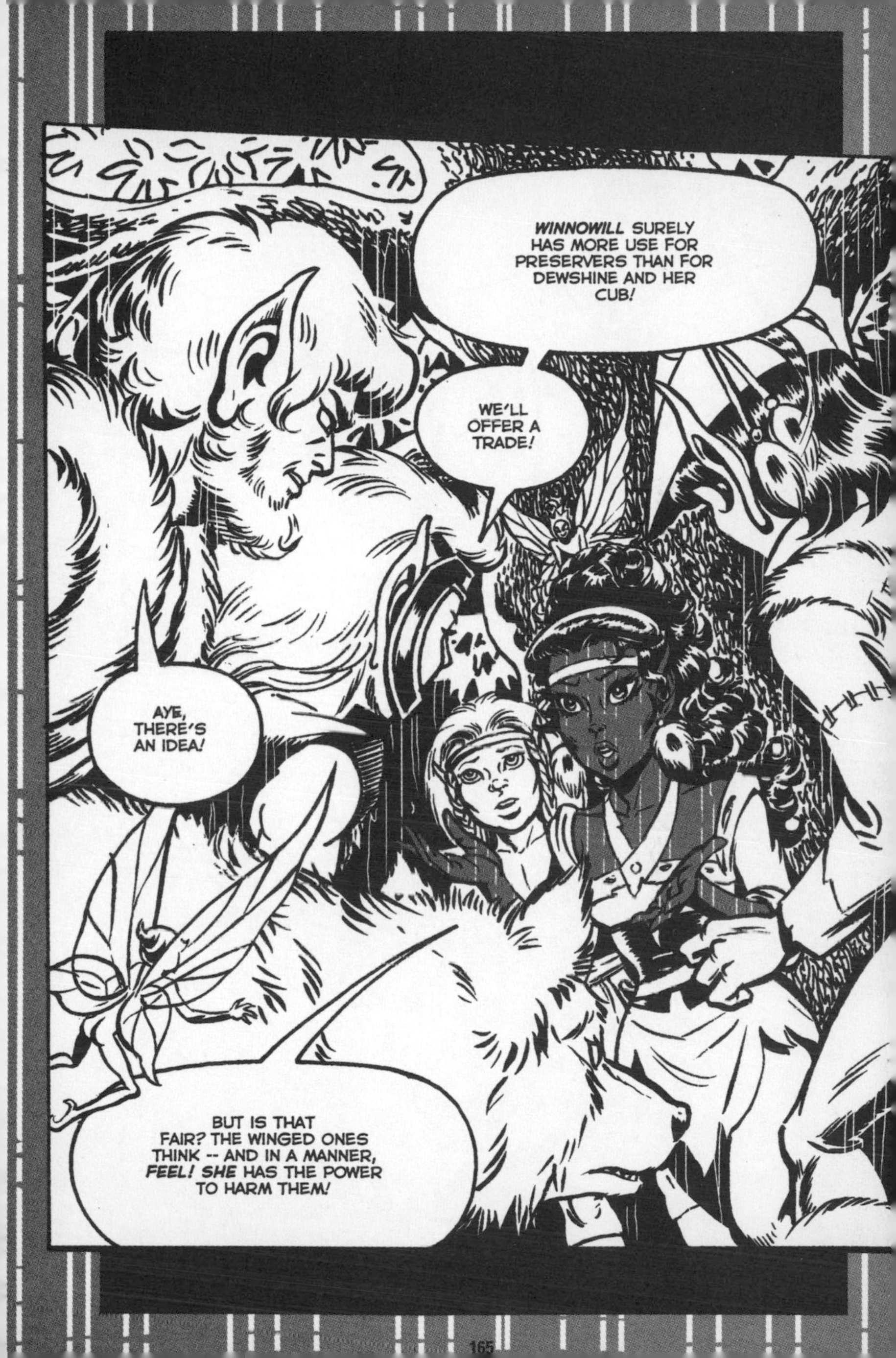
WINNOWILL SURELY HAS MORE USE FOR PRESERVERS THAN FOR DEWSHINE AND HER CUB!
WE'LL OFFER A TRADE!
AYE, THERE'S AN IDEA!
BUT IS THAT FAIR? THE WINGED ONES THINK -- AND IN A MANNER, FEEL! SHE HAS THE POWER TO HARM THEM!

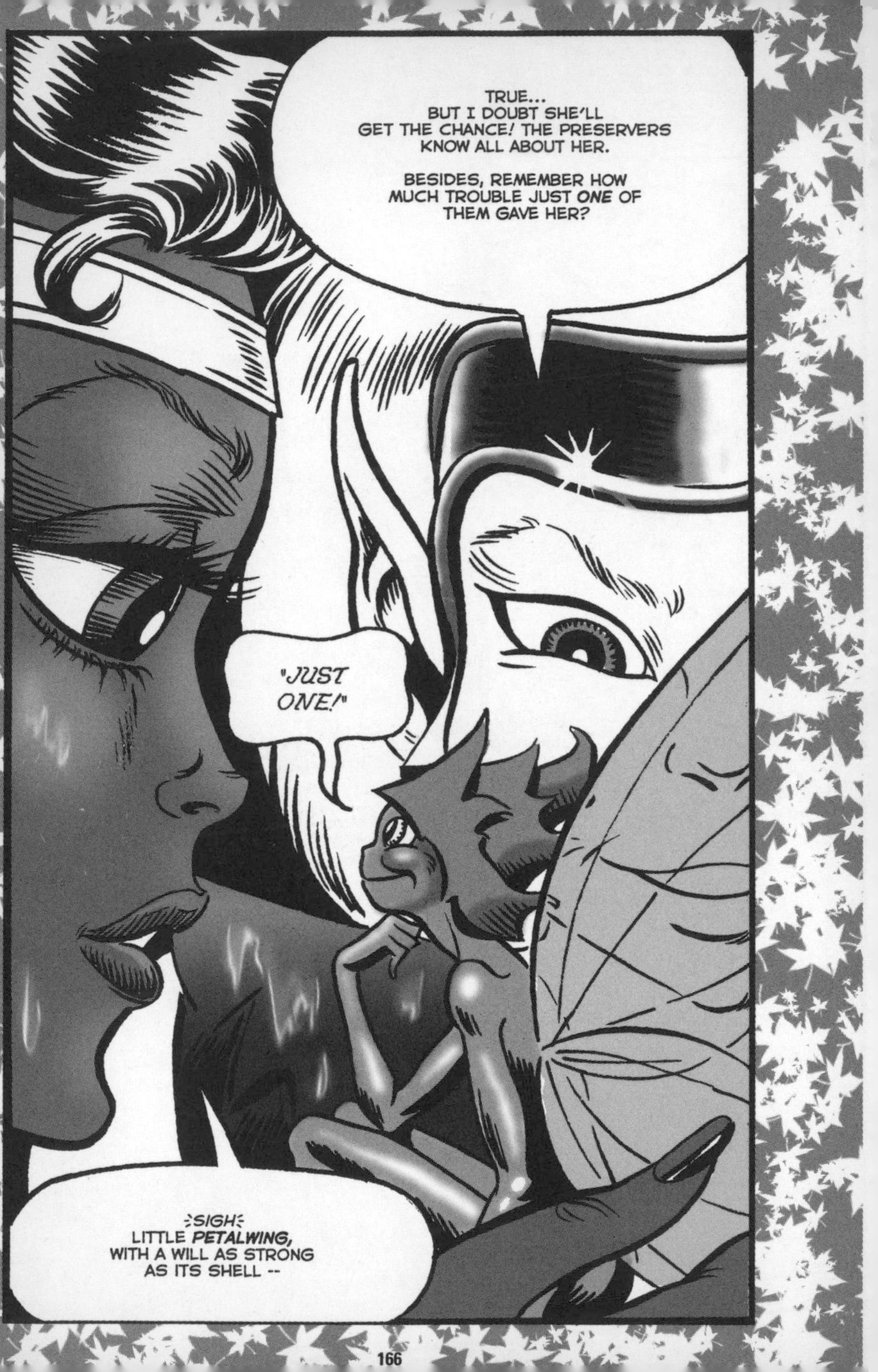
TRUE... BUT I DOUBT SHE'LL GET THE CHANCE! THE PRESERVERS KNOW ALL ABOUT HER.
BESIDES, REMEMBER HOW MUCH TROUBLE JUST *ONE* OF THEM GAVE HER?
"JUST ONE!"
SIGH LITTLE **PETALWING**, WITH A WILL AS STRONG AS ITS SHELL --

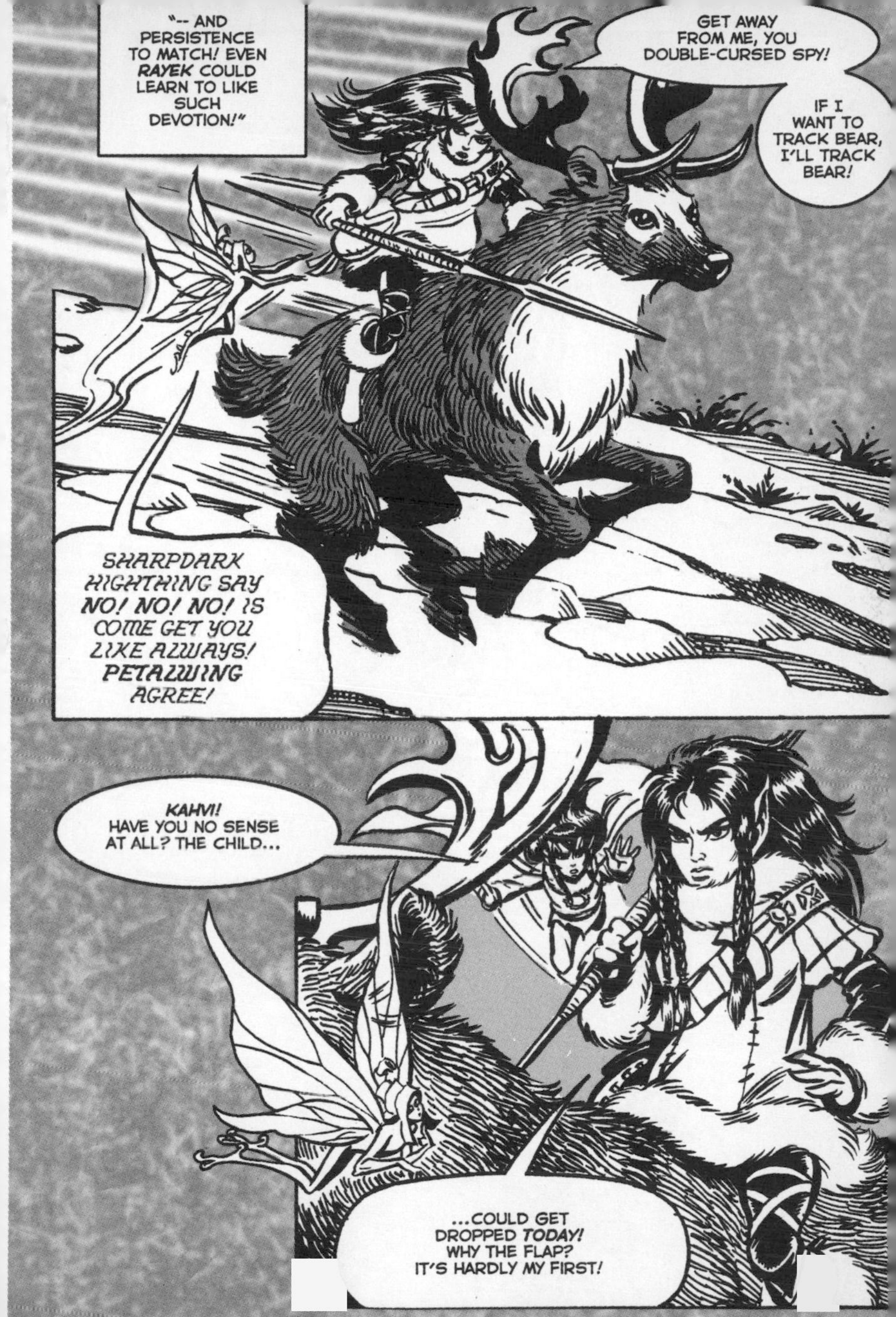
"-- AND PERSISTENCE TO MATCH! EVEN RAYEK COULD LEARN TO LIKE SUCH DEVOTION!"
GET AWAY FROM ME, YOU DOUBLE-CURSED SPY!
IF I WANT TO TRACK BEAR, I'LL TRACK BEAR!
SHARPDARK HIGHTHING SAY NO! NO! NO! IS COME GET YOU LIKE ALWAYS! PETALWING AGREE!
KAHVI! HAVE YOU NO SENSE AT ALL? THE CHILD...
...COULD GET DROPPED TODAY! WHY THE FLAP? IT'S HARDLY MY FIRST!

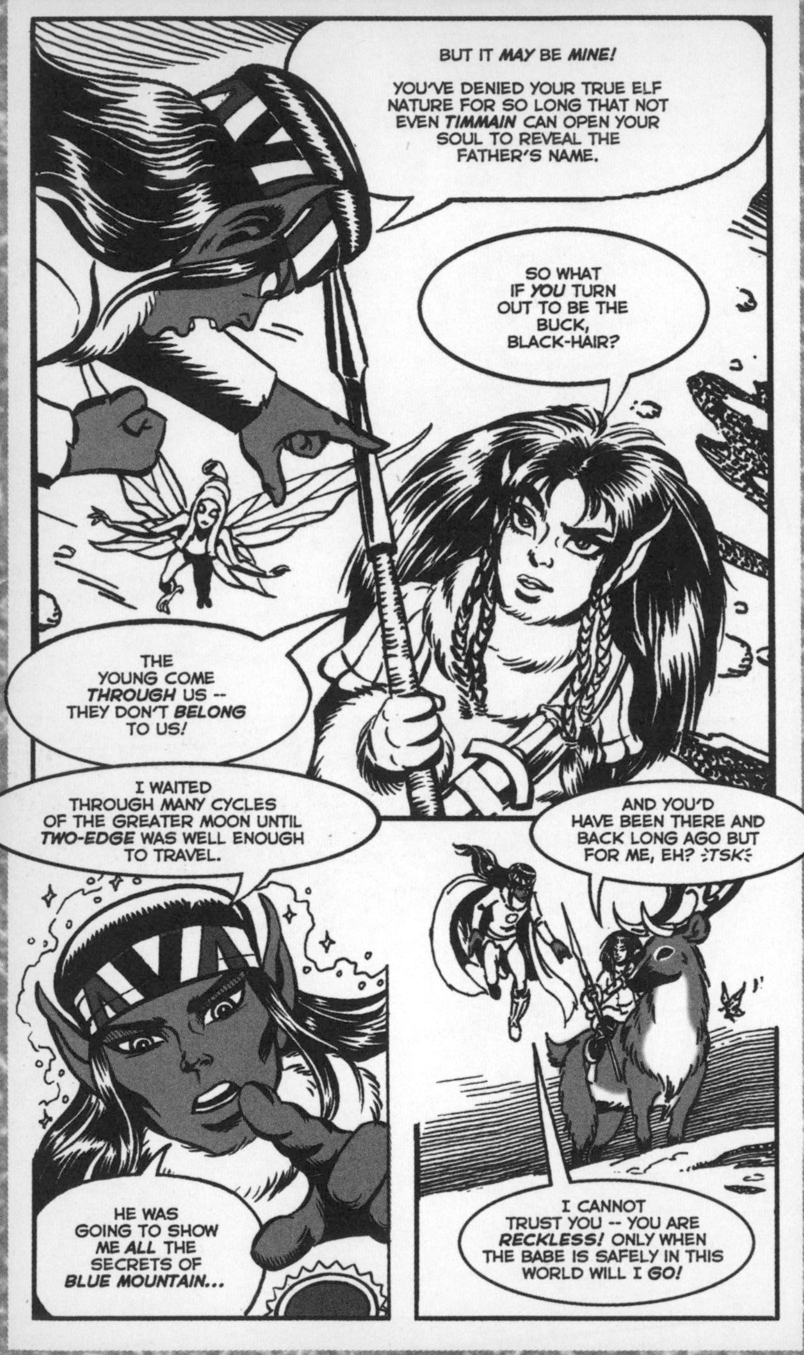
BUT IT MAY BE MINE!
YOU'VE DENIED YOUR TRUE ELF NATURE FOR SO LONG THAT NOT EVEN TIMMAIN CAN OPEN YOUR SOUL TO REVEAL THE FATHER'S NAME.
SO WHAT IF YOU TURN OUT TO BE THE BUCK, BLACK-HAIR?
THE YOUNG COME THROUGH US -- THEY DON'T BELONG TO US!
I WAITED THROUGH MANY CYCLES OF THE GREATER MOON UNTIL TWO-EDGE WAS WELL ENOUGH TO TRAVEL.
HE WAS GOING TO SHOW ME ALL THE SECRETS OF BLUE MOUNTAIN...
AND YOU'D HAVE BEEN THERE AND BACK LONG AGO BUT FOR ME, EH? TSK
I CANNOT TRUST YOU -- YOU ARE RECKLESS! ONLY WHEN THE BABE IS SAFELY IN THIS WORLD WILL I GO!

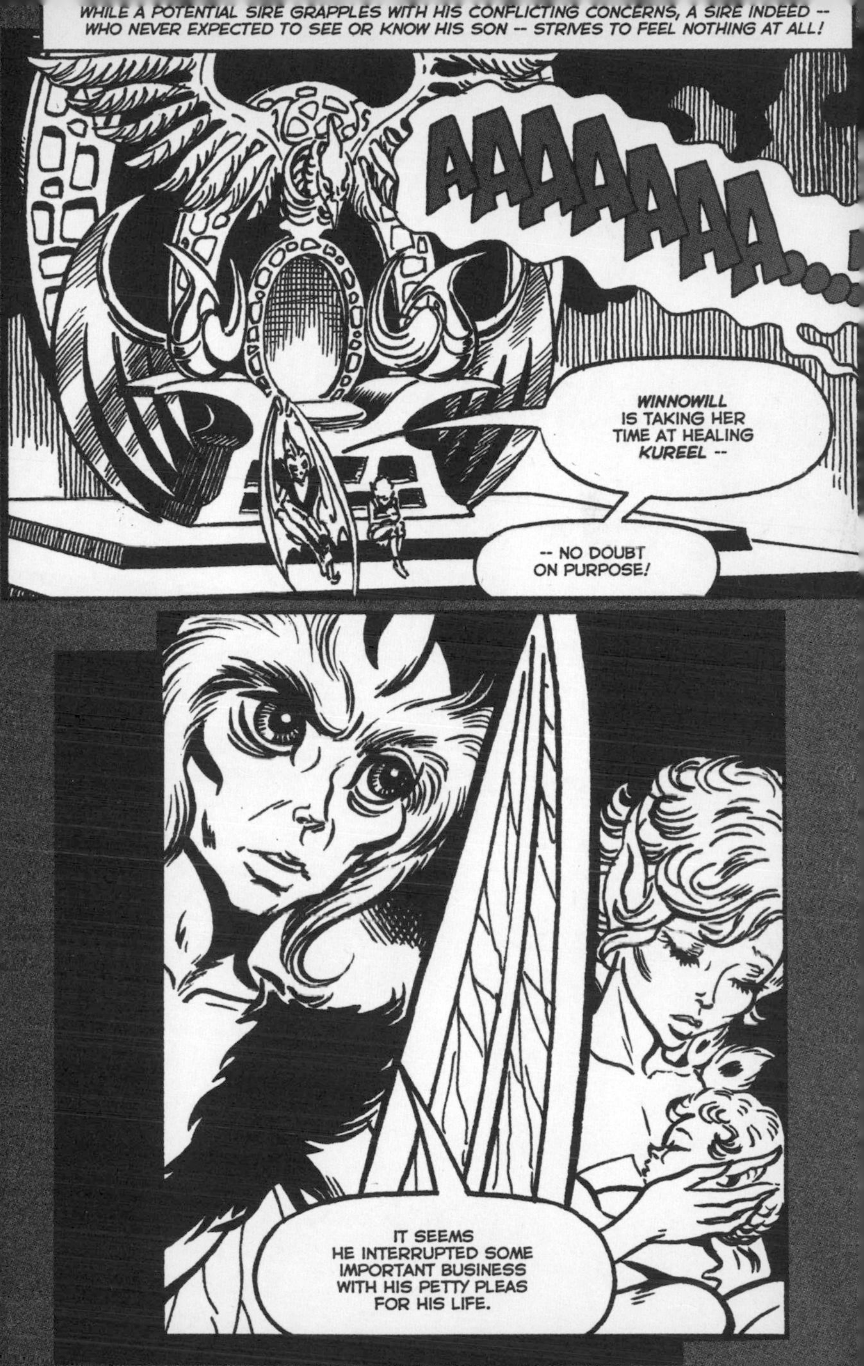
WHILE A POTENTIAL SIRE GRAPPLES WITH HIS CONFLICTING CONCERNS, A SIRE INDEED -- WHO NEVER EXPECTED TO SEE OR KNOW HIS SON -- STRIVES TO FEEL NOTHING AT ALL!
AAAAAAAA...
WINNOWILL IS TAKING HER TIME AT HEALING KUREEL --
-- NO DOUBT ON PURPOSE!
IT SEEMS HE INTERRUPTED SOME IMPORTANT BUSINESS WITH HIS PETTY PLEAS FOR HIS LIFE.

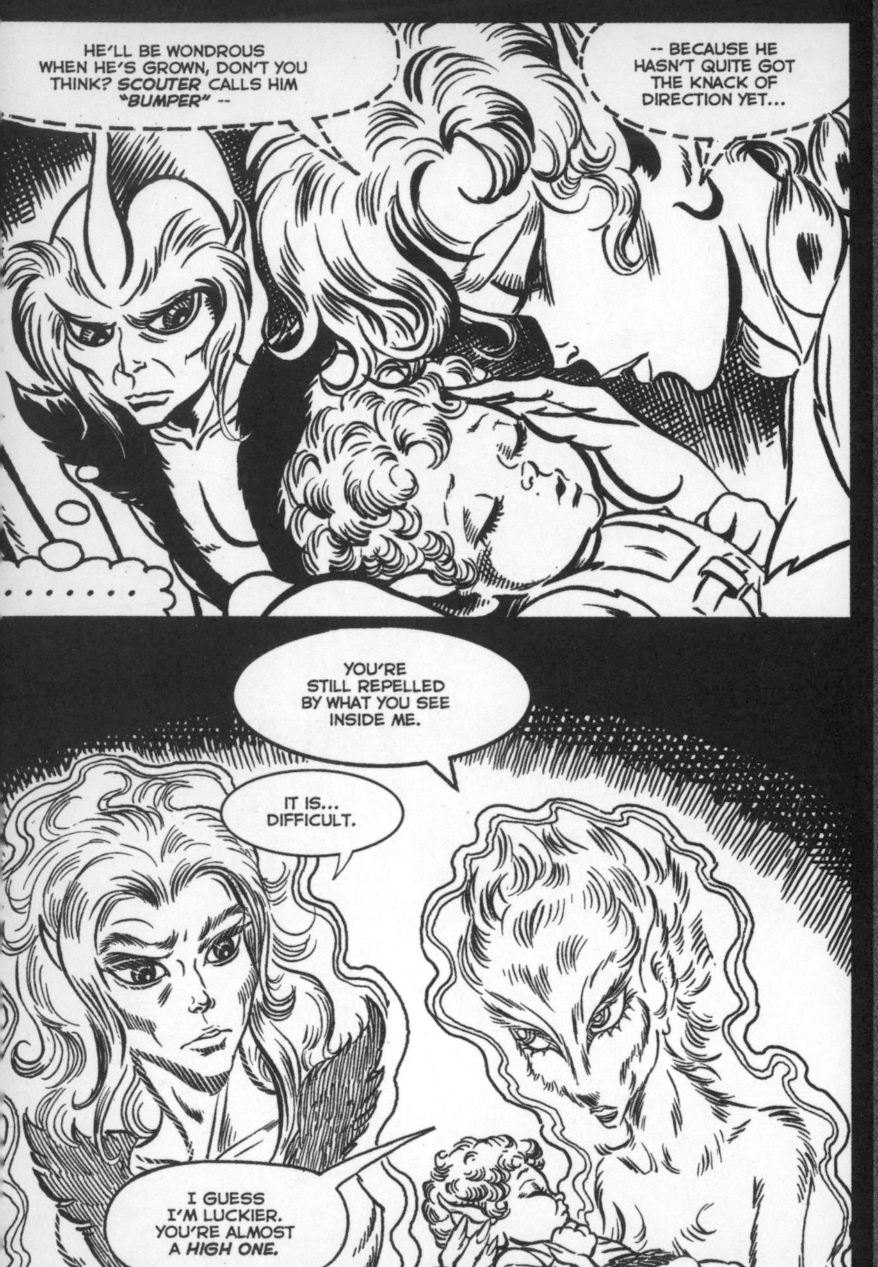
HE'LL BE WONDROUS WHEN HE'S GROWN, DON'T YOU THINK? *SCOUTER* CALLS HIM *"BUMPER"* --
-- BECAUSE HE HASN'T QUITE GOT THE KNACK OF DIRECTION YET...
YOU'RE STILL REPELLED BY WHAT YOU SEE INSIDE ME.
IT IS... DIFFICULT.
I GUESS I'M LUCKIER. YOU'RE ALMOST A *HIGH ONE.*

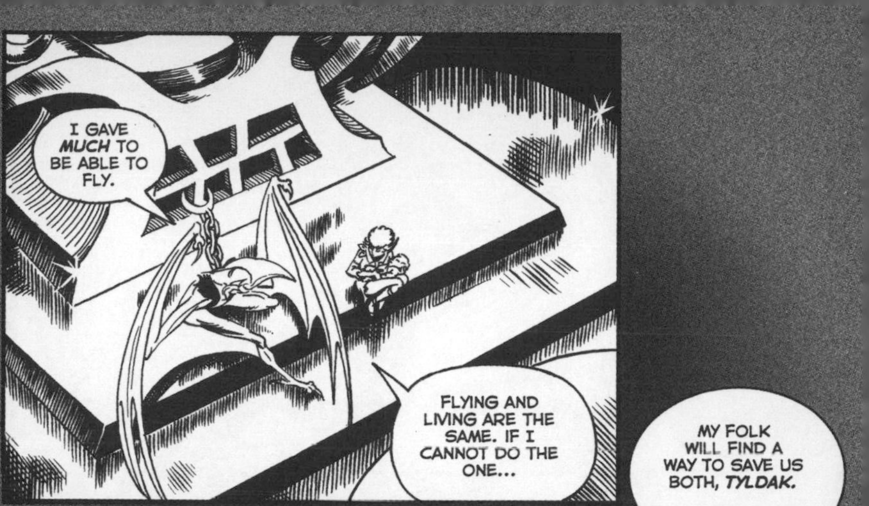
I GAVE MUCH TO BE ABLE TO FLY.
FLYING AND LIVING ARE THE SAME. IF I CANNOT DO THE ONE...

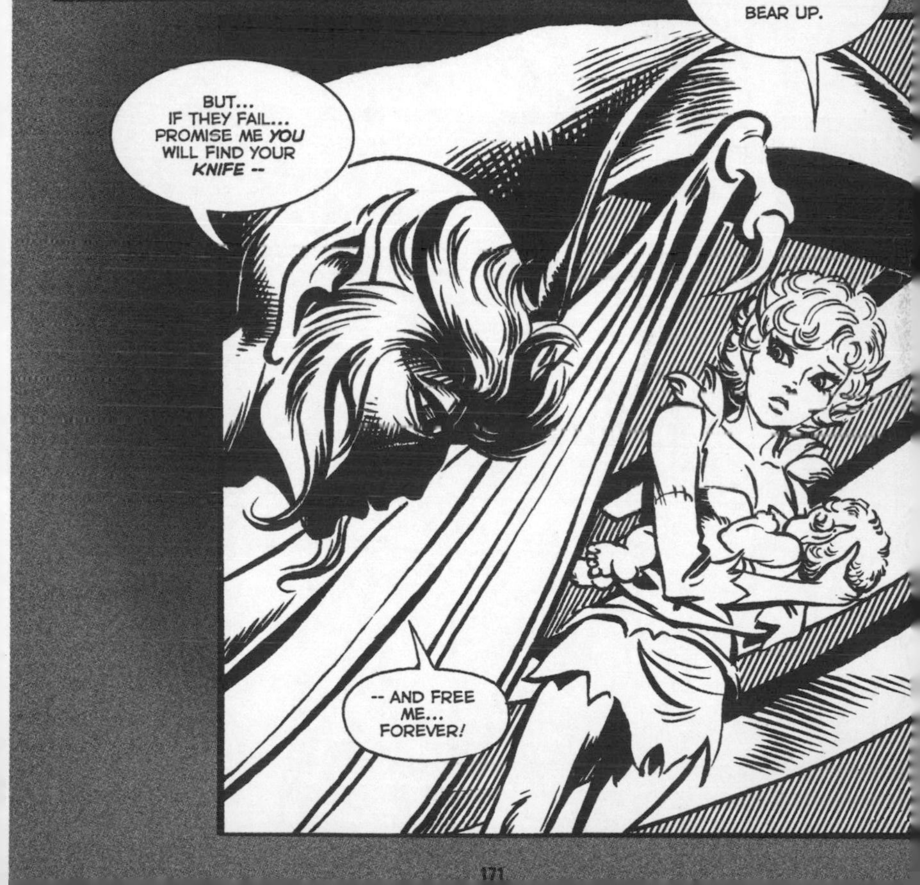
MY FOLK WILL FIND A WAY TO SAVE US BOTH, TYLDAK.
BEAR UP.
BUT... IF THEY FAIL... PROMISE ME YOU WILL FIND YOUR KNIFE --
-- AND FREE ME... FOREVER!

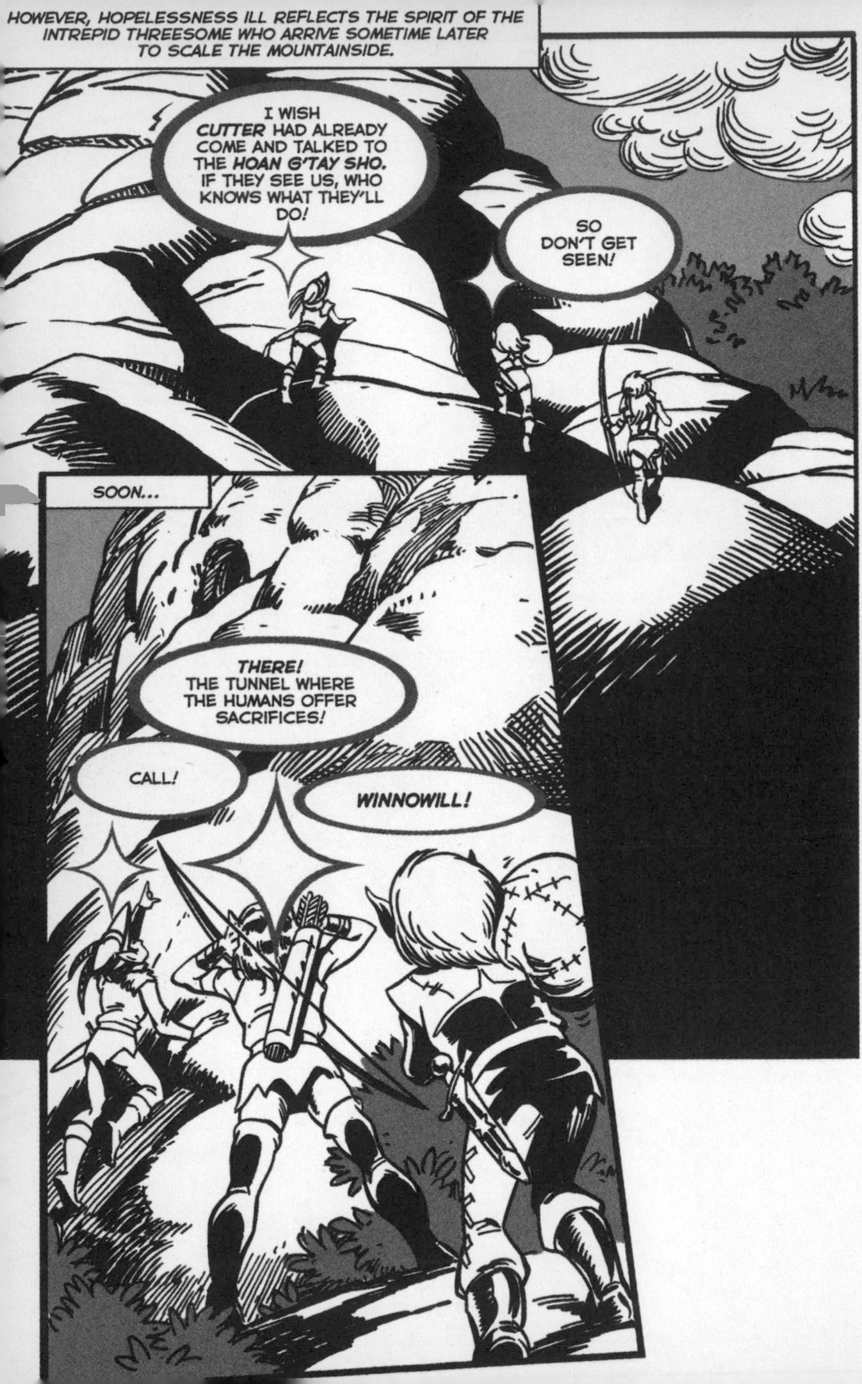
HOWEVER, HOPELESSNESS ILL REFLECTS THE SPIRIT OF THE INTREPID THREESOME WHO ARRIVE SOMETIME LATER TO SCALE THE MOUNTAINSIDE.
I WISH CUTTER HAD ALREADY COME AND TALKED TO THE HOAN G'TAY SHO. IF THEY SEE US, WHO KNOWS WHAT THEY'LL DO!
SO DON'T GET SEEN!
SOON...
THERE! THE TUNNEL WHERE THE HUMANS OFFER SACRIFICES!
CALL!
WINNOWILL!

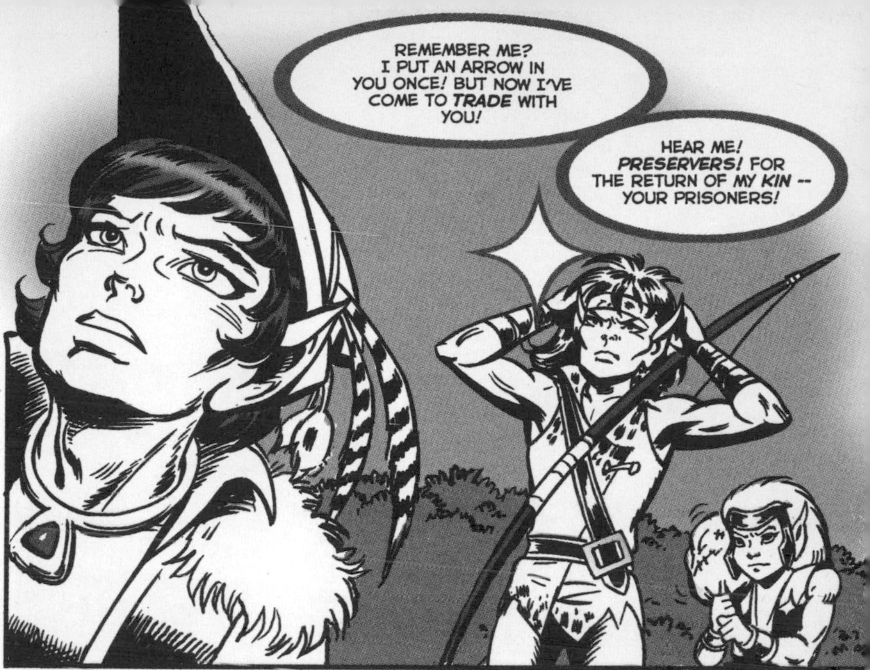
REMEMBER ME? I PUT AN ARROW IN YOU ONCE! BUT NOW I'VE COME TO *TRADE* WITH YOU!
HEAR ME! *PRESERVERS!* FOR THE RETURN OF *MY KIN* -- YOUR PRISONERS!

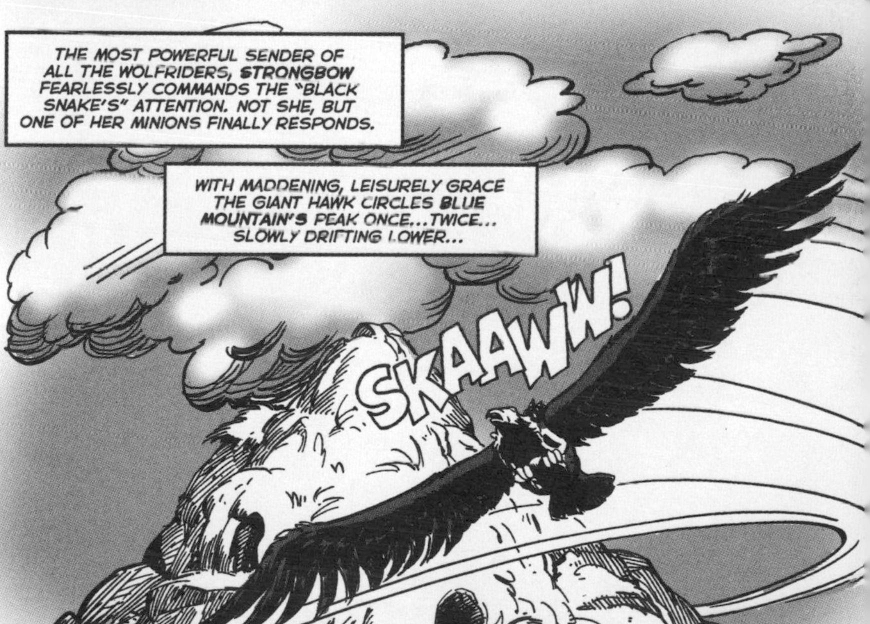
THE MOST POWERFUL SENDER OF ALL THE WOLFRIDERS, STRONGBOW FEARLESSLY COMMANDS THE "BLACK SNAKE'S" ATTENTION. NOT SHE, BUT ONE OF HER MINIONS FINALLY RESPONDS.
WITH MADDENING, LEISURELY GRACE THE GIANT HAWK CIRCLES BLUE MOUNTAIN'S PEAK ONCE...TWICE... SLOWLY DRIFTING LOWER...
SKAAAWW!

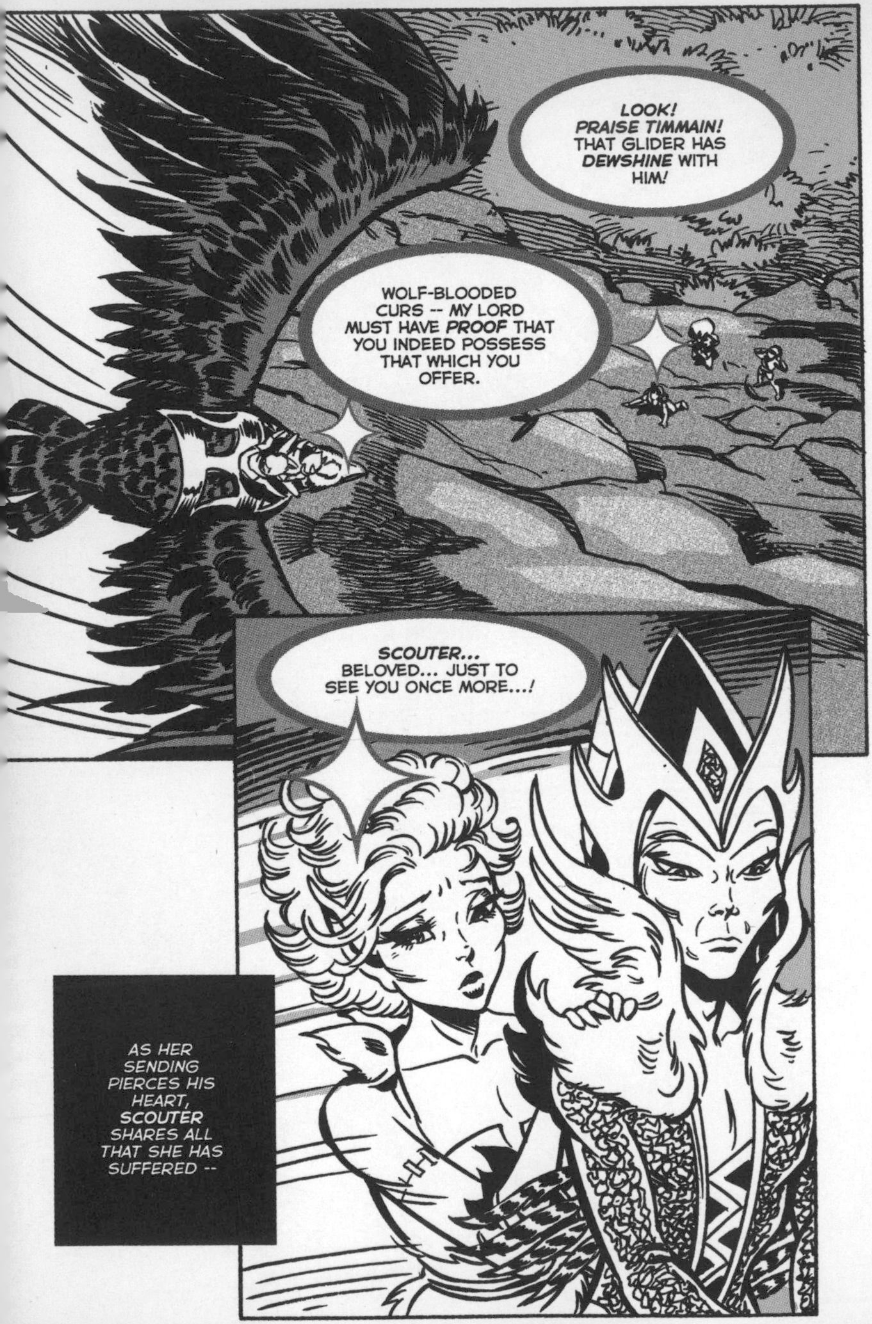
LOOK! PRAISE TIMMAIN! THAT GLIDER HAS DEWSHINE WITH HIM!
WOLF-BLOODED CURS -- MY LORD MUST HAVE PROOF THAT YOU INDEED POSSESS THAT WHICH YOU OFFER.
SCOUTER... BELOVED... JUST TO SEE YOU ONCE MORE...!
AS HER SENDING PIERCES HIS HEART, SCOUTER SHARES ALL THAT SHE HAS SUFFERED --

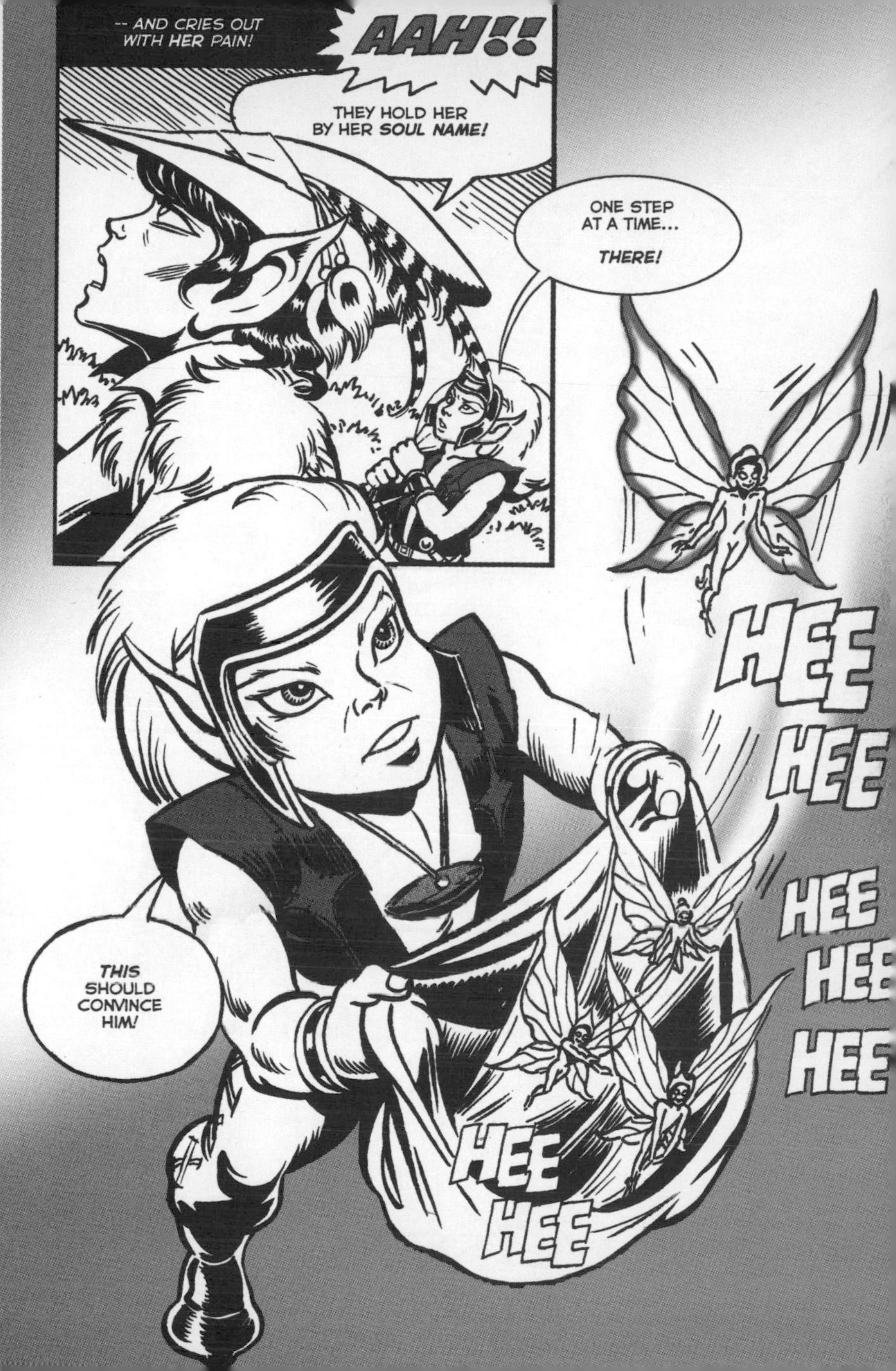
-- AND CRIES OUT WITH HER PAIN!
AAH!!
THEY HOLD HER BY HER SOUL NAME!
ONE STEP AT A TIME... THERE!
HEE HEE
HEE HEE HEE
THIS SHOULD CONVINCE HIM!
HEE HEE

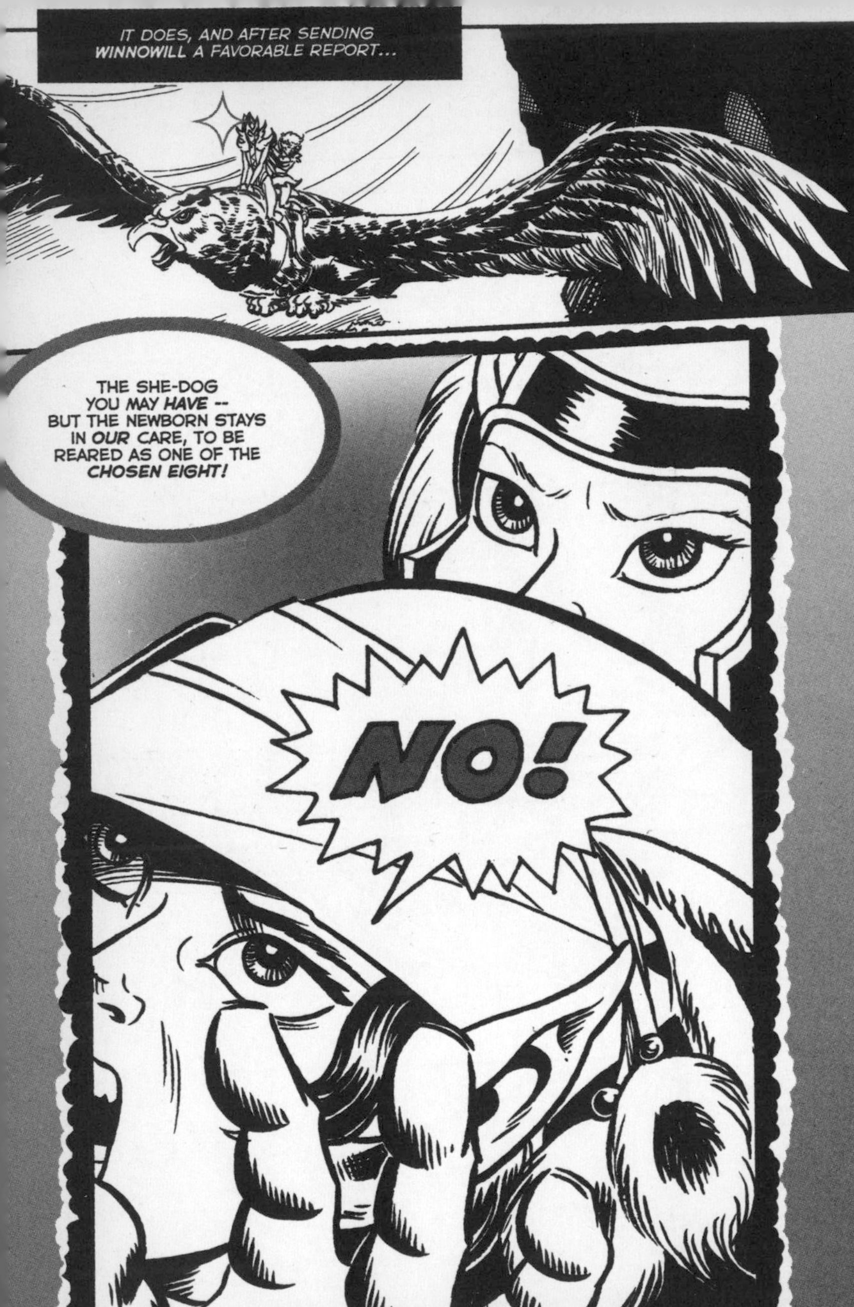
IT DOES, AND AFTER SENDING WINNOWILL A FAVORABLE REPORT...
THE SHE-DOG YOU MAY HAVE -- BUT THE NEWBORN STAYS IN OUR CARE, TO BE REARED AS ONE OF THE CHOSEN EIGHT!
NO!

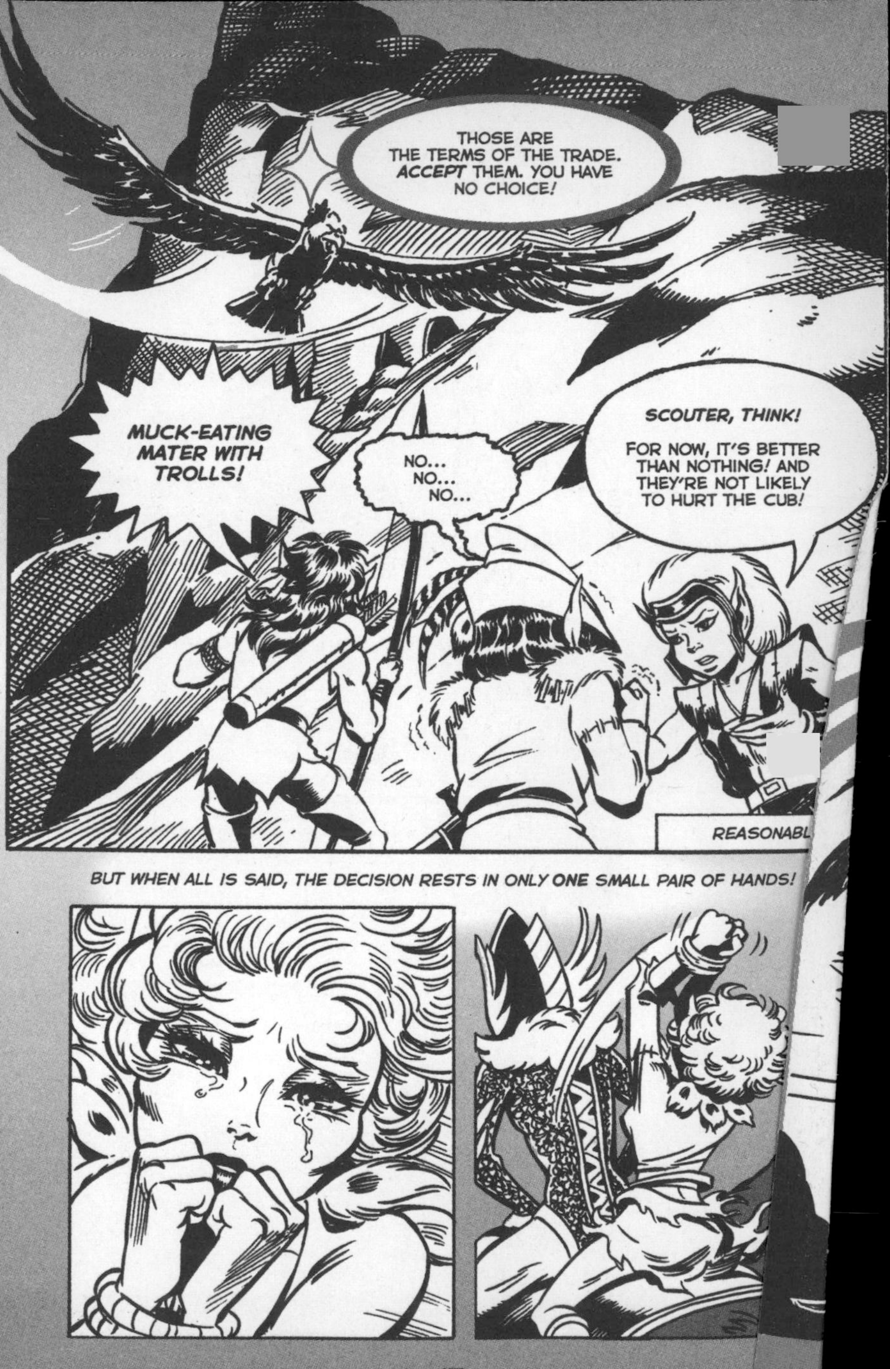
THOSE ARE THE TERMS OF THE TRADE. ACCEPT THEM. YOU HAVE NO CHOICE!
MUCK-EATING MATER WITH TROLLS!
NO... NO... NO...
SCOUTER, THINK!
FOR NOW, IT'S BETTER THAN NOTHING! AND THEY'RE NOT LIKELY TO HURT THE CUB!
REASONABL
BUT WHEN ALL IS SAID, THE DECISION RESTS IN ONLY ONE SMALL PAIR OF HANDS!

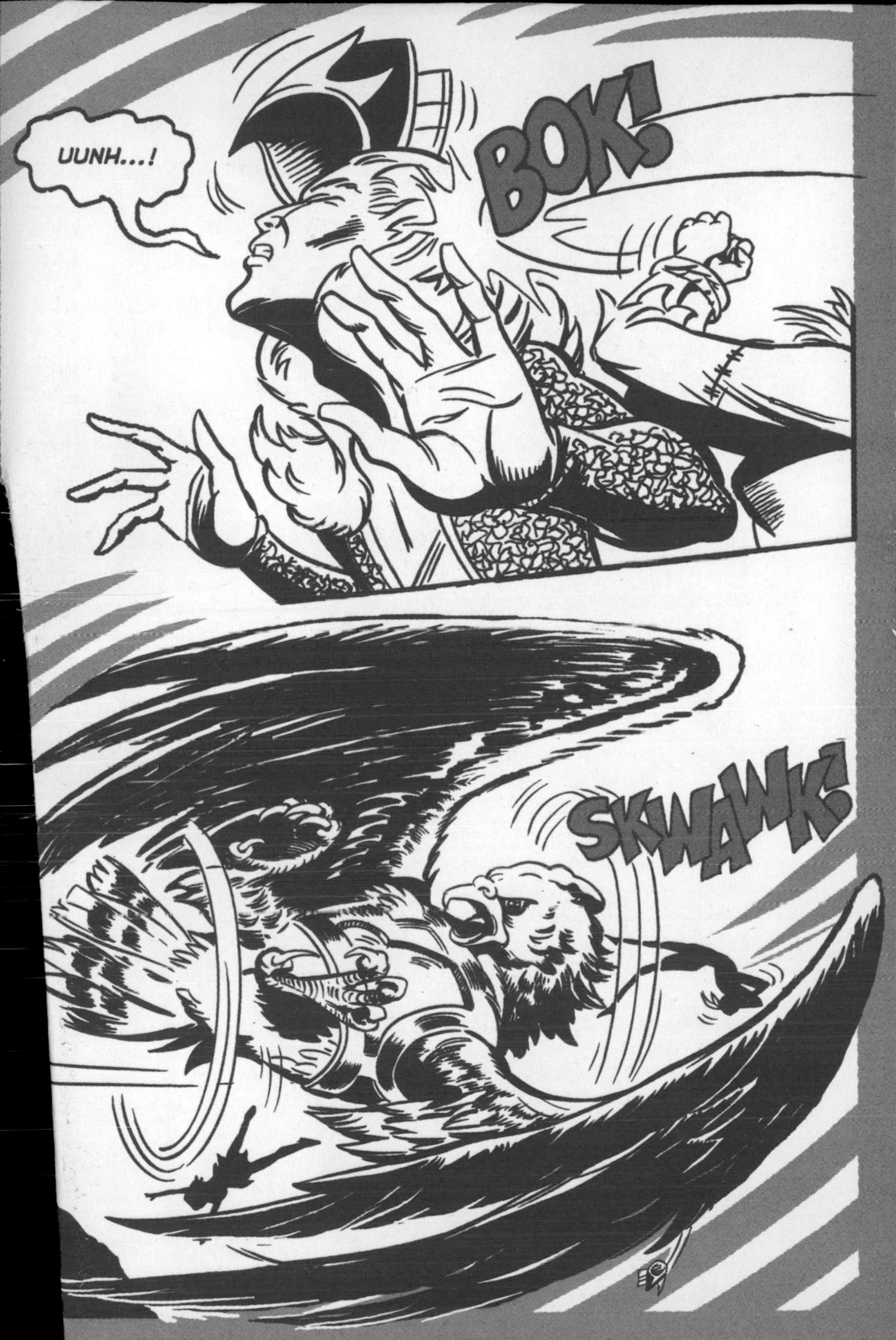
UUNH...!
BOK!
SKWAWK!

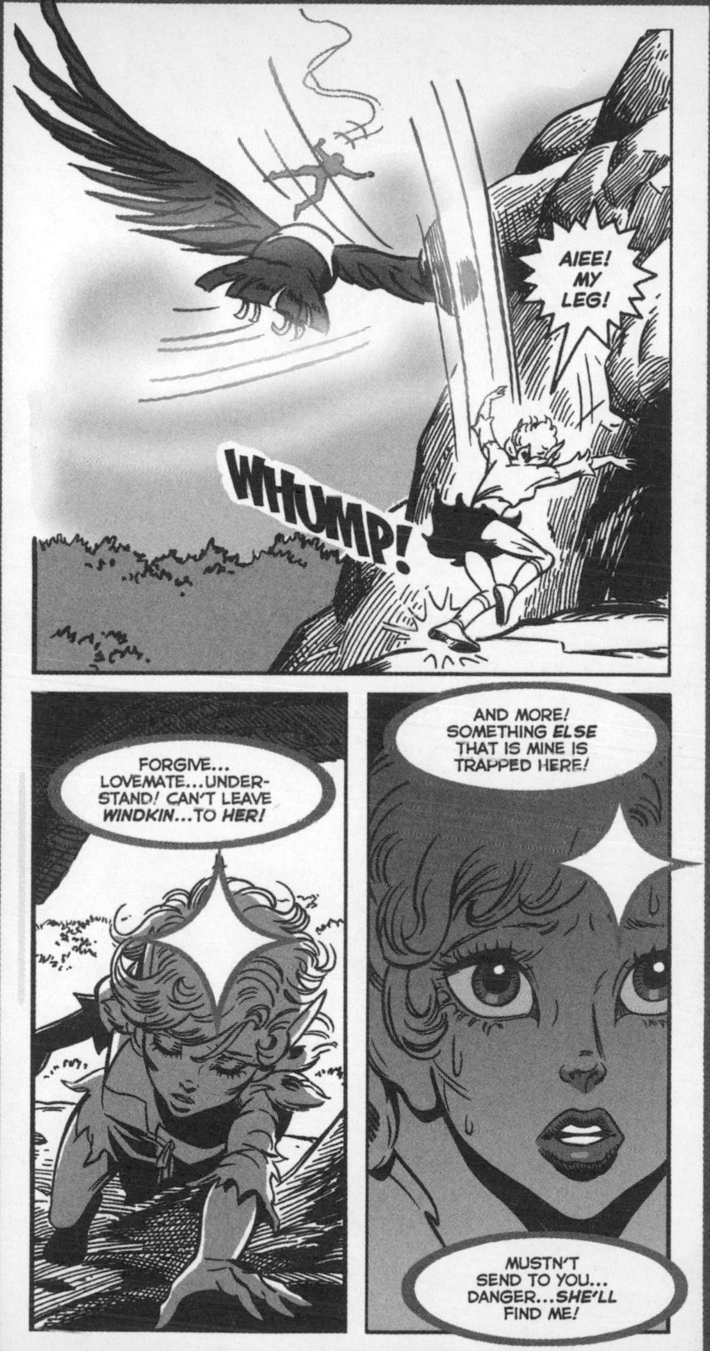
AIEE! MY LEG!
WHUMP!
FORGIVE... LOVEMATE...UNDER-STAND! CAN'T LEAVE WINDKIN...TO HER!
AND MORE! SOMETHING ELSE THAT IS MINE IS TRAPPED HERE!
MUSTN'T SEND TO YOU... DANGER...SHE'LL FIND ME!

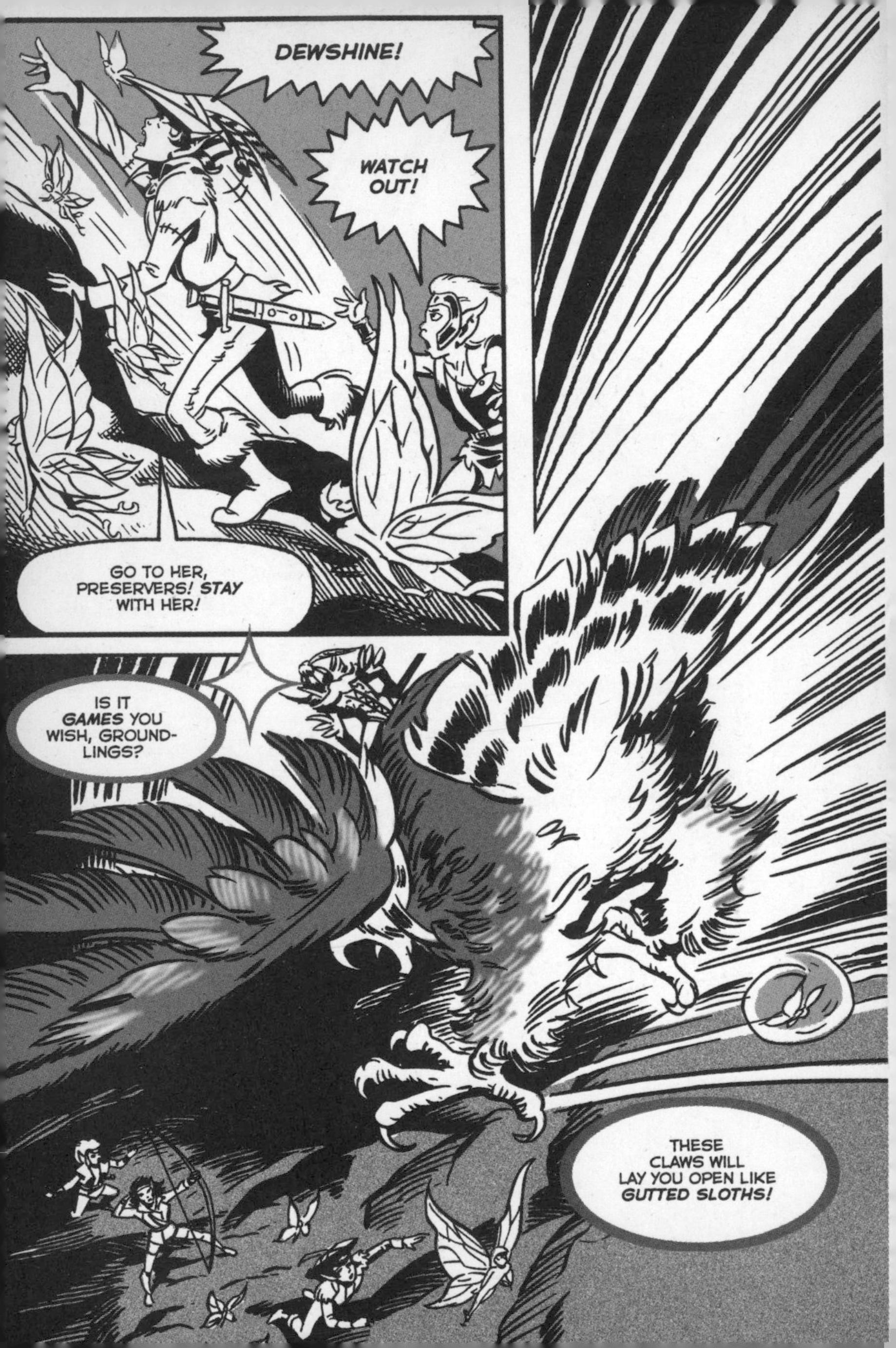
DEWSHINE!
WATCH OUT!
GO TO HER, PRESERVERS! STAY WITH HER!
IS IT GAMES YOU WISH, GROUND-LINGS?
THESE CLAWS WILL LAY YOU OPEN LIKE GUTTED SLOTHS!

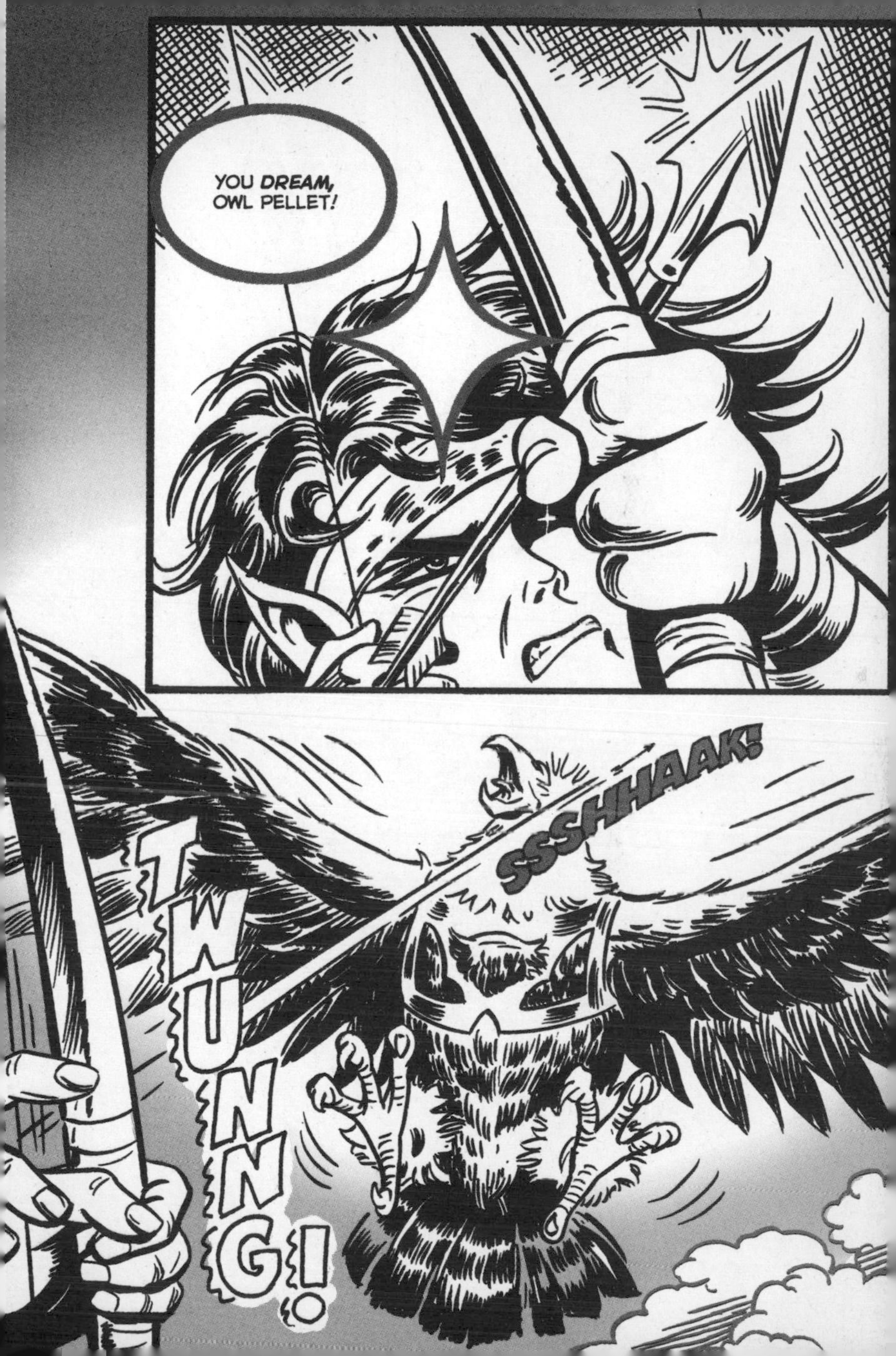
YOU DREAM, OWL PELLET!
SSSHHAAK!
TWUNNNG!

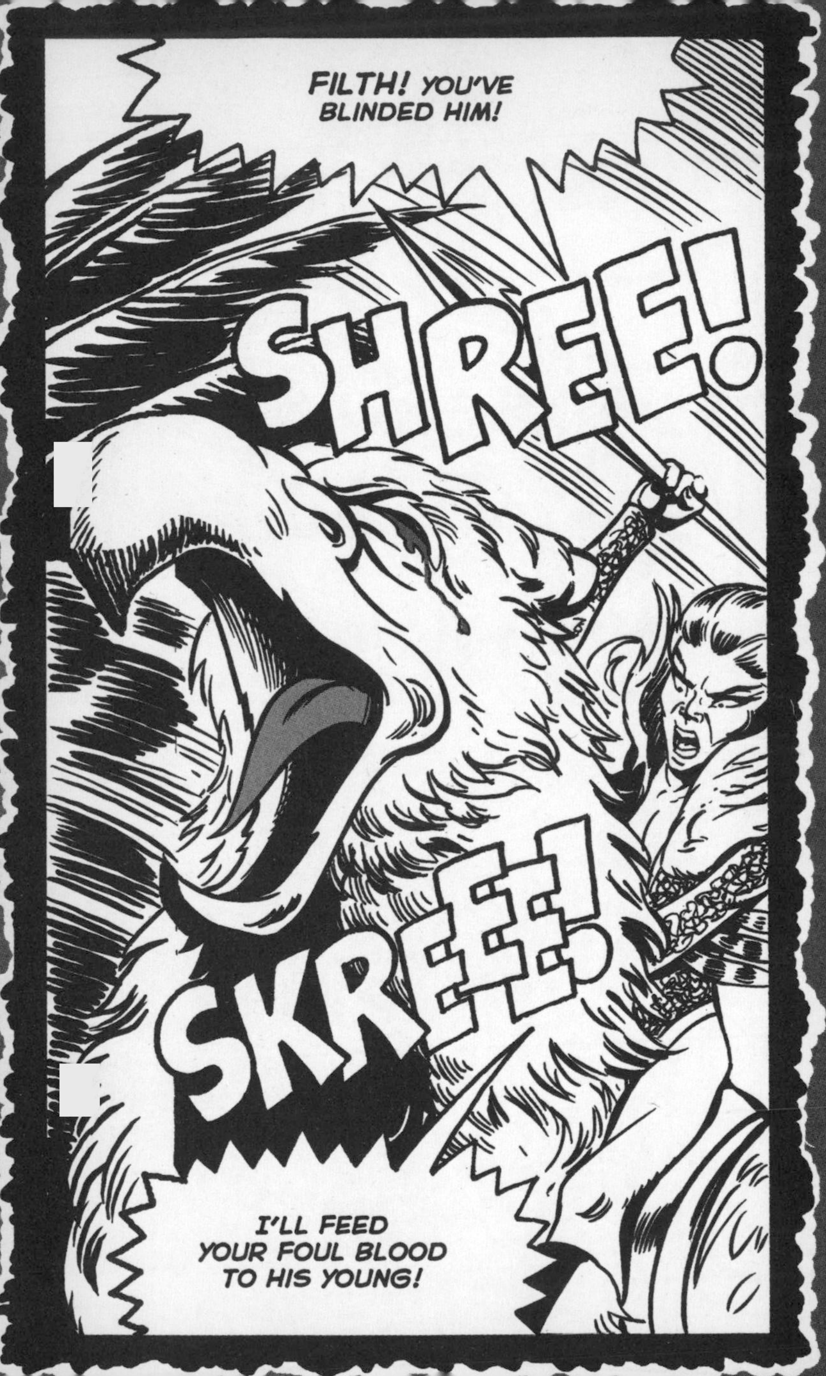
FILTH! YOU'VE BLINDED HIM!
SHREEE!
SKREEEE!
I'LL FEED YOUR FOUL BLOOD TO HIS YOUNG!

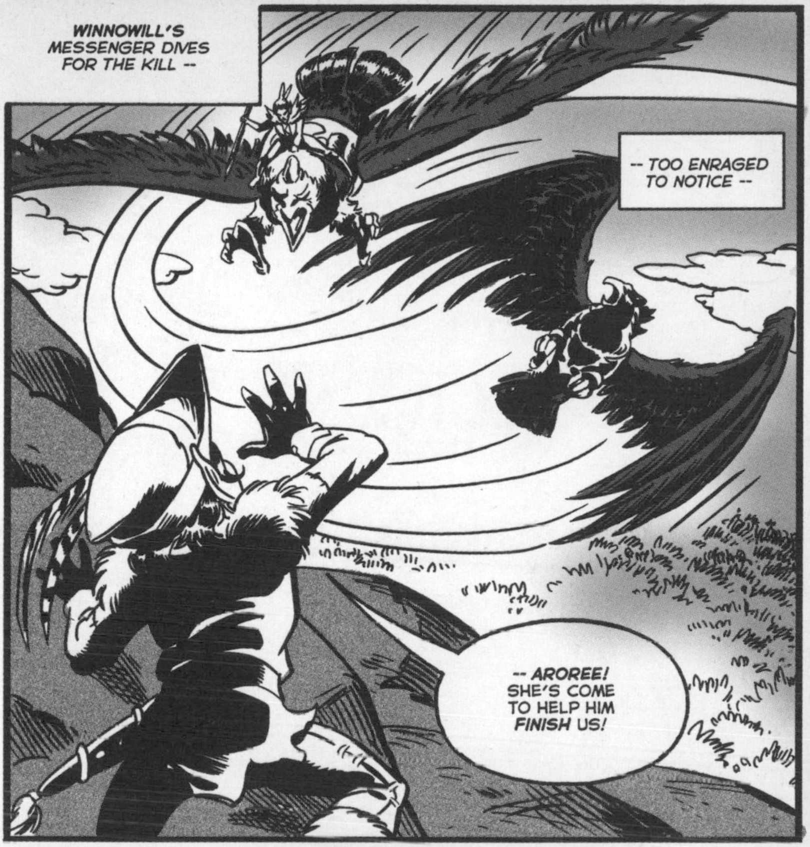
WINNOWILL'S MESSENGER DIVES FOR THE KILL --
-- TOO ENRAGED TO NOTICE --
-- AROREE! SHE'S COME TO HELP HIM FINISH US!

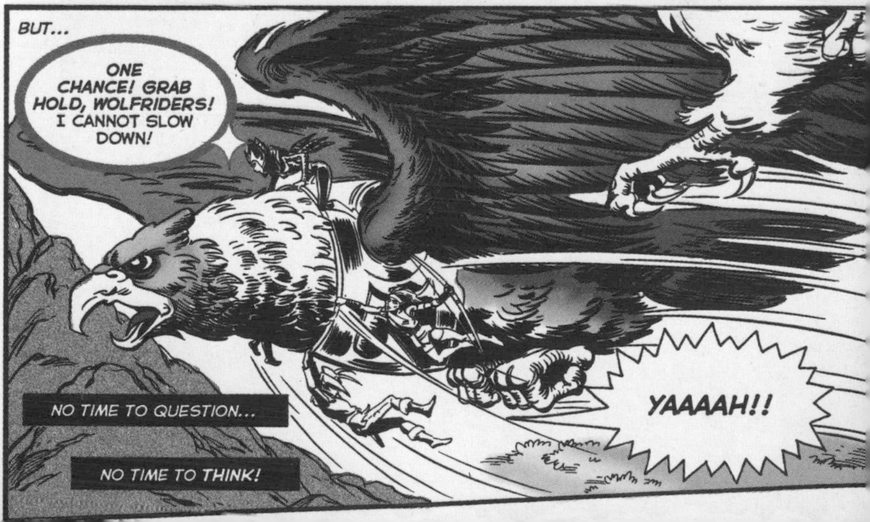
BUT...
ONE CHANCE! GRAB HOLD, WOLFRIDERS! I CANNOT SLOW DOWN!
YAAAAH!!
NO TIME TO QUESTION...
NO TIME TO THINK!

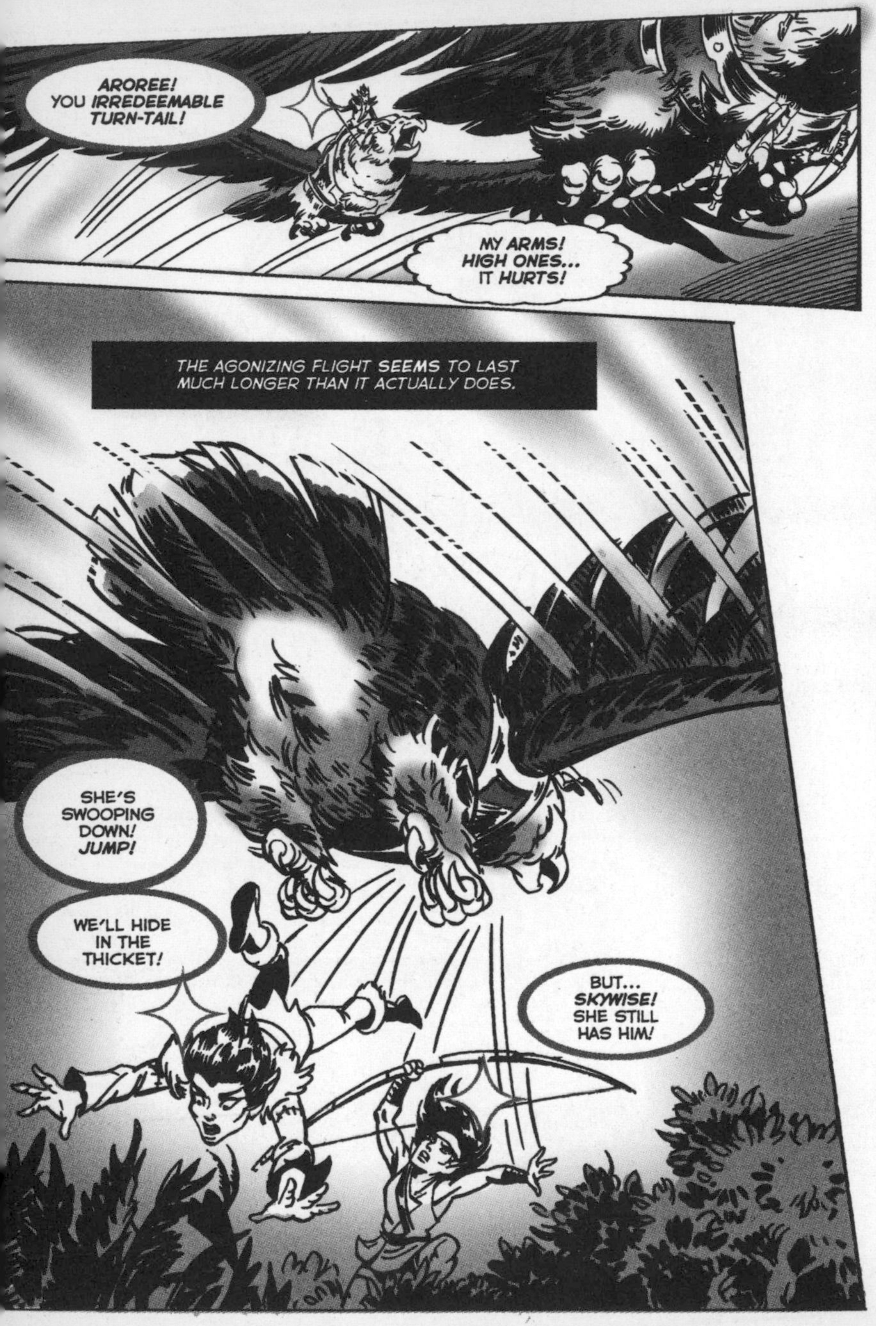
AROREE! YOU IRREDEEMABLE TURN-TAIL!
MY ARMS! HIGH ONES... IT HURTS!
THE AGONIZING FLIGHT SEEMS TO LAST MUCH LONGER THAN IT ACTUALLY DOES.
SHE'S SWOOPING DOWN! JUMP!
WE'LL HIDE IN THE THICKET!
BUT... SKYWISE! SHE STILL HAS HIM!

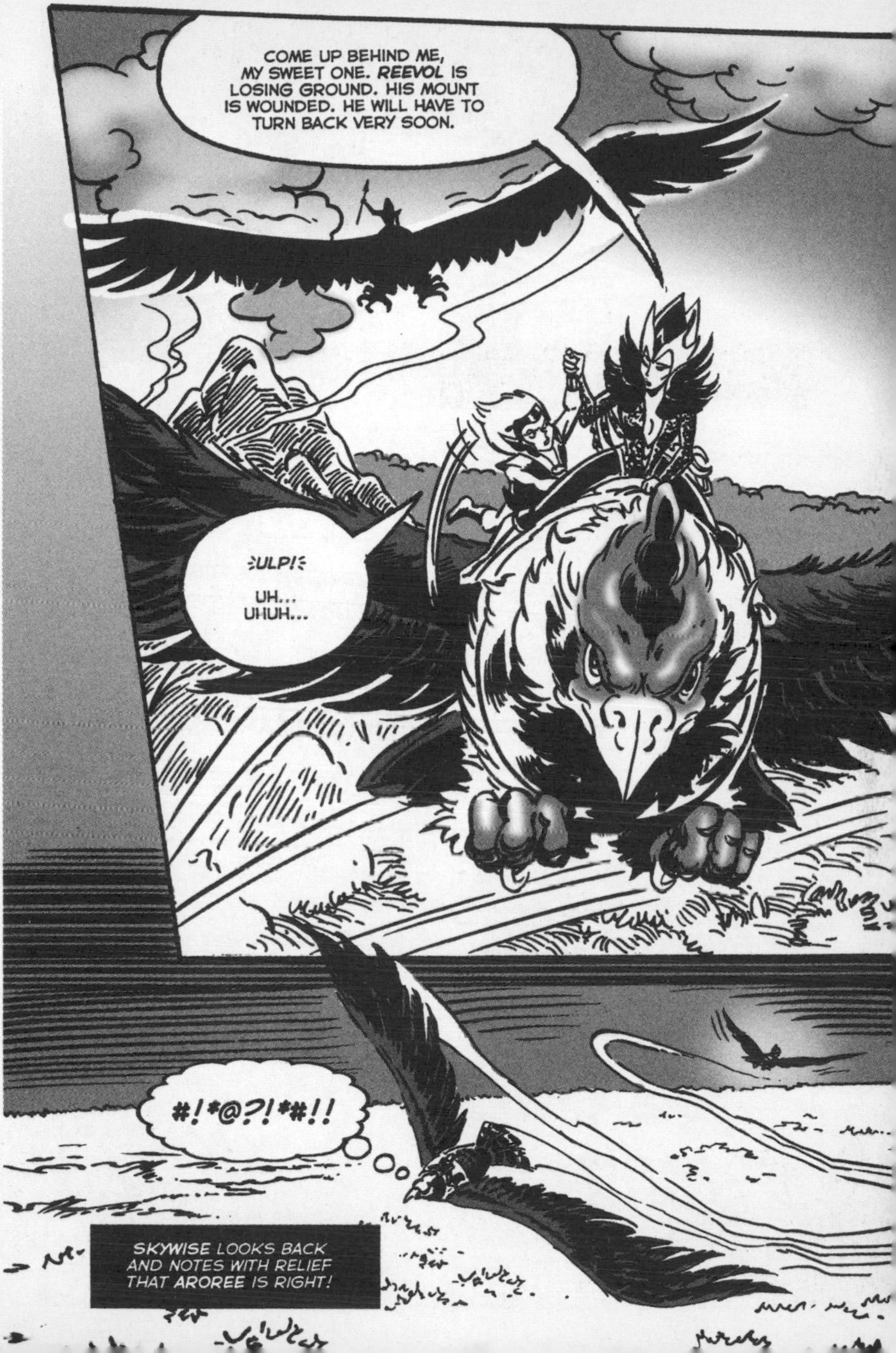
COME UP BEHIND ME, MY SWEET ONE. *REEVOL* IS LOSING GROUND. HIS MOUNT IS WOUNDED. HE WILL HAVE TO TURN BACK VERY SOON.
ULP!
UH... UHUH...
#!*@?!*#!!
SKYWISE LOOKS BACK AND NOTES WITH RELIEF THAT *AROREE* IS RIGHT!

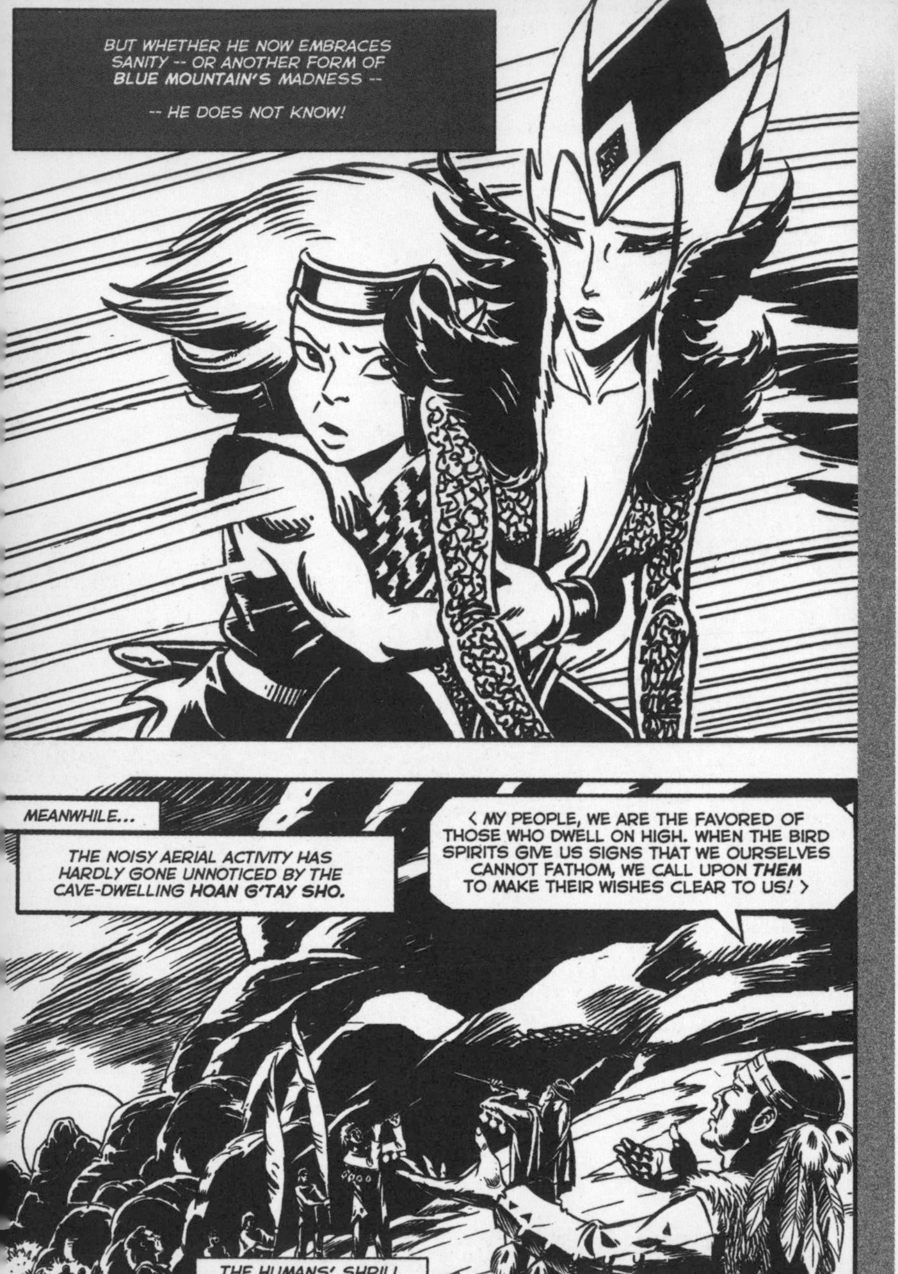

BUT WHETHER HE NOW EMBRACES SANITY -- OR ANOTHER FORM OF BLUE MOUNTAIN'S MADNESS --
-- HE DOES NOT KNOW!
MEANWHILE...
THE NOISY AERIAL ACTIVITY HAS HARDLY GONE UNNOTICED BY THE CAVE-DWELLING HOAN G'TAY SHO.
< MY PEOPLE, WE ARE THE FAVORED OF THOSE WHO DWELL ON HIGH. WHEN THE BIRD SPIRITS GIVE US SIGNS THAT WE OURSELVES CANNOT FATHOM, WE CALL UPON THEM TO MAKE THEIR WISHES CLEAR TO US! >
THE HUMANS' SHRILL PIPES CRY OUT --

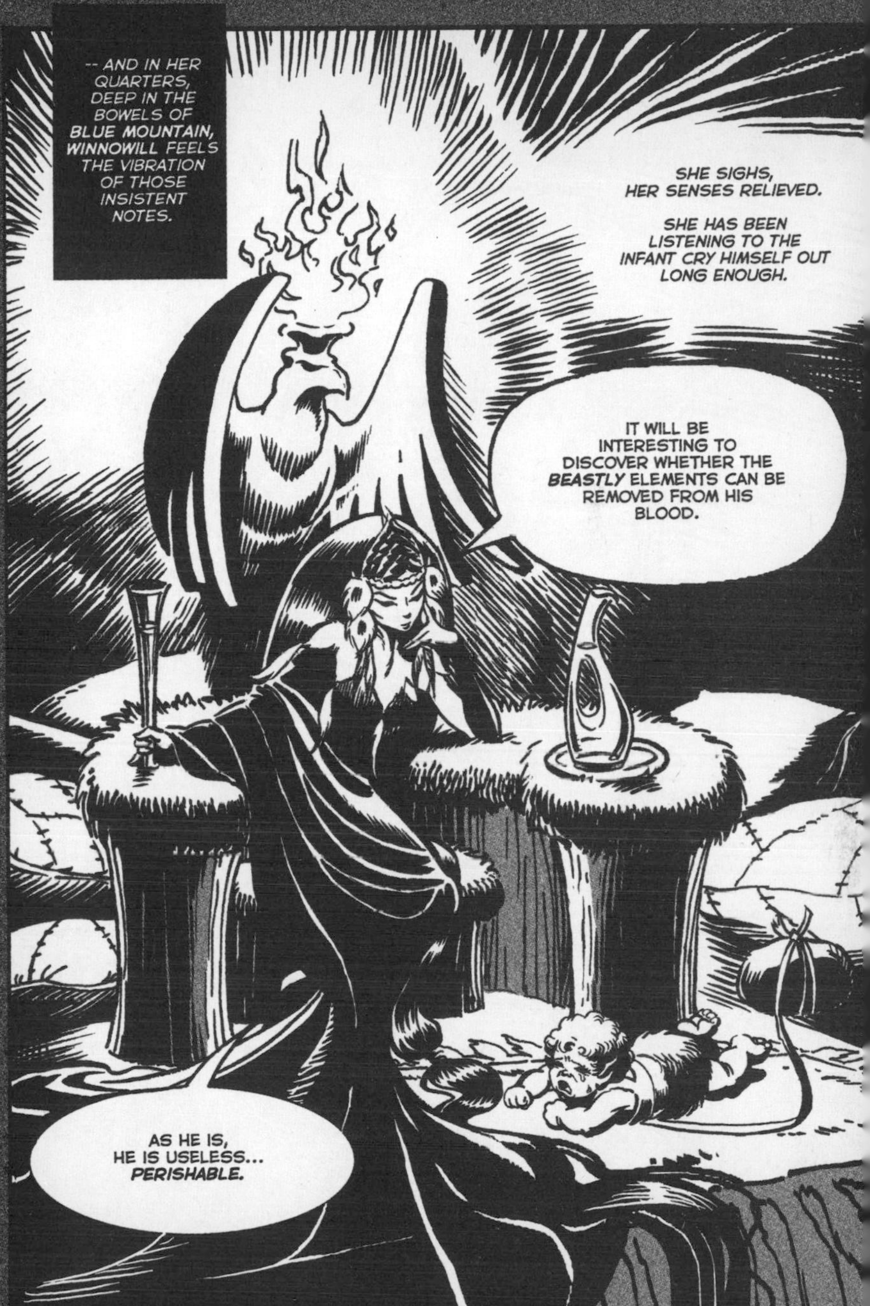
-- AND IN HER QUARTERS, DEEP IN THE BOWELS OF BLUE MOUNTAIN, WINNOWILL FEELS THE VIBRATION OF THOSE INSISTENT NOTES.
SHE SIGHS, HER SENSES RELIEVED.
SHE HAS BEEN LISTENING TO THE INFANT CRY HIMSELF OUT LONG ENOUGH.
IT WILL BE INTERESTING TO DISCOVER WHETHER THE *BEASTLY* ELEMENTS CAN BE REMOVED FROM HIS BLOOD.
AS HE IS, HE IS USELESS... *PERISHABLE.*

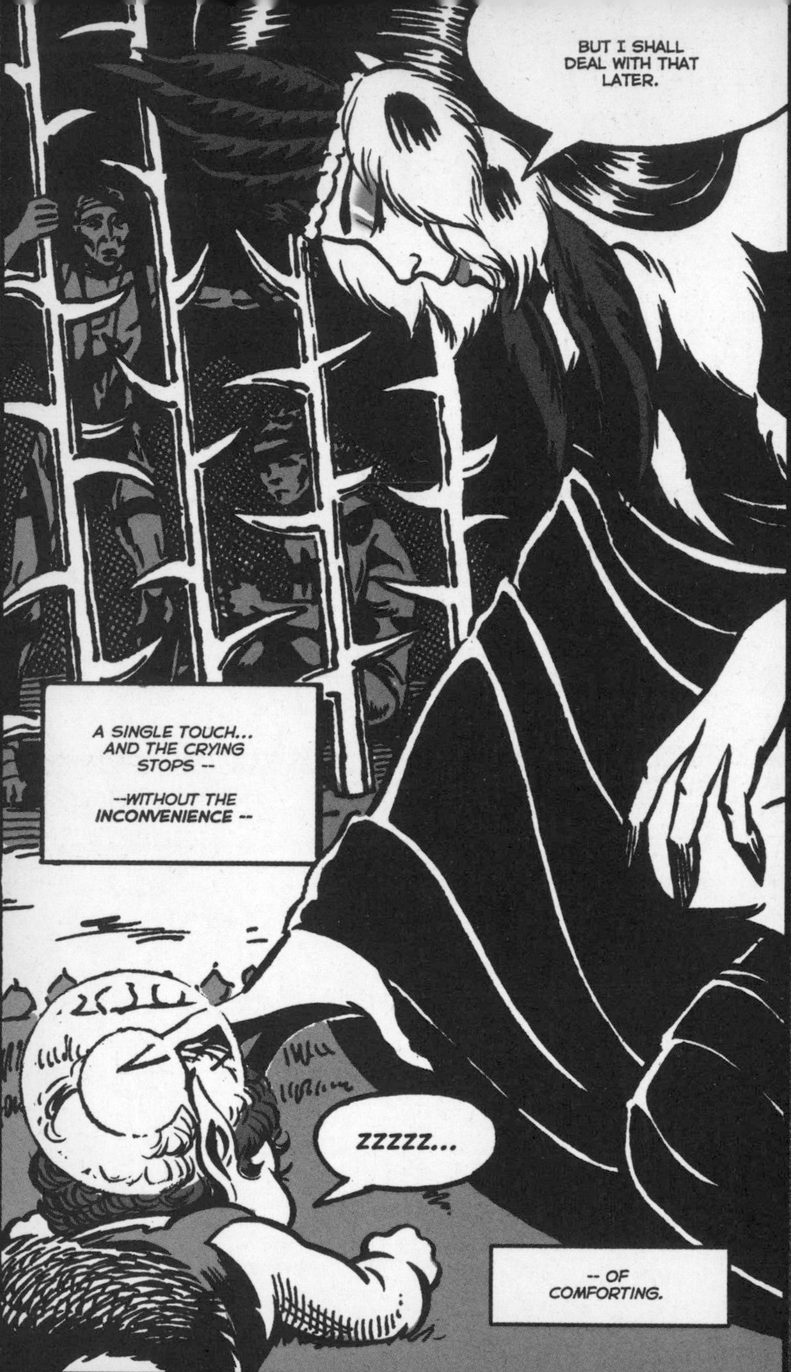
BUT I SHALL DEAL WITH THAT LATER.
A SINGLE TOUCH... AND THE CRYING STOPS --
--WITHOUT THE INCONVENIENCE --
ZZZZZ...
-- OF COMFORTING.

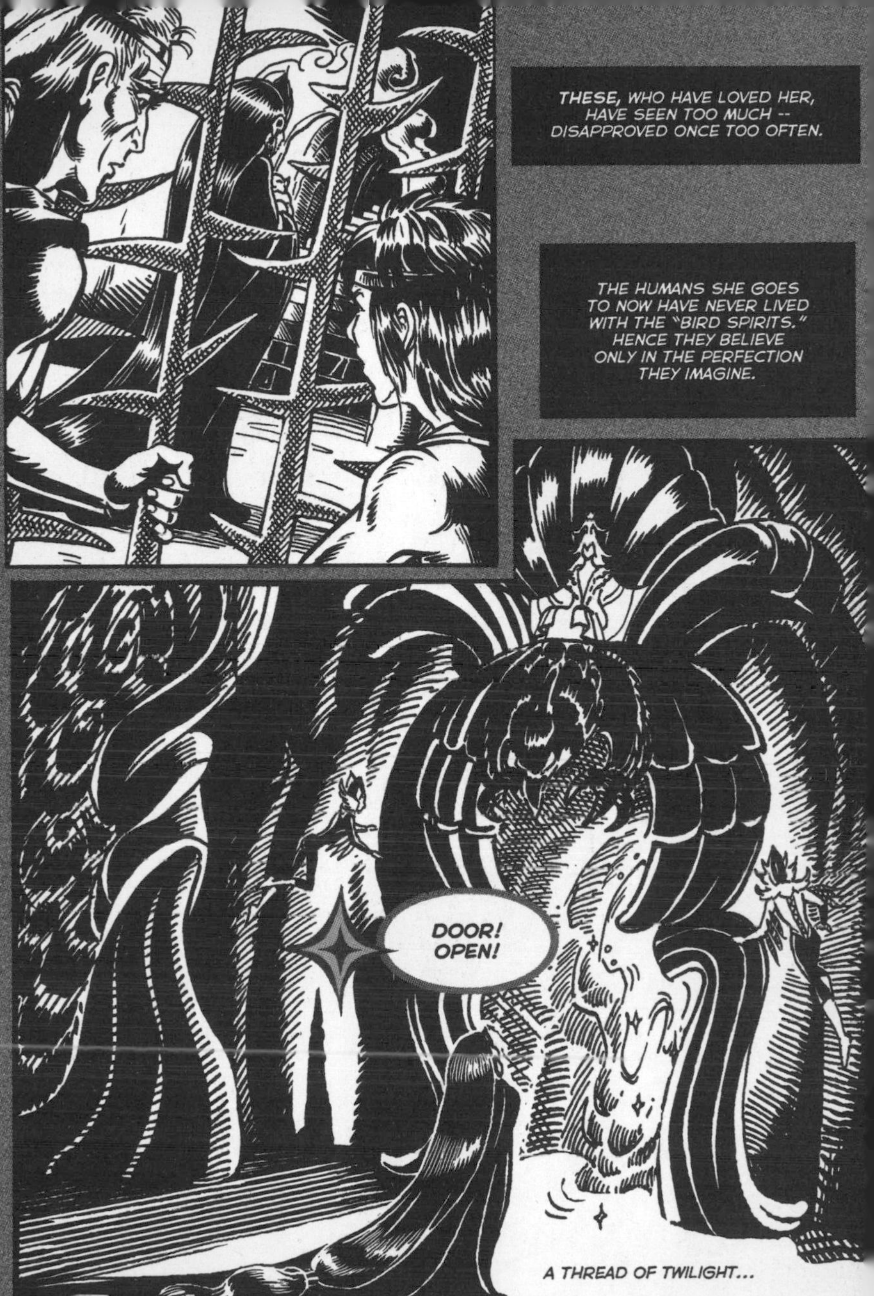
THESE, WHO HAVE LOVED HER, HAVE SEEN TOO MUCH -- DISAPPROVED ONCE TOO OFTEN.
THE HUMANS SHE GOES TO NOW HAVE NEVER LIVED WITH THE "BIRD SPIRITS." HENCE THEY BELIEVE ONLY IN THE PERFECTION THEY IMAGINE.
DOOR! OPEN!
A THREAD OF TWILIGHT...

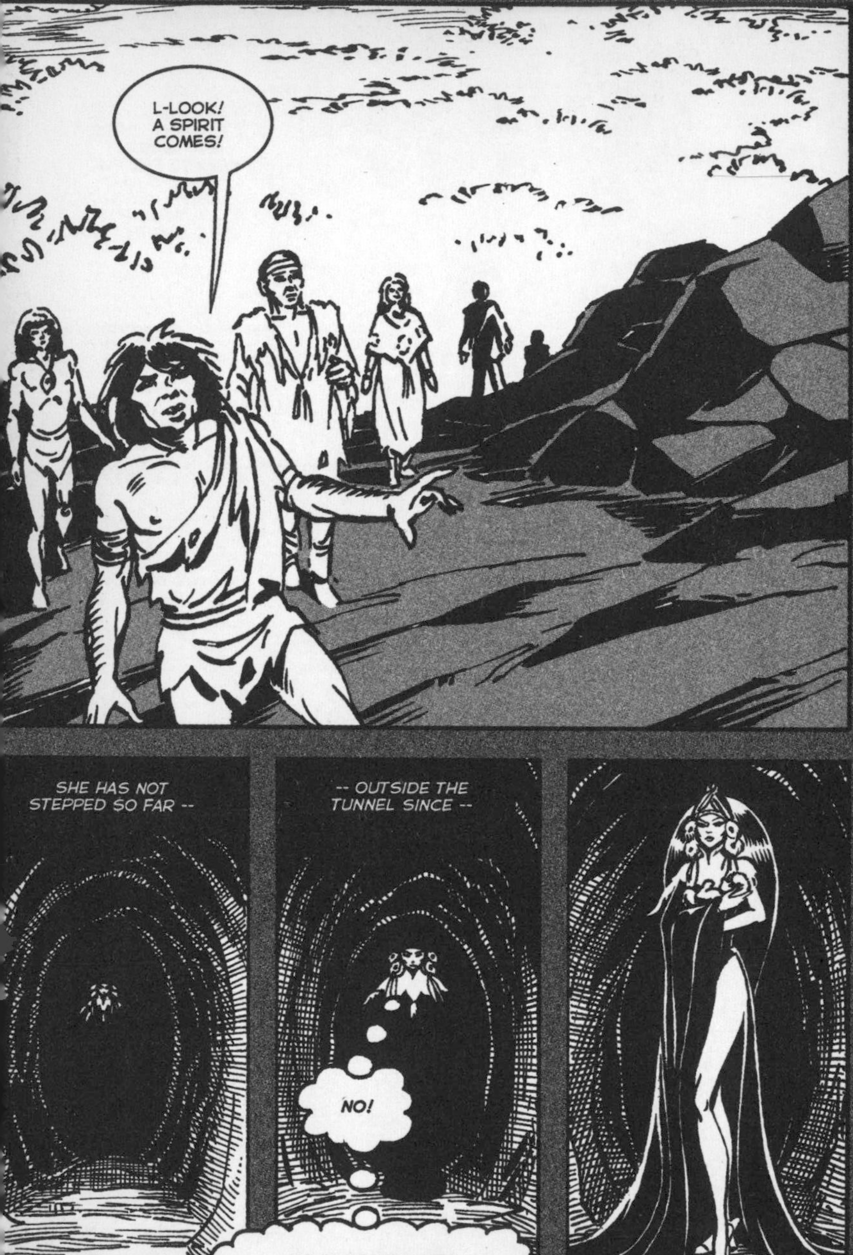
L-LOOK! A SPIRIT COMES!
SHE HAS NOT STEPPED SO FAR --
-- OUTSIDE THE TUNNEL SINCE --
NO!
NO REMEMBERING!

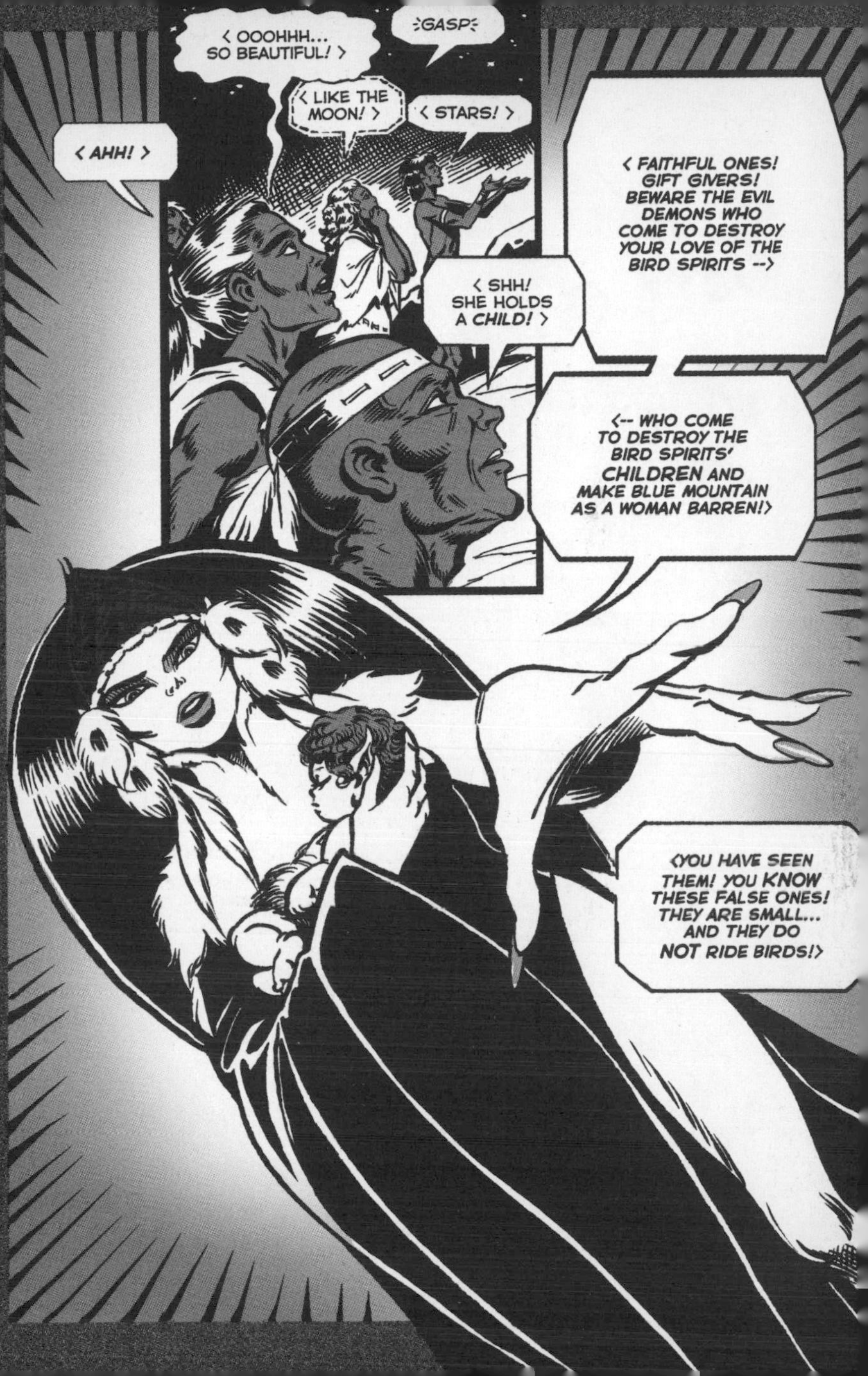
< OOOHHH... SO BEAUTIFUL! >
GASP
< LIKE THE MOON! >
< STARS! >
< AHH! >
< FAITHFUL ONES! GIFT GIVERS! BEWARE THE EVIL DEMONS WHO COME TO DESTROY YOUR LOVE OF THE BIRD SPIRITS -->
< SHH! SHE HOLDS A CHILD! >
<-- WHO COME TO DESTROY THE BIRD SPIRITS' CHILDREN AND MAKE BLUE MOUNTAIN AS A WOMAN BARREN!>
<YOU HAVE SEEN THEM! YOU KNOW THESE FALSE ONES! THEY ARE SMALL... AND THEY DO NOT RIDE BIRDS!>

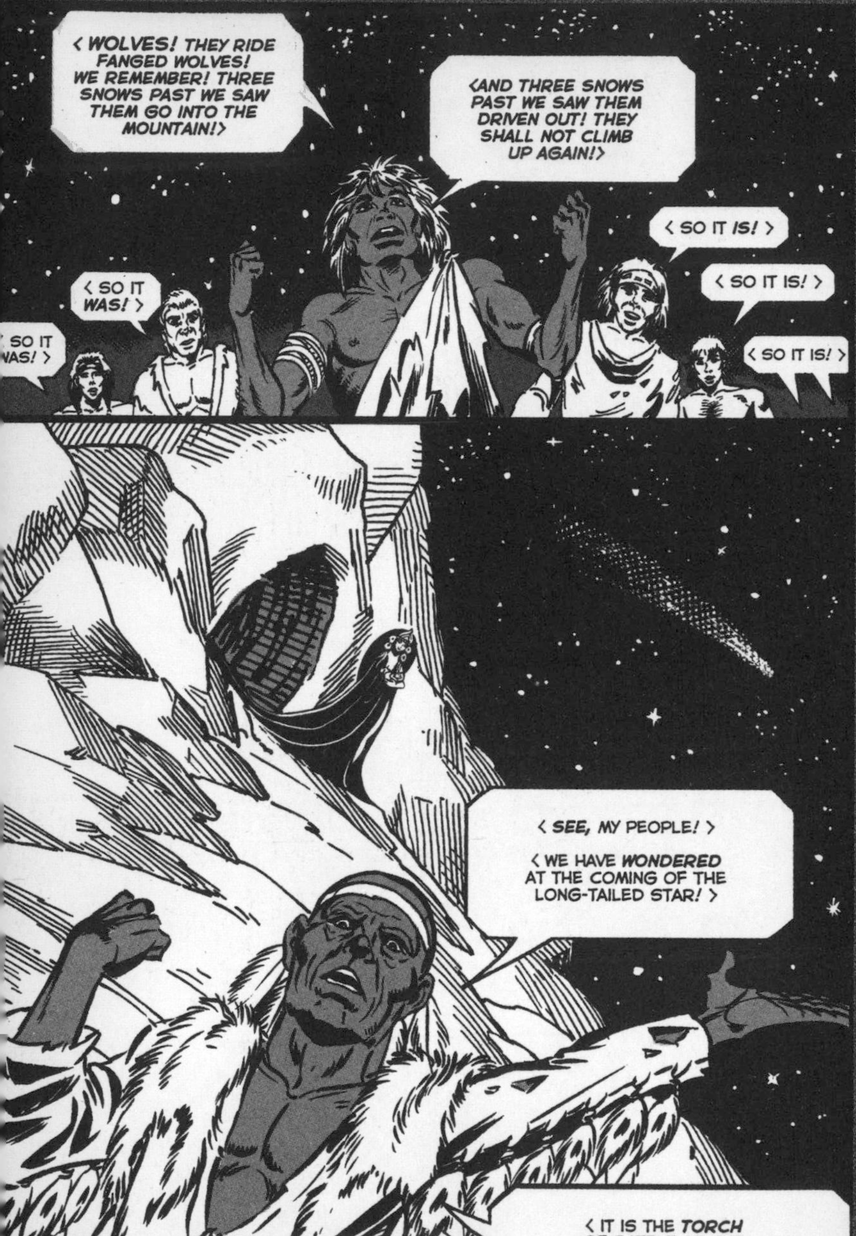
< WOLVES! THEY RIDE FANGED WOLVES! WE REMEMBER! THREE SNOWS PAST WE SAW THEM GO INTO THE MOUNTAIN!>
<AND THREE SNOWS PAST WE SAW THEM DRIVEN OUT! THEY SHALL NOT CLIMB UP AGAIN!>
SO IT WAS! >
< SO IT WAS! >
< SO IT IS! >
< SO IT IS! >
< SO IT IS! >
< SEE, MY PEOPLE! >
< WE HAVE WONDERED AT THE COMING OF THE LONG-TAILED STAR! >
< IT IS THE TORCH OF BATTLE AS THE SHAMAN FORETOLD! >

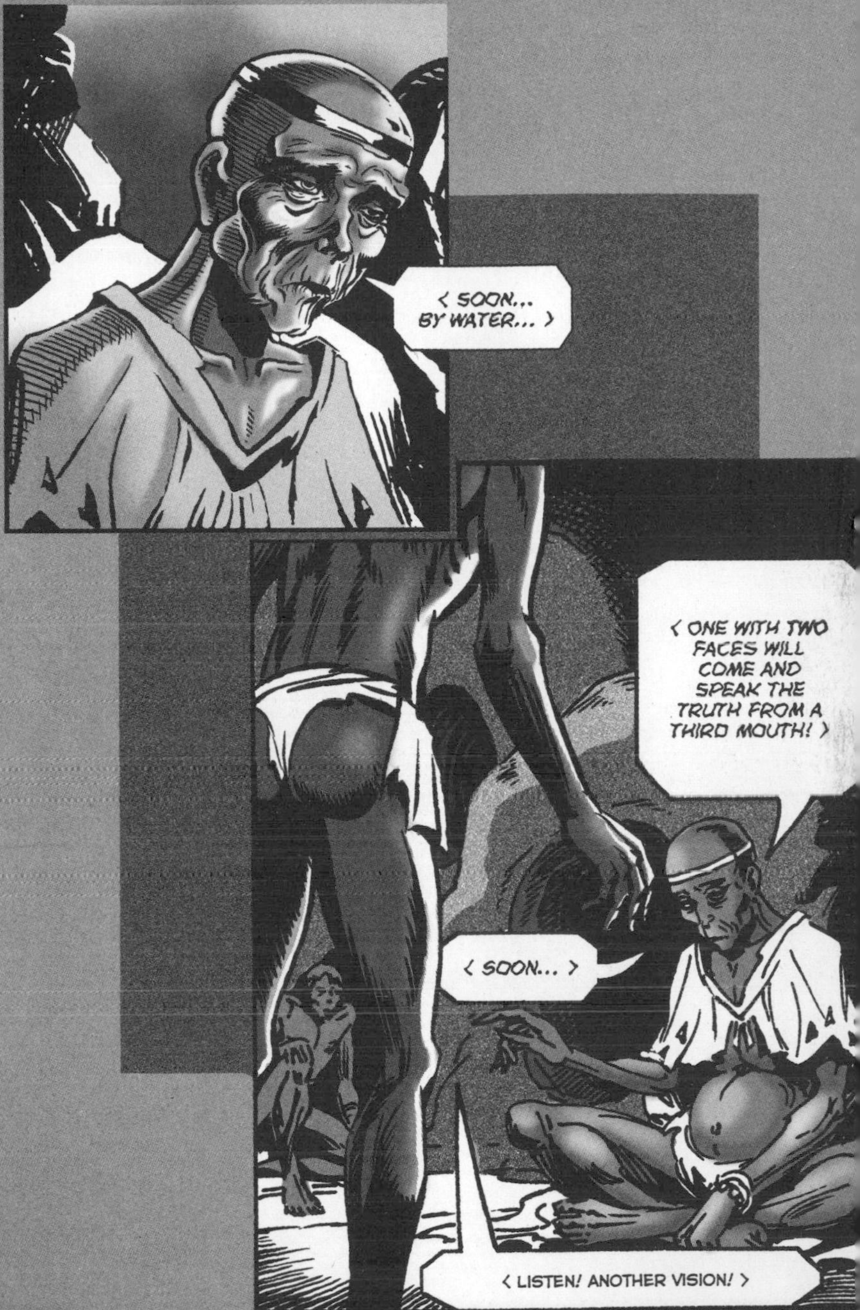
< SOON... BY WATER... >
< ONE WITH TWO FACES WILL COME AND SPEAK THE TRUTH FROM A THIRD MOUTH! >
< SOON... >
< LISTEN! ANOTHER VISION! >

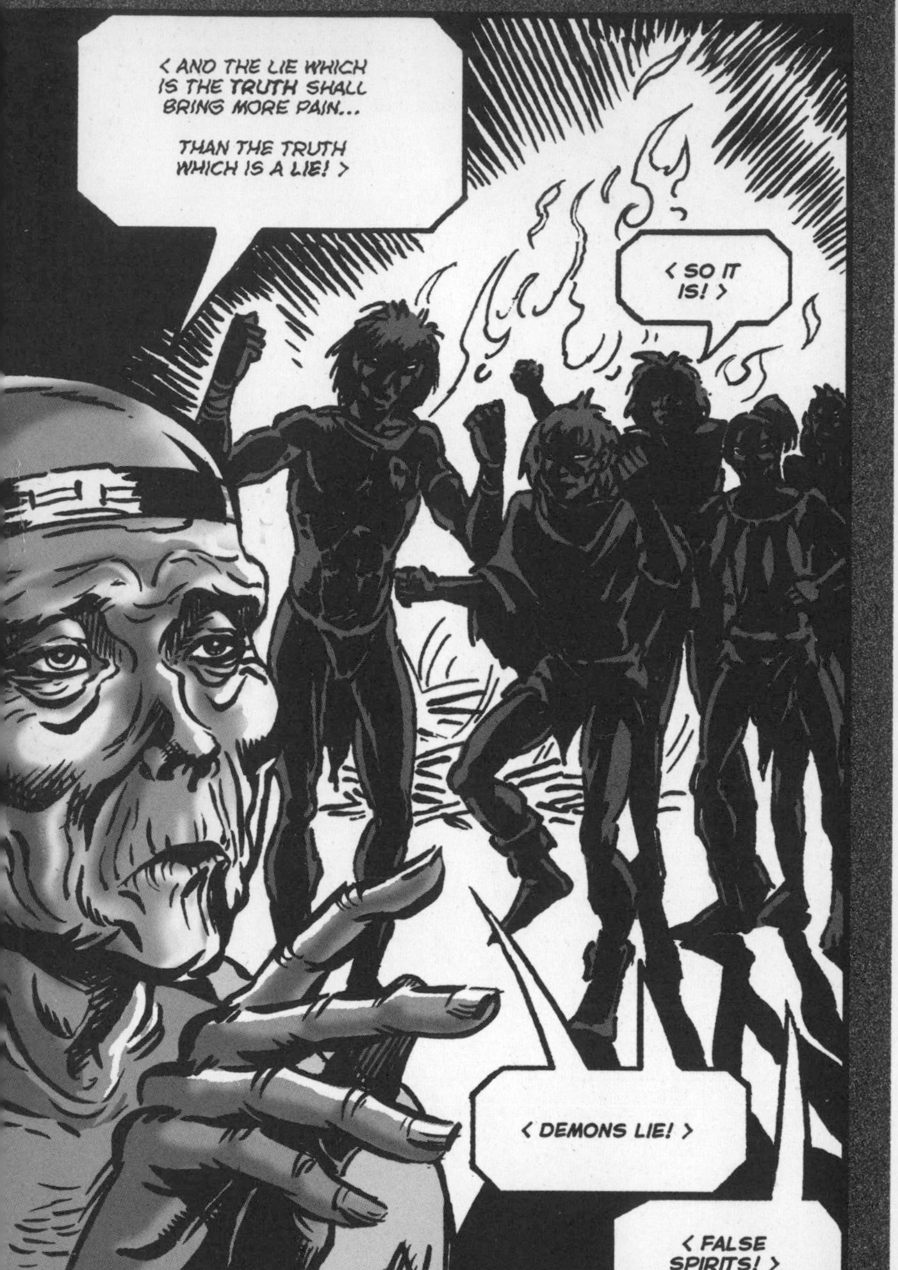
< AND THE LIE WHICH IS THE TRUTH SHALL BRING MORE PAIN...
THAN THE TRUTH WHICH IS A LIE! >
< SO IT IS! >
< DEMONS LIE! >
< FALSE SPIRITS! >

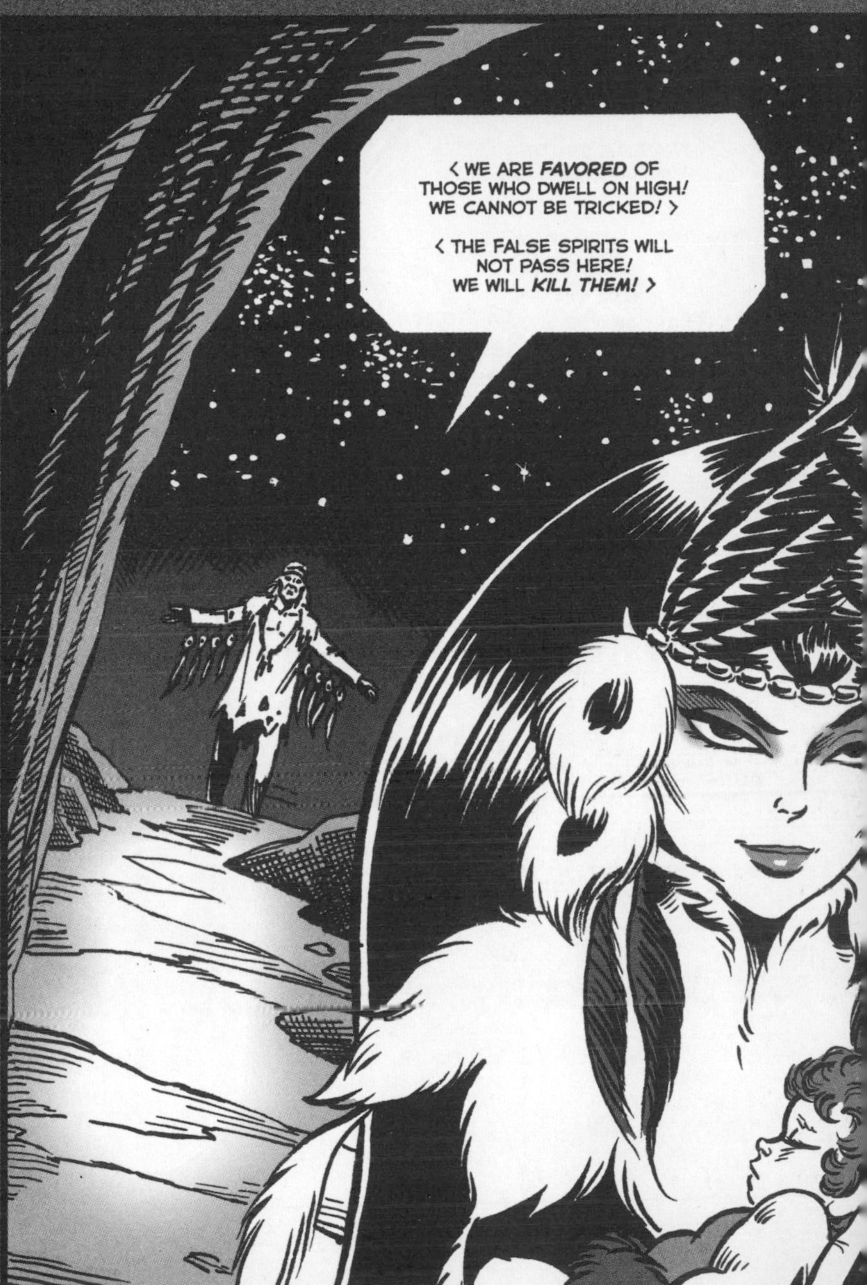
< WE ARE FAVORED OF THOSE WHO DWELL ON HIGH! WE CANNOT BE TRICKED! >
< THE FALSE SPIRITS WILL NOT PASS HERE! WE WILL KILL THEM! >

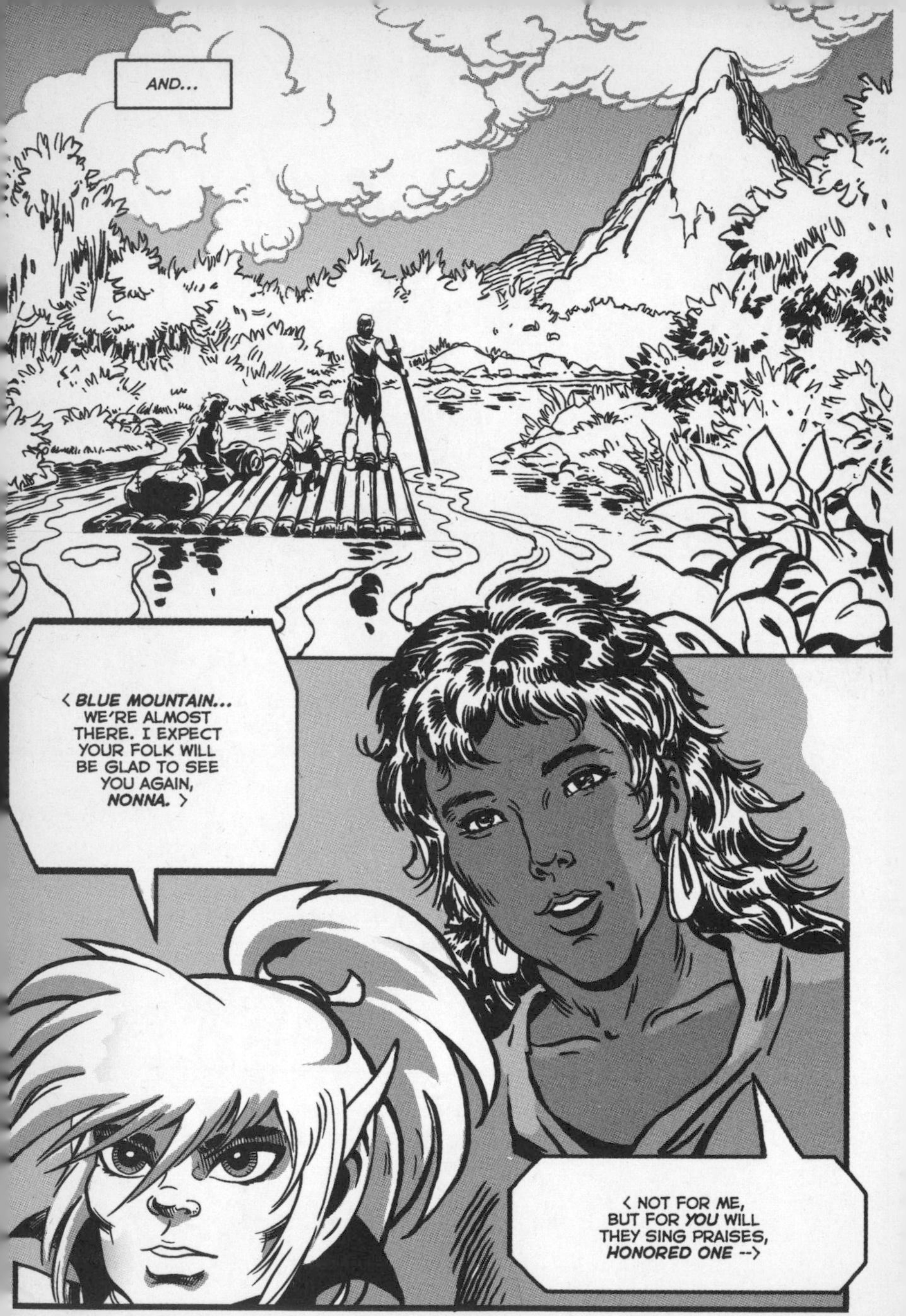
AND...
< BLUE MOUNTAIN... WE'RE ALMOST THERE. I EXPECT YOUR FOLK WILL BE GLAD TO SEE YOU AGAIN, NONNA. >
< NOT FOR ME, BUT FOR YOU WILL THEY SING PRAISES, HONORED ONE -->

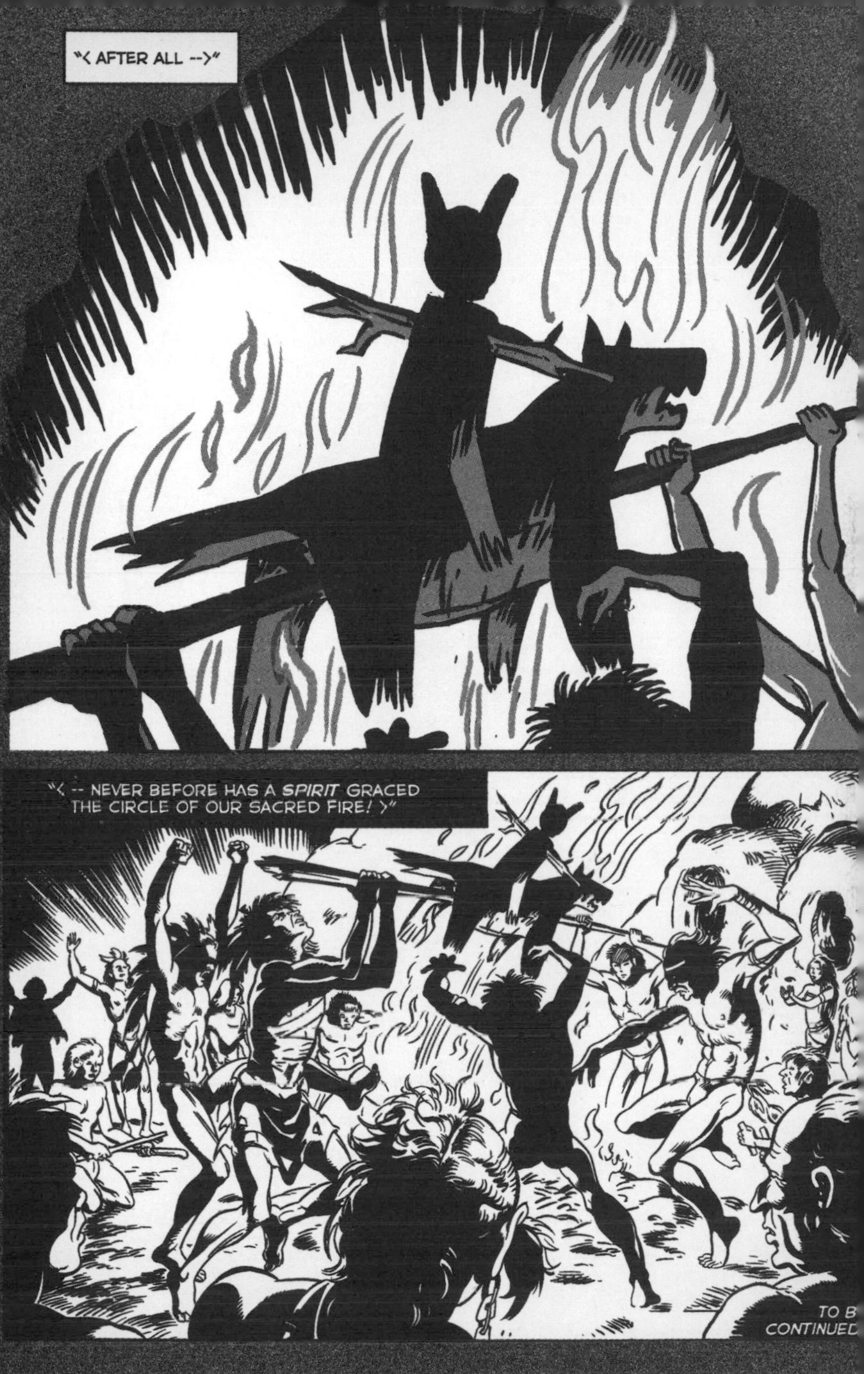
"< AFTER ALL -->"
"< -- NEVER BEFORE HAS A *SPIRIT* GRACED THE CIRCLE OF OUR SACRED FIRE! >"
TO B
CONTINUED

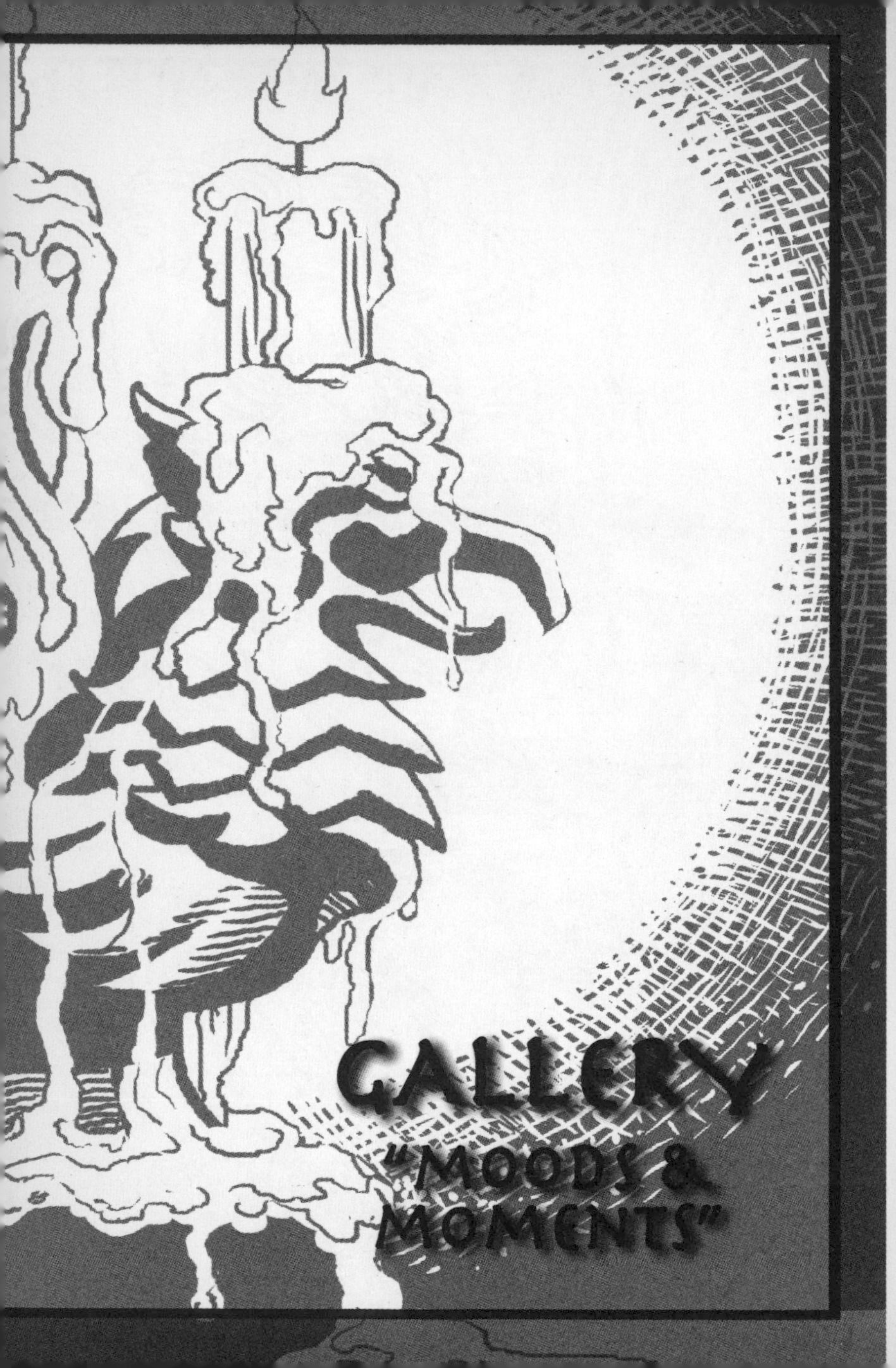
GALLERY
"MOODS &
MOMENTS"

DEWSHINE AND WINDKIN

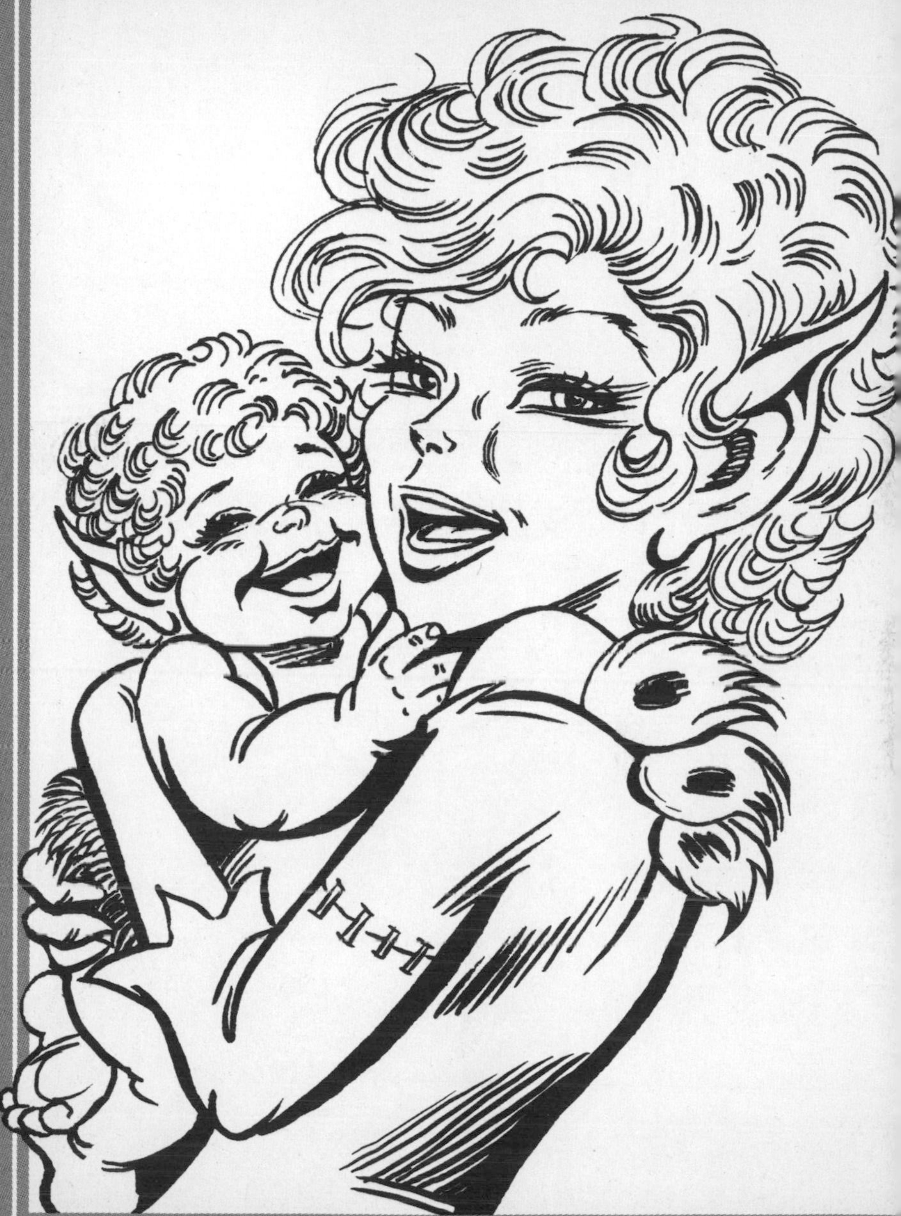

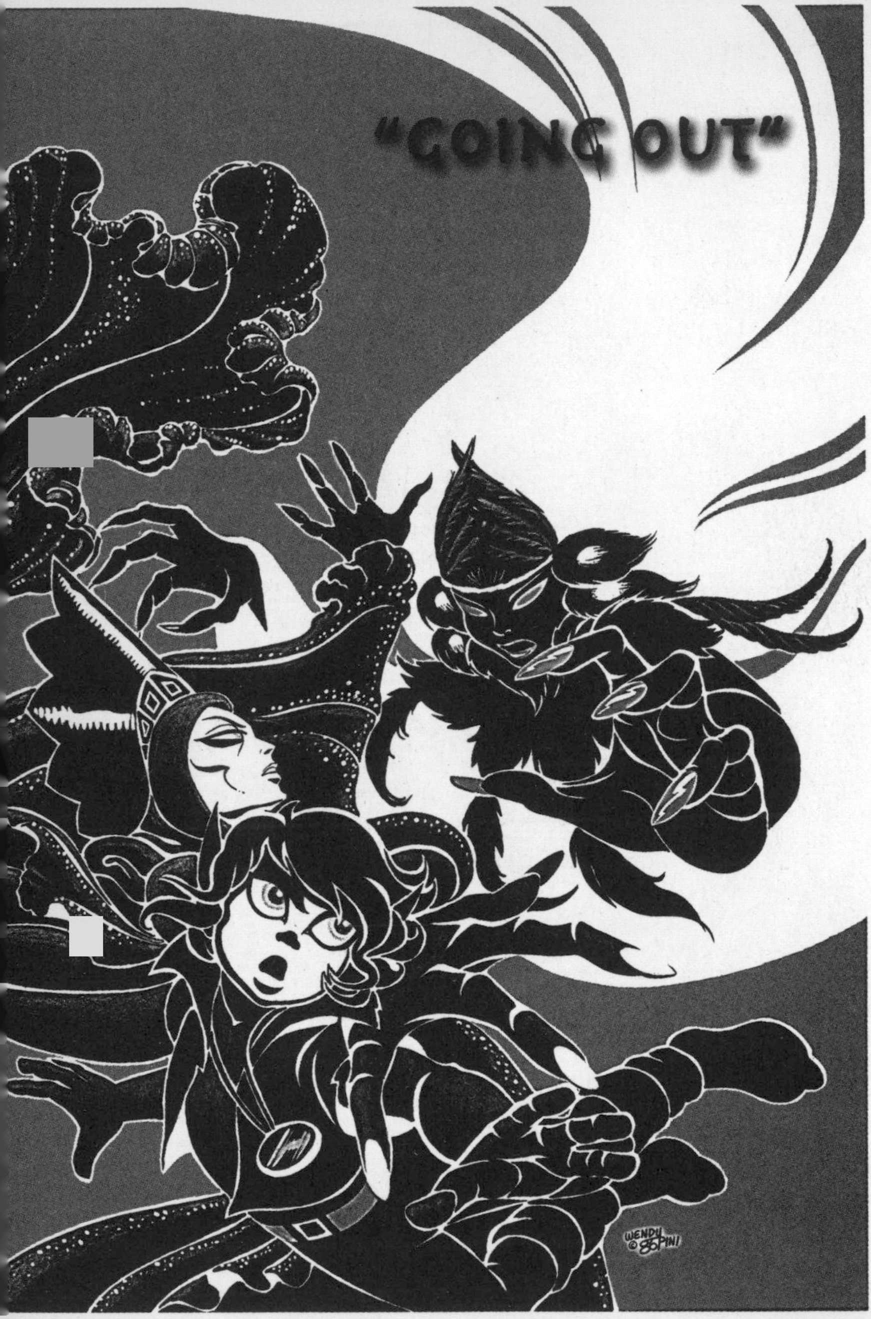
"GOING OUT"
WENDY © 85 PINI

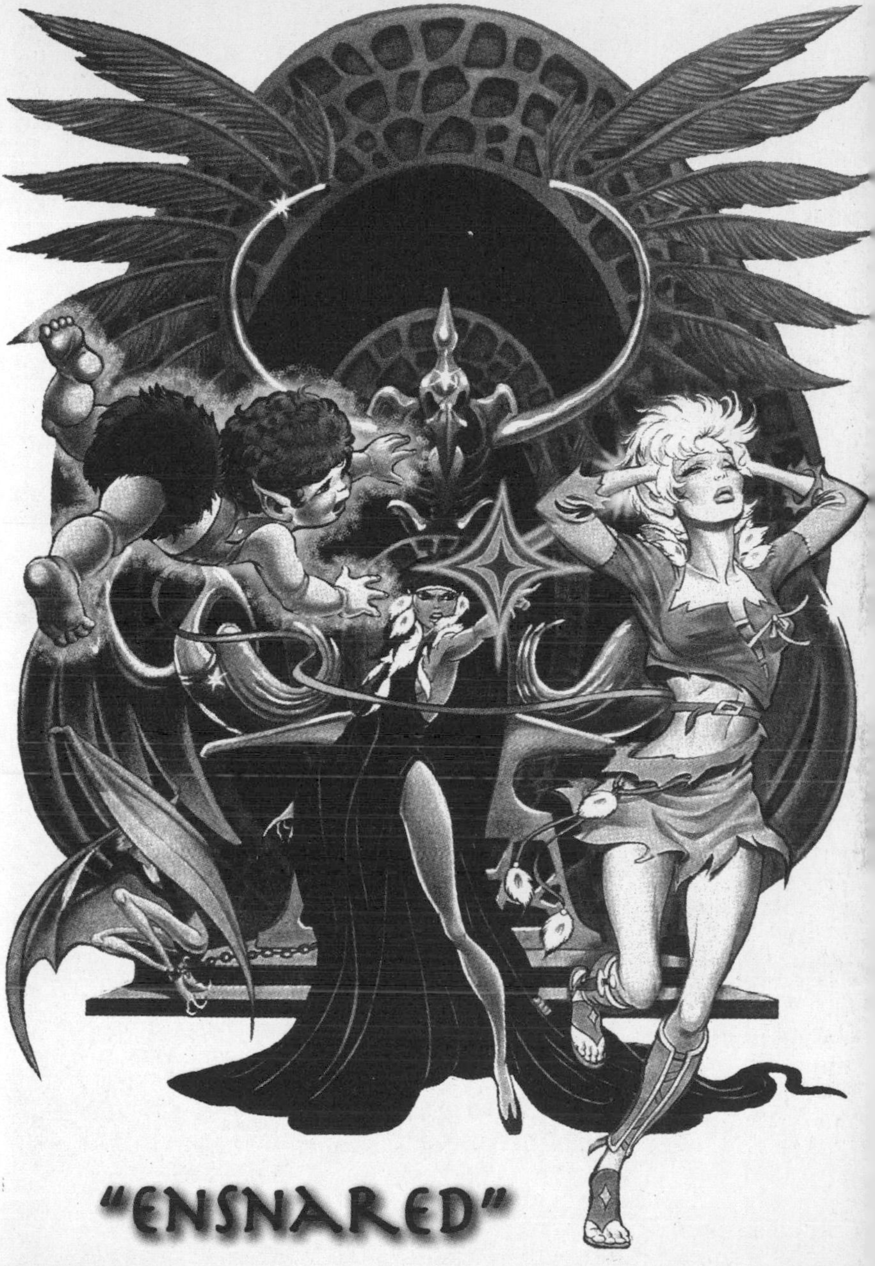
"ENSNARED"

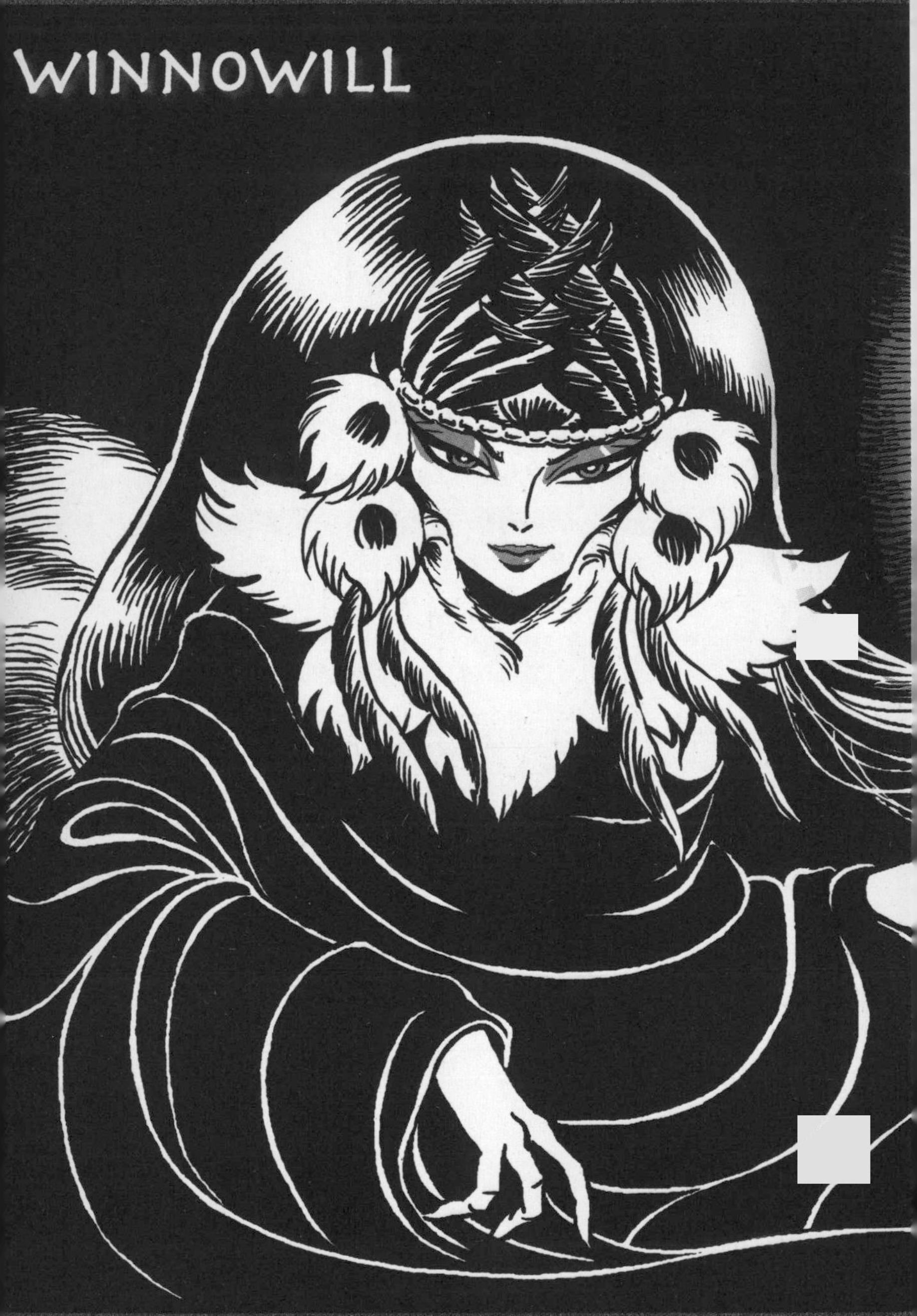
WINNOWILL

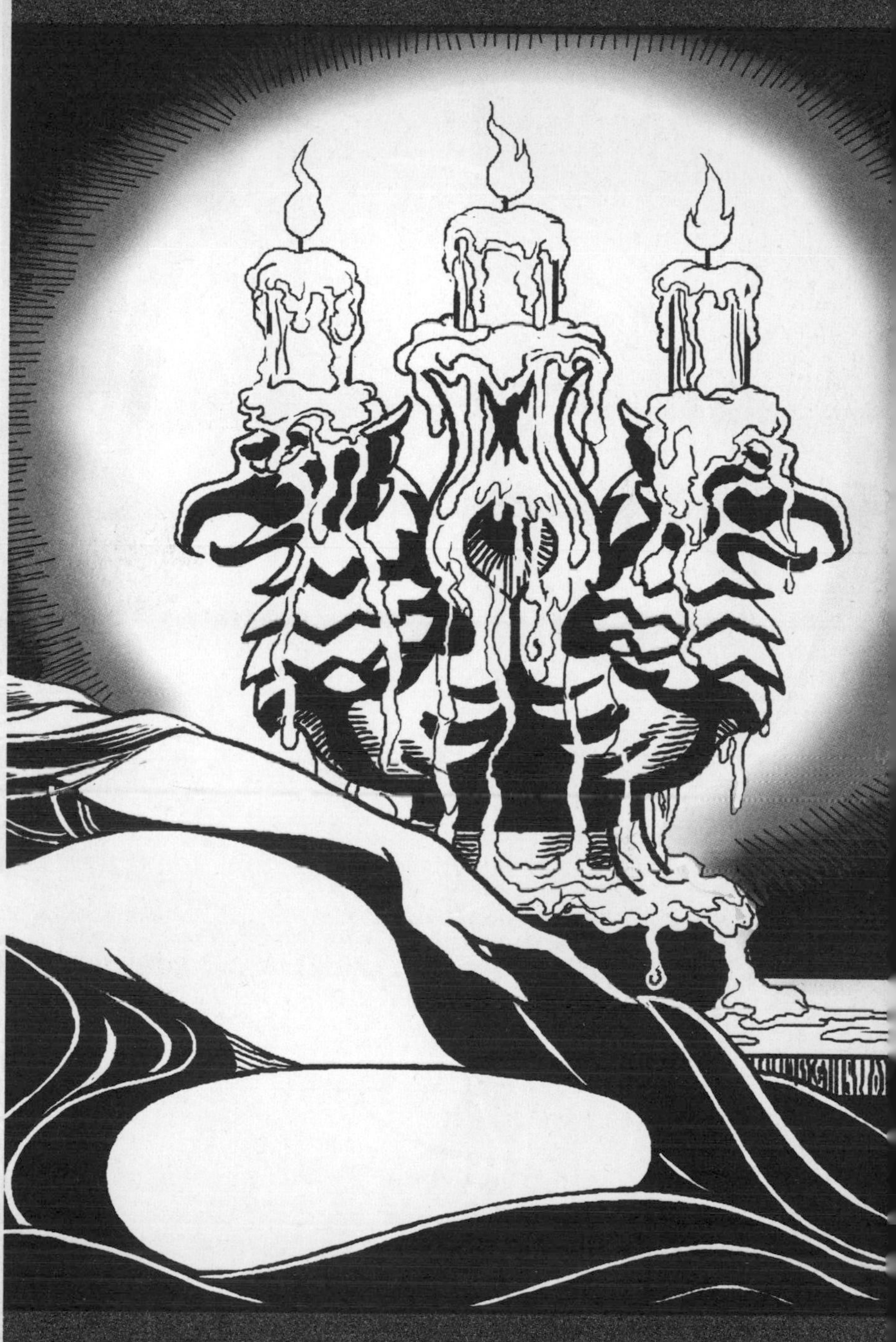

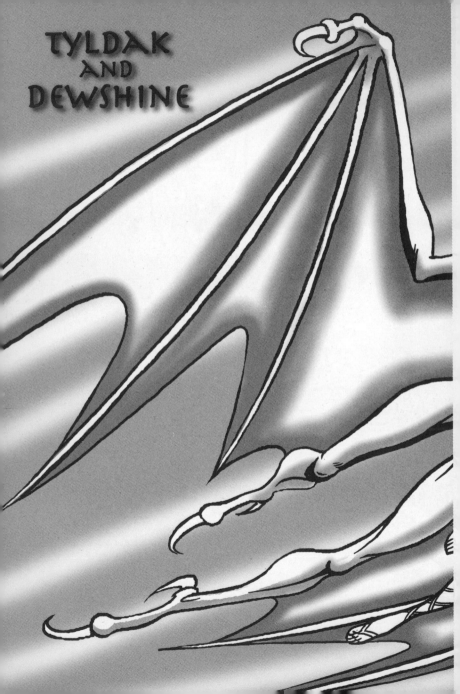

TYLDAK
AND
DEWSHINE

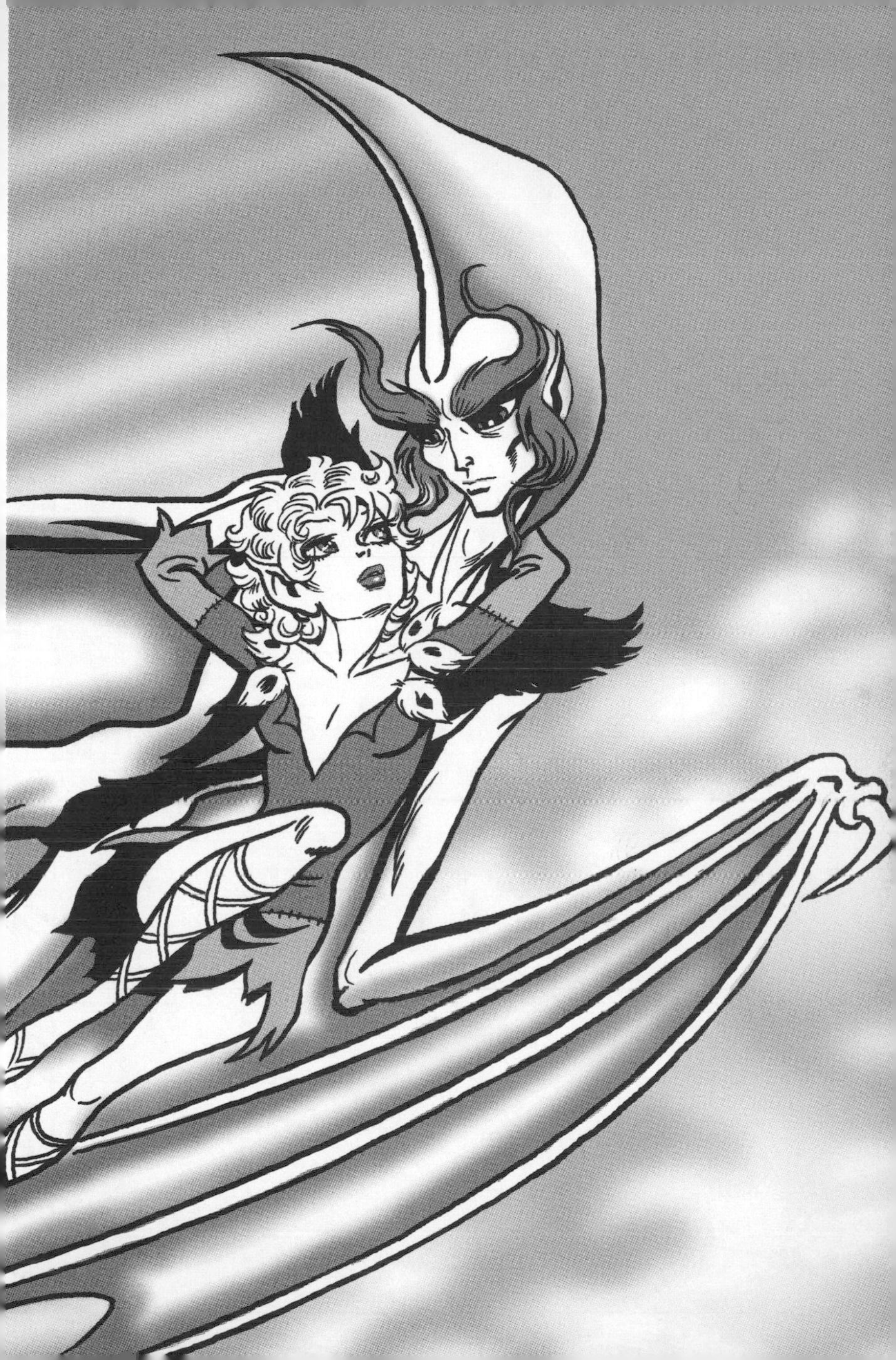

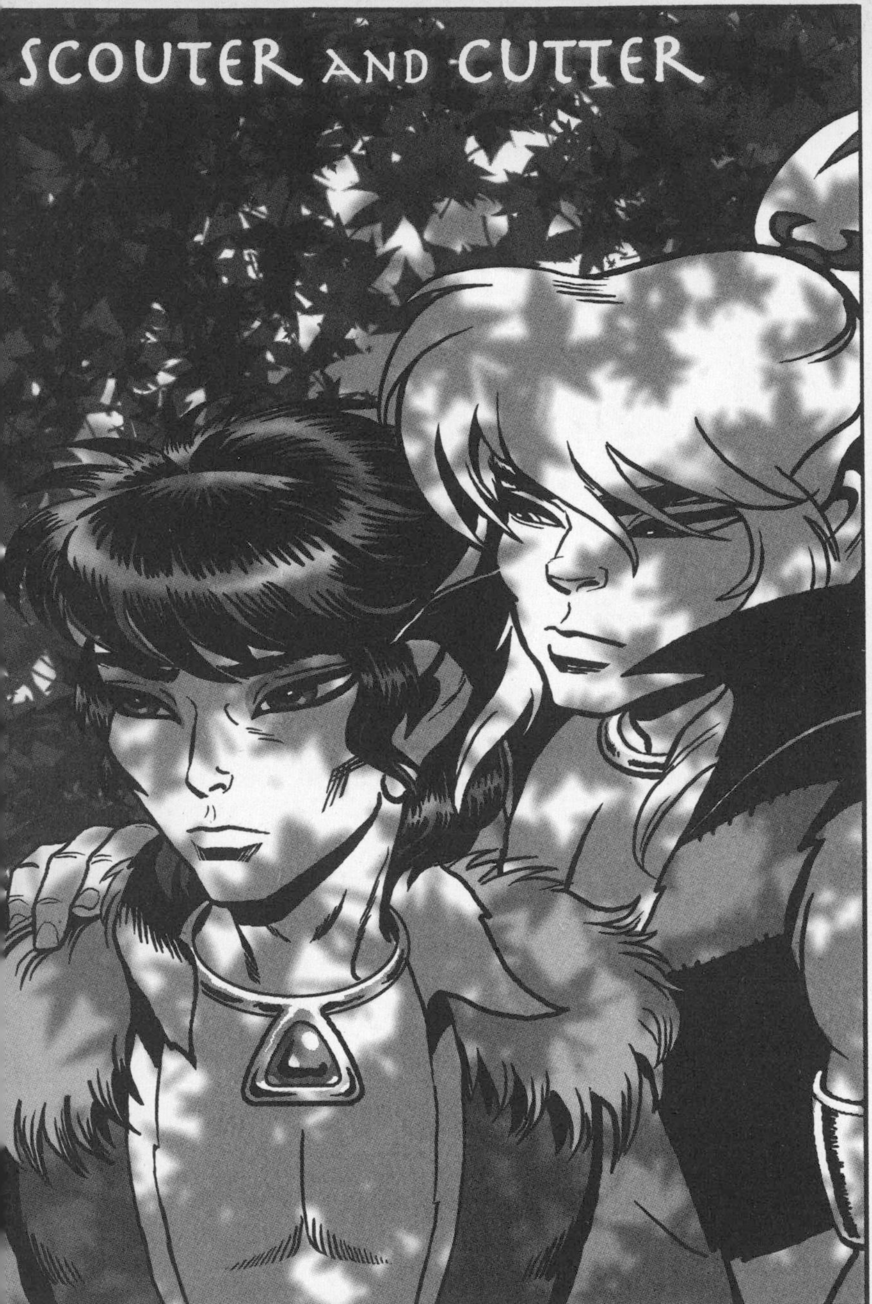
SCOUTER AND CUTTER